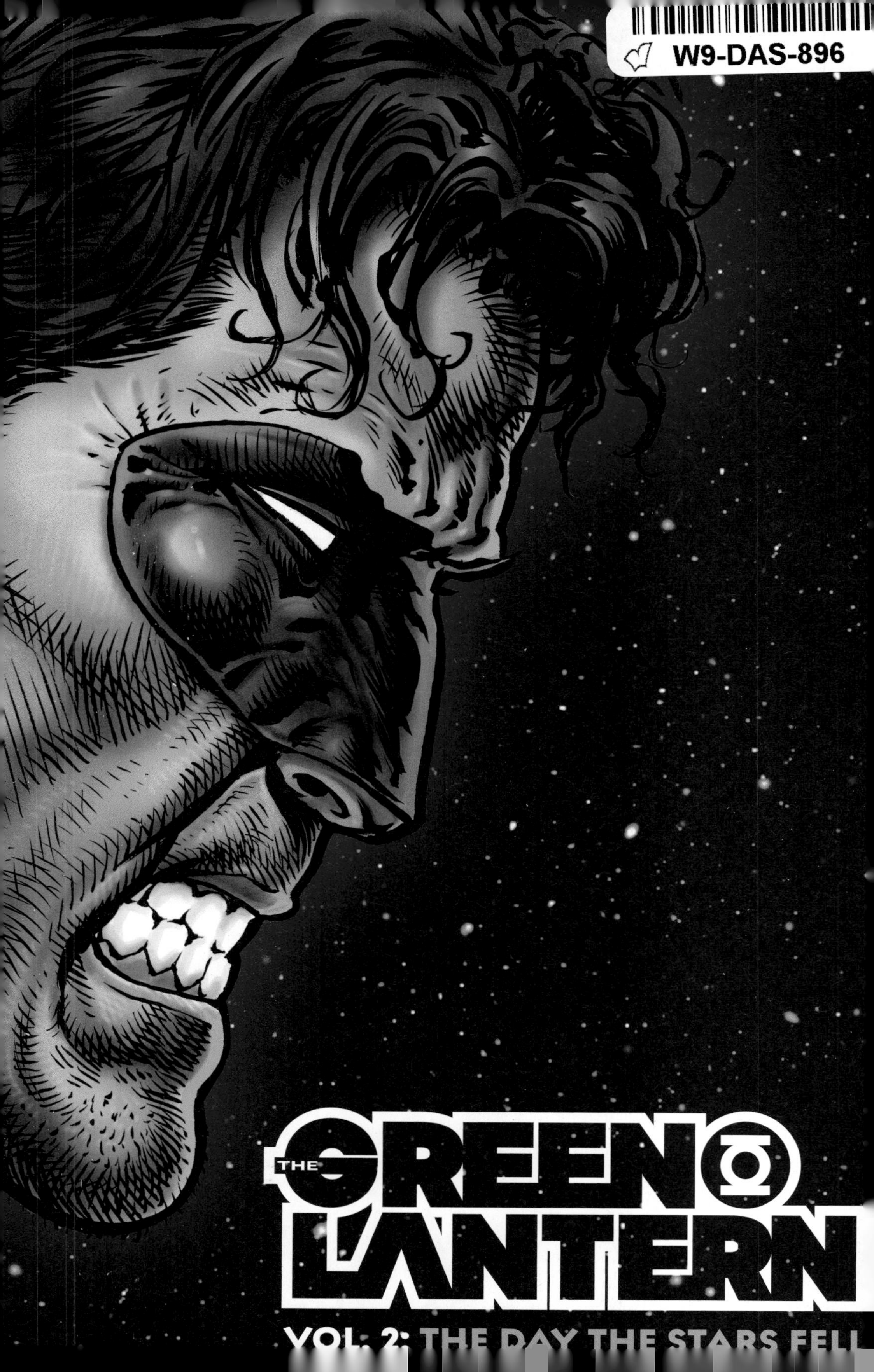
THE GREEN LANTERN
VOL. 2: THE DAY THE STARS FELL

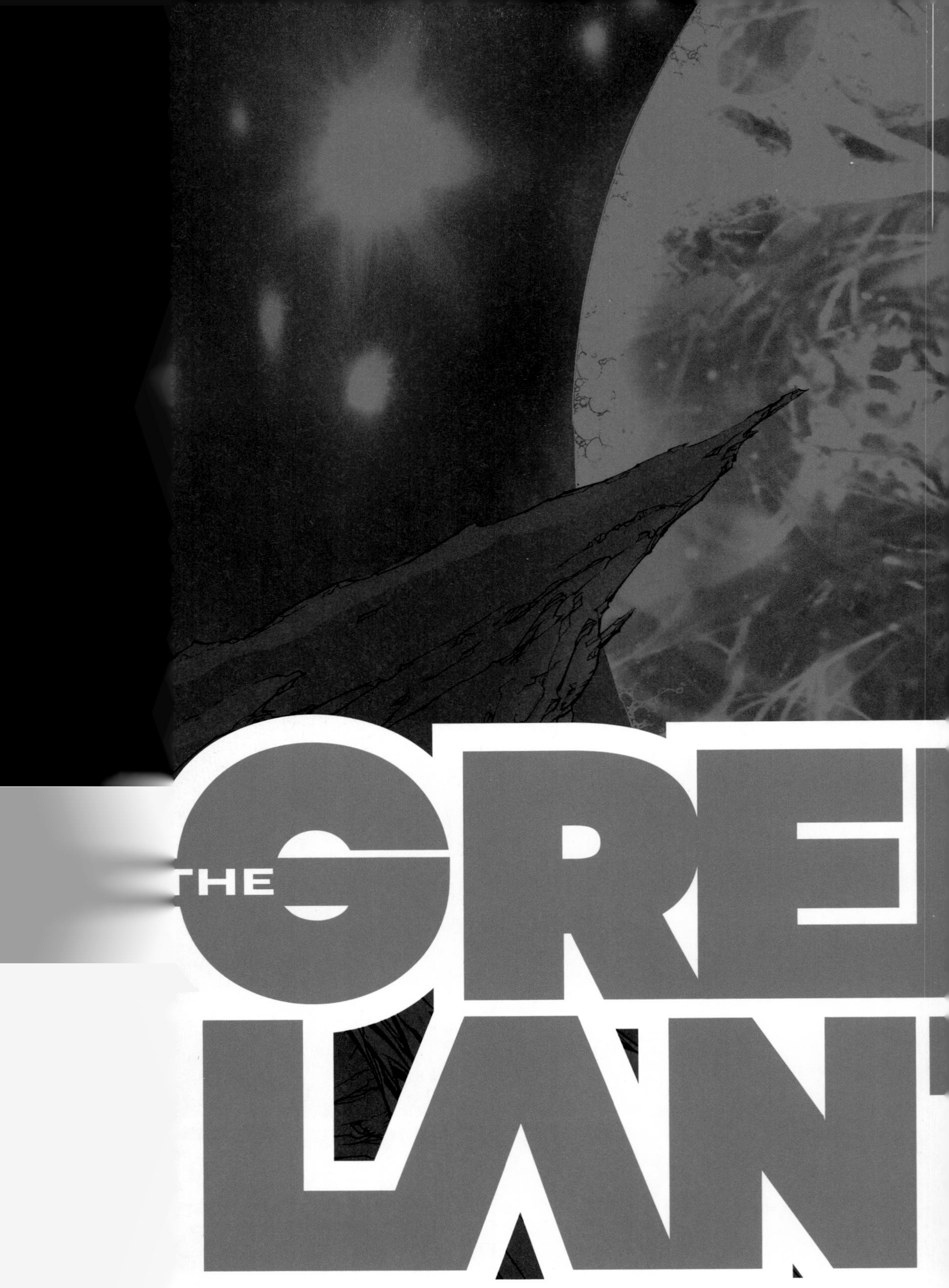
THE
GRE
LAN

VOL. 2: THE DAY THE STARS FELL

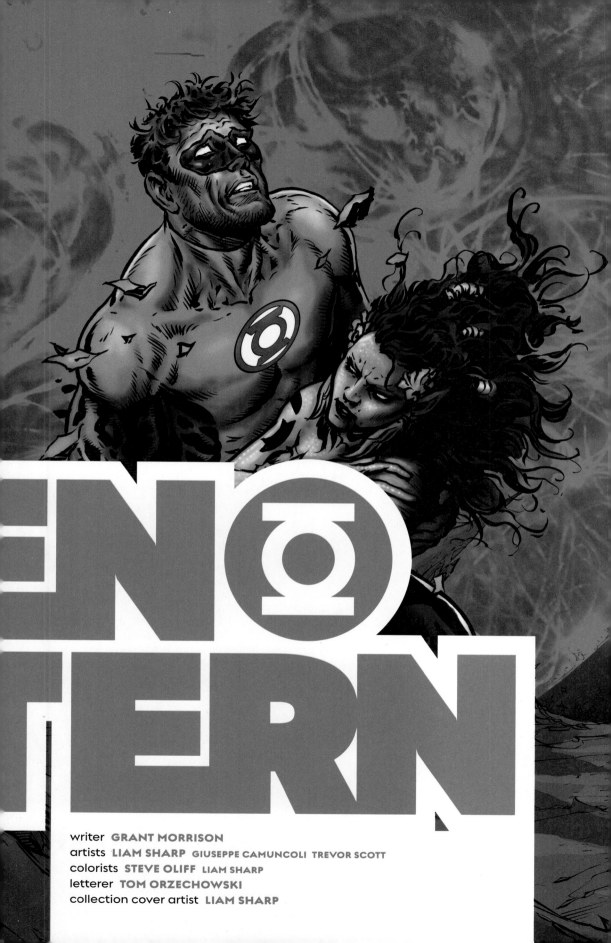

writer **GRANT MORRISON**
artists **LIAM SHARP** GIUSEPPE CAMUNCOLI TREVOR SCOTT
colorists **STEVE OLIFF** LIAM SHARP
letterer **TOM ORZECHOWSKI**
collection cover artist **LIAM SHARP**

BRIAN CUNNINGHAM Editor – Original Series
JESSICA CHEN Associate Editor – Original Series
JEB WOODARD Group Editor – Collected Editions
ROBIN WILDMAN Editor – Collected Edition
STEVE COOK Design Director – Books
JOHN J. HILL Publication Design
ERIN VANOVER Publication Production

BOB HARRAS Senior VP – Editor-in-Chief, DC Comics
PAT McCALLUM Executive Editor, DC Comics

DAN DiDIO Publisher
JIM LEE Publisher & Chief Creative Officer
BOBBIE CHASE VP – New Publishing Initiatives & Talent Development
DON FALLETTI VP – Manufacturing Operations & Workflow Management
LAWRENCE GANEM VP – Talent Services
ALISON GILL Senior VP – Manufacturing & Operations
HANK KANALZ Senior VP – Publishing Strategy & Support Services
DAN MIRON VP – Publishing Operations
NICK J. NAPOLITANO VP – Manufacturing Administration & Design
NANCY SPEARS VP – Sales
MICHELE R. WELLS VP & Executive Editor, Young Reader

THE GREEN LANTERN VOL. 2: THE DAY THE STARS FELL

DC Comics, 2900 West Alameda Ave., Burbank, CA 91505
Printed by LSC Communications, Kendallville, IN, USA. 11/15/19. First Printing.
ISBN: 978-1-4012-9535-6

Library of Congress Cataloging-in-Publication Data is available.

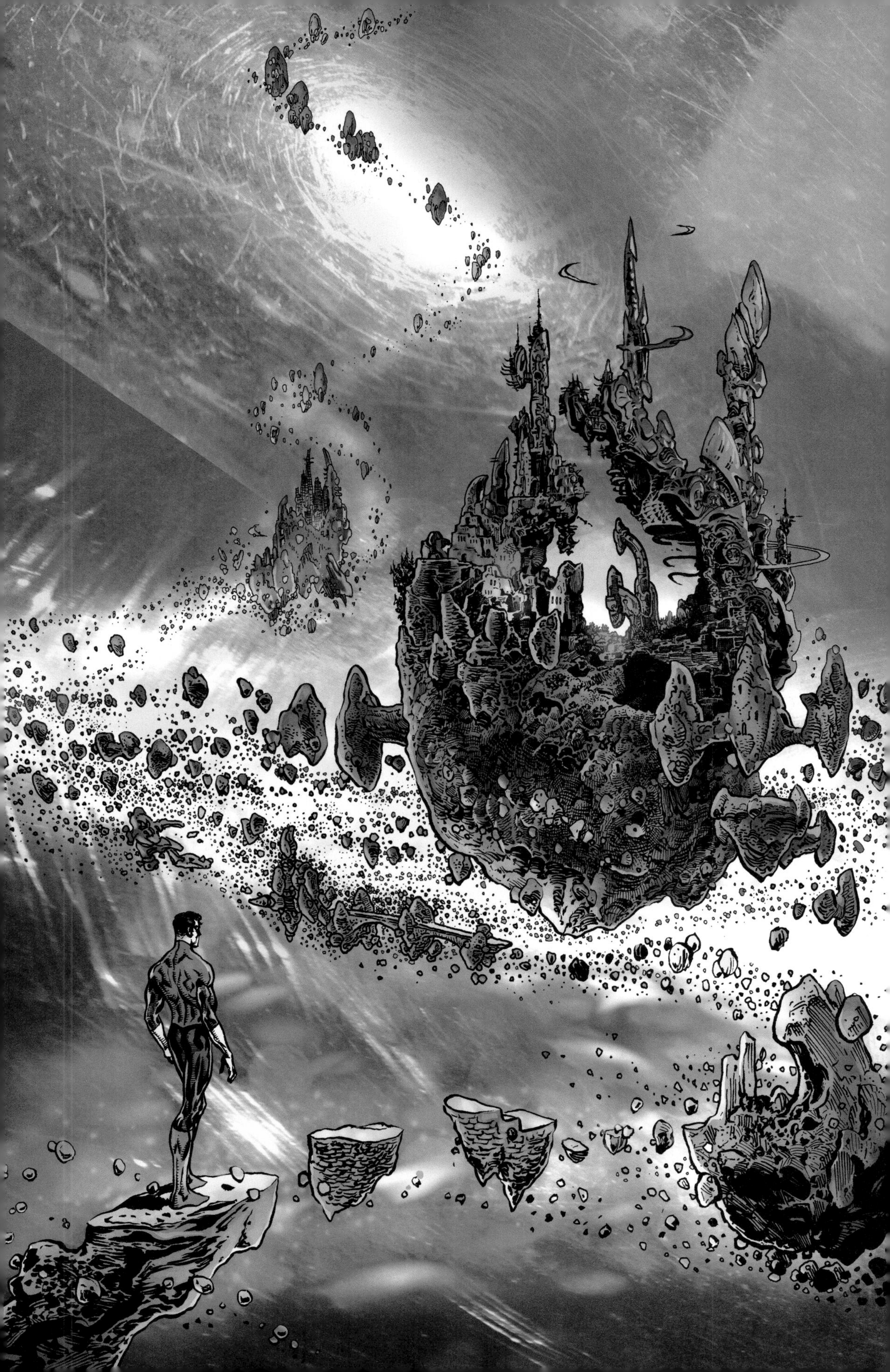

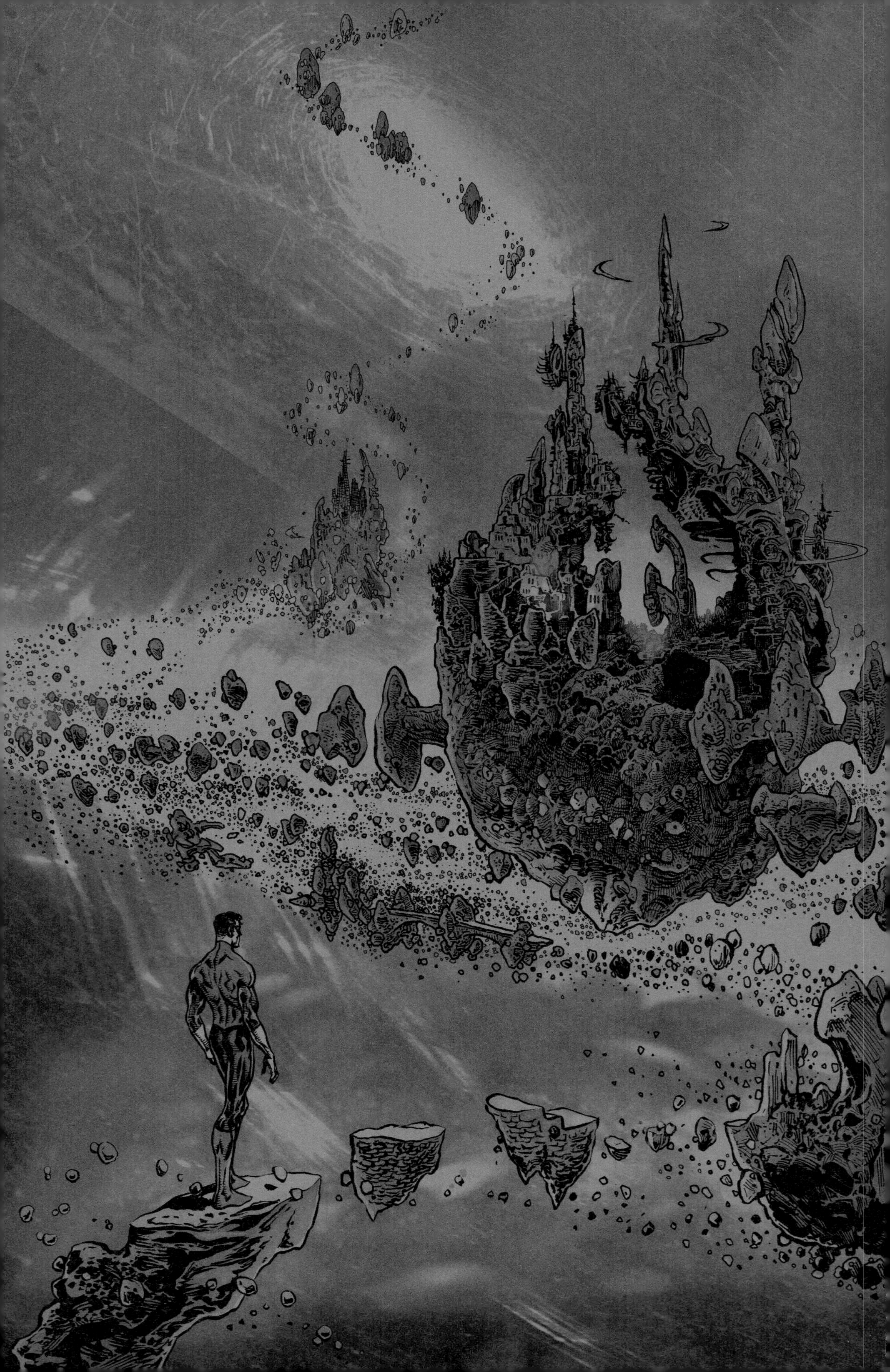

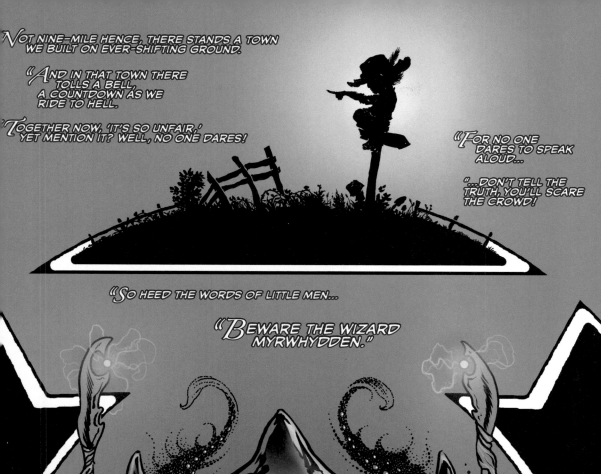

"Not nine-mile hence, there stands a town we built on ever-shifting ground.

"And in that town there tolls a bell, a countdown as we ride to hell.

"Together now, 'It's so unfair,' yet mention it? Well, no one dares!

"For no one dares to speak aloud...

"...don't tell the truth, you'll scare the crowd!

"So heed the words of little men...

"Beware the wizard Myrwhydden."

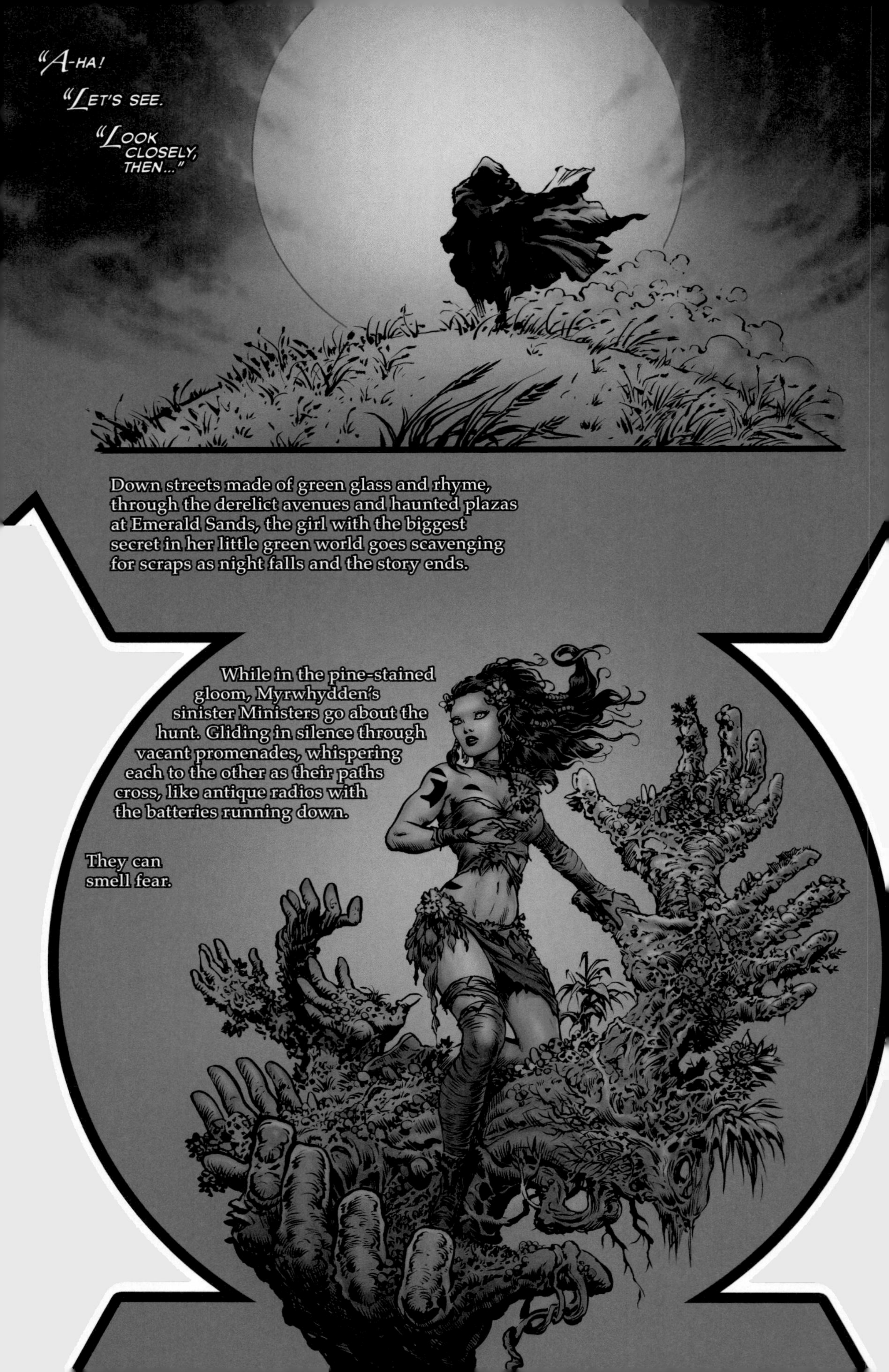
"A-HA!
"LET'S SEE.
"LOOK CLOSELY, THEN..."
Down streets made of green glass and rhyme, through the derelict avenues and haunted plazas at Emerald Sands, the girl with the biggest secret in her little green world goes scavenging for scraps as night falls and the story ends.
While in the pine-stained gloom, Myrwhydden's sinister Ministers go about the hunt. Gliding in silence through vacant promenades, whispering each to the other as their paths cross, like antique radios with the batteries running down.
They can smell fear.

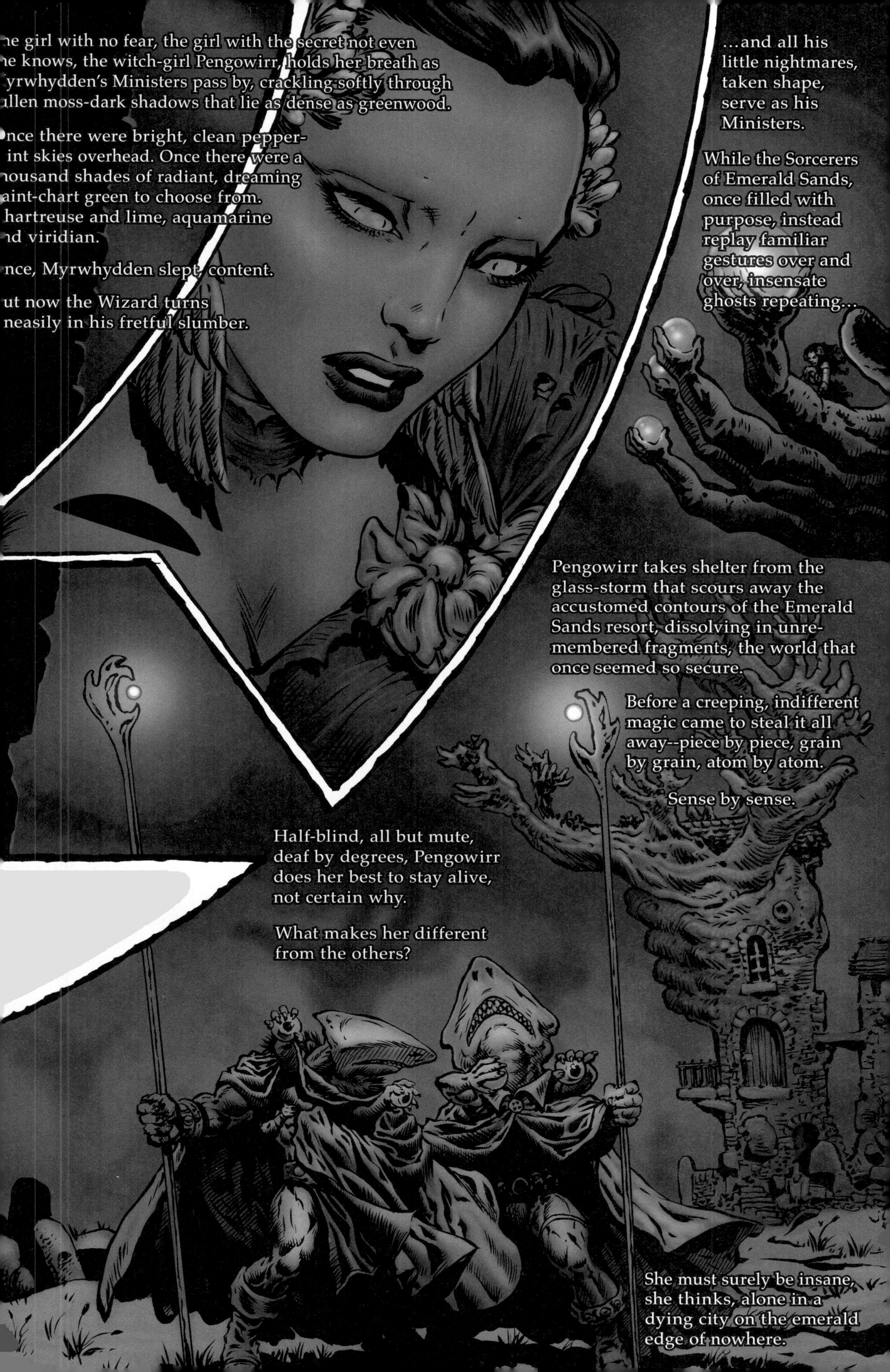
ne girl with no fear, the girl with the secret not even
ne knows, the witch-girl Pengowirr, holds her breath as
yrwhydden's Ministers pass by, crackling softly through
ullen moss-dark shadows that lie as dense as greenwood.
nce there were bright, clean pepper-
int skies overhead. Once there were a
housand shades of radiant, dreaming
aint-chart green to choose from.
hartreuse and lime, aquamarine
nd viridian.
nce, Myrwhydden slept, content.
ut now the Wizard turns
neasily in his fretful slumber.
...and all his little nightmares, taken shape, serve as his Ministers.
While the Sorcerers of Emerald Sands, once filled with purpose, instead replay familiar gestures over and over, insensate ghosts repeating...
Pengowirr takes shelter from the glass-storm that scours away the accustomed contours of the Emerald Sands resort, dissolving in unre-membered fragments, the world that once seemed so secure.
Before a creeping, indifferent magic came to steal it all away--piece by piece, grain by grain, atom by atom.
Sense by sense.
Half-blind, all but mute, deaf by degrees, Pengowirr does her best to stay alive, not certain why.
What makes her different from the others?
She must surely be insane, she thinks, alone in a dying city on the emerald edge of nowhere.

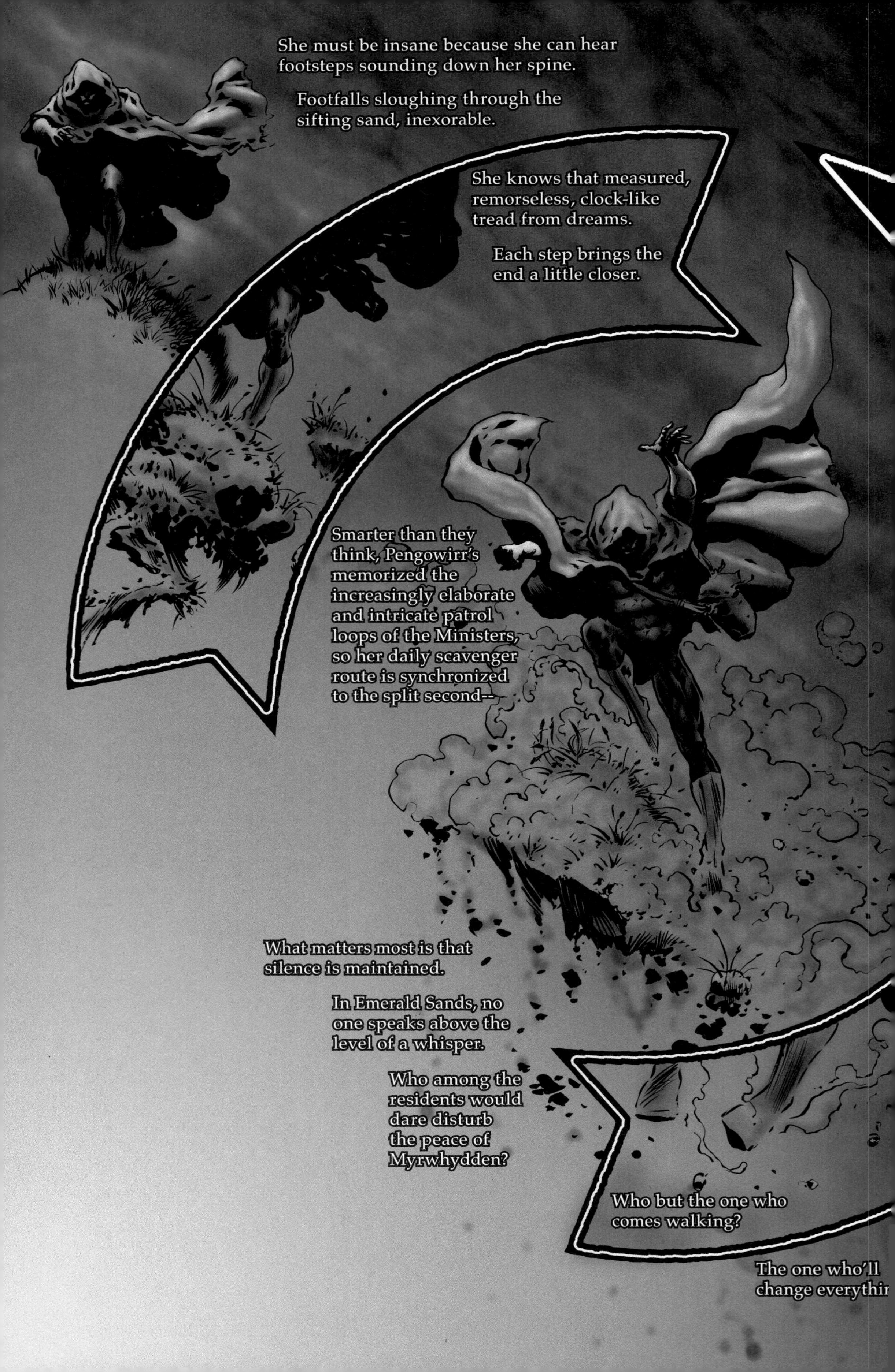
She must be insane because she can hear footsteps sounding down her spine.
Footfalls sloughing through the sifting sand, inexorable.
She knows that measured, remorseless, clock-like tread from dreams.
Each step brings the end a little closer.
Smarter than they think, Pengowirr's memorized the increasingly elaborate and intricate patrol loops of the Ministers, so her daily scavenger route is synchronized to the split second--
What matters most is that silence is maintained.
In Emerald Sands, no one speaks above the level of a whisper.
Who among the residents would dare disturb the peace of Myrwhydden?
Who but the one who comes walking?
The one who'll change everythi

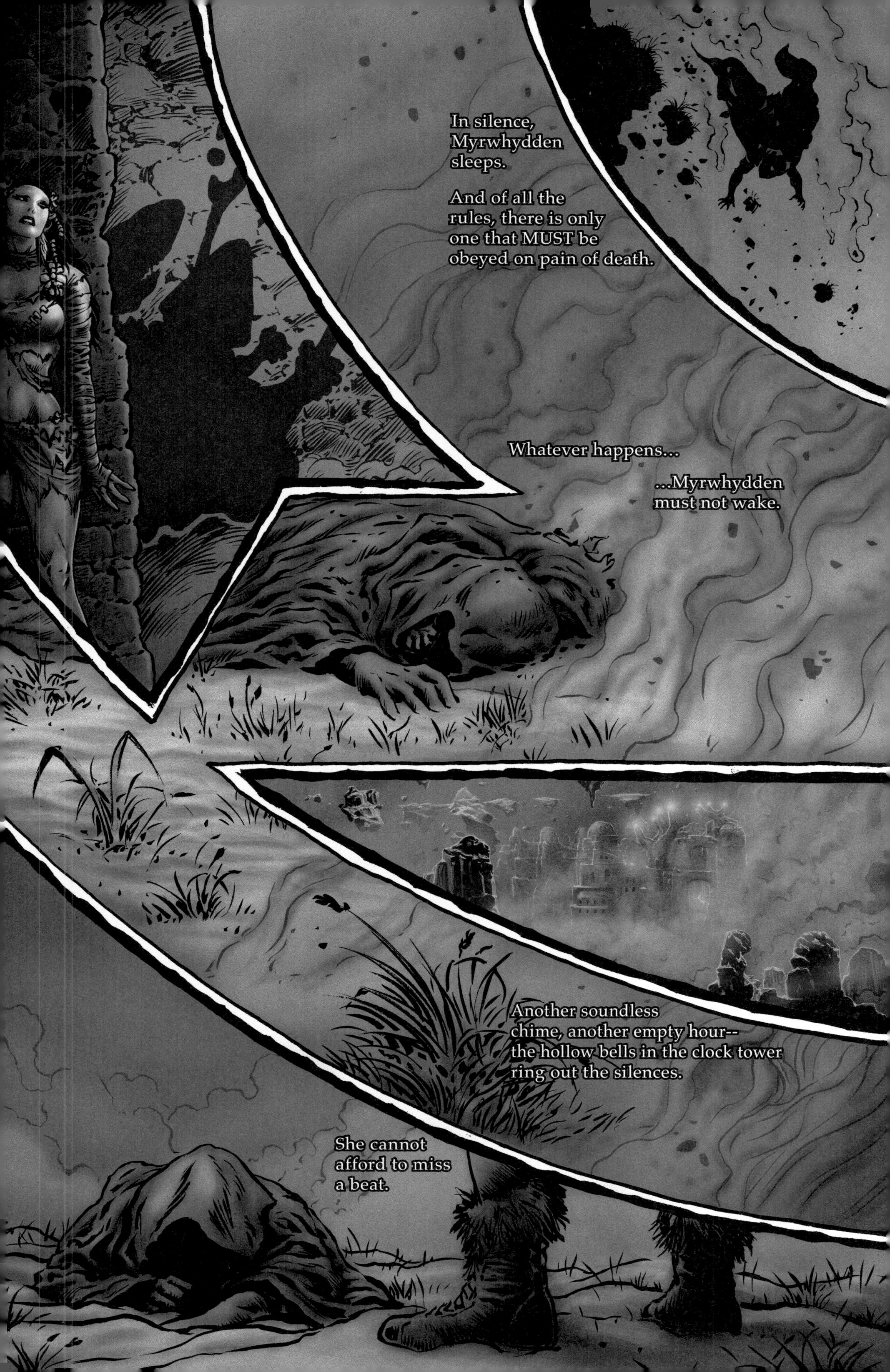
In silence, Myrwhydden sleeps.
And of all the rules, there is only one that MUST be obeyed on pain of death.
Whatever happens...
...Myrwhydden must not wake.
Another soundless chime, another empty hour-- the hollow bells in the clock tower ring out the silences.
She cannot afford to miss a beat.

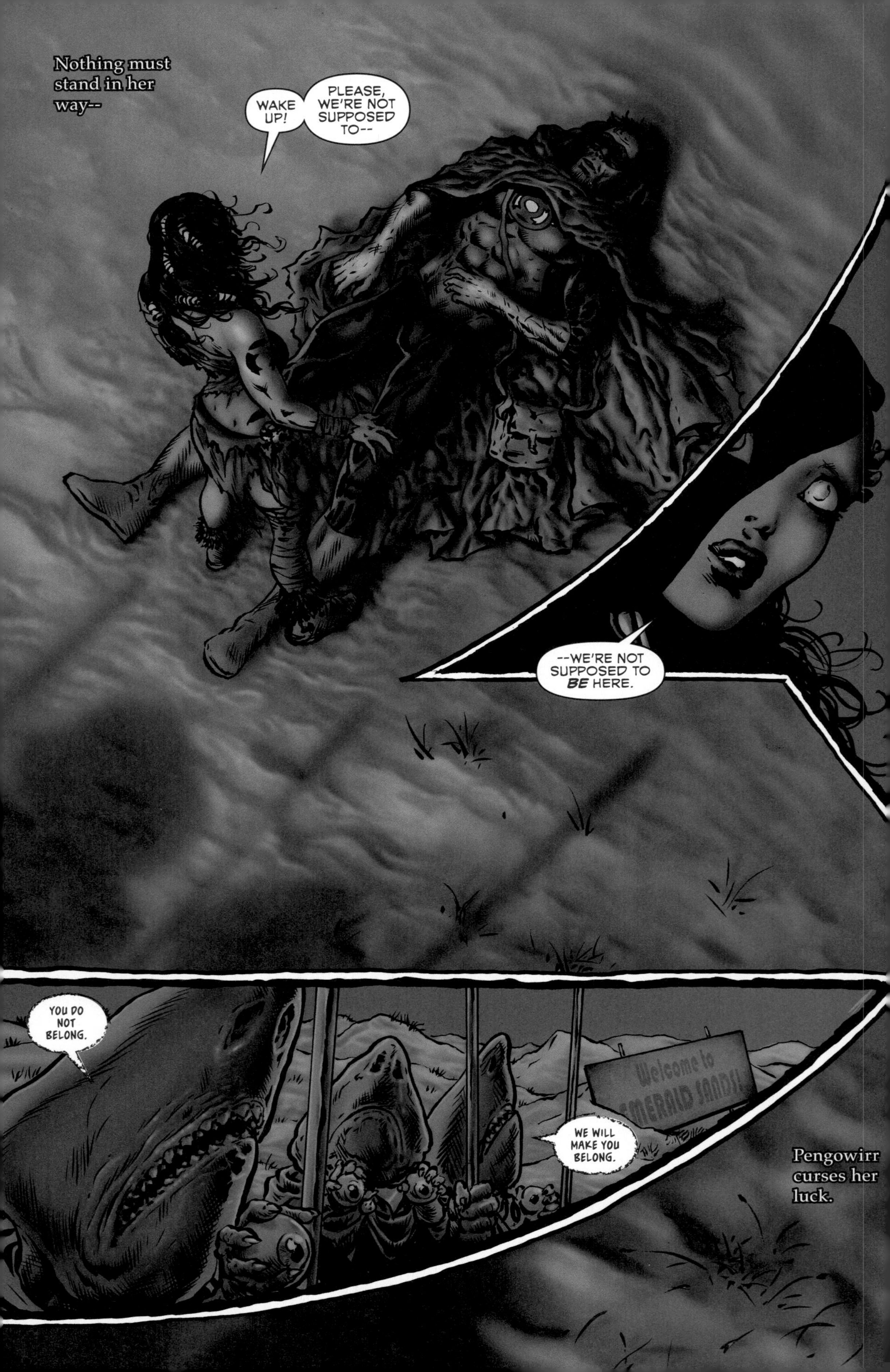
Nothing must stand in her way--
WAKE UP!
PLEASE, WE'RE NOT SUPPOSED TO--
--WE'RE NOT SUPPOSED TO *BE* HERE.
YOU DO NOT BELONG.
Welcome to
MERALD SANDS!
WE WILL MAKE YOU BELONG.
Pengowirr curses her luck.

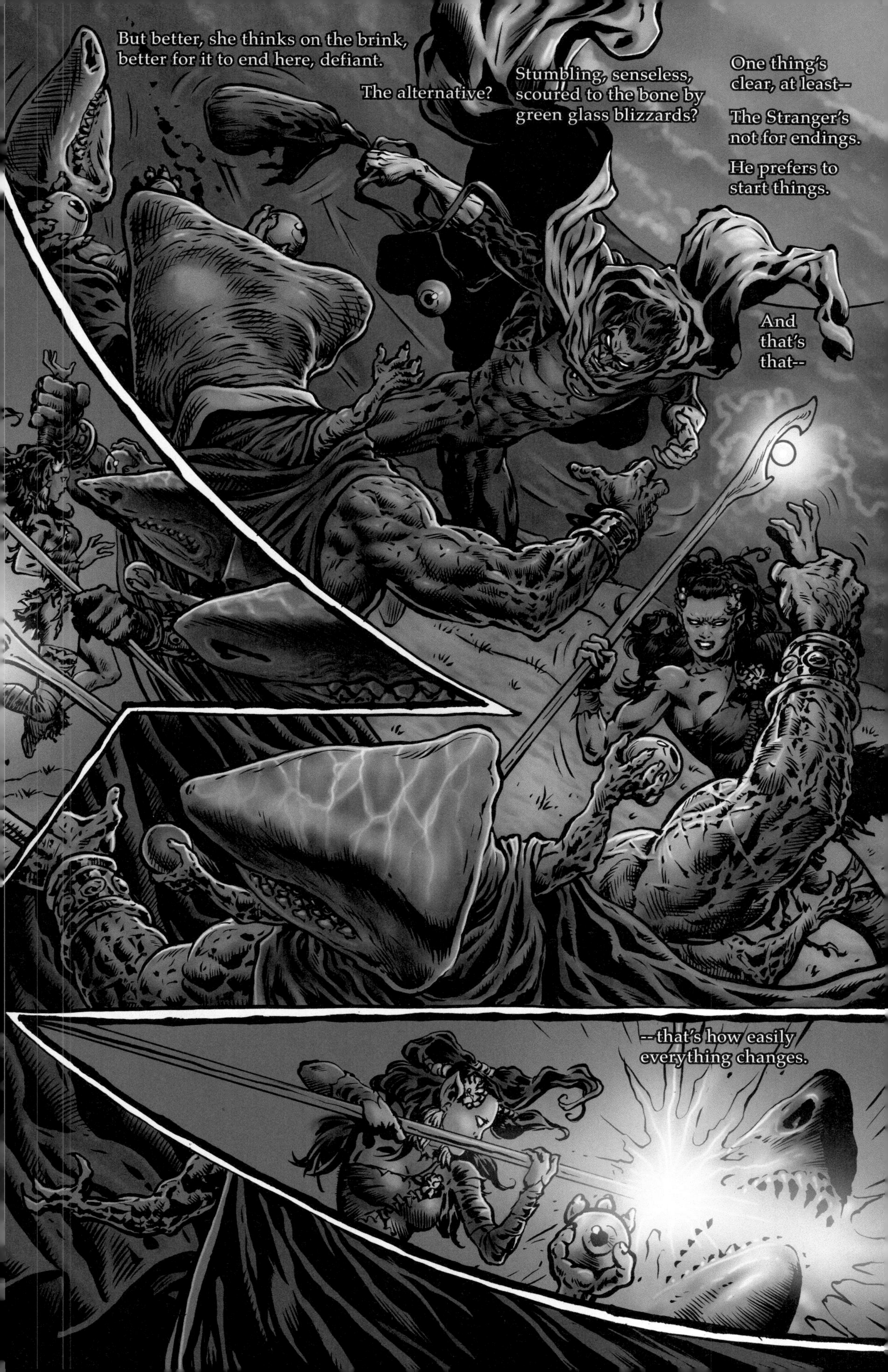
But better, she thinks on the brink, better for it to end here, defiant.
The alternative?
Stumbling, senseless, scoured to the bone by green glass blizzards?
One thing's clear, at least--
The Stranger's not for endings.
He prefers to start things.
And that's that--
--that's how easily everything changes.

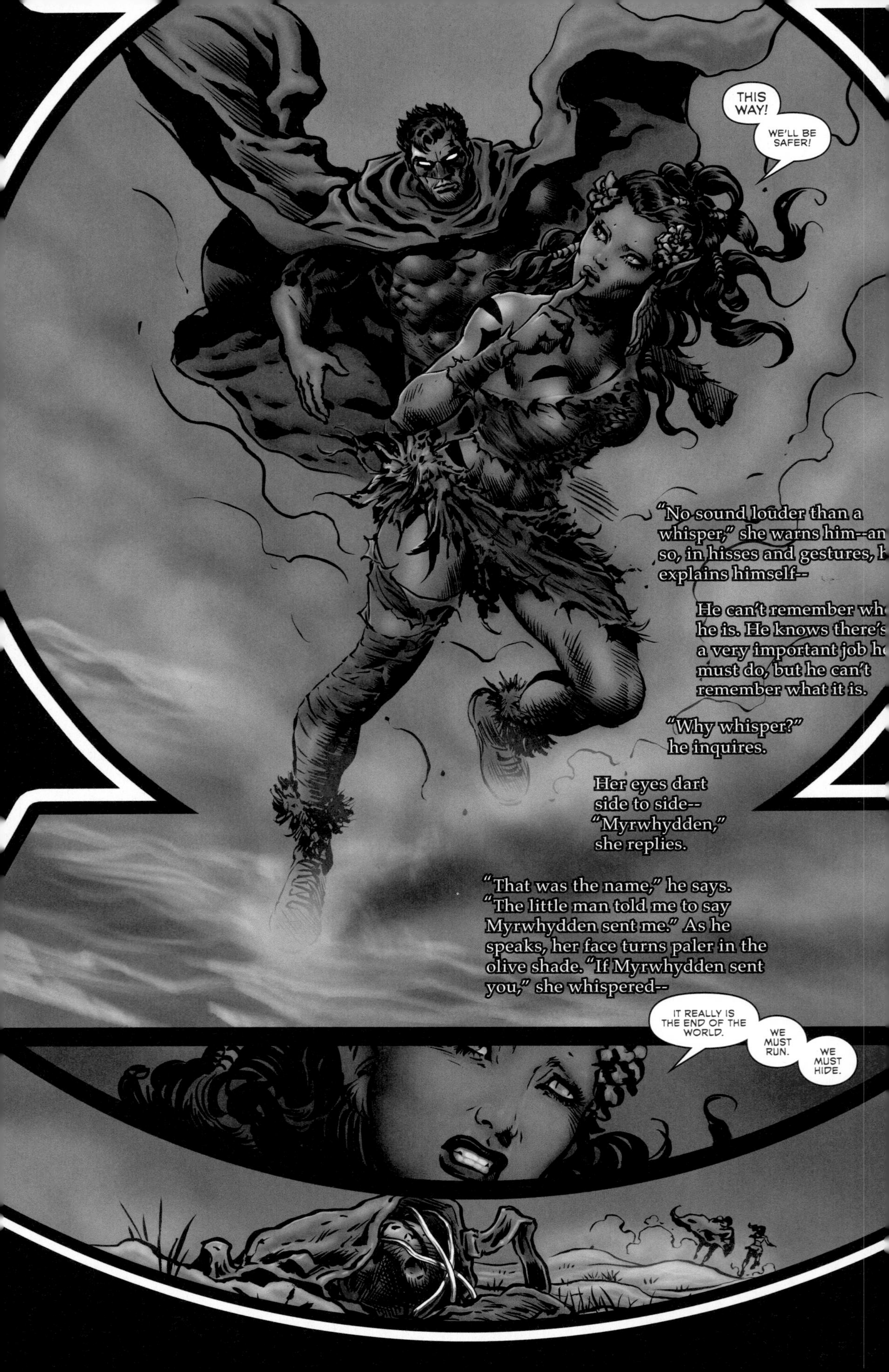
THIS WAY!
WE'LL BE SAFER!
"No sound louder than a whisper," she warns him--an so, in hisses and gestures, h explains himself--
He can't remember wh he is. He knows there's a very important job h must do, but he can't remember what it is.
"Why whisper?" he inquires.
Her eyes dart side to side-- "Myrwhydden," she replies.
"That was the name," he says. "The little man told me to say Myrwhydden sent me." As he speaks, her face turns paler in the olive shade. "If Myrwhydden sent you," she whispered--
IT REALLY IS THE END OF THE WORLD.
WE MUST RUN.
WE MUST HIDE.

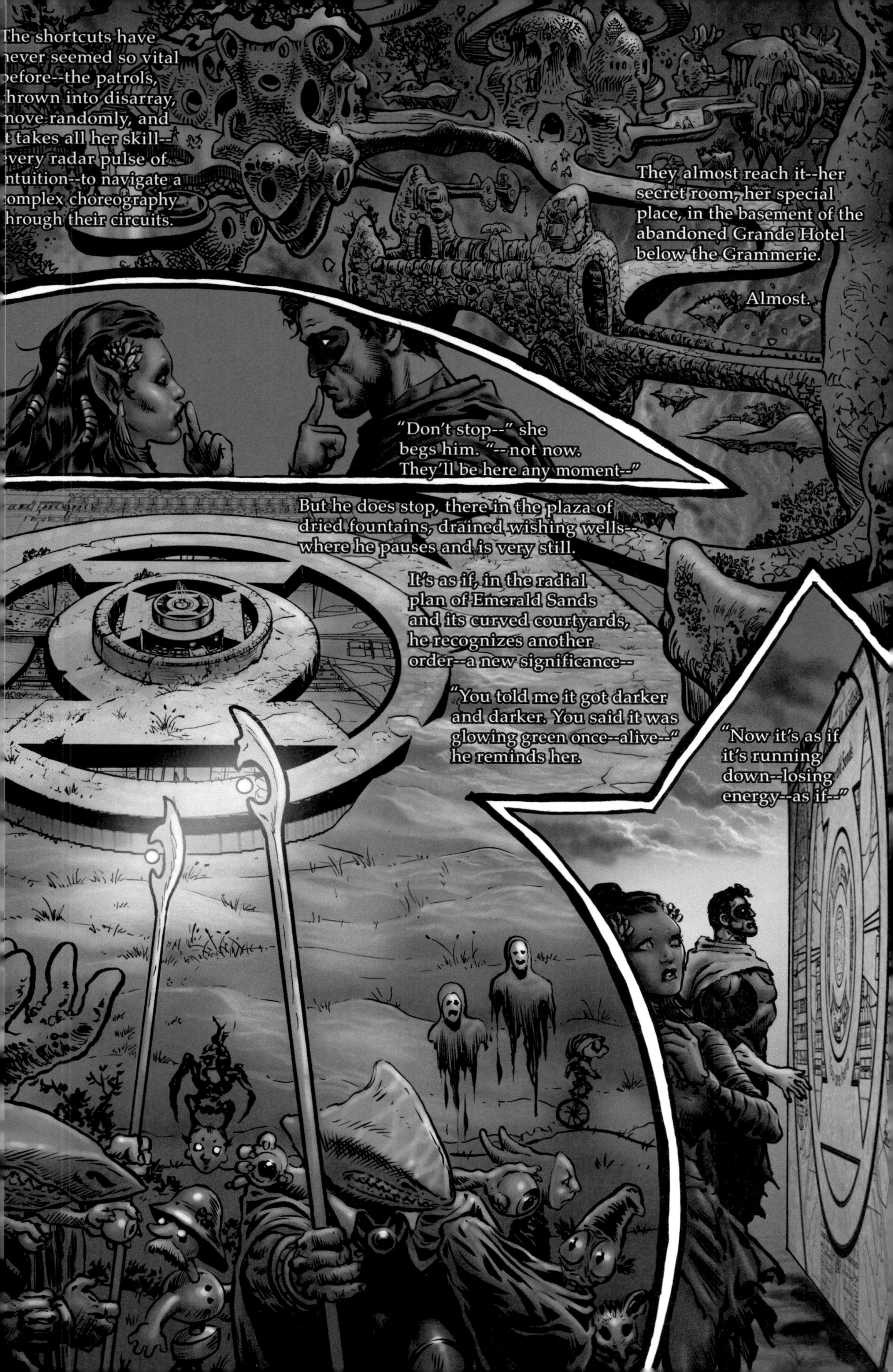
The shortcuts have
never seemed so vital
before--the patrols,
thrown into disarray,
move randomly, and
it takes all her skill--
every radar pulse of
intuition--to navigate a
complex choreography
through their circuits.
They almost reach it--her secret room, her special place, in the basement of the abandoned Grande Hotel below the Grammerie.
Almost.
"Don't stop--" she begs him. "--not now. They'll be here any moment--"
But he does stop, there in the plaza of dried fountains, drained wishing wells--where he pauses and is very still.
It's as if, in the radial plan of Emerald Sands and its curved courtyards, he recognizes another order--a new significance--
"You told me it got darker and darker. You said it was glowing green once--alive--" he reminds her.
"Now it's as if it's running down--losing energy--as if--"

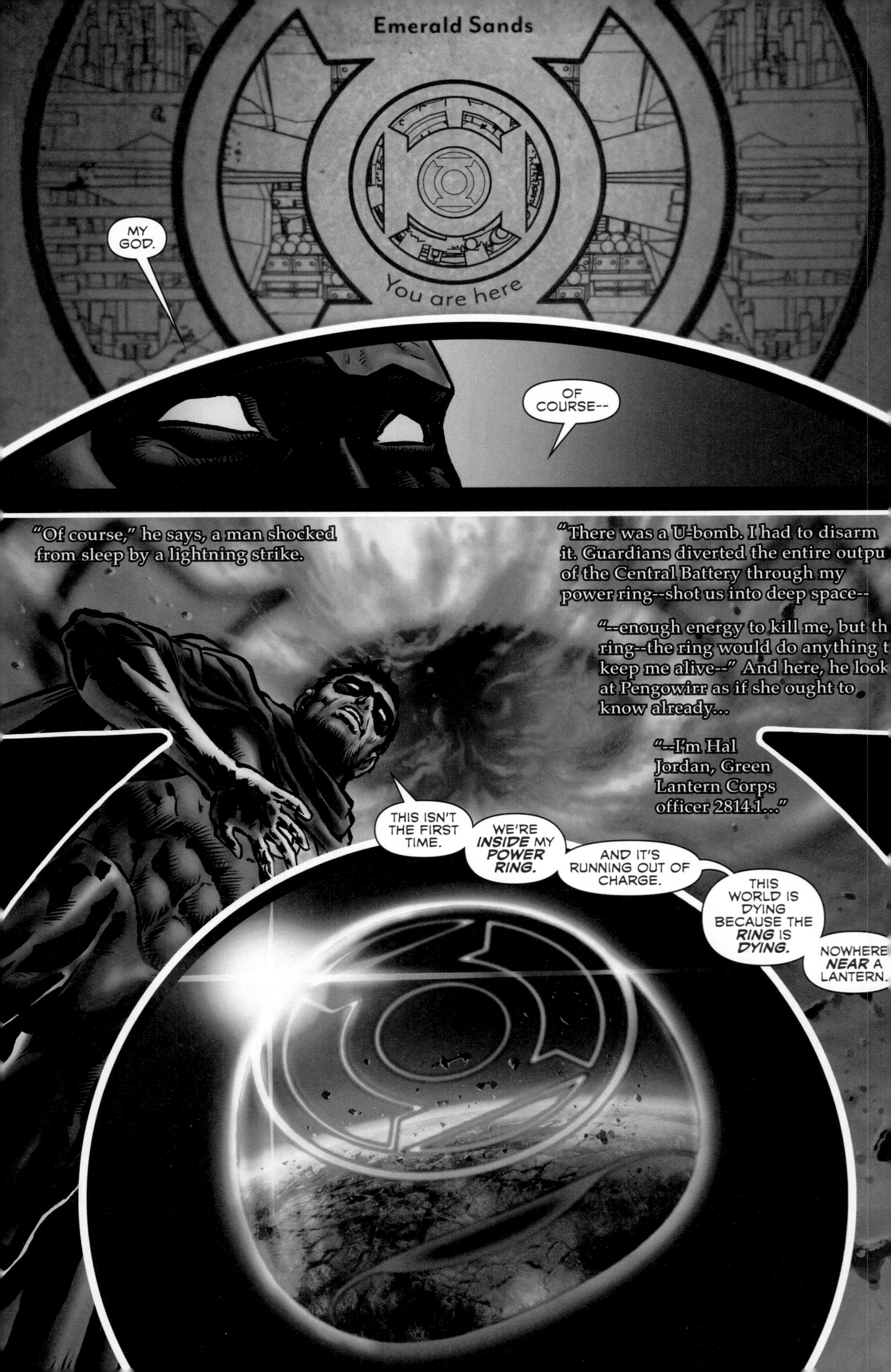
Emerald Sands
You are here
MY GOD.
OF COURSE--
"Of course," he says, a man shocked from sleep by a lightning strike.
"There was a U-bomb. I had to disarm it. Guardians diverted the entire outpu of the Central Battery through my power ring--shot us into deep space--
"--enough energy to kill me, but th ring--the ring would do anything t keep me alive--" And here, he look at Pengowirr as if she ought to know already...
"--I'm Hal Jordan, Green Lantern Corps officer 2814.1..."
THIS ISN'T THE FIRST TIME.
WE'RE *INSIDE* MY *POWER RING.*
AND IT'S RUNNING OUT OF CHARGE.
THIS WORLD IS DYING BECAUSE THE *RING* IS *DYING.*
NOWHERE *NEAR* A LANTERN.

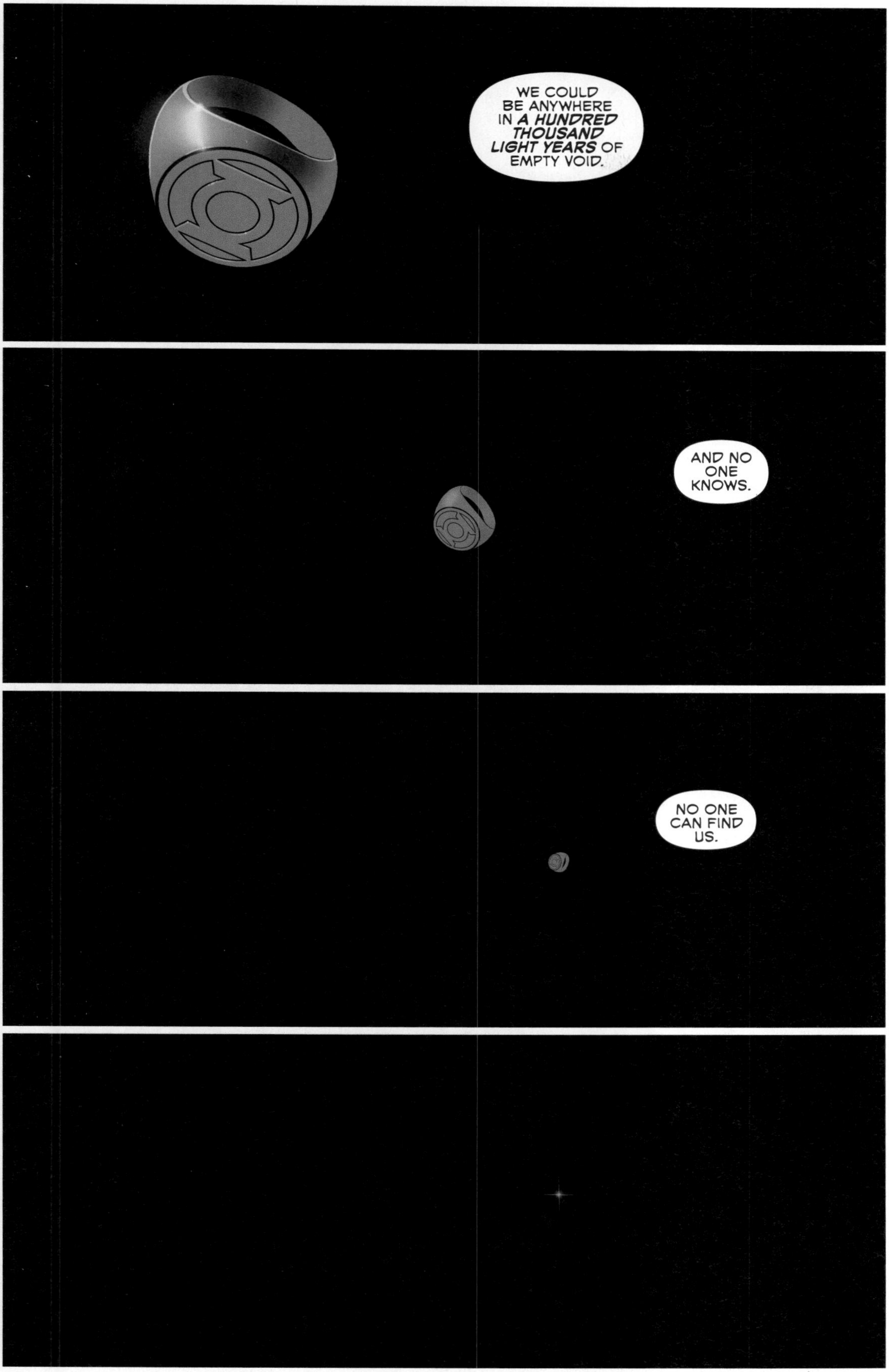
WE COULD BE ANYWHERE IN A HUNDRED THOUSAND LIGHT YEARS OF EMPTY VOID.
AND NO ONE KNOWS.
NO ONE CAN FIND US.

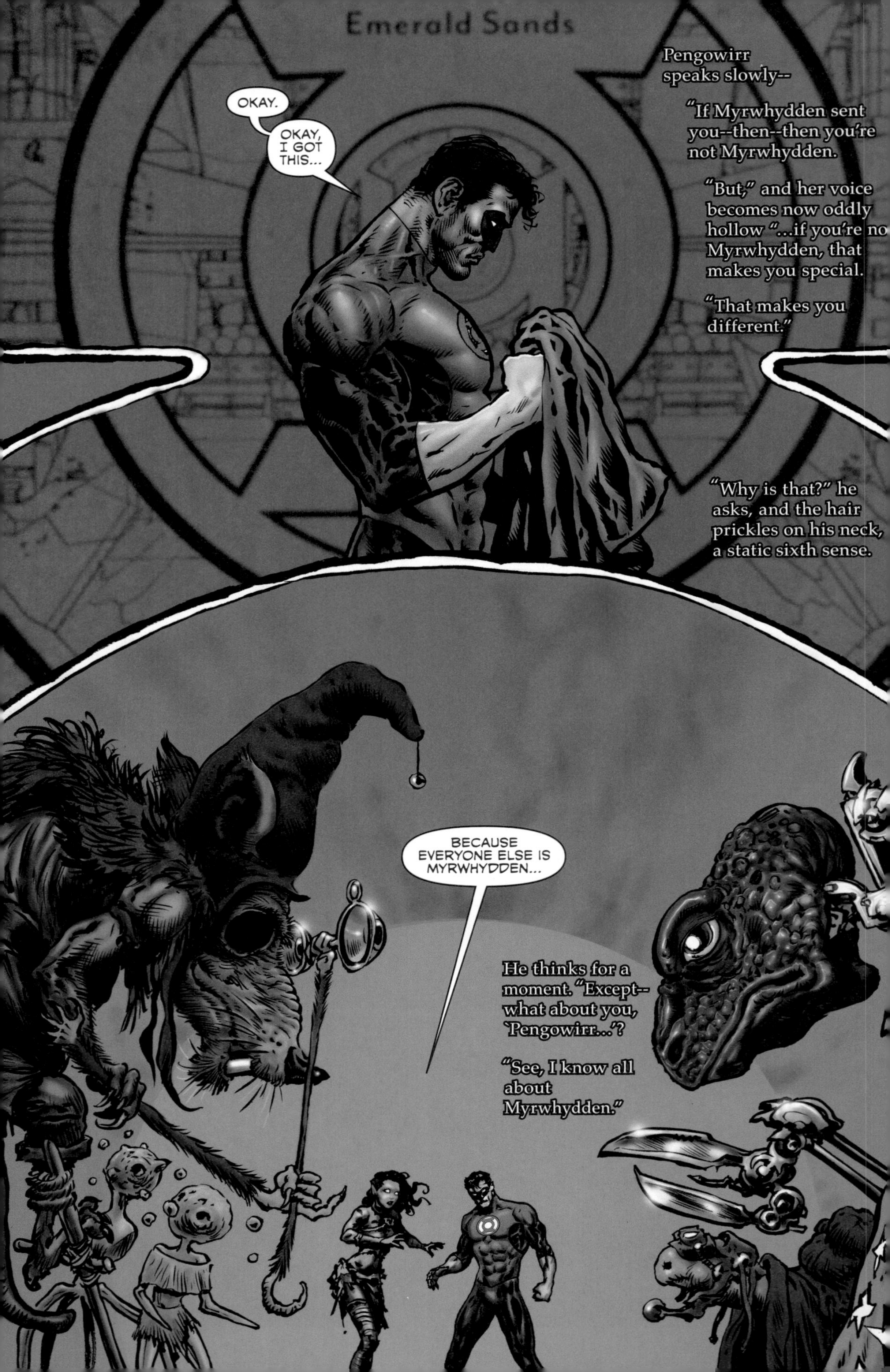

Emerald Sands
Pengowirr speaks slowly--
"If Myrwhydden sent you--then--then you're not Myrwhydden.
"But," and her voice becomes now oddly hollow "...if you're no Myrwhydden, that makes you special.
"That makes you different."
OKAY.
OKAY, I GOT THIS...
"Why is that?" he asks, and the hair prickles on his neck, a static sixth sense.
BECAUSE EVERYONE ELSE IS MYRWHYDDEN...
He thinks for a moment. "Except--what about you, `Pengowirr...'?
"See, I know all about Myrwhydden."

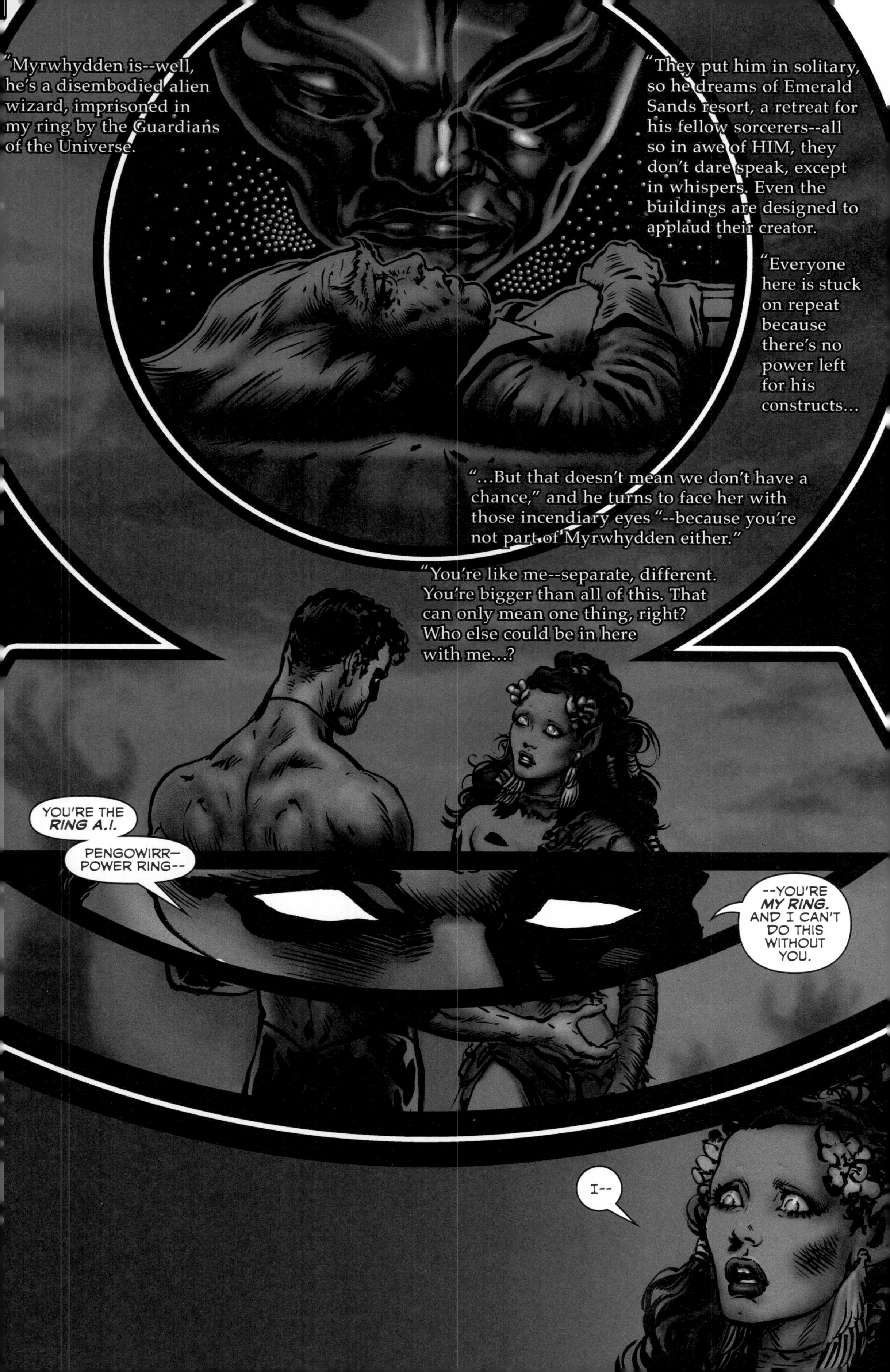
"Myrwhydden is--well, he's a disembodied alien wizard, imprisoned in my ring by the Guardians of the Universe.
"They put him in solitary, so he dreams of Emerald Sands resort, a retreat for his fellow sorcerers--all so in awe of HIM, they don't dare speak, except in whispers. Even the buildings are designed to applaud their creator.
"Everyone here is stuck on repeat because there's no power left for his constructs...
"...But that doesn't mean we don't have a chance," and he turns to face her with those incendiary eyes "--because you're not part of Myrwhydden either."
"You're like me--separate, different. You're bigger than all of this. That can only mean one thing, right? Who else could be in here with me...?
YOU'RE THE RING A.I.
PENGOWIRR— POWER RING--
--YOU'RE MY RING. AND I CAN'T DO THIS WITHOUT YOU.
I--

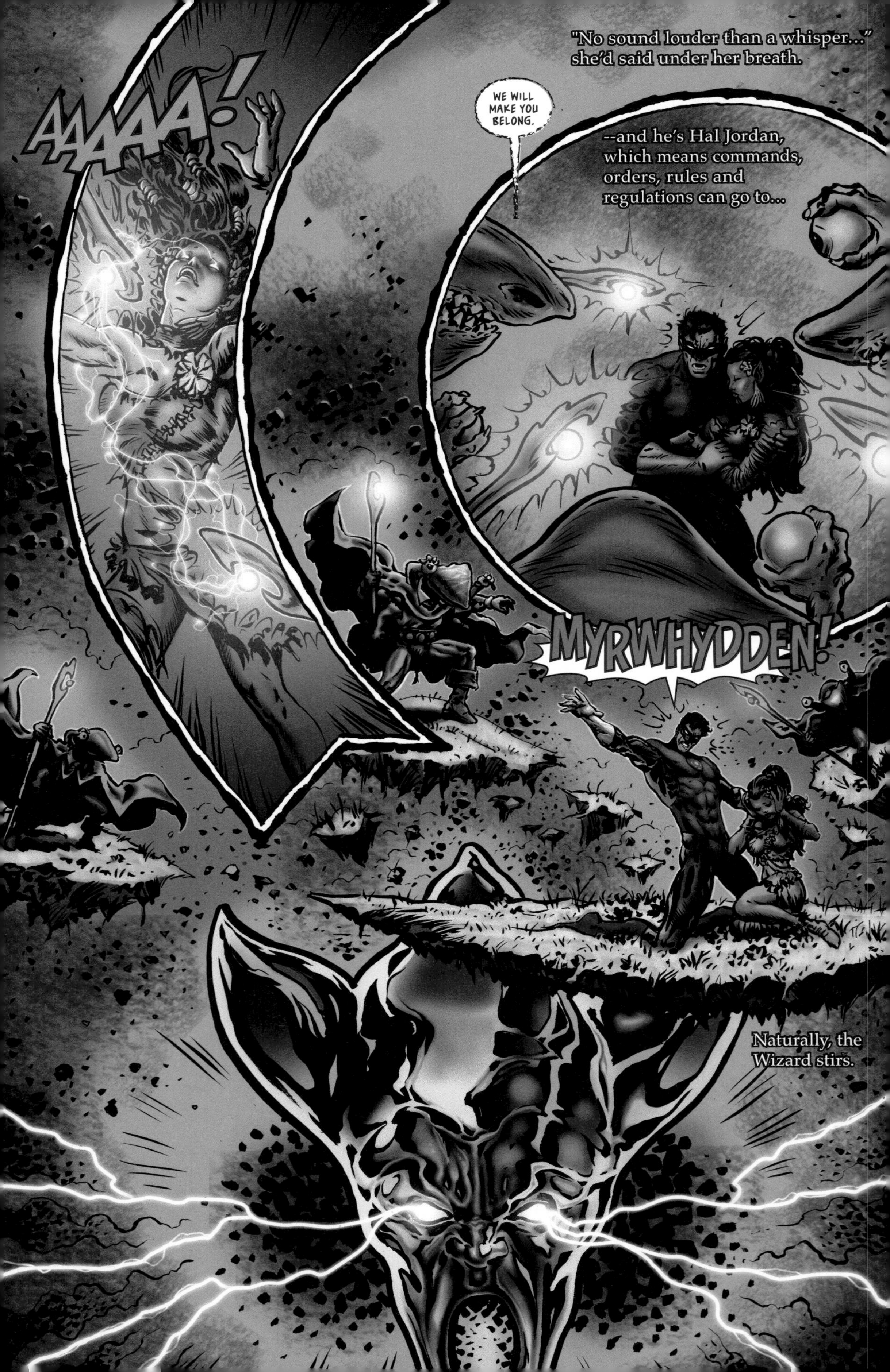
AAAAA!
"No sound louder than a whisper..." she'd said under her breath.
WE WILL MAKE YOU BELONG.
--and he's Hal Jordan, which means commands, orders, rules and regulations can go to...
MYRWHYDDEN!
Naturally, the Wizard stirs.

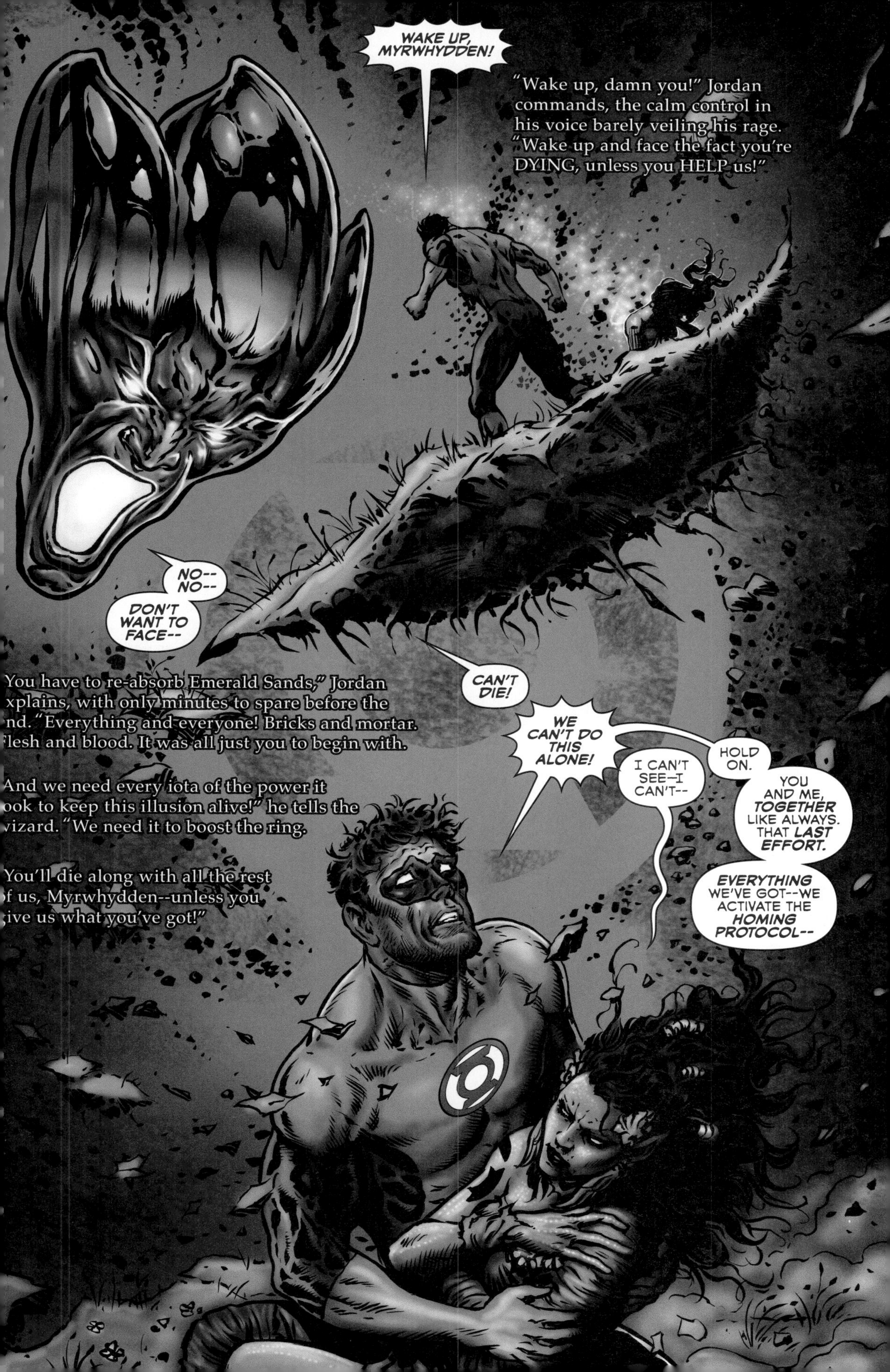
WAKE UP, MYRWHYDDEN!
"Wake up, damn you!" Jordan commands, the calm control in his voice barely veiling his rage. "Wake up and face the fact you're DYING, unless you HELP us!"
NO-- NO--
DON'T WANT TO FACE--
You have to re-absorb Emerald Sands," Jordan xplains, with only minutes to spare before the nd. "Everything and everyone! Bricks and mortar. lesh and blood. It was all just you to begin with.
And we need every iota of the power it ook to keep this illusion alive!" he tells the vizard. "We need it to boost the ring.
You'll die along with all the rest f us, Myrwhydden--unless you ive us what you've got!"
CAN'T DIE!
WE CAN'T DO THIS ALONE!
I CAN'T SEE--I CAN'T--
HOLD ON.
YOU AND ME, TOGETHER LIKE ALWAYS. THAT LAST EFFORT.
EVERYTHING WE'VE GOT--WE ACTIVATE THE HOMING PROTOCOL--

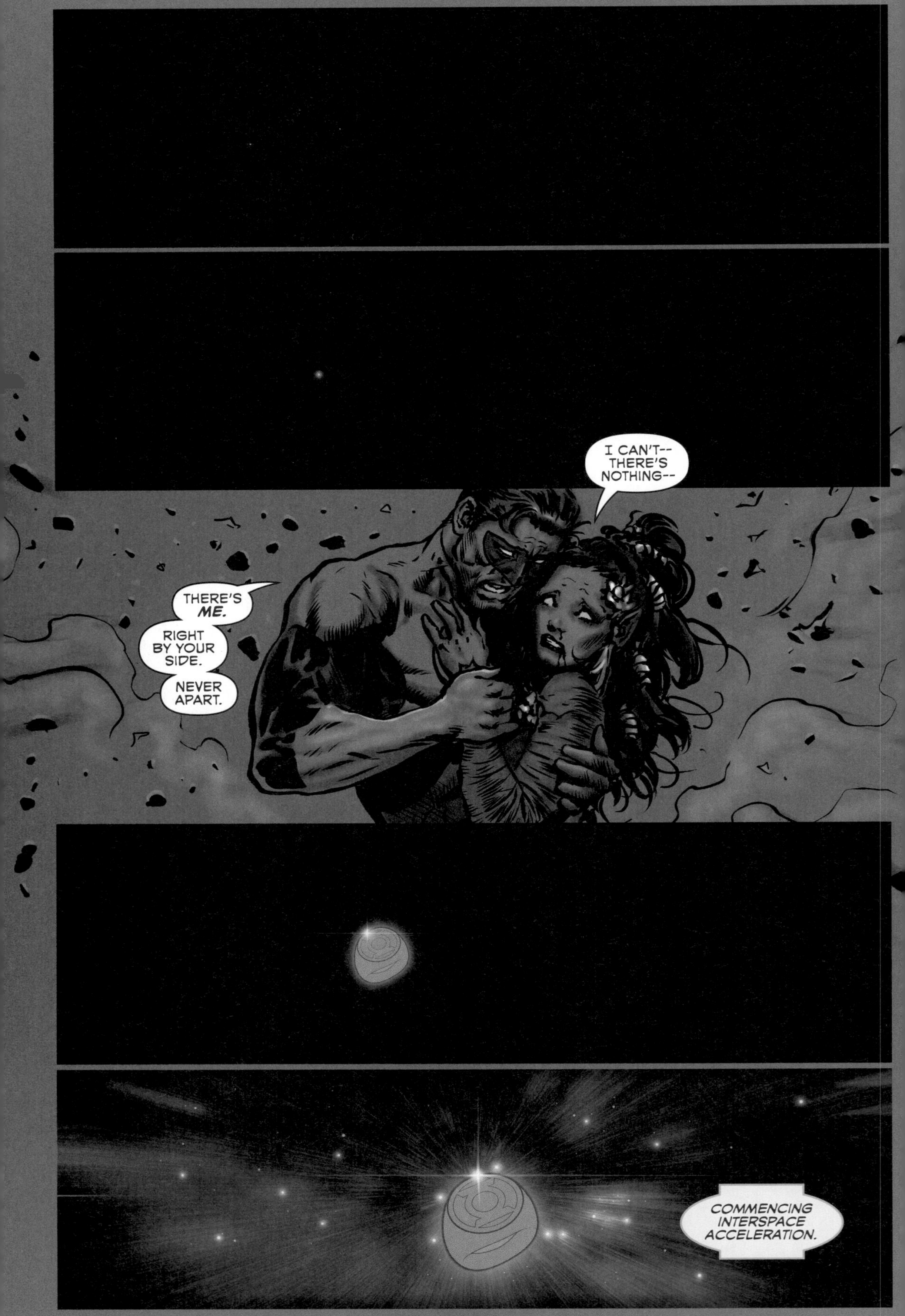
I CAN'T-- THERE'S NOTHING--
THERE'S *ME.*
RIGHT BY YOUR SIDE.
NEVER APART.
COMMENCING INTERSPACE ACCELERATION.

Together, they watch the world fall down, and together hear Myrwhydden's terrible death-denying howls.

EVEN MYRWHYDDEN'S POWER--IT ISN'T ENOUGH!

THEN IT ALL COMES DOWN TO *US!*

PURE WILL AND GENIUS TECHNOLOGY.

EVERYTHING WE'VE *GOT,* REMEMBER?

POWER 0.5%

0.3%

AND WHEN WE'VE GIVEN *EVERYTHING* AND THERE'S *NO MORE* LEFT TO GIVE--

WE GO THE *EXTRA MILE!*

"Hell yeah!" he says as if he knows they're already home, already safe, just somewhere up ahead. "Lock course to OA!

"All remaining power accelerate to space fold NOW--"

SEE?

SAY WHAT, PERDOO?...
SEE? I SAID!
I SAW!
A RING APPEARED FROM NOWHERE!
RING DEPLETED.
IMMEDIATE ATTENTION REQUIRED!
HAL JORDAN!
JORDAN IS INSIDE THE RING!
...REVERSE MINIATURIZATION--
EMERGENCY PROTOCOL O-900.
BRINGING HIM UP NOW!

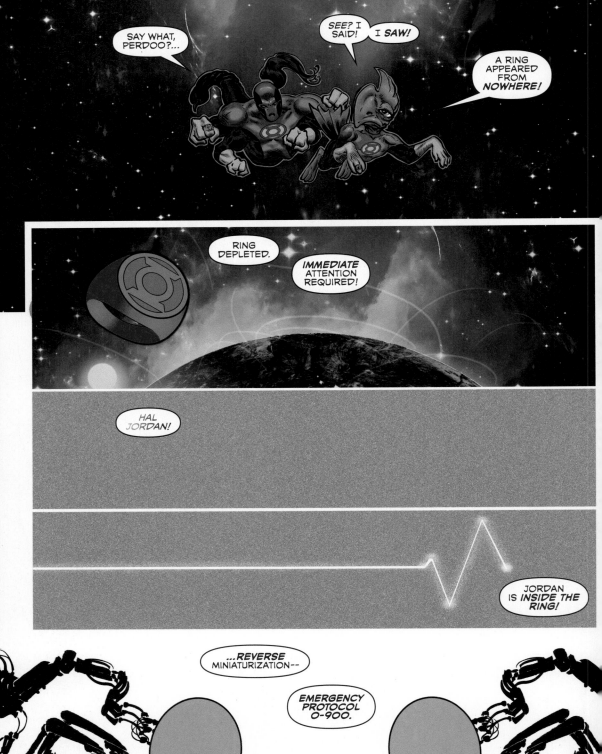

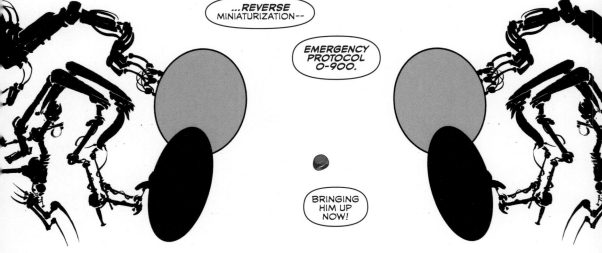

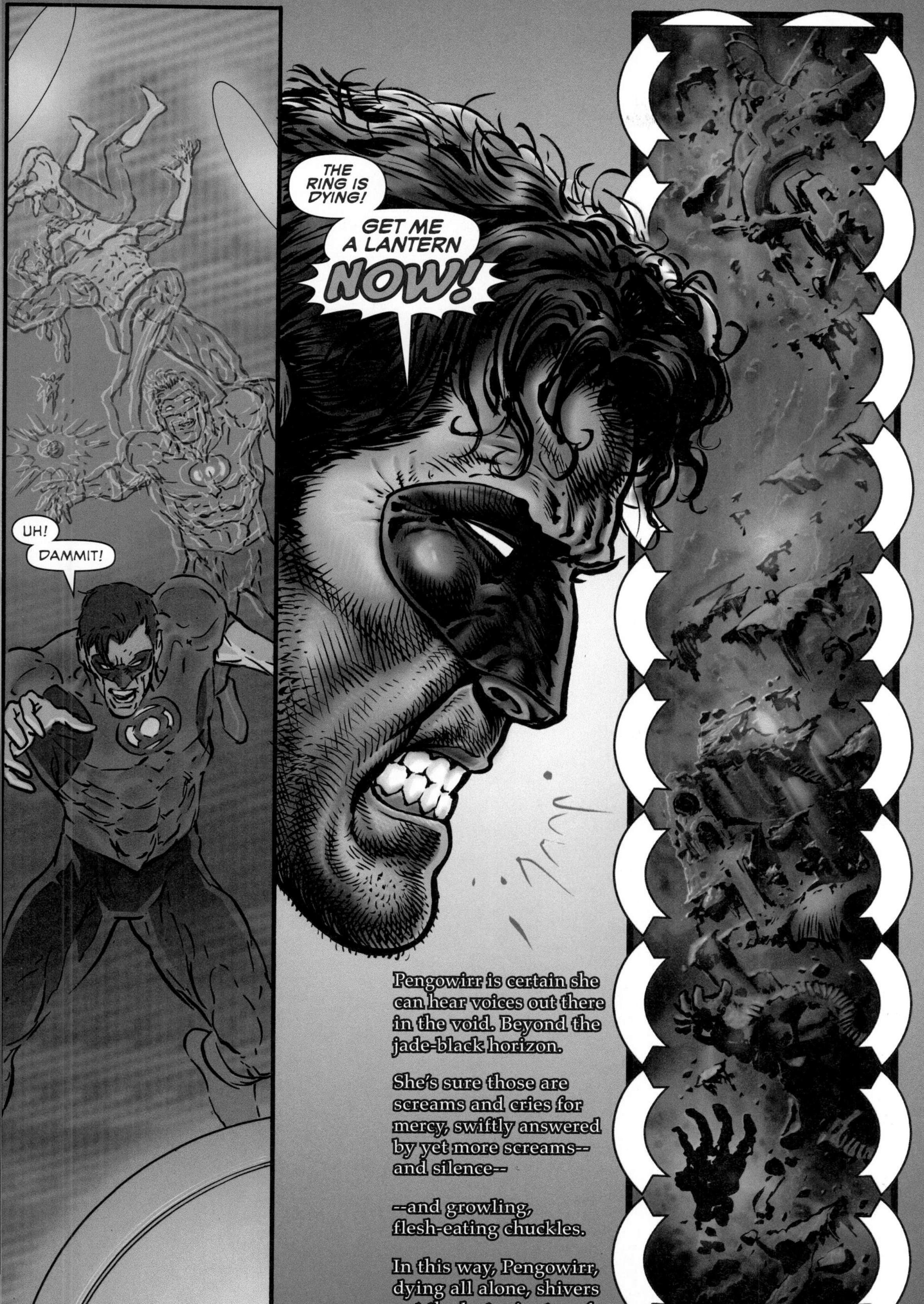

THE RING IS DYING!
GET ME A LANTERN NOW!
UH! DAMMIT!
Pengowirr is certain she can hear voices out there in the void. Beyond the jade-black horizon.
She's sure those are screams and cries for mercy, swiftly answered by yet more screams-- and silence--
--and growling, flesh-eating chuckles.
In this way, Pengowirr, dying all alone, shivers out the last minutes of existence.

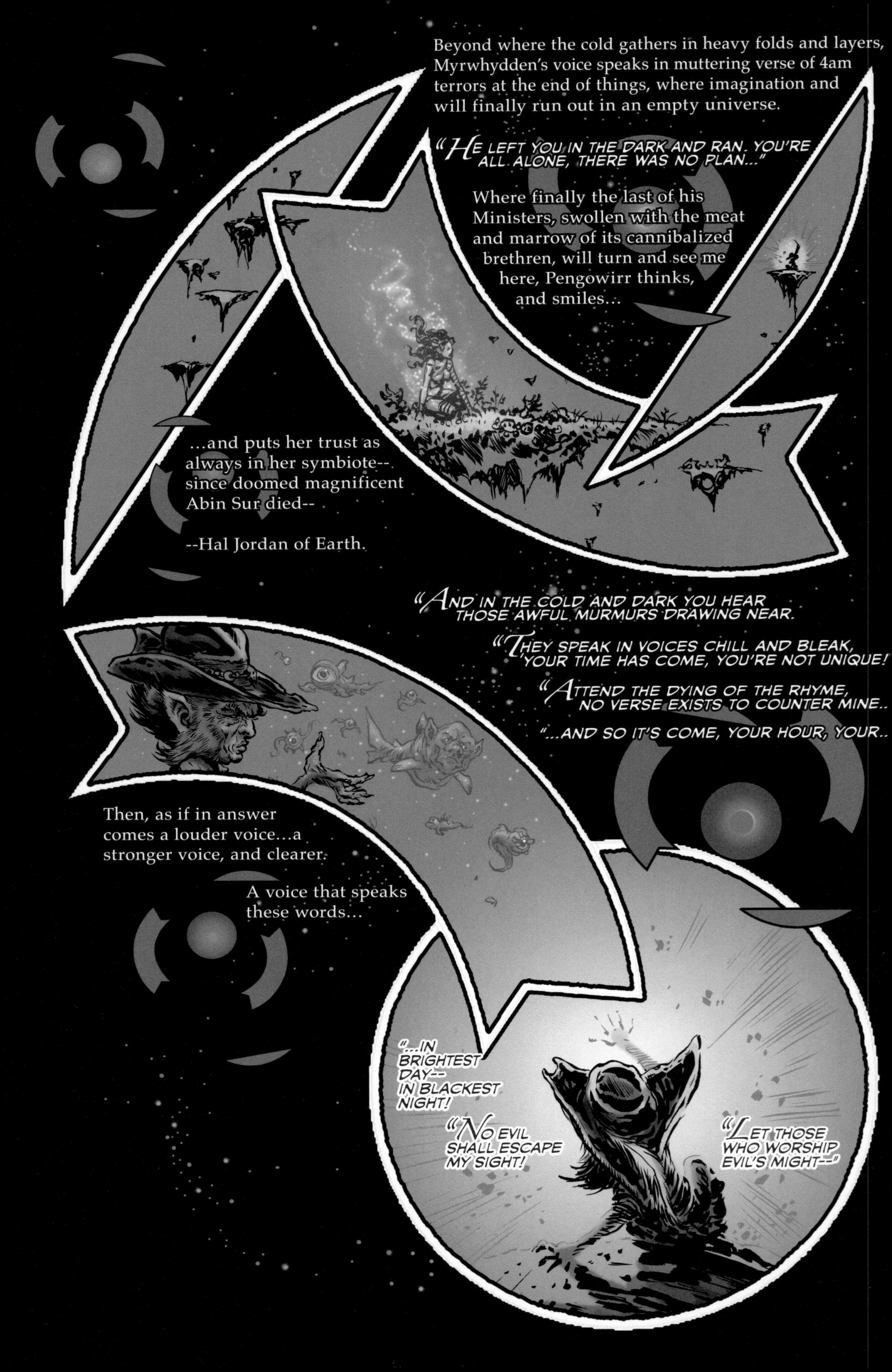

Beyond where the cold gathers in heavy folds and layers, Myrwhydden's voice speaks in muttering verse of 4am terrors at the end of things, where imagination and will finally run out in an empty universe.
"He left you in the dark and ran. You're all alone, there was no plan..."
Where finally the last of his Ministers, swollen with the meat and marrow of its cannibalized brethren, will turn and see me here, Pengowirr thinks, and smiles...
...and puts her trust as always in her symbiote-- since doomed magnificent Abin Sur died--
--Hal Jordan of Earth.
"And in the cold and dark you hear those awful murmurs drawing near.
"They speak in voices chill and bleak, 'your time has come, you're not unique!
"Attend the dying of the rhyme, no verse exists to counter mine..
"...and so it's come, your hour, your..
Then, as if in answer comes a louder voice...a stronger voice, and clearer.
A voice that speaks these words...
"...In brightest day-- in blackest night!
"No evil shall escape my sight!
"Let those who worship evil's might--"

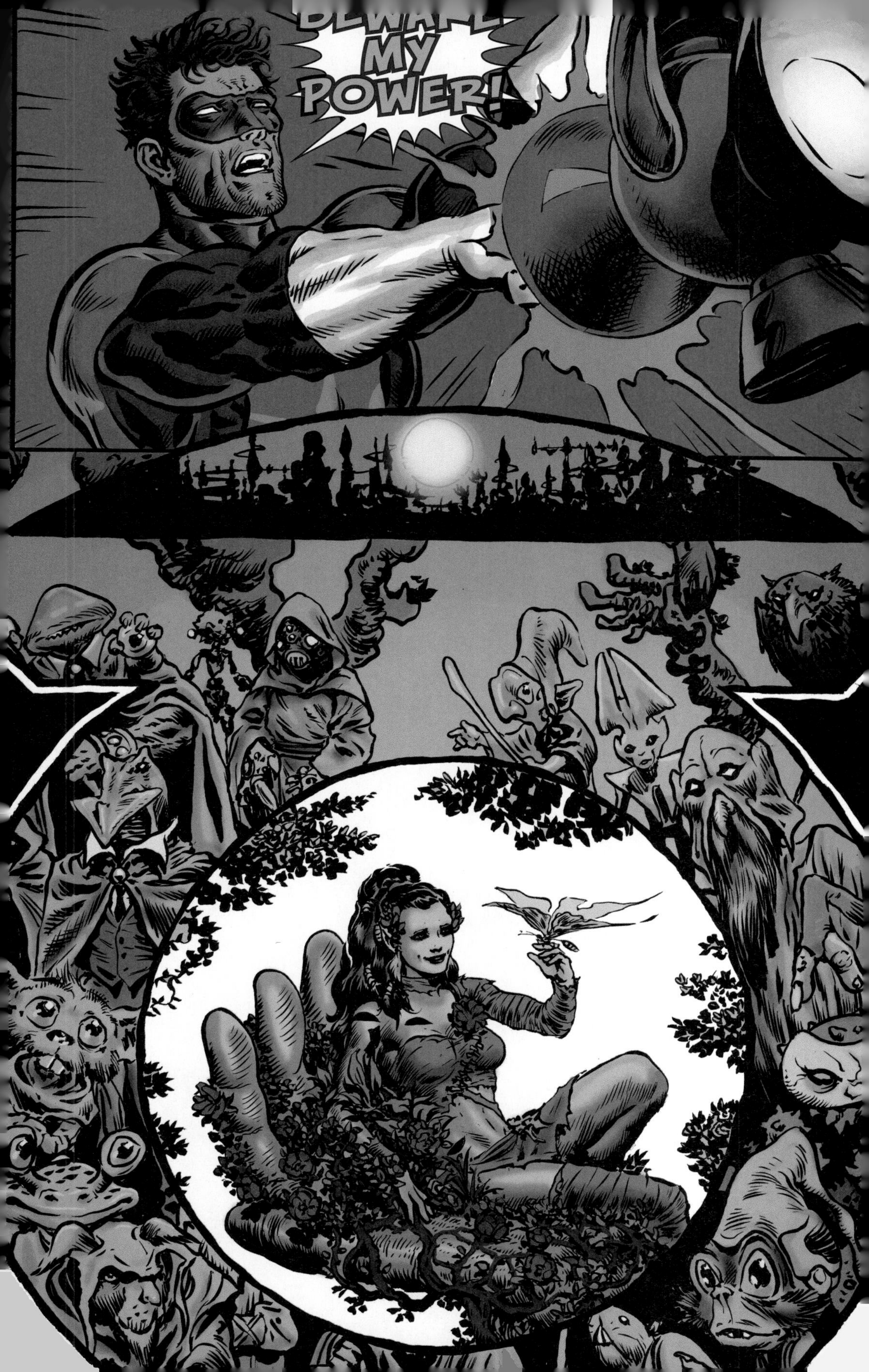
MY POWER!

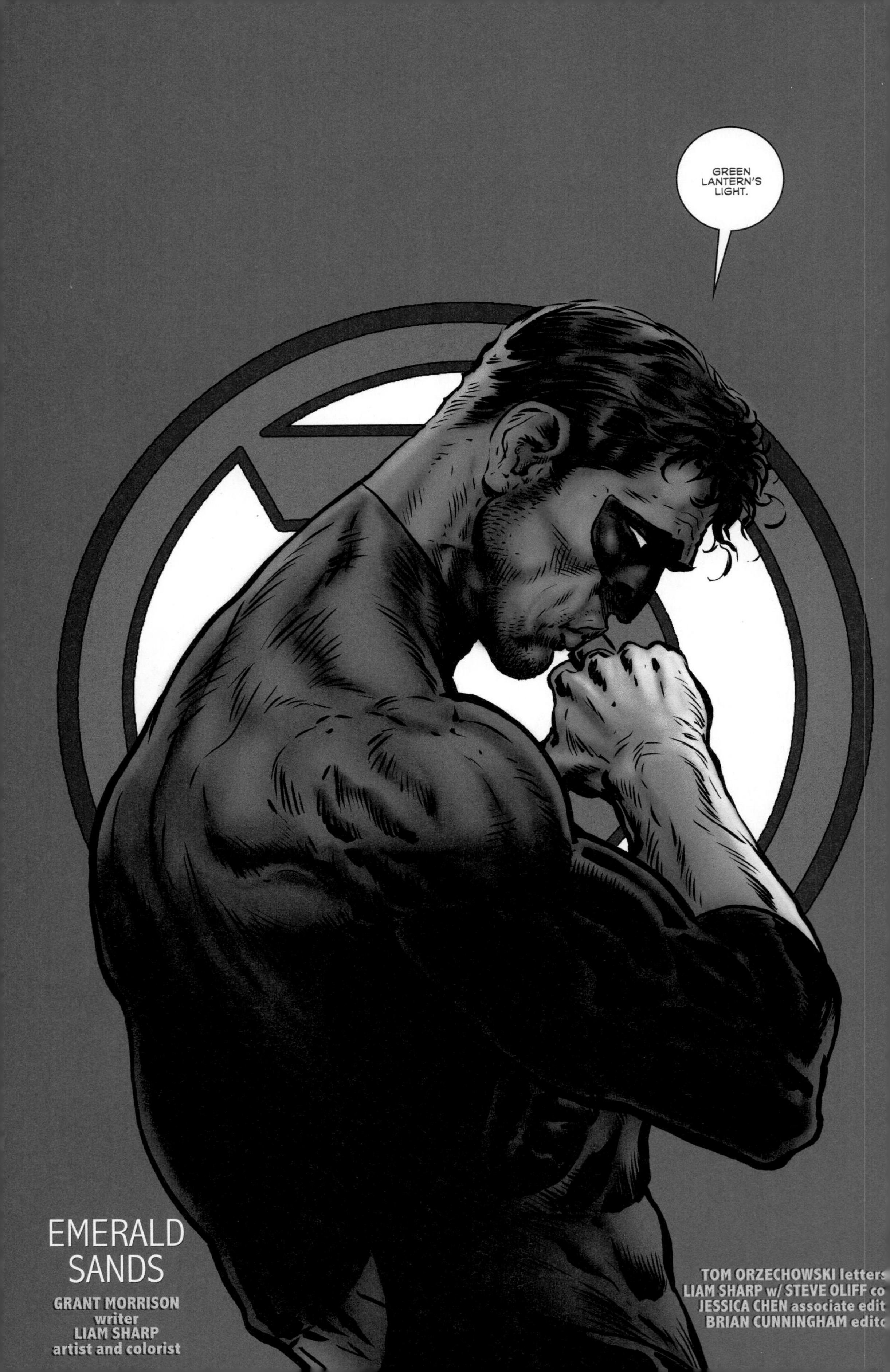

GREEN LANTERN'S LIGHT.
EMERALD SANDS
GRANT MORRISON writer
LIAM SHARP artist and colorist
TOM ORZECHOWSKI letters
LIAM SHARP w/ STEVE OLIFF co
JESSICA CHEN associate edit
BRIAN CUNNINGHAM edit

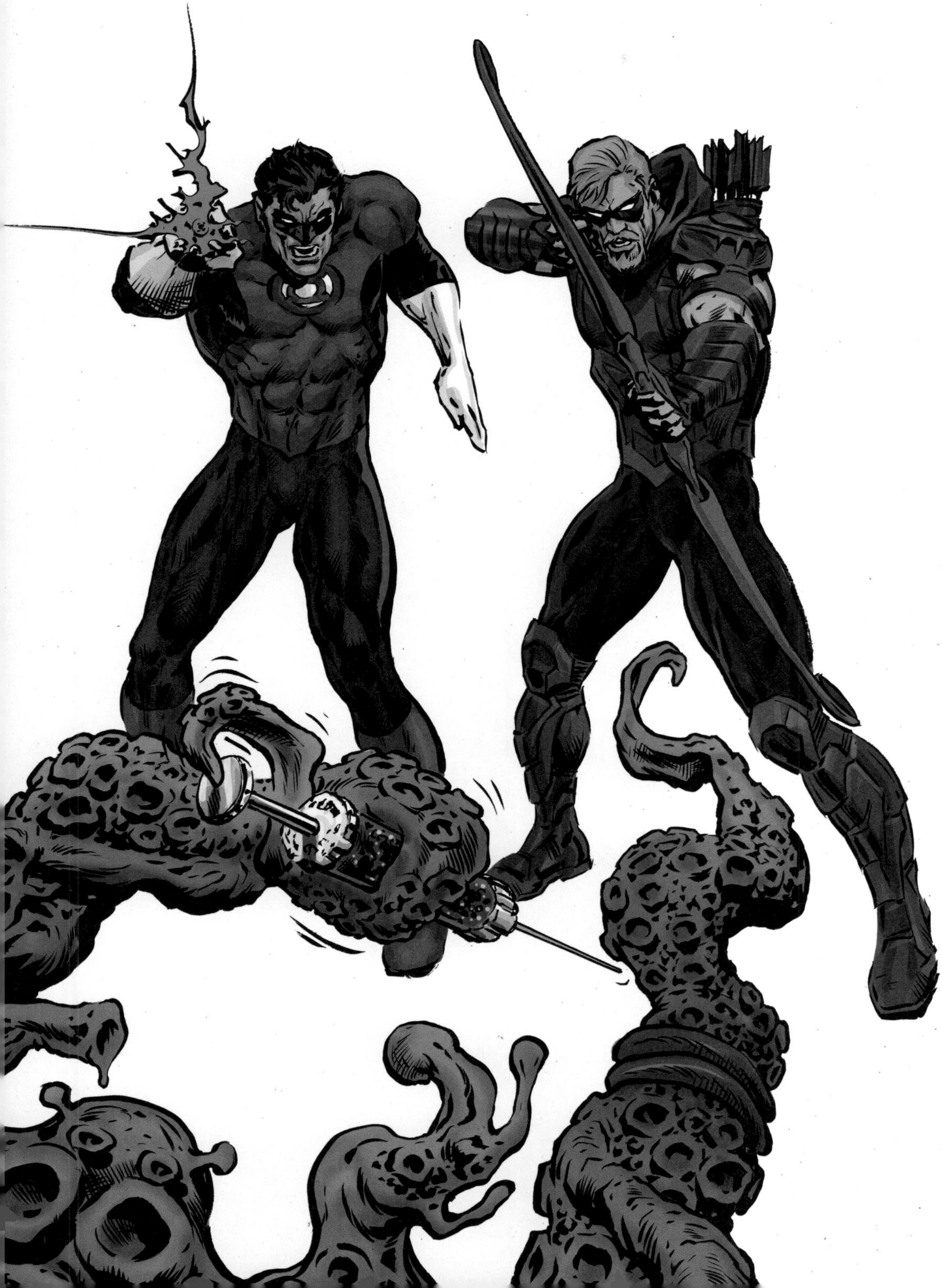

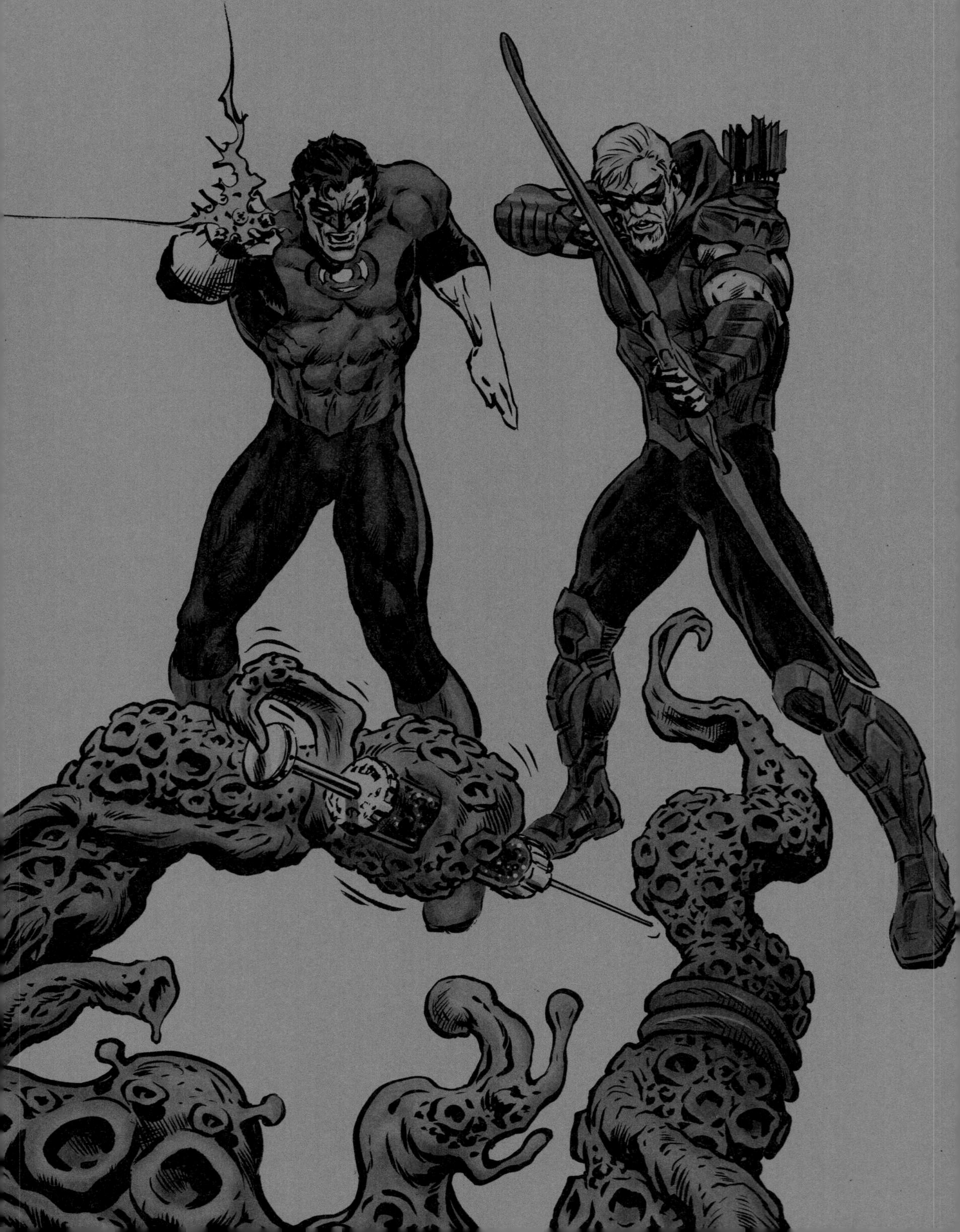

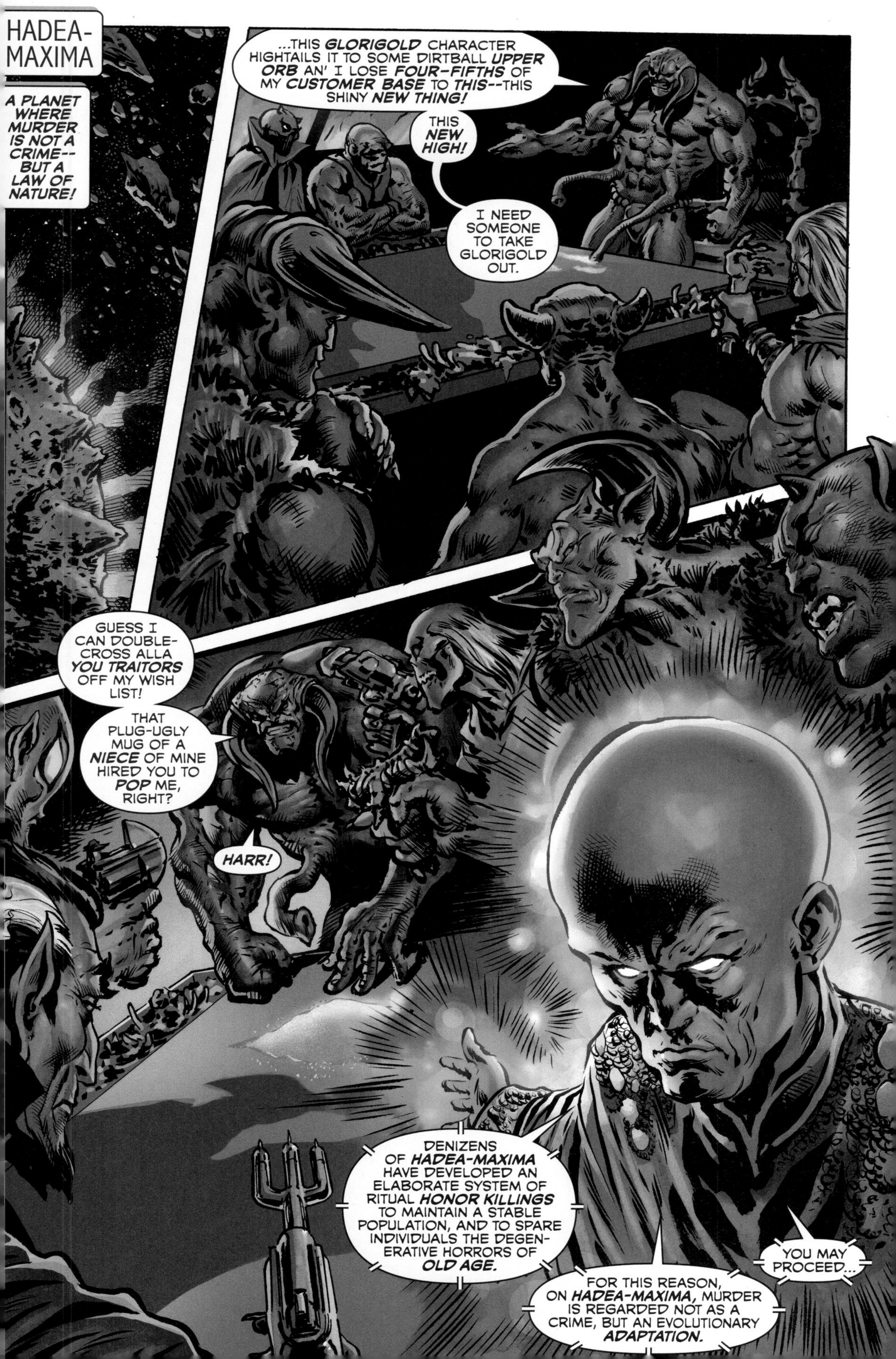
HADEA-MAXIMA
A PLANET WHERE MURDER IS NOT A CRIME--BUT A LAW OF NATURE!
...THIS GLORIGOLD CHARACTER HIGHTAILS IT TO SOME DIRTBALL UPPER ORB AN' I LOSE FOUR-FIFTHS OF MY CUSTOMER BASE TO THIS--THIS SHINY NEW THING!
THIS NEW HIGH!
I NEED SOMEONE TO TAKE GLORIGOLD OUT.
GUESS I CAN DOUBLE-CROSS ALLA YOU TRAITORS OFF MY WISH LIST!
THAT PLUG-UGLY MUG OF A NIECE OF MINE HIRED YOU TO POP ME, RIGHT?
HARR!
DENIZENS OF HADEA-MAXIMA HAVE DEVELOPED AN ELABORATE SYSTEM OF RITUAL HONOR KILLINGS TO MAINTAIN A STABLE POPULATION, AND TO SPARE INDIVIDUALS THE DEGENERATIVE HORRORS OF OLD AGE.
FOR THIS REASON, ON HADEA-MAXIMA, MURDER IS REGARDED NOT AS A CRIME, BUT AN EVOLUTIONARY ADAPTATION.
YOU MAY PROCEED...

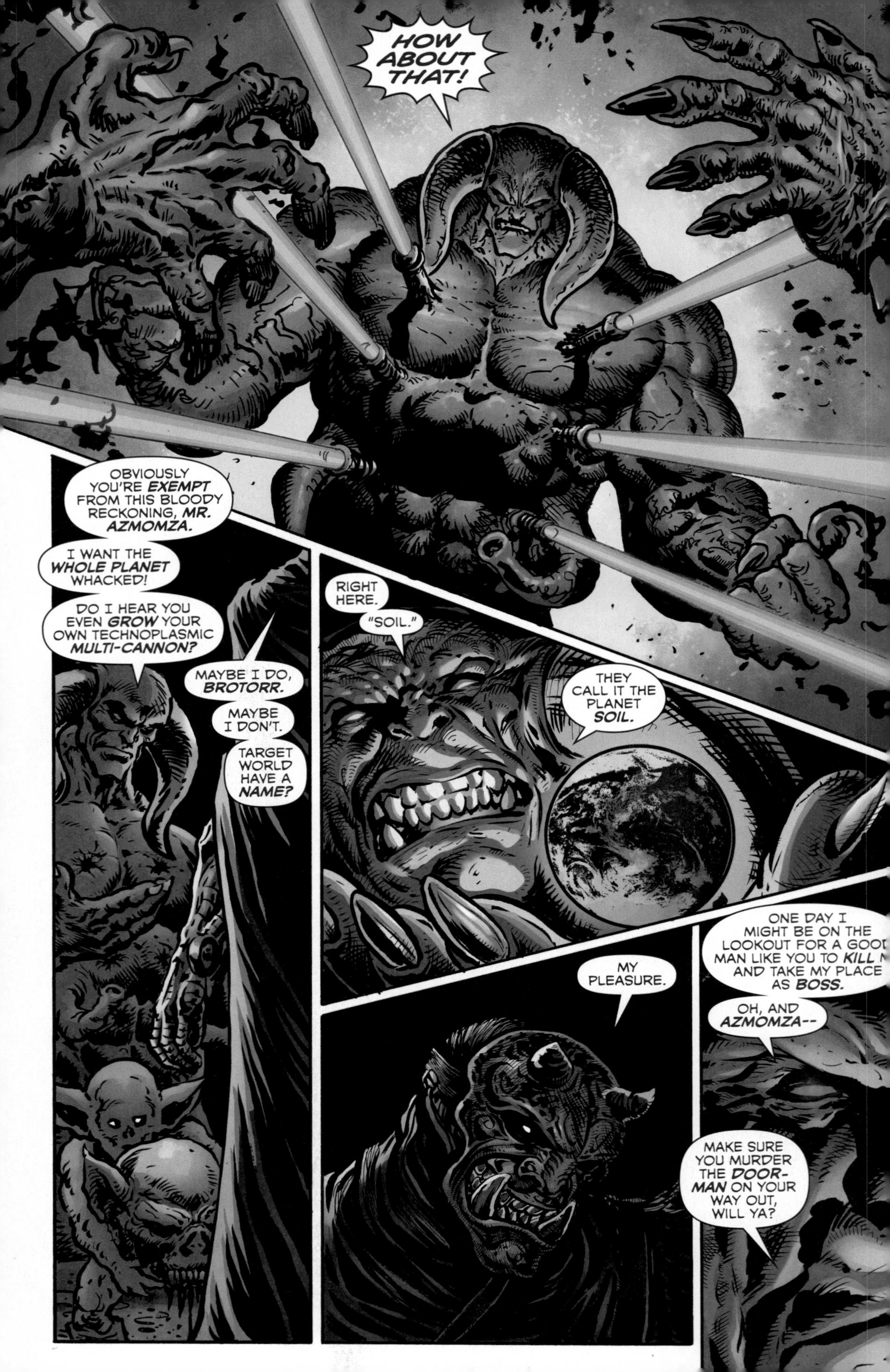
HOW ABOUT THAT!
OBVIOUSLY YOU'RE EXEMPT FROM THIS BLOODY RECKONING, MR. AZMOMZA.
I WANT THE WHOLE PLANET WHACKED!
DO I HEAR YOU EVEN GROW YOUR OWN TECHNOPLASMIC MULTI-CANNON?
MAYBE I DO, BROTORR.
MAYBE I DON'T.
TARGET WORLD HAVE A NAME?
RIGHT HERE.
"SOIL."
THEY CALL IT THE PLANET SOIL.
MY PLEASURE.
OH, AND AZMOMZA--
MAKE SURE YOU MURDER THE DOOR-MAN ON YOUR WAY OUT, WILL YA?

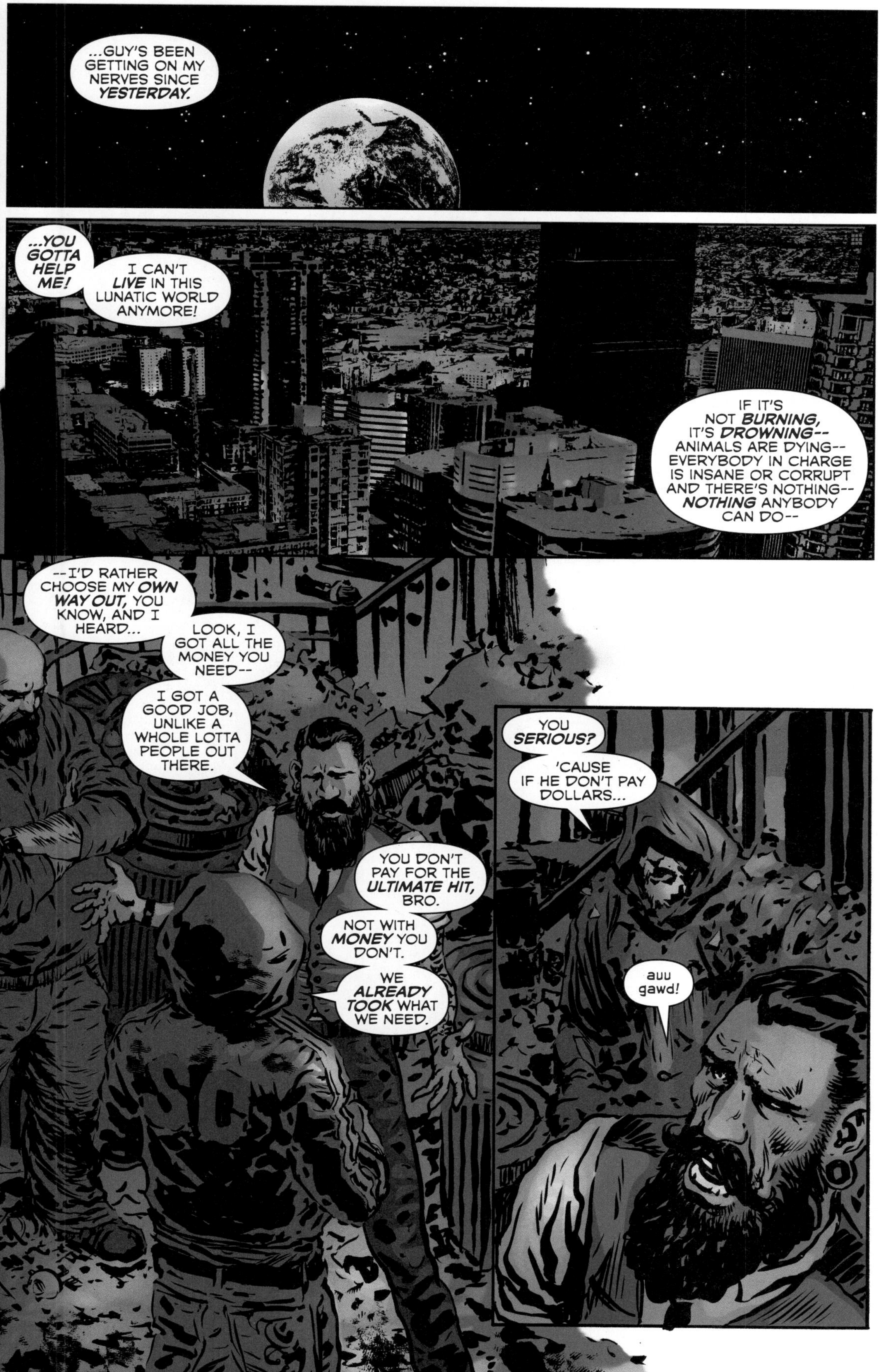
...GUY'S BEEN GETTING ON MY NERVES SINCE *YESTERDAY.*
...YOU GOTTA HELP ME!
I CAN'T *LIVE* IN THIS LUNATIC WORLD ANYMORE!
IF IT'S NOT *BURNING,* IT'S *DROWNING--* ANIMALS ARE DYING-- EVERYBODY IN CHARGE IS INSANE OR CORRUPT AND THERE'S NOTHING-- *NOTHING* ANYBODY CAN DO--
--I'D RATHER CHOOSE MY *OWN WAY OUT,* YOU KNOW, AND I HEARD...
LOOK, I GOT ALL THE MONEY YOU NEED--
I GOT A GOOD JOB, UNLIKE A WHOLE LOTTA PEOPLE OUT THERE.
YOU DON'T PAY FOR THE *ULTIMATE HIT,* BRO.
NOT WITH *MONEY* YOU DON'T.
WE *ALREADY TOOK* WHAT WE NEED.
YOU *SERIOUS?*
'CAUSE IF HE DON'T PAY DOLLARS...
auu gawd!

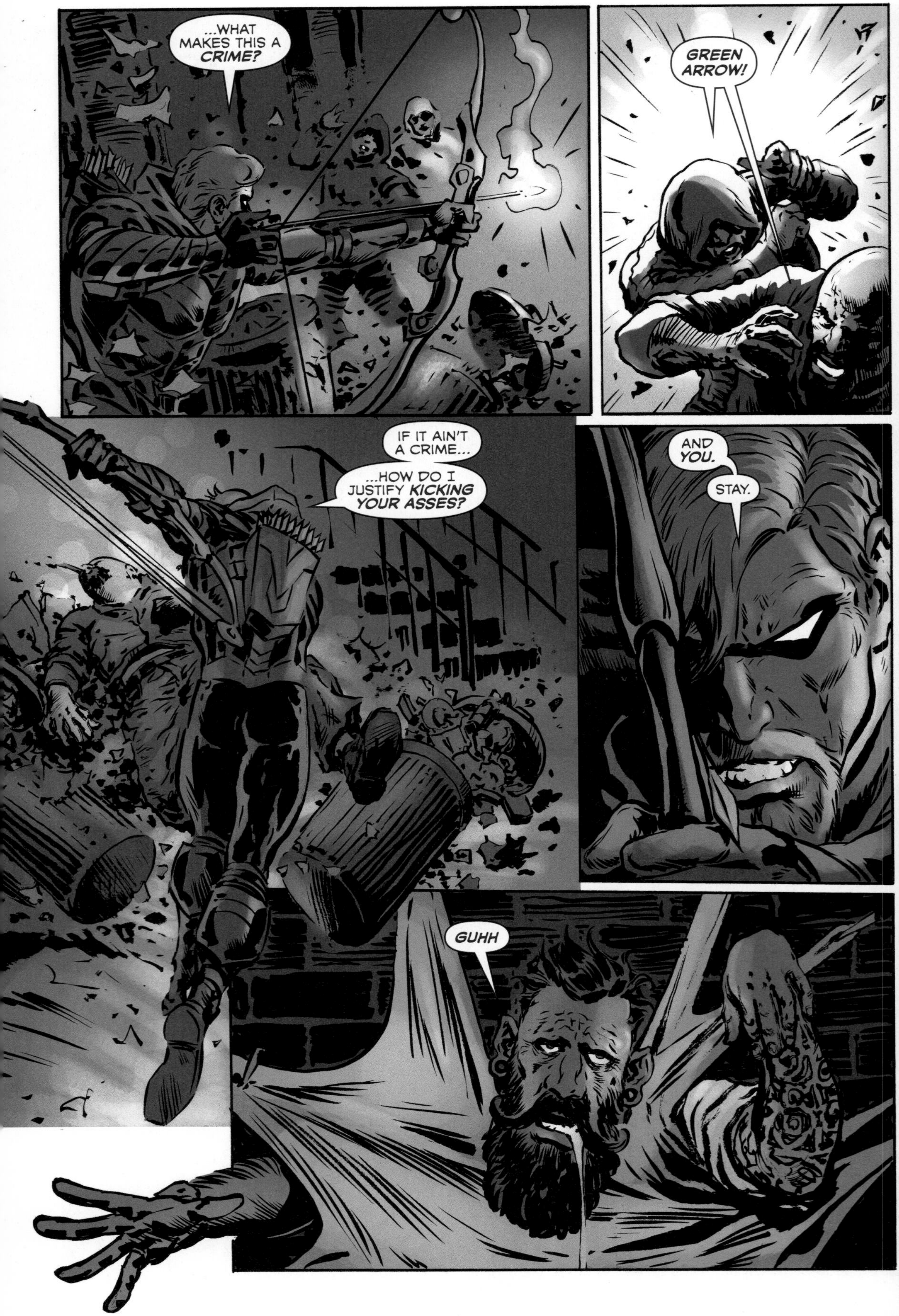

...WHAT MAKES THIS A *CRIME?*
GREEN ARROW!
IF IT AIN'T A CRIME...
...HOW DO I JUSTIFY *KICKING YOUR ASSES?*
AND *YOU.*
STAY.
GUHH

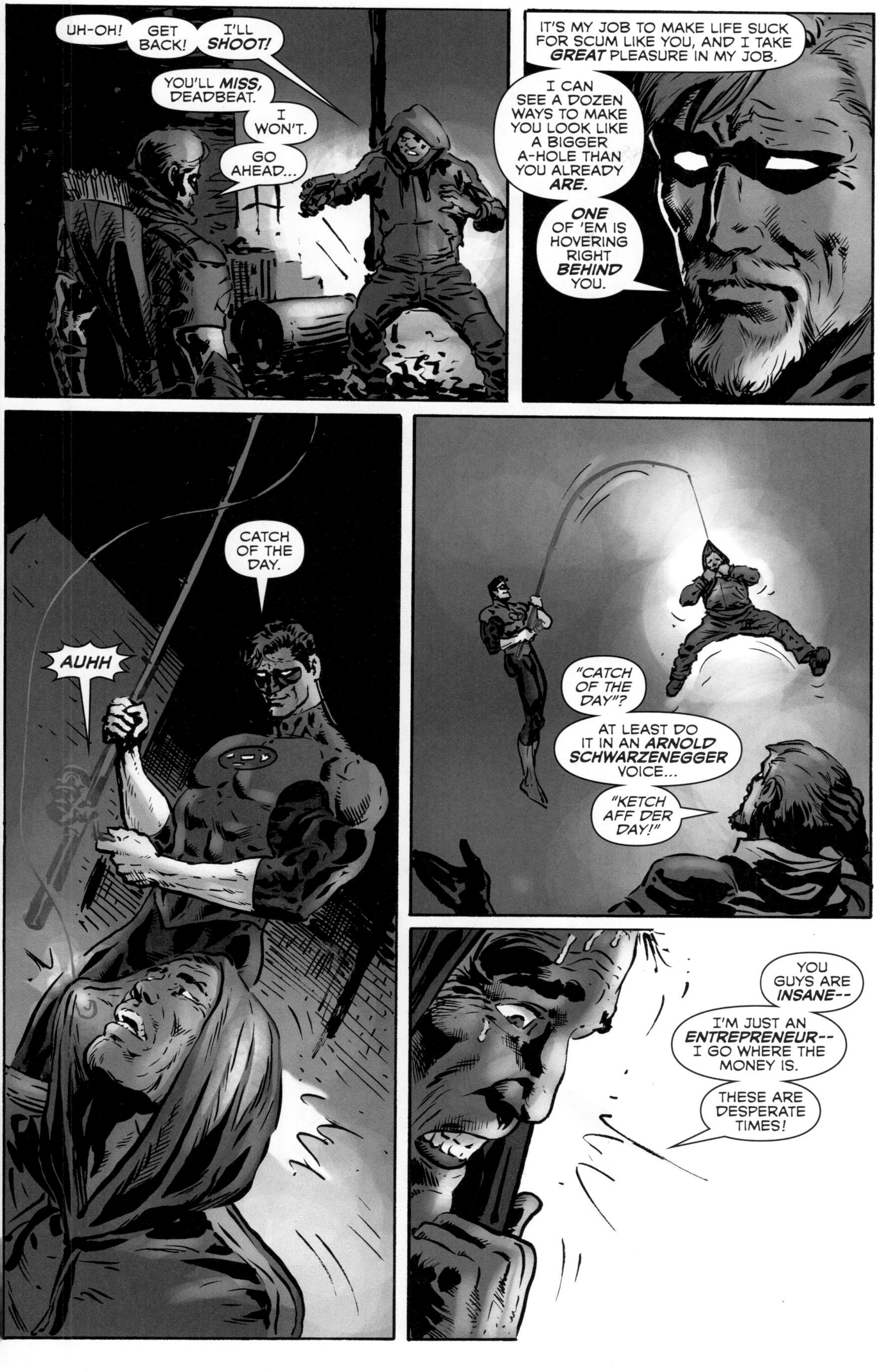
UH-OH!
GET BACK!
I'LL SHOOT!
YOU'LL MISS, DEADBEAT.
I WON'T.
GO AHEAD...
IT'S MY JOB TO MAKE LIFE SUCK FOR SCUM LIKE YOU, AND I TAKE GREAT PLEASURE IN MY JOB.
I CAN SEE A DOZEN WAYS TO MAKE YOU LOOK LIKE A BIGGER A-HOLE THAN YOU ALREADY ARE.
ONE OF 'EM IS HOVERING RIGHT BEHIND YOU.
CATCH OF THE DAY.
AUHH
"CATCH OF THE DAY"?
AT LEAST DO IT IN AN ARNOLD SCHWARZENEGGER VOICE...
"KETCH AFF DER DAY!"
YOU GUYS ARE INSANE--
I'M JUST AN ENTREPRENEUR-- I GO WHERE THE MONEY IS.
THESE ARE DESPERATE TIMES!

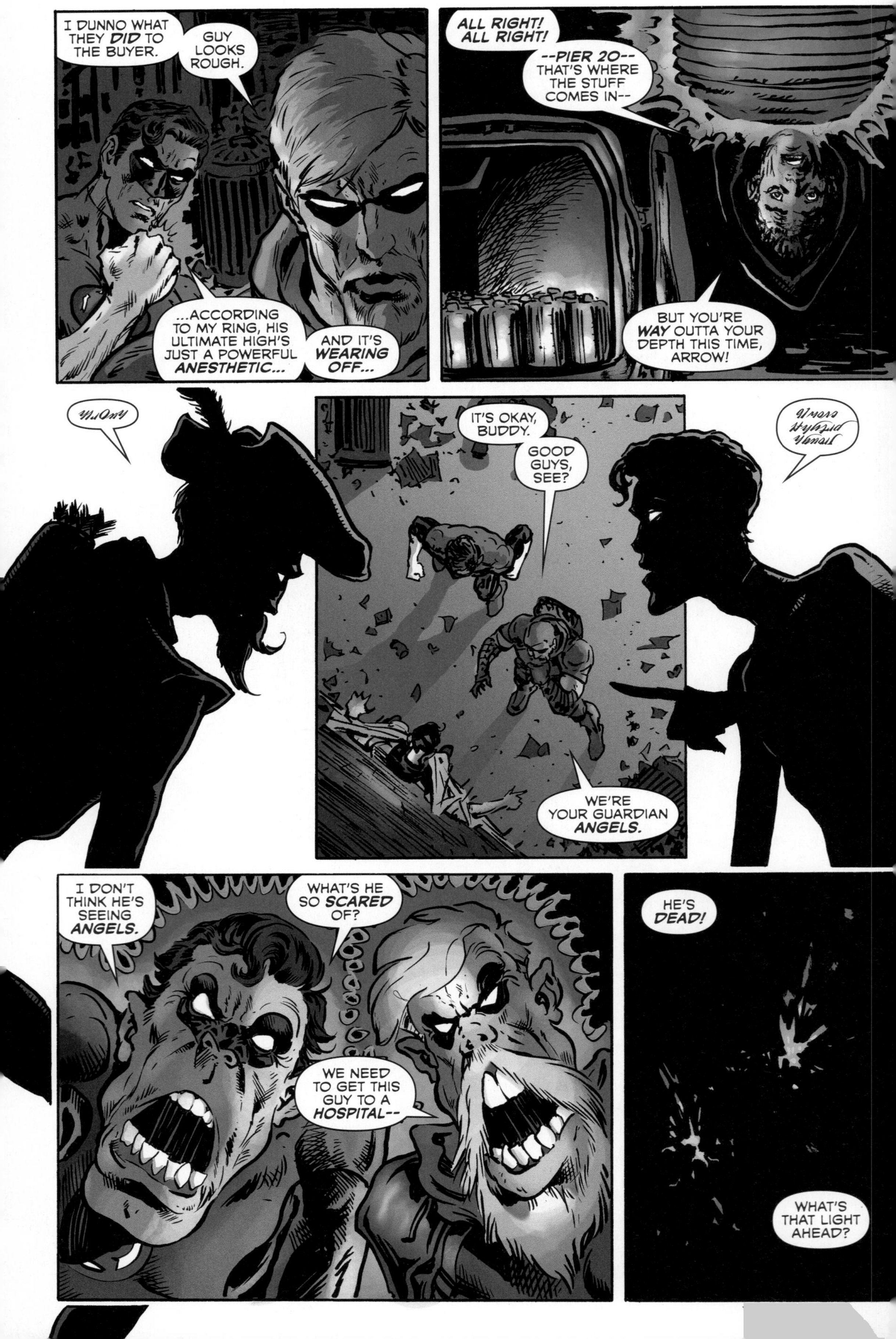
I DUNNO WHAT THEY DID TO THE BUYER.
GUY LOOKS ROUGH.
...ACCORDING TO MY RING, HIS ULTIMATE HIGH'S JUST A POWERFUL ANESTHETIC...
AND IT'S WEARING OFF...
ALL RIGHT! ALL RIGHT!
--PIER 20-- THAT'S WHERE THE STUFF COMES IN--
BUT YOU'RE WAY OUTTA YOUR DEPTH THIS TIME, ARROW!
IT'S OKAY, BUDDY.
GOOD GUYS, SEE?
WE'RE YOUR GUARDIAN ANGELS.
I DON'T THINK HE'S SEEING ANGELS.
WHAT'S HE SO SCARED OF?
WE NEED TO GET THIS GUY TO A HOSPITAL--
HE'S DEAD!
WHAT'S THAT LIGHT AHEAD?

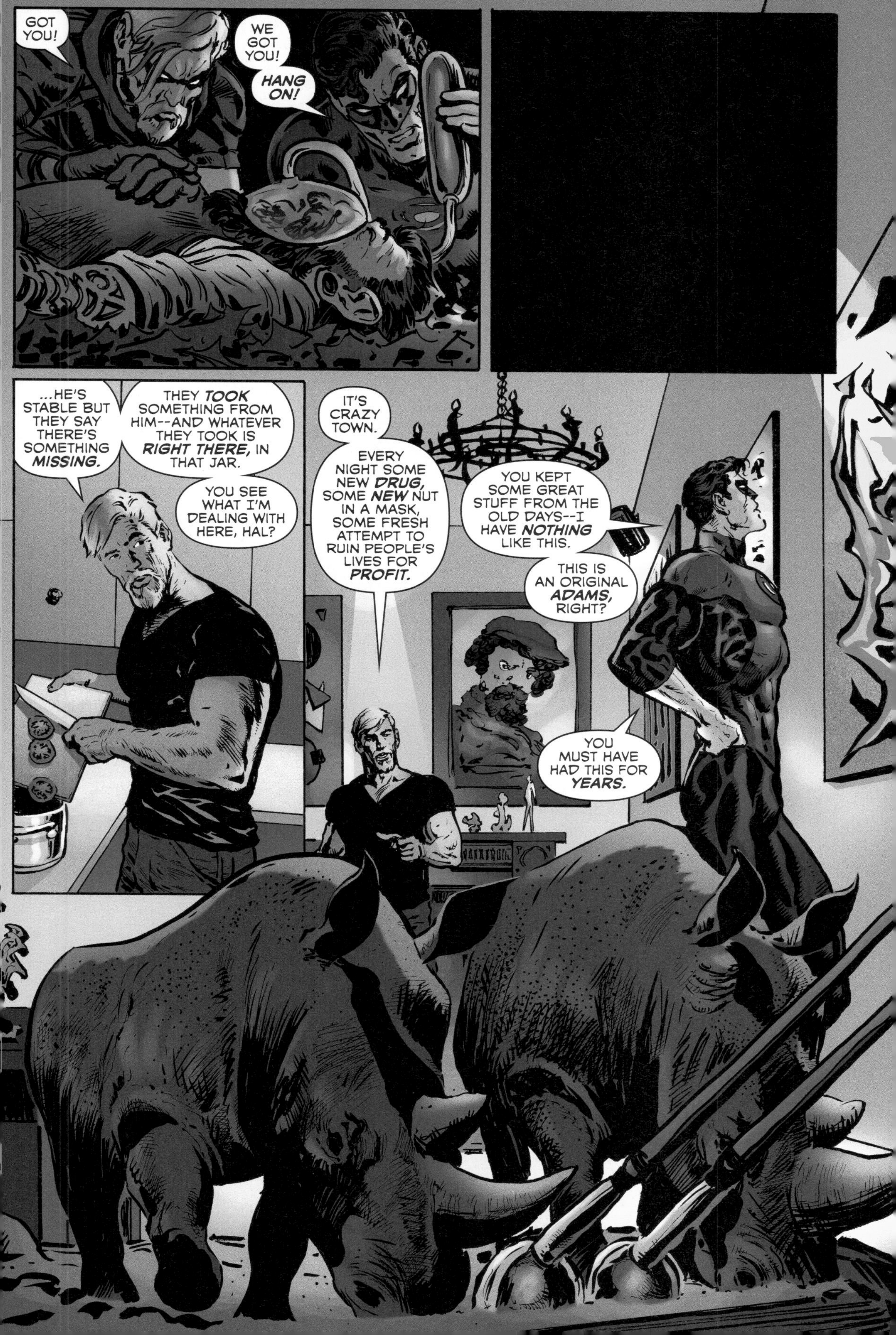
GOT YOU!
WE GOT YOU!
HANG ON!
...HE'S STABLE BUT THEY SAY THERE'S SOMETHING MISSING.
THEY TOOK SOMETHING FROM HIM--AND WHATEVER THEY TOOK IS RIGHT THERE, IN THAT JAR.
YOU SEE WHAT I'M DEALING WITH HERE, HAL?
IT'S CRAZY TOWN.
EVERY NIGHT SOME NEW DRUG, SOME NEW NUT IN A MASK, SOME FRESH ATTEMPT TO RUIN PEOPLE'S LIVES FOR PROFIT.
YOU KEPT SOME GREAT STUFF FROM THE OLD DAYS--I HAVE NOTHING LIKE THIS.
THIS IS AN ORIGINAL ADAMS, RIGHT?
YOU MUST HAVE HAD THIS FOR YEARS.

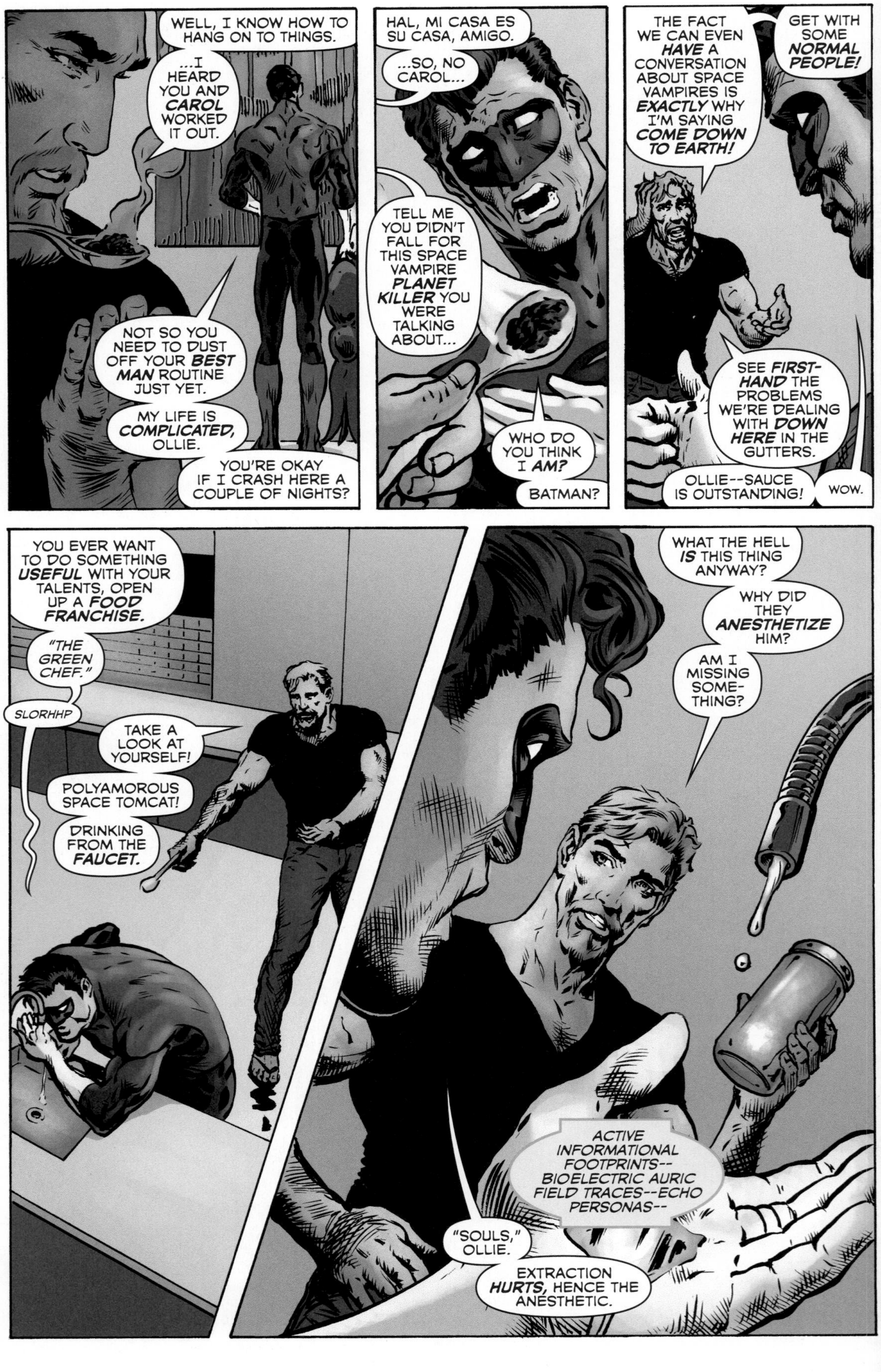
WELL, I KNOW HOW TO HANG ON TO THINGS.
...I HEARD YOU AND CAROL WORKED IT OUT.
NOT SO YOU NEED TO DUST OFF YOUR BEST MAN ROUTINE JUST YET.
MY LIFE IS COMPLICATED, OLLIE.
YOU'RE OKAY IF I CRASH HERE A COUPLE OF NIGHTS?
HAL, MI CASA ES SU CASA, AMIGO.
...SO, NO CAROL...
TELL ME YOU DIDN'T FALL FOR THIS SPACE VAMPIRE PLANET KILLER YOU WERE TALKING ABOUT...
WHO DO YOU THINK I AM?
BATMAN?
THE FACT WE CAN EVEN HAVE A CONVERSATION ABOUT SPACE VAMPIRES IS EXACTLY WHY I'M SAYING COME DOWN TO EARTH!
GET WITH SOME NORMAL PEOPLE!
SEE FIRST-HAND THE PROBLEMS WE'RE DEALING WITH DOWN HERE IN THE GUTTERS.
OLLIE--SAUCE IS OUTSTANDING!
WOW.
YOU EVER WANT TO DO SOMETHING USEFUL WITH YOUR TALENTS, OPEN UP A FOOD FRANCHISE.
"THE GREEN CHEF."
SLORHHP
TAKE A LOOK AT YOURSELF!
POLYAMOROUS SPACE TOMCAT!
DRINKING FROM THE FAUCET.
WHAT THE HELL IS THIS THING ANYWAY?
WHY DID THEY ANESTHETIZE HIM?
AM I MISSING SOME-THING?
ACTIVE INFORMATIONAL FOOTPRINTS-- BIOELECTRIC AURIC FIELD TRACES--ECHO PERSONAS--
"SOULS," OLLIE.
EXTRACTION HURTS, HENCE THE ANESTHETIC.

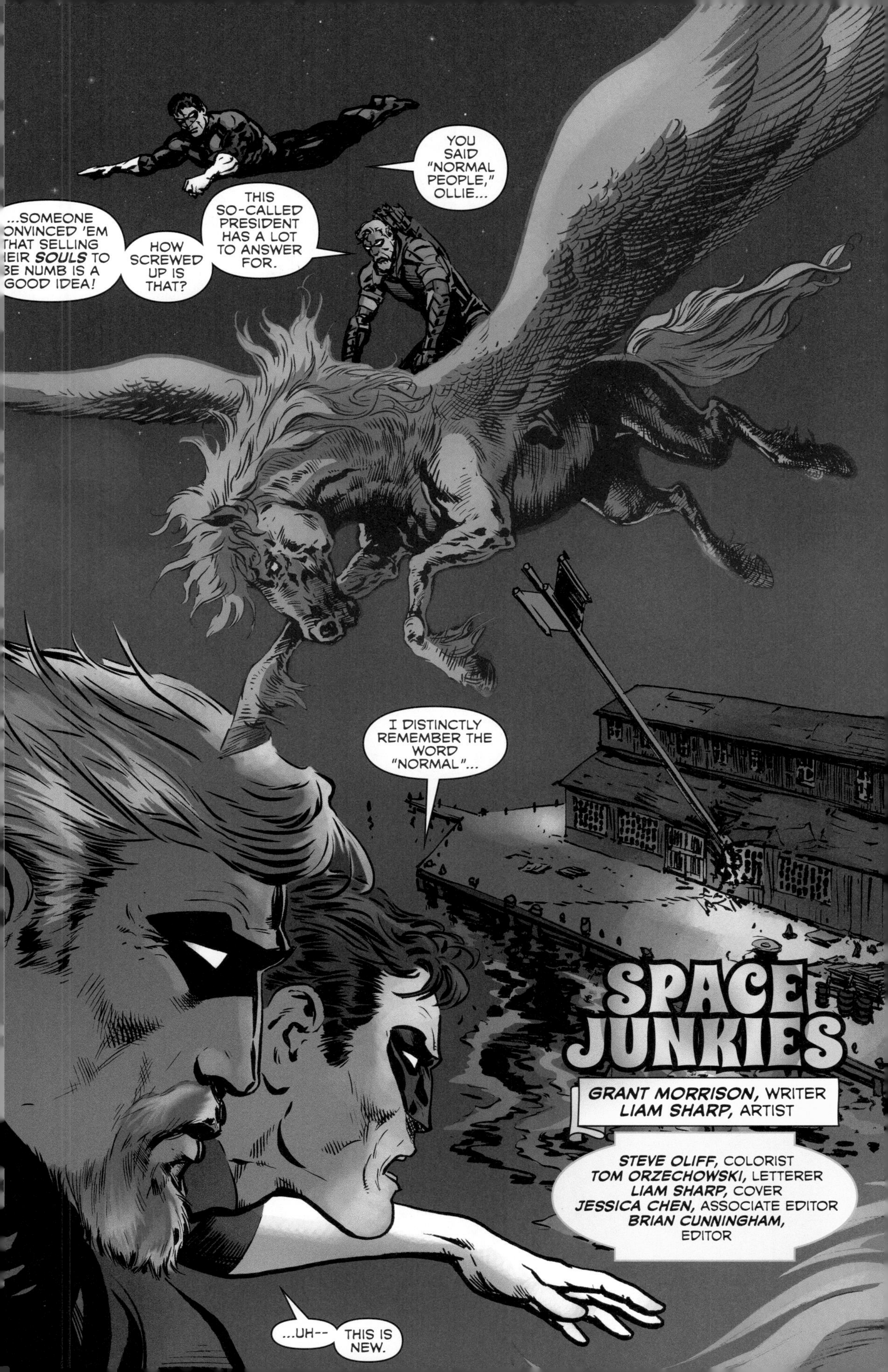
YOU SAID "NORMAL PEOPLE," OLLIE...
THIS SO-CALLED PRESIDENT HAS A LOT TO ANSWER FOR.
HOW SCREWED UP IS THAT?
...SOMEONE ONVINCED 'EM THAT SELLING IEIR SOULS TO BE NUMB IS A GOOD IDEA!
I DISTINCTLY REMEMBER THE WORD "NORMAL"...
SPACE JUNKIES
GRANT MORRISON, WRITER
LIAM SHARP, ARTIST
STEVE OLIFF, COLORIST
TOM ORZECHOWSKI, LETTERER
LIAM SHARP, COVER
JESSICA CHEN, ASSOCIATE EDITOR
BRIAN CUNNINGHAM, EDITOR
...UH--
THIS IS NEW.

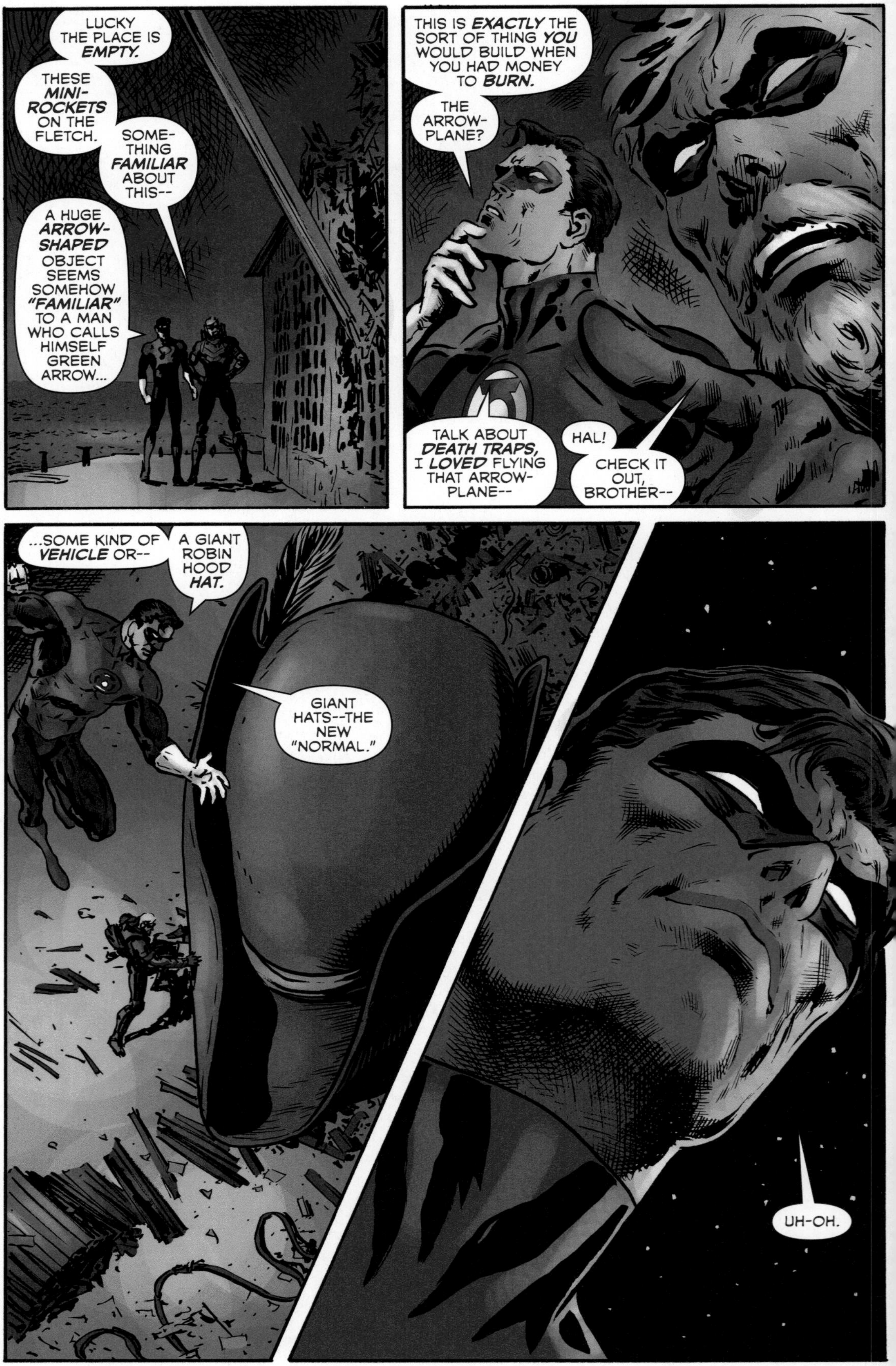
LUCKY THE PLACE IS EMPTY.
THESE MINI-ROCKETS ON THE FLETCH.
SOME-THING FAMILIAR ABOUT THIS--
A HUGE ARROW-SHAPED OBJECT SEEMS SOMEHOW "FAMILIAR" TO A MAN WHO CALLS HIMSELF GREEN ARROW...
THIS IS EXACTLY THE SORT OF THING YOU WOULD BUILD WHEN YOU HAD MONEY TO BURN.
THE ARROW-PLANE?
TALK ABOUT DEATH TRAPS, I LOVED FLYING THAT ARROW-PLANE--
HAL!
CHECK IT OUT, BROTHER--
...SOME KIND OF VEHICLE OR--
A GIANT ROBIN HOOD HAT.
GIANT HATS--THE NEW "NORMAL."
UH-OH.

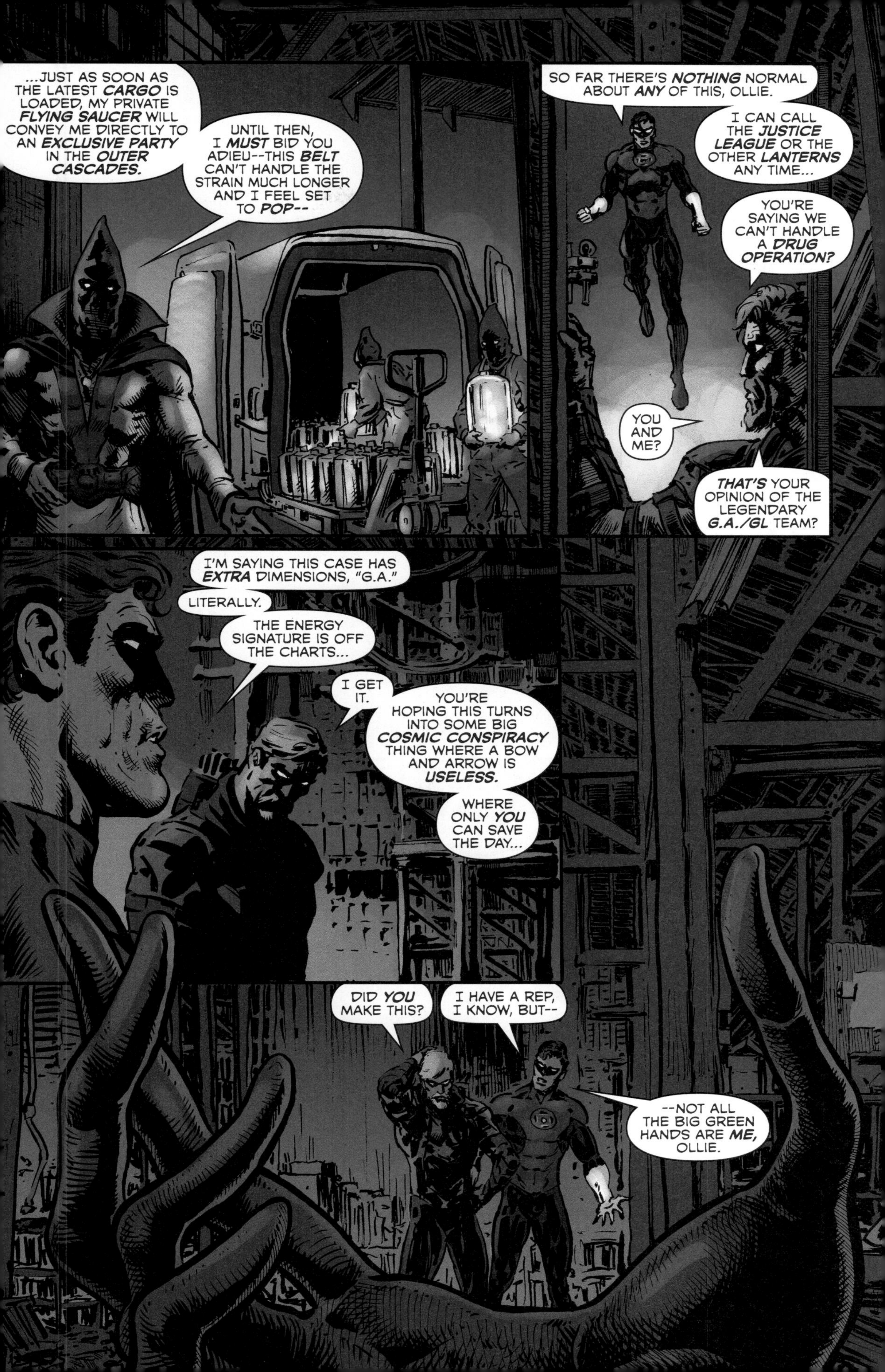
...JUST AS SOON AS THE LATEST CARGO IS LOADED, MY PRIVATE FLYING SAUCER WILL CONVEY ME DIRECTLY TO AN EXCLUSIVE PARTY IN THE OUTER CASCADES.
UNTIL THEN, I MUST BID YOU ADIEU--THIS BELT CAN'T HANDLE THE STRAIN MUCH LONGER AND I FEEL SET TO POP--
SO FAR THERE'S NOTHING NORMAL ABOUT ANY OF THIS, OLLIE.
I CAN CALL THE JUSTICE LEAGUE OR THE OTHER LANTERNS ANY TIME...
YOU'RE SAYING WE CAN'T HANDLE A DRUG OPERATION?
YOU AND ME?
THAT'S YOUR OPINION OF THE LEGENDARY G.A./GL TEAM?
I'M SAYING THIS CASE HAS EXTRA DIMENSIONS, "G.A."
LITERALLY.
THE ENERGY SIGNATURE IS OFF THE CHARTS...
I GET IT.
YOU'RE HOPING THIS TURNS INTO SOME BIG COSMIC CONSPIRACY THING WHERE A BOW AND ARROW IS USELESS.
WHERE ONLY YOU CAN SAVE THE DAY...
DID YOU MAKE THIS?
I HAVE A REP, I KNOW, BUT--
--NOT ALL THE BIG GREEN HANDS ARE ME, OLLIE.

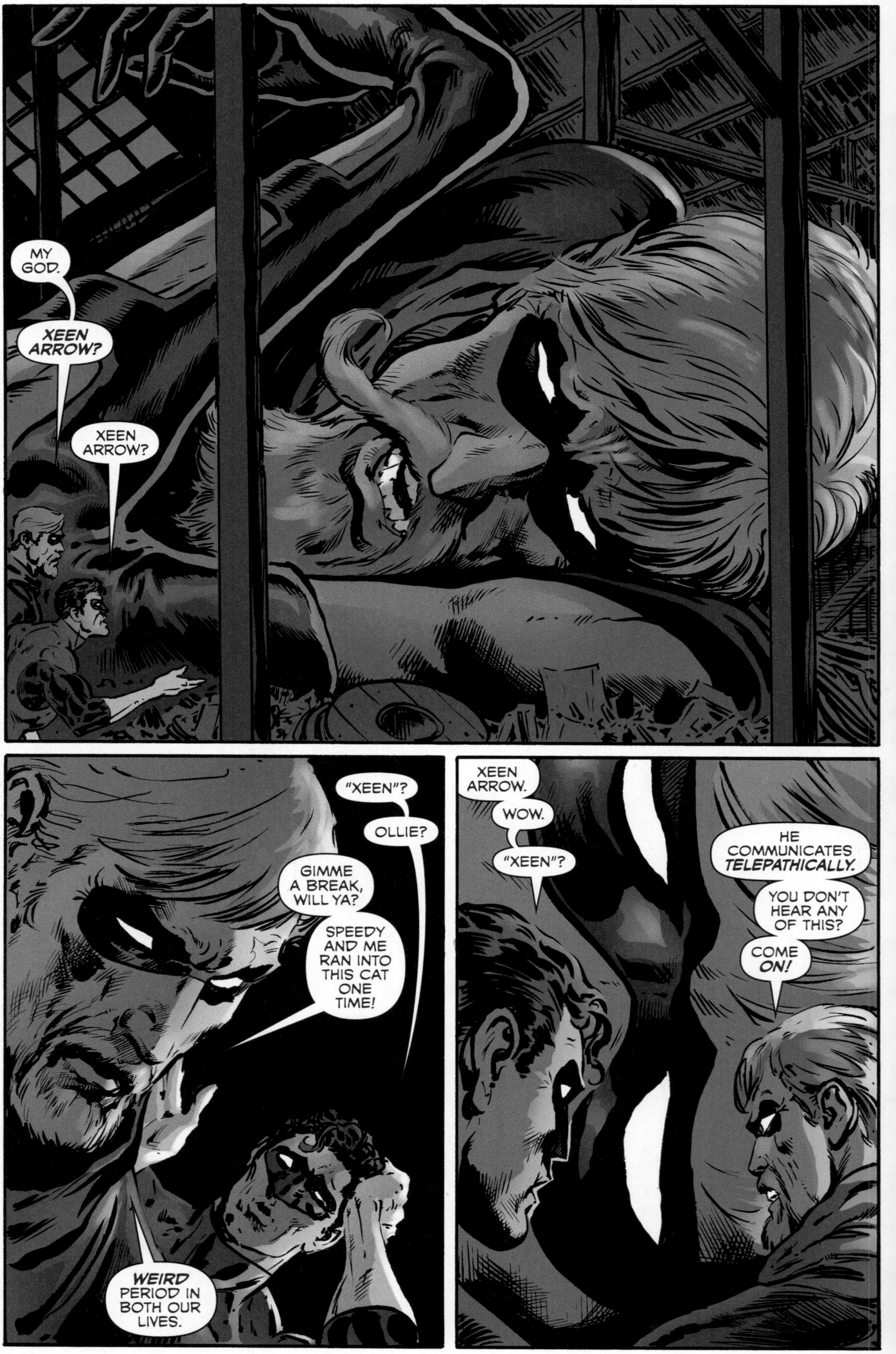
MY GOD.
XEEN ARROW?
XEEN ARROW?
"XEEN"?
OLLIE?
GIMME A BREAK, WILL YA?
SPEEDY AND ME RAN INTO THIS CAT ONE TIME!
WEIRD PERIOD IN BOTH OUR LIVES.
XEEN ARROW.
WOW.
"XEEN"?
HE COMMUNICATES TELEPATHICALLY.
YOU DON'T HEAR ANY OF THIS?
COME ON!

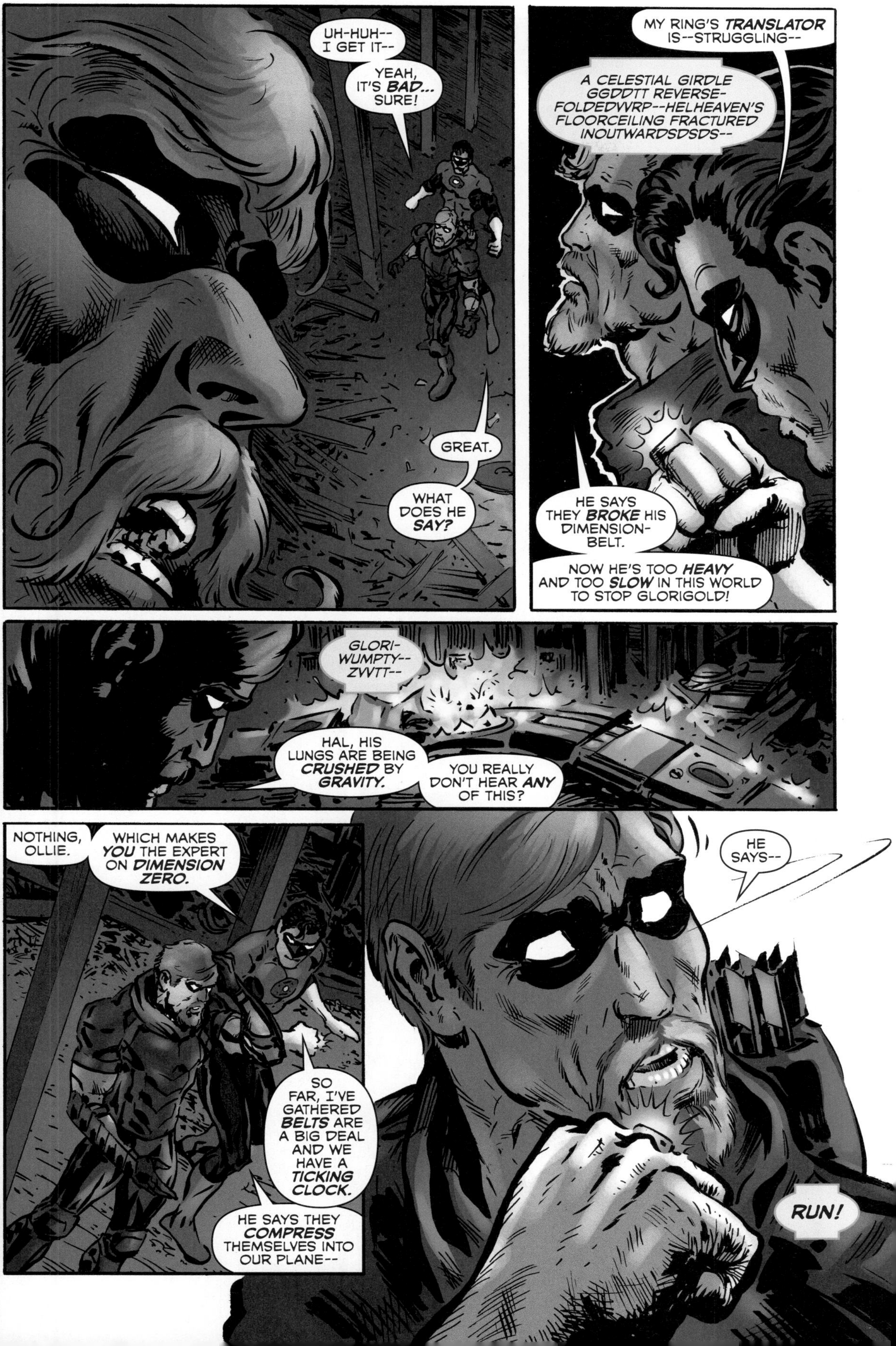
UH-HUH-- I GET IT--
YEAH, IT'S BAD... SURE!
GREAT.
WHAT DOES HE SAY?
MY RING'S TRANSLATOR IS--STRUGGLING--
A CELESTIAL GIRDLE GGDDTT REVERSE-FOLDEDVVRP--HELHEAVEN'S FLOORCEILING FRACTURED INOUTWARDSDSDS--
HE SAYS THEY BROKE HIS DIMENSION-BELT.
NOW HE'S TOO HEAVY AND TOO SLOW IN THIS WORLD TO STOP GLORIGOLD!
GLORI-WUMPTY--ZVVTT--
HAL, HIS LUNGS ARE BEING CRUSHED BY GRAVITY.
YOU REALLY DON'T HEAR ANY OF THIS?
NOTHING, OLLIE.
WHICH MAKES YOU THE EXPERT ON DIMENSION ZERO.
SO FAR, I'VE GATHERED BELTS ARE A BIG DEAL AND WE HAVE A TICKING CLOCK.
HE SAYS THEY COMPRESS THEMSELVES INTO OUR PLANE--
HE SAYS--
RUN!

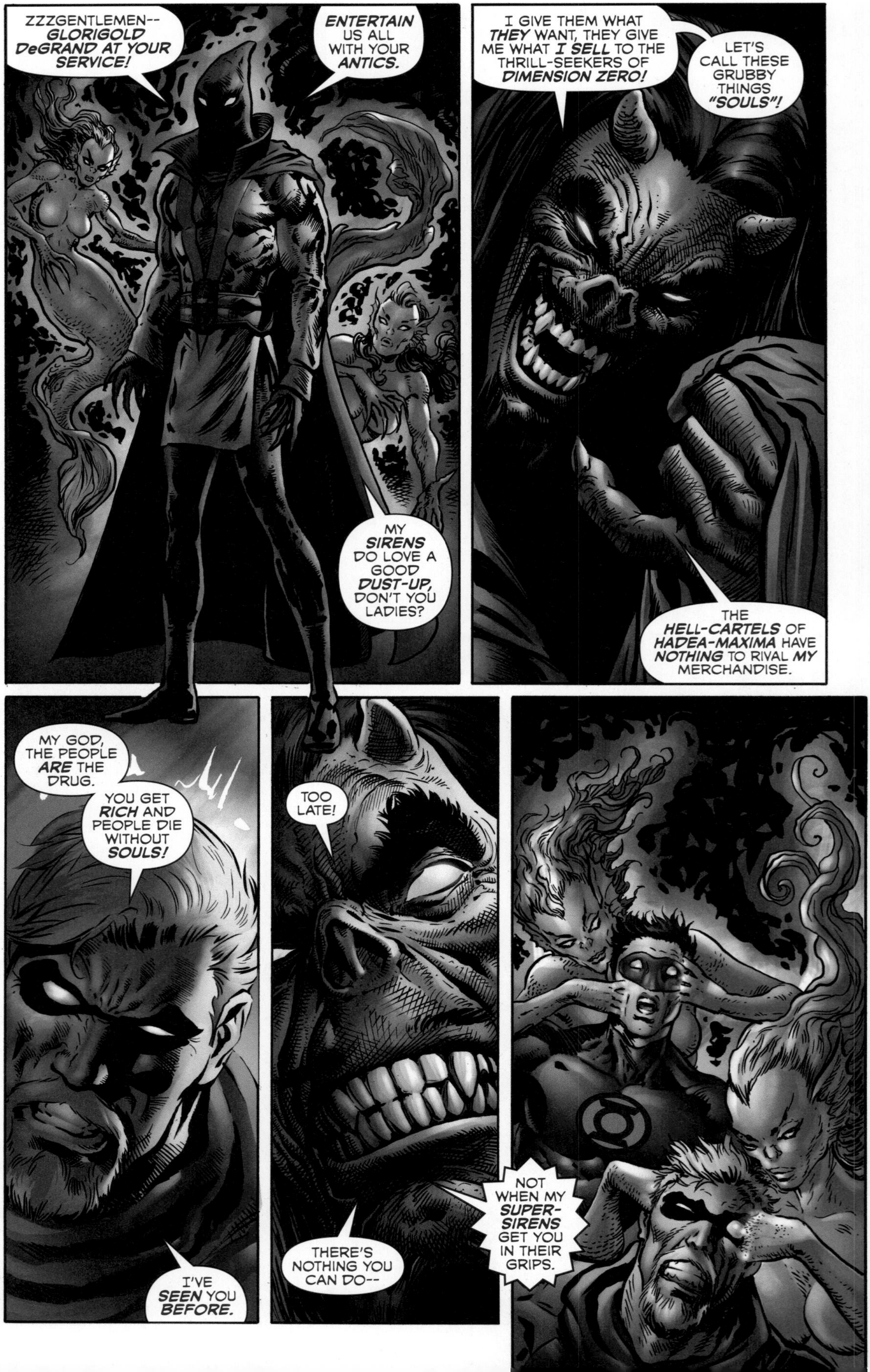
ZZZGENTLEMEN-- GLORIGOLD DeGRAND AT YOUR SERVICE!
ENTERTAIN US ALL WITH YOUR ANTICS.
MY SIRENS DO LOVE A GOOD DUST-UP, DON'T YOU LADIES?
I GIVE THEM WHAT THEY WANT, THEY GIVE ME WHAT I SELL TO THE THRILL-SEEKERS OF DIMENSION ZERO!
LET'S CALL THESE GRUBBY THINGS "SOULS"!
THE HELL-CARTELS OF HADEA-MAXIMA HAVE NOTHING TO RIVAL MY MERCHANDISE.
MY GOD, THE PEOPLE ARE THE DRUG.
YOU GET RICH AND PEOPLE DIE WITHOUT SOULS!
I'VE SEEN YOU BEFORE.
TOO LATE!
THERE'S NOTHING YOU CAN DO--
NOT WHEN MY SUPER-SIRENS GET YOU IN THEIR GRIPS.

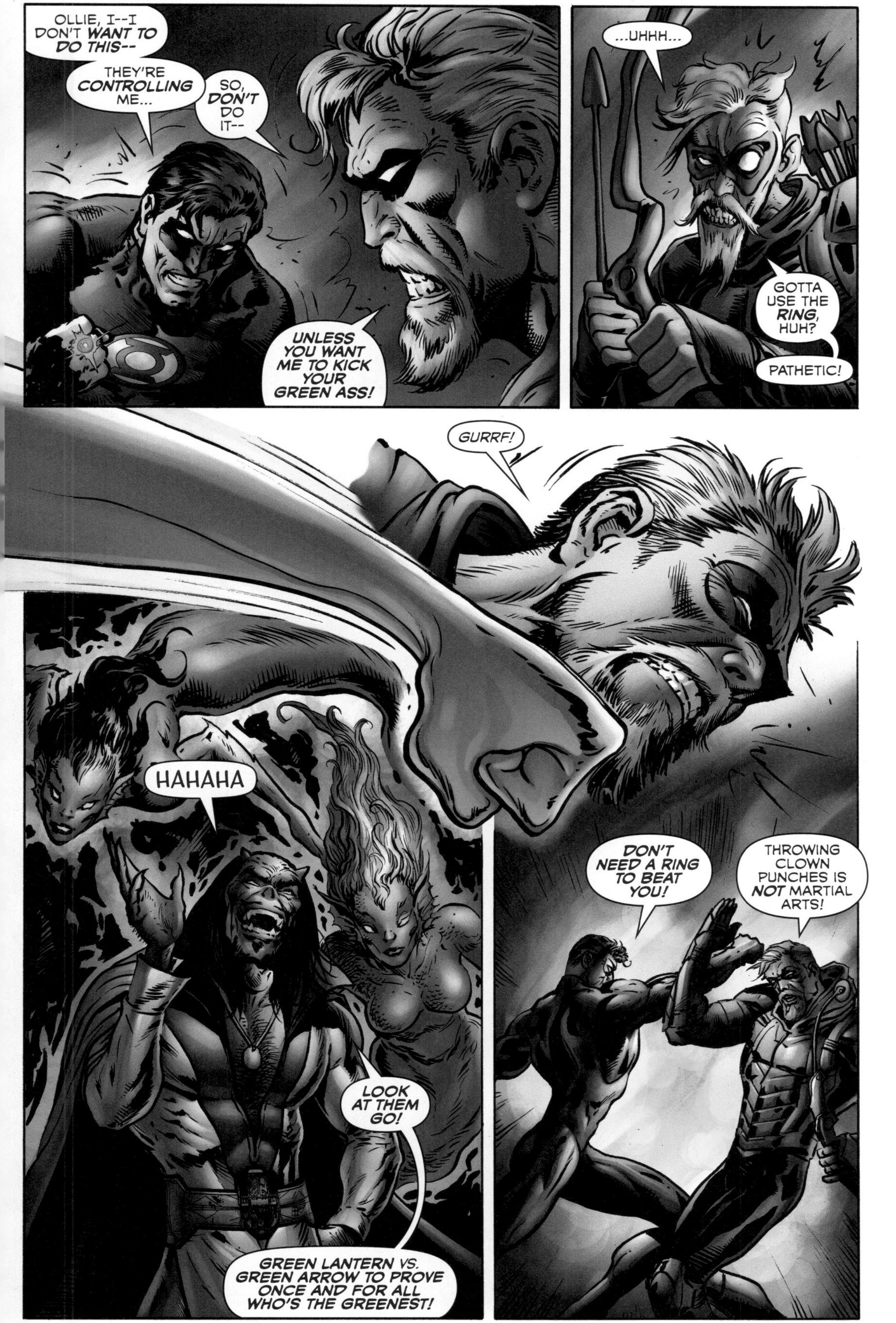
OLLIE, I--I DON'T WANT TO DO THIS--
THEY'RE CONTROLLING ME...
SO, DON'T DO IT--
UNLESS YOU WANT ME TO KICK YOUR GREEN ASS!
...UHHH...
GOTTA USE THE RING, HUH?
PATHETIC!
GURRF!
HAHAHA
LOOK AT THEM GO!
GREEN LANTERN VS. GREEN ARROW TO PROVE ONCE AND FOR ALL WHO'S THE GREENEST!
DON'T NEED A RING TO BEAT YOU!
THROWING CLOWN PUNCHES IS NOT MARTIAL ARTS!

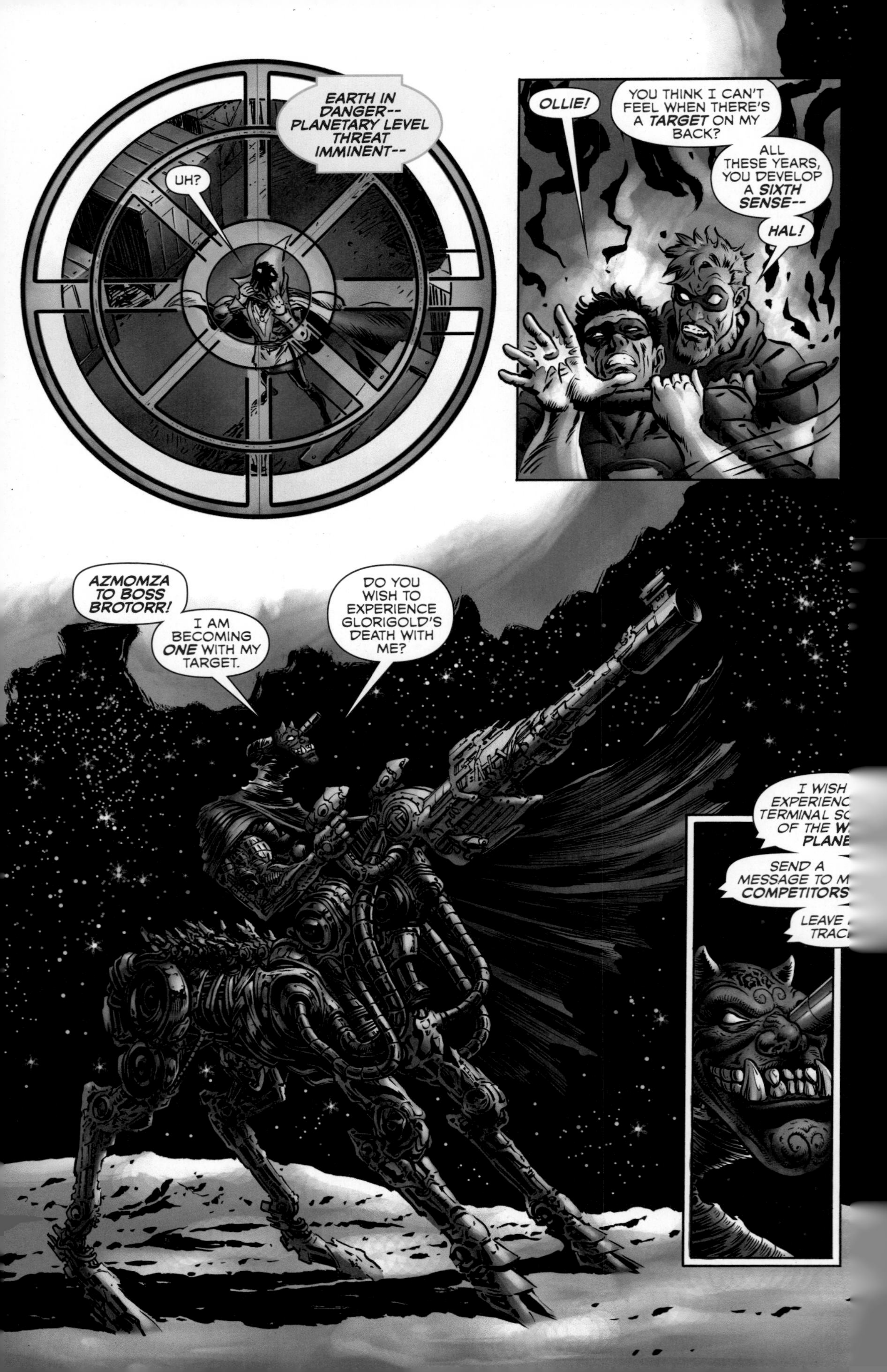
EARTH IN DANGER-- PLANETARY LEVEL THREAT IMMINENT--
UH?
OLLIE!
YOU THINK I CAN'T FEEL WHEN THERE'S A TARGET ON MY BACK?
ALL THESE YEARS, YOU DEVELOP A SIXTH SENSE--
HAL!
AZMOMZA TO BOSS BROTORR!
I AM BECOMING ONE WITH MY TARGET.
DO YOU WISH TO EXPERIENCE GLORIGOLD'S DEATH WITH ME?
I WISH
EXPERIENC
TERMINAL SC
OF THE W
PLANE
SEND A MESSAGE TO M
COMPETITORS
LEAVE
TRAC

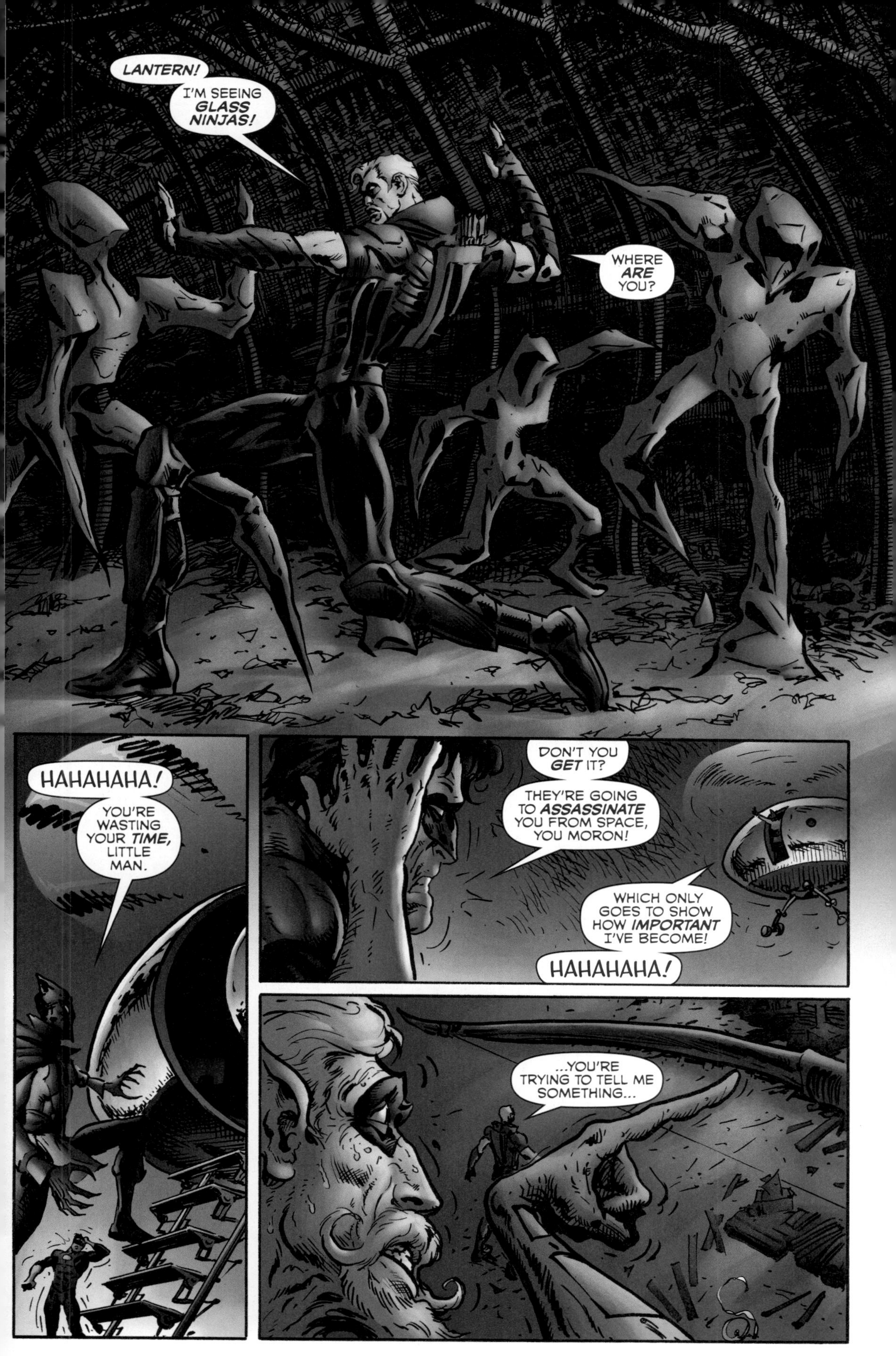

LANTERN!
I'M SEEING GLASS NINJAS!
WHERE ARE YOU?
HAHAHAHA!
YOU'RE WASTING YOUR TIME, LITTLE MAN.
DON'T YOU GET IT?
THEY'RE GOING TO ASSASSINATE YOU FROM SPACE, YOU MORON!
WHICH ONLY GOES TO SHOW HOW IMPORTANT I'VE BECOME!
HAHAHAHA!
...YOU'RE TRYING TO TELL ME SOMETHING...

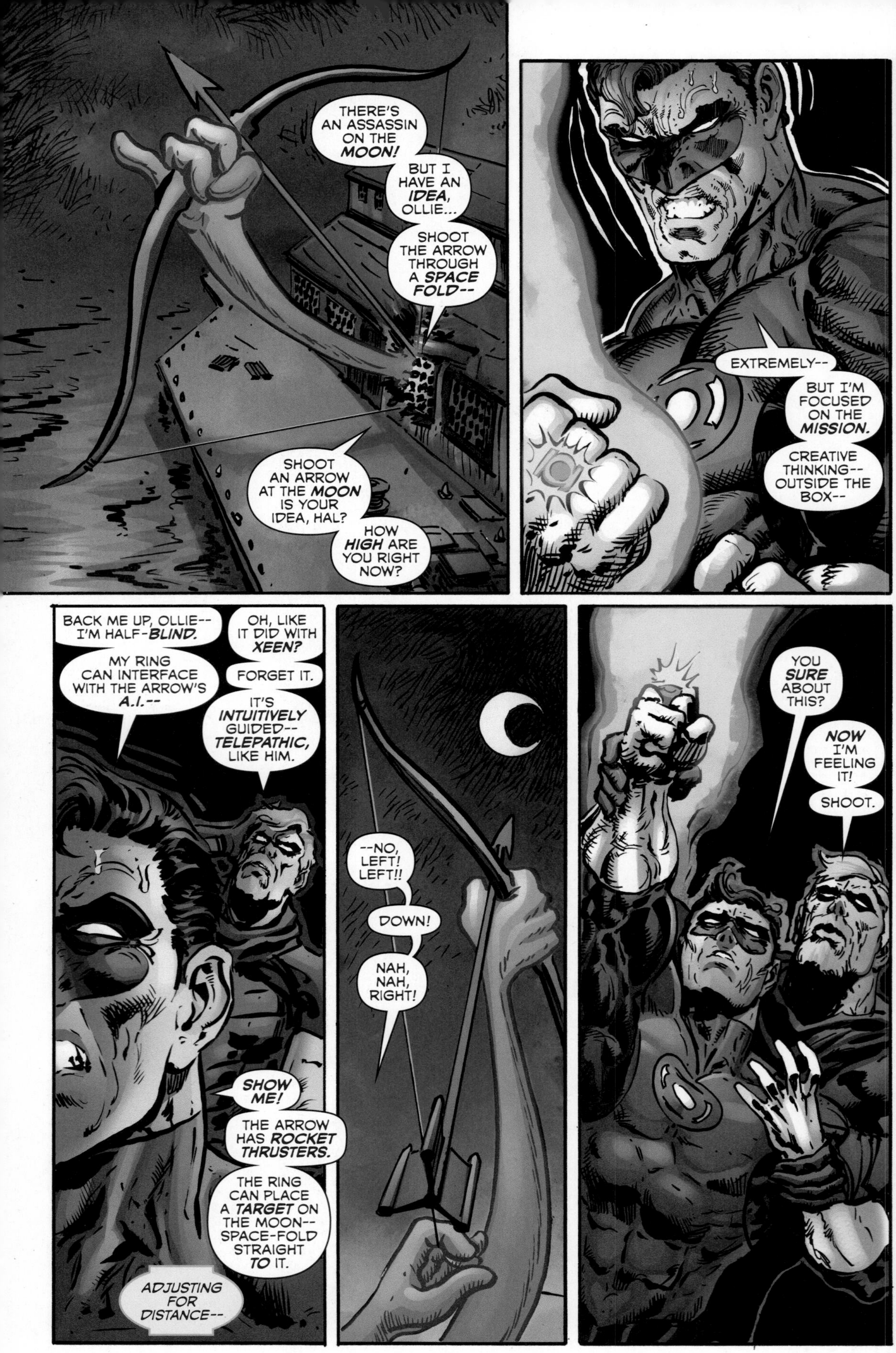

THERE'S AN ASSASSIN ON THE MOON!
BUT I HAVE AN IDEA, OLLIE...
SHOOT THE ARROW THROUGH A SPACE FOLD--
SHOOT AN ARROW AT THE MOON IS YOUR IDEA, HAL?
HOW HIGH ARE YOU RIGHT NOW?
EXTREMELY--
BUT I'M FOCUSED ON THE MISSION.
CREATIVE THINKING-- OUTSIDE THE BOX--
BACK ME UP, OLLIE-- I'M HALF-BLIND.
MY RING CAN INTERFACE WITH THE ARROW'S A.I.--
OH, LIKE IT DID WITH XEEN?
FORGET IT.
IT'S INTUITIVELY GUIDED-- TELEPATHIC, LIKE HIM.
SHOW ME!
THE ARROW HAS ROCKET THRUSTERS.
THE RING CAN PLACE A TARGET ON THE MOON-- SPACE-FOLD STRAIGHT TO IT.
ADJUSTING FOR DISTANCE--
--NO, LEFT! LEFT!!
DOWN!
NAH, NAH, RIGHT!
YOU SURE ABOUT THIS?
NOW I'M FEELING IT!
SHOOT.

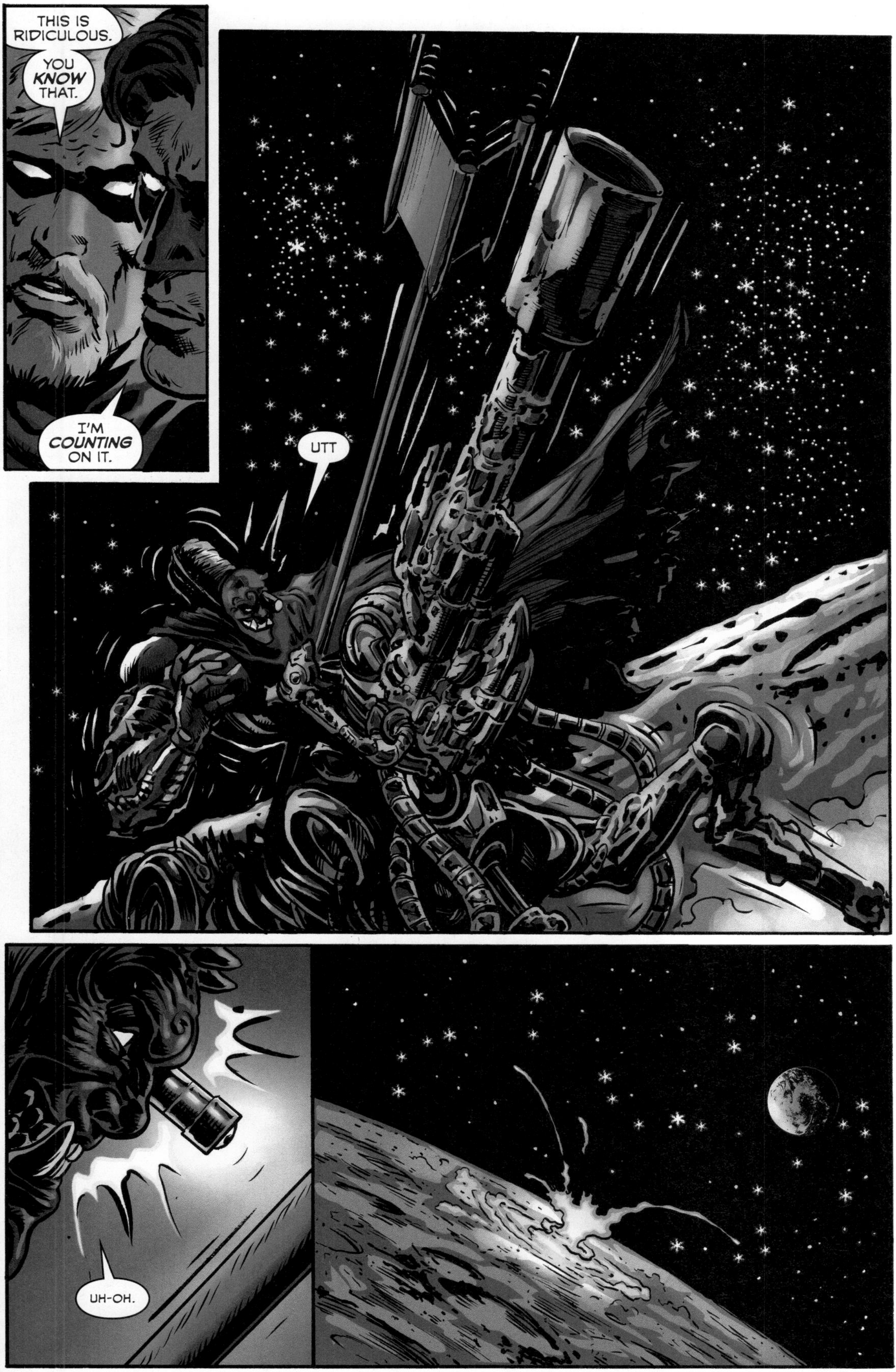
THIS IS RIDICULOUS.
YOU KNOW THAT.
I'M COUNTING ON IT.
UTT
UH-OH.

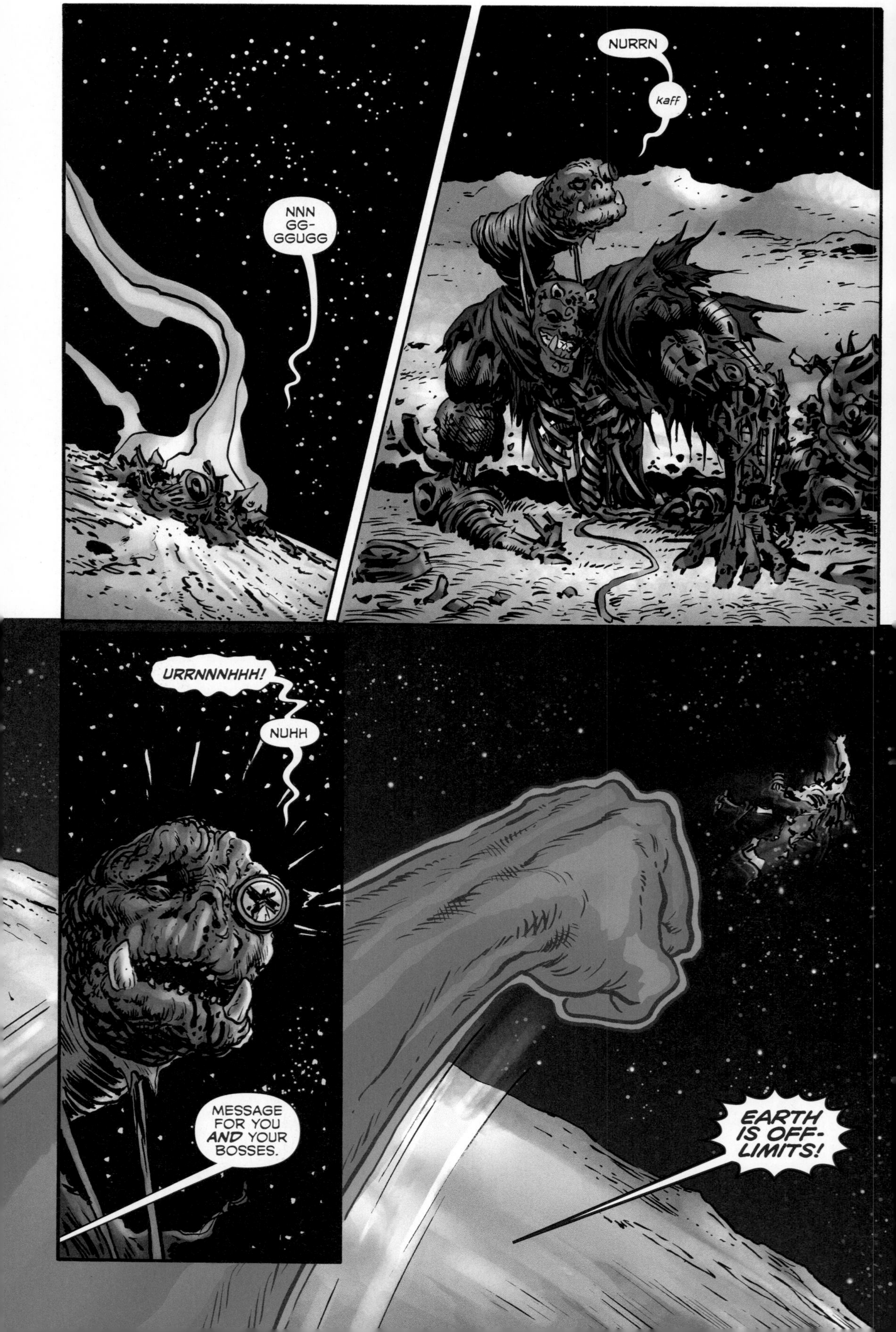
NNN GG- GGUGG
NURRN
kaff
URRNNNHHH!
NUHH
MESSAGE FOR YOU AND YOUR BOSSES.
EARTH IS OFF-LIMITS!

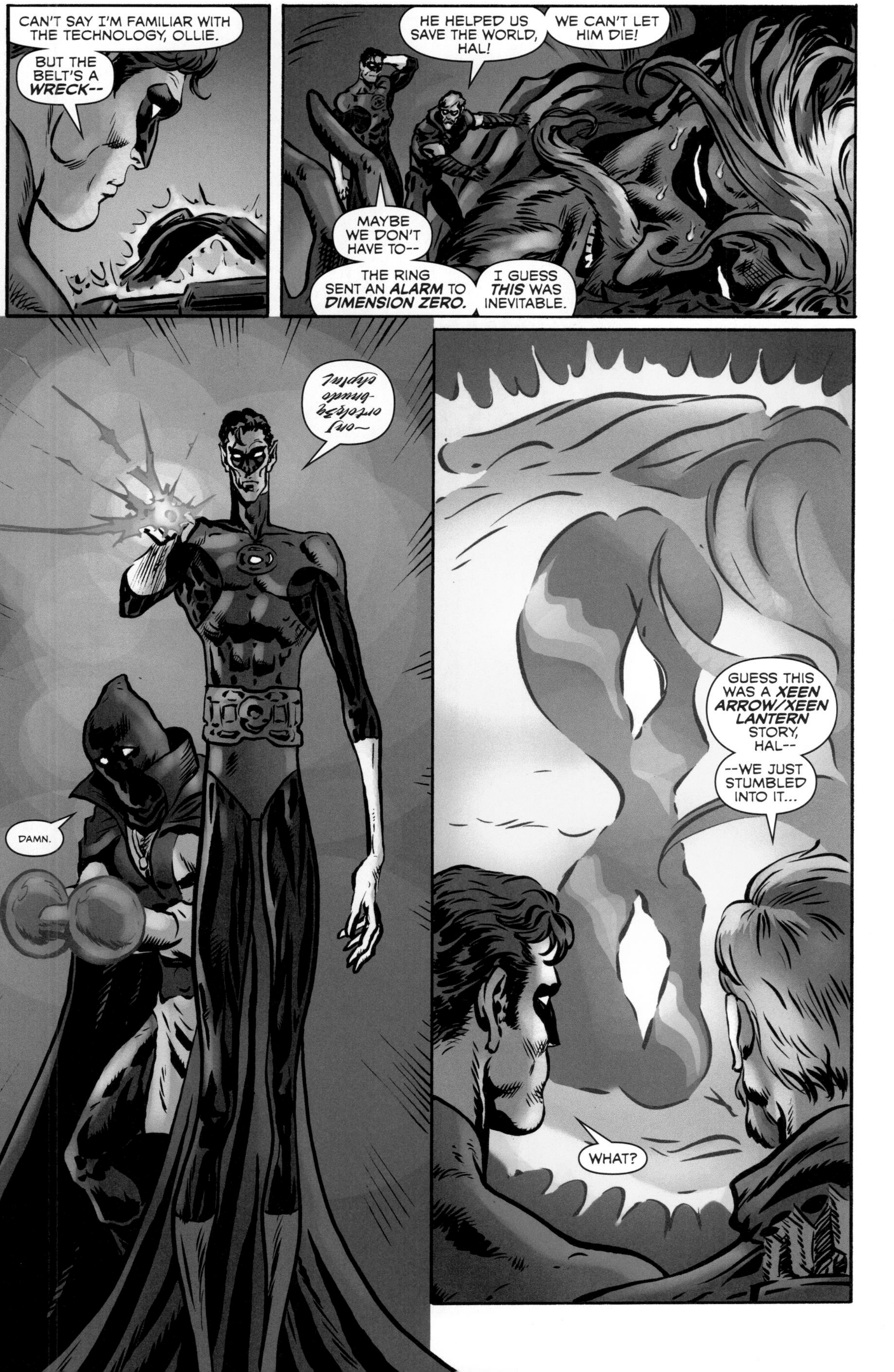
CAN'T SAY I'M FAMILIAR WITH THE TECHNOLOGY, OLLIE.
BUT THE BELT'S A *WRECK*--
HE HELPED US SAVE THE WORLD, HAL!
WE CAN'T LET HIM DIE!
MAYBE WE DON'T HAVE TO--
THE RING SENT AN *ALARM* TO *DIMENSION ZERO.*
I GUESS *THIS* WAS INEVITABLE.
DAMN.
GUESS THIS WAS A *XEEN ARROW/XEEN LANTERN* STORY, HAL--
--WE JUST STUMBLED INTO IT...
WHAT?

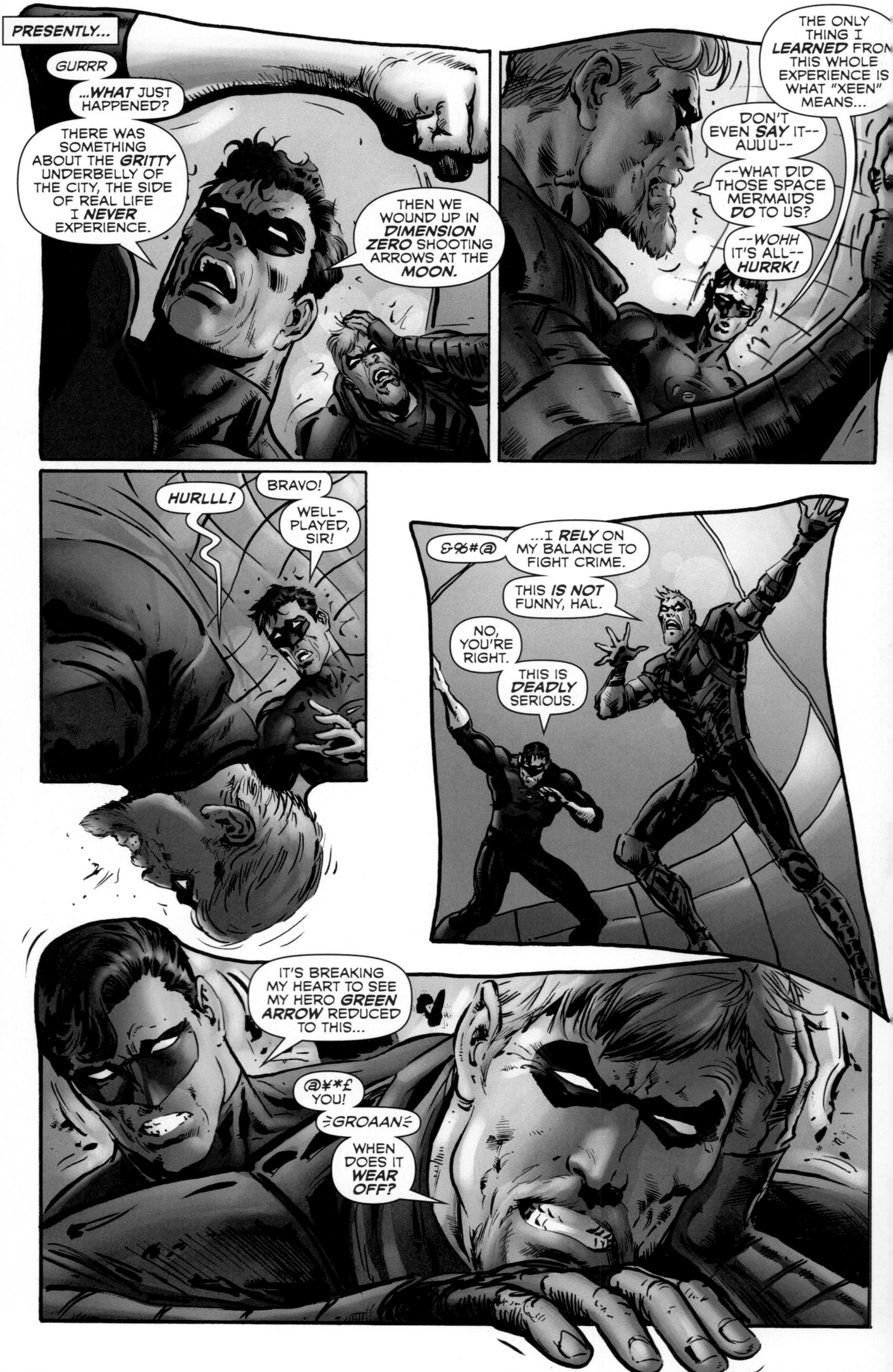
PRESENTLY...
GURRR
...WHAT JUST HAPPENED?
THERE WAS SOMETHING ABOUT THE GRITTY UNDERBELLY OF THE CITY, THE SIDE OF REAL LIFE I NEVER EXPERIENCE.
THEN WE WOUND UP IN DIMENSION ZERO SHOOTING ARROWS AT THE MOON.
THE ONLY THING I LEARNED FROM THIS WHOLE EXPERIENCE IS WHAT "XEEN" MEANS...
DON'T EVEN SAY IT-- AUUU--
--WHAT DID THOSE SPACE MERMAIDS DO TO US?
--WOHH IT'S ALL-- HURRK!
HURLLL!
BRAVO!
WELL-PLAYED, SIR!
&%#@
...I RELY ON MY BALANCE TO FIGHT CRIME.
THIS IS NOT FUNNY, HAL.
NO, YOU'RE RIGHT.
THIS IS DEADLY SERIOUS.
IT'S BREAKING MY HEART TO SEE MY HERO GREEN ARROW REDUCED TO THIS...
@¥*£ YOU!
GROAAN
WHEN DOES IT WEAR OFF?

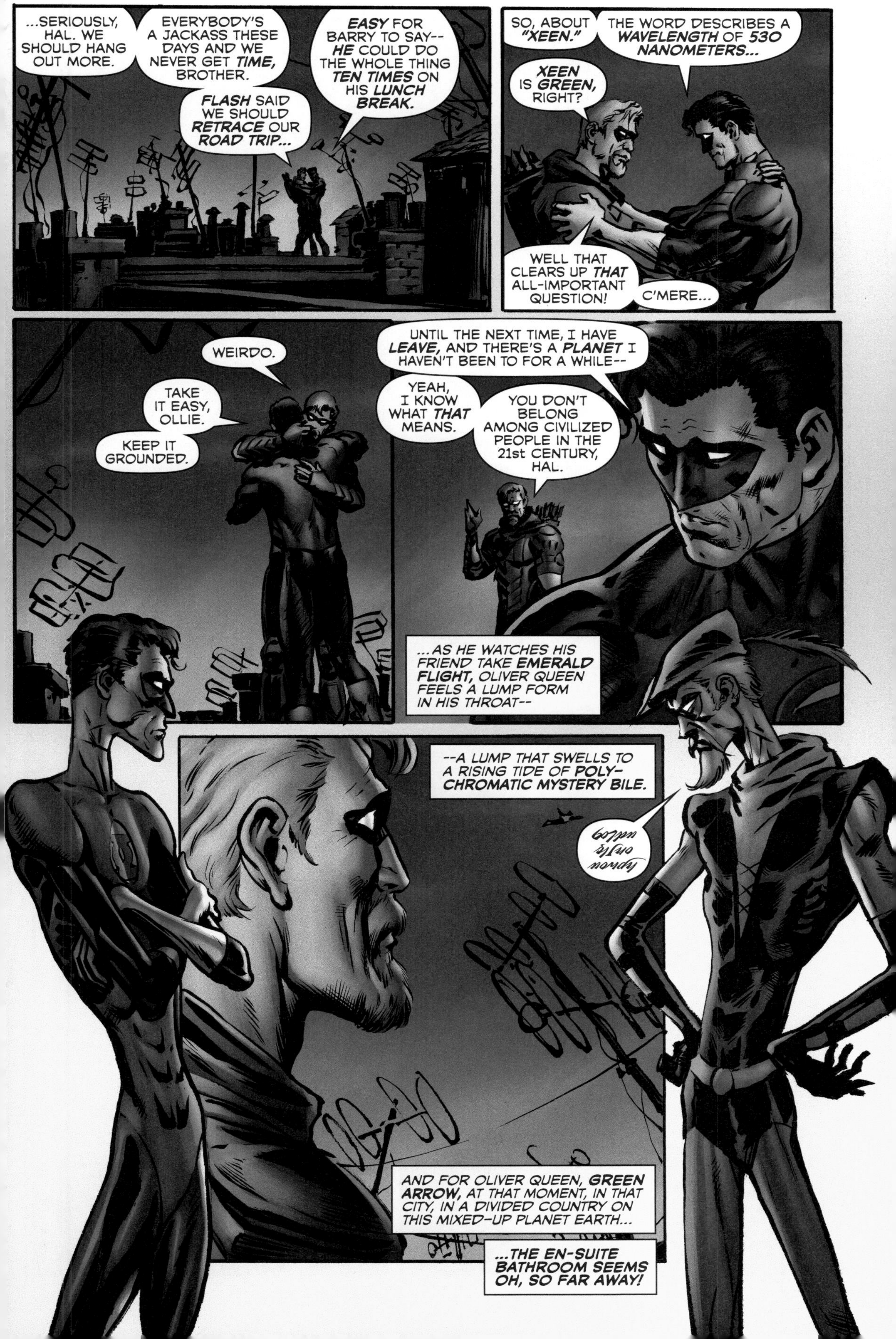
...SERIOUSLY, HAL. WE SHOULD HANG OUT MORE.
EVERYBODY'S A JACKASS THESE DAYS AND WE NEVER GET TIME, BROTHER.
FLASH SAID WE SHOULD RETRACE OUR ROAD TRIP...
EASY FOR BARRY TO SAY-- HE COULD DO THE WHOLE THING TEN TIMES ON HIS LUNCH BREAK.
SO, ABOUT "XEEN."
THE WORD DESCRIBES A WAVELENGTH OF 530 NANOMETERS...
XEEN IS GREEN, RIGHT?
WELL THAT CLEARS UP THAT ALL-IMPORTANT QUESTION!
C'MERE...
WEIRDO.
TAKE IT EASY, OLLIE.
KEEP IT GROUNDED.
UNTIL THE NEXT TIME, I HAVE LEAVE, AND THERE'S A PLANET I HAVEN'T BEEN TO FOR A WHILE--
YEAH, I KNOW WHAT THAT MEANS.
YOU DON'T BELONG AMONG CIVILIZED PEOPLE IN THE 21st CENTURY, HAL.
...AS HE WATCHES HIS FRIEND TAKE EMERALD FLIGHT, OLIVER QUEEN FEELS A LUMP FORM IN HIS THROAT--
--A LUMP THAT SWELLS TO A RISING TIDE OF POLY-CHROMATIC MYSTERY BILE.
AND FOR OLIVER QUEEN, GREEN ARROW, AT THAT MOMENT, IN THAT CITY, IN A DIVIDED COUNTRY ON THIS MIXED-UP PLANET EARTH...
...THE EN-SUITE BATHROOM SEEMS OH, SO FAR AWAY!

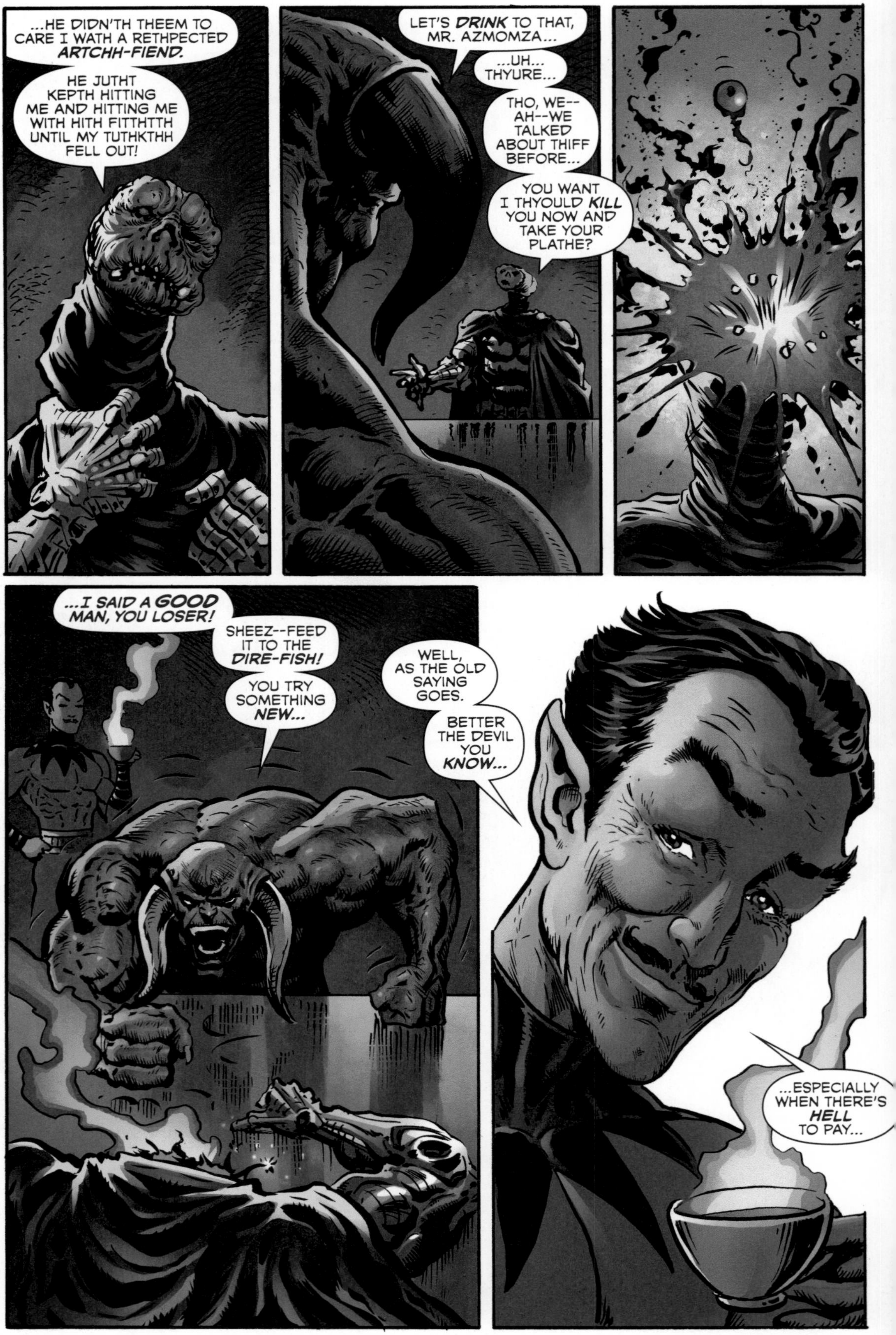
...HE DIDN'TH THEEM TO CARE I WATH A RETHPECTED ARTCHH-FIEND.
HE JUTHT KEPTH HITTING ME AND HITTING ME WITH HITH FITTHTTH UNTIL MY TUTHKTHH FELL OUT!
LET'S DRINK TO THAT, MR. AZMOMZA...
...UH... THYURE...
THO, WE-- AH--WE TALKED ABOUT THIFF BEFORE...
YOU WANT I THYOULD KILL YOU NOW AND TAKE YOUR PLATHE?
...I SAID A GOOD MAN, YOU LOSER!
SHEEZ--FEED IT TO THE DIRE-FISH!
YOU TRY SOMETHING NEW...
WELL, AS THE OLD SAYING GOES.
BETTER THE DEVIL YOU KNOW...
...ESPECIALLY WHEN THERE'S HELL TO PAY...

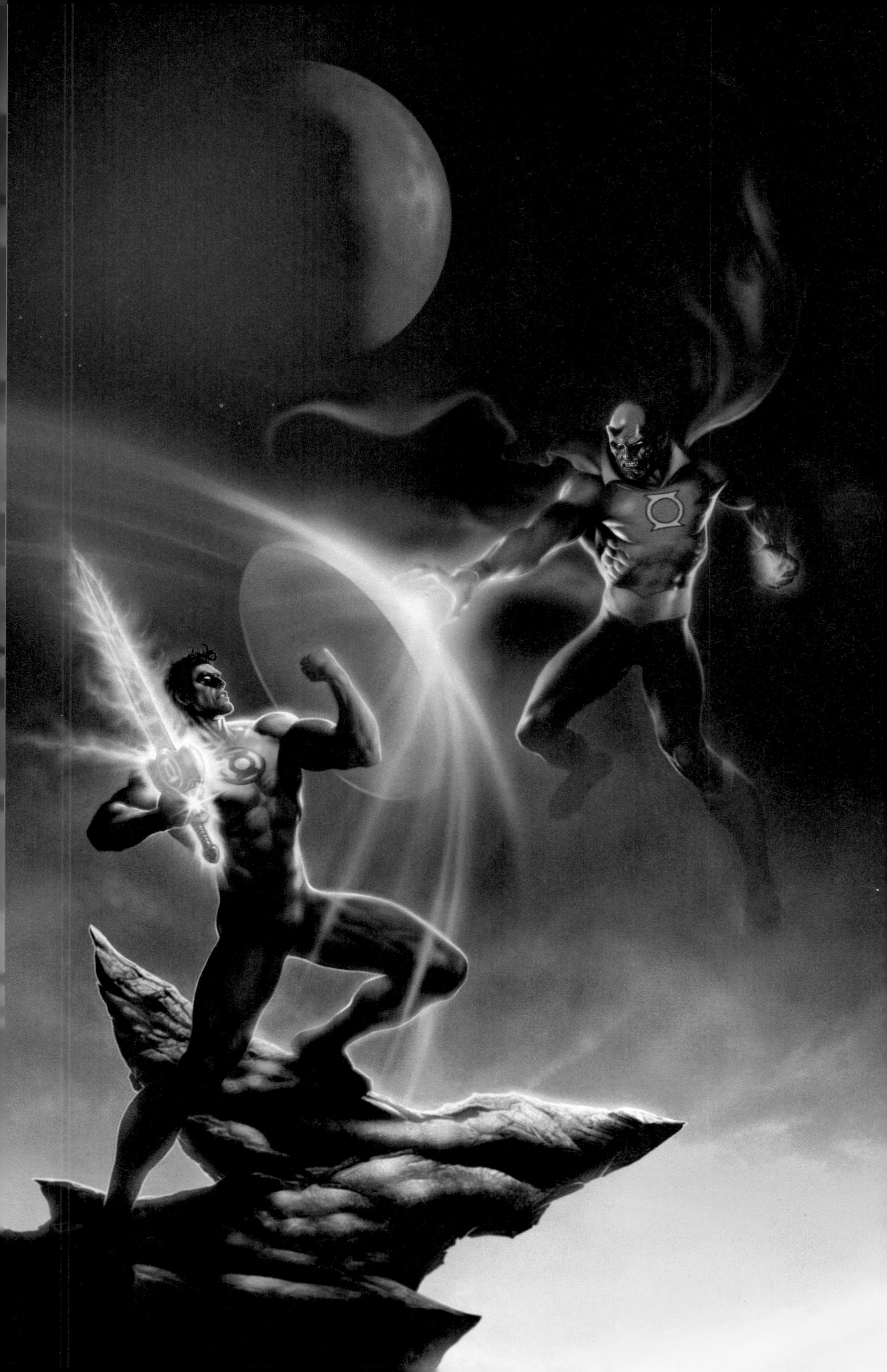

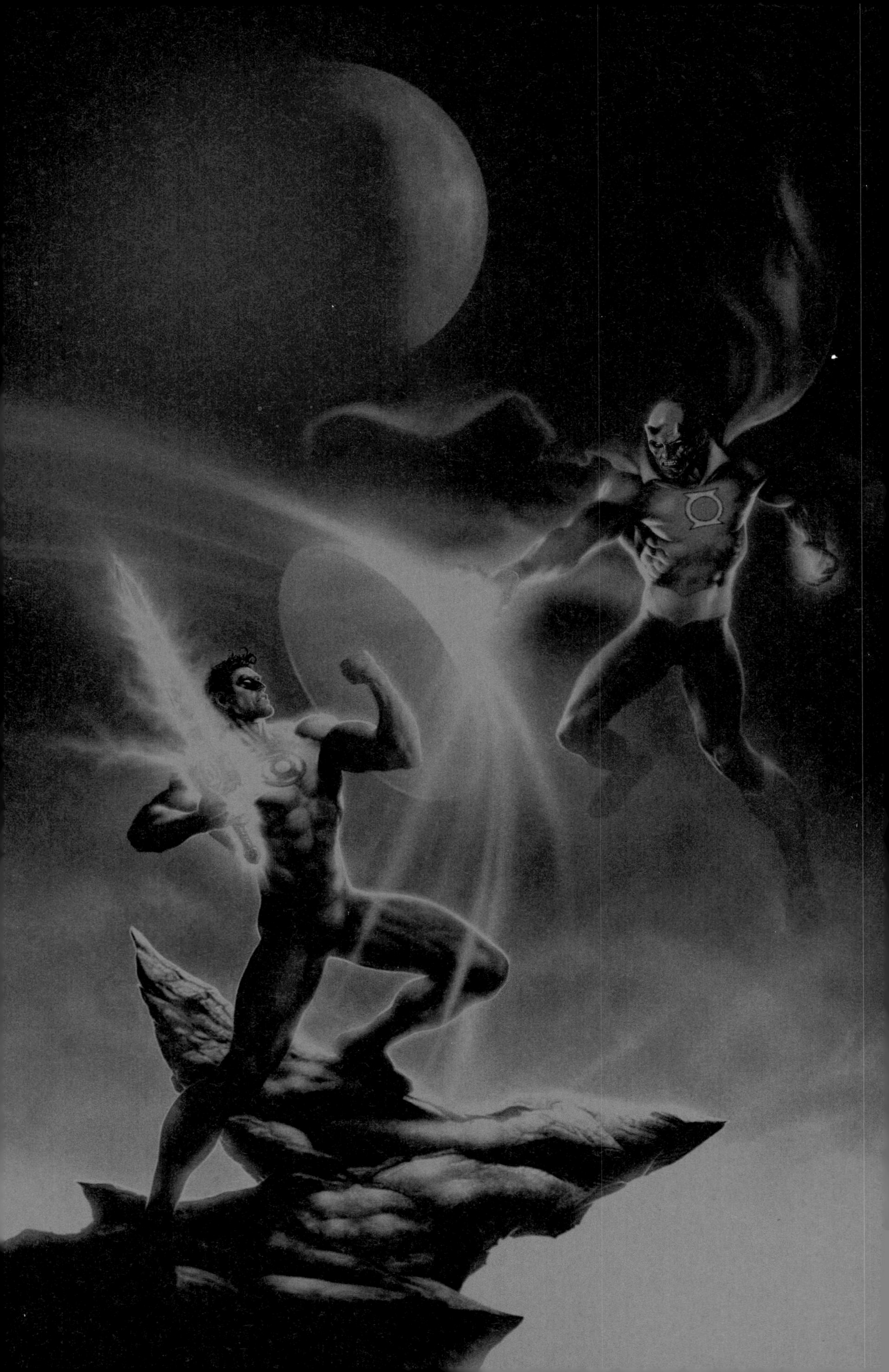

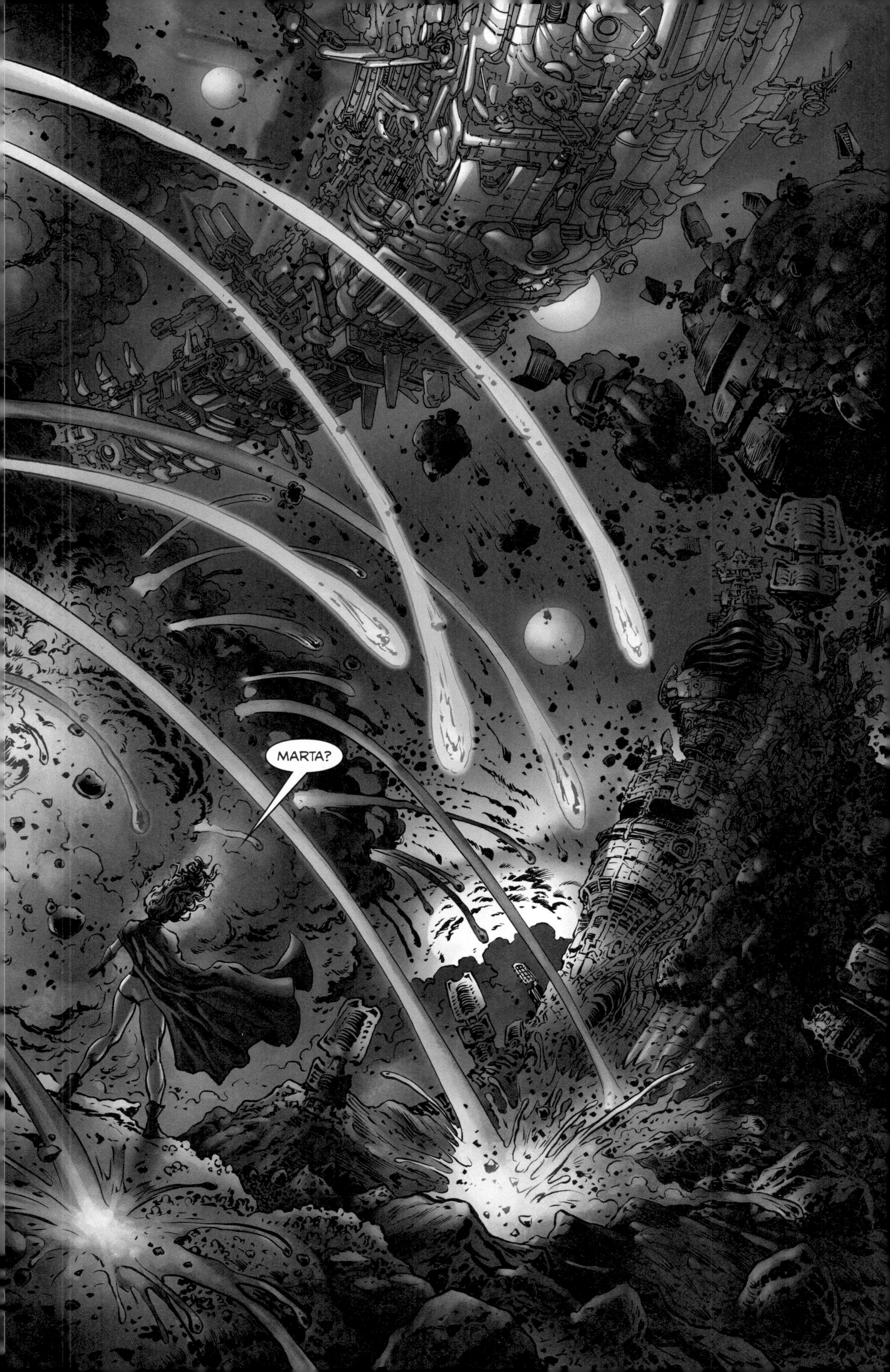
MARTA?

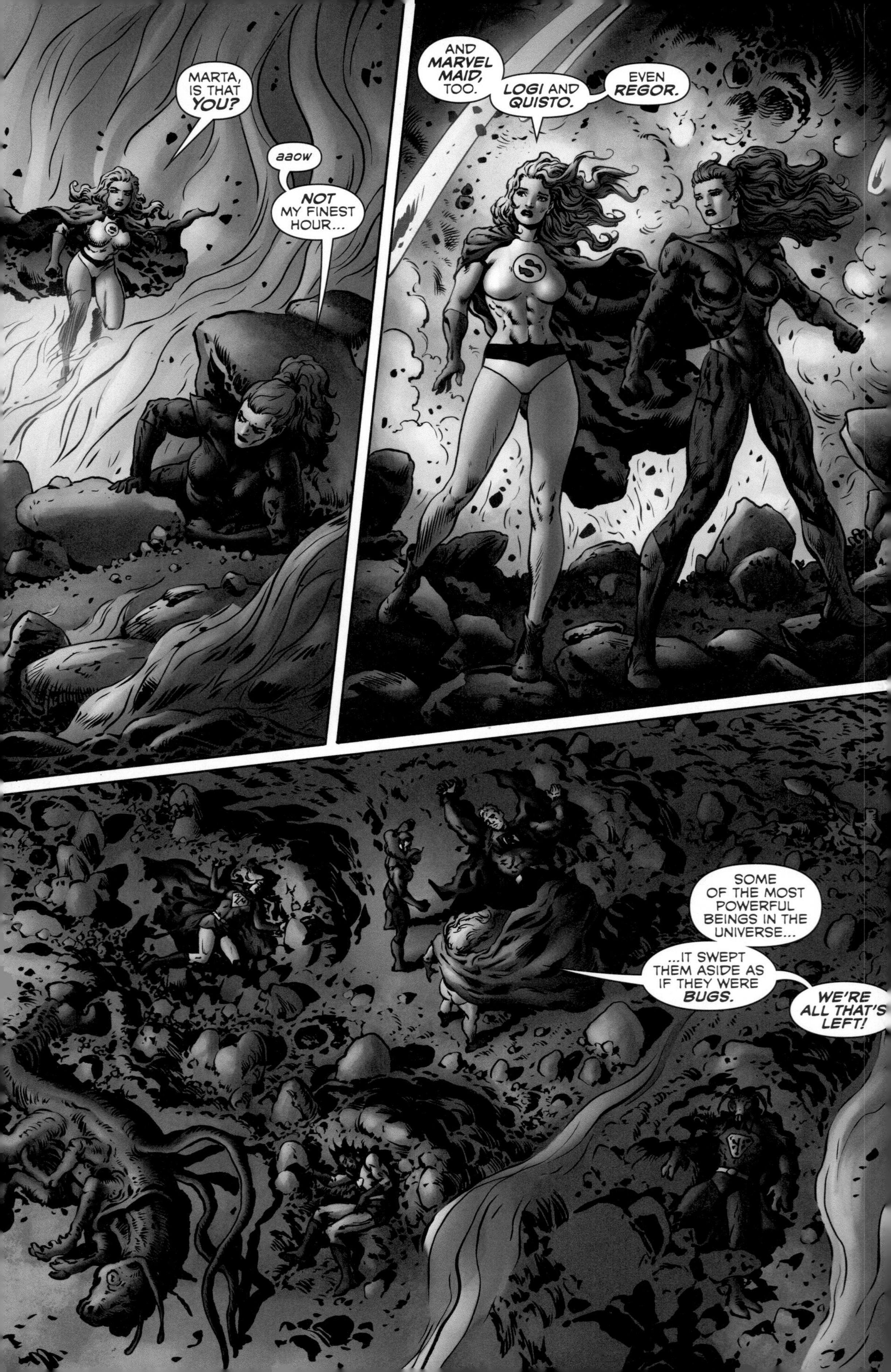

MARTA, IS THAT YOU?
aaow
NOT MY FINEST HOUR...
AND MARVEL MAID, TOO.
LOGI AND QUISTO.
EVEN REGOR.
SOME OF THE MOST POWERFUL BEINGS IN THE UNIVERSE...
...IT SWEPT THEM ASIDE AS IF THEY WERE BUGS.
WE'RE ALL THAT'S LEFT!

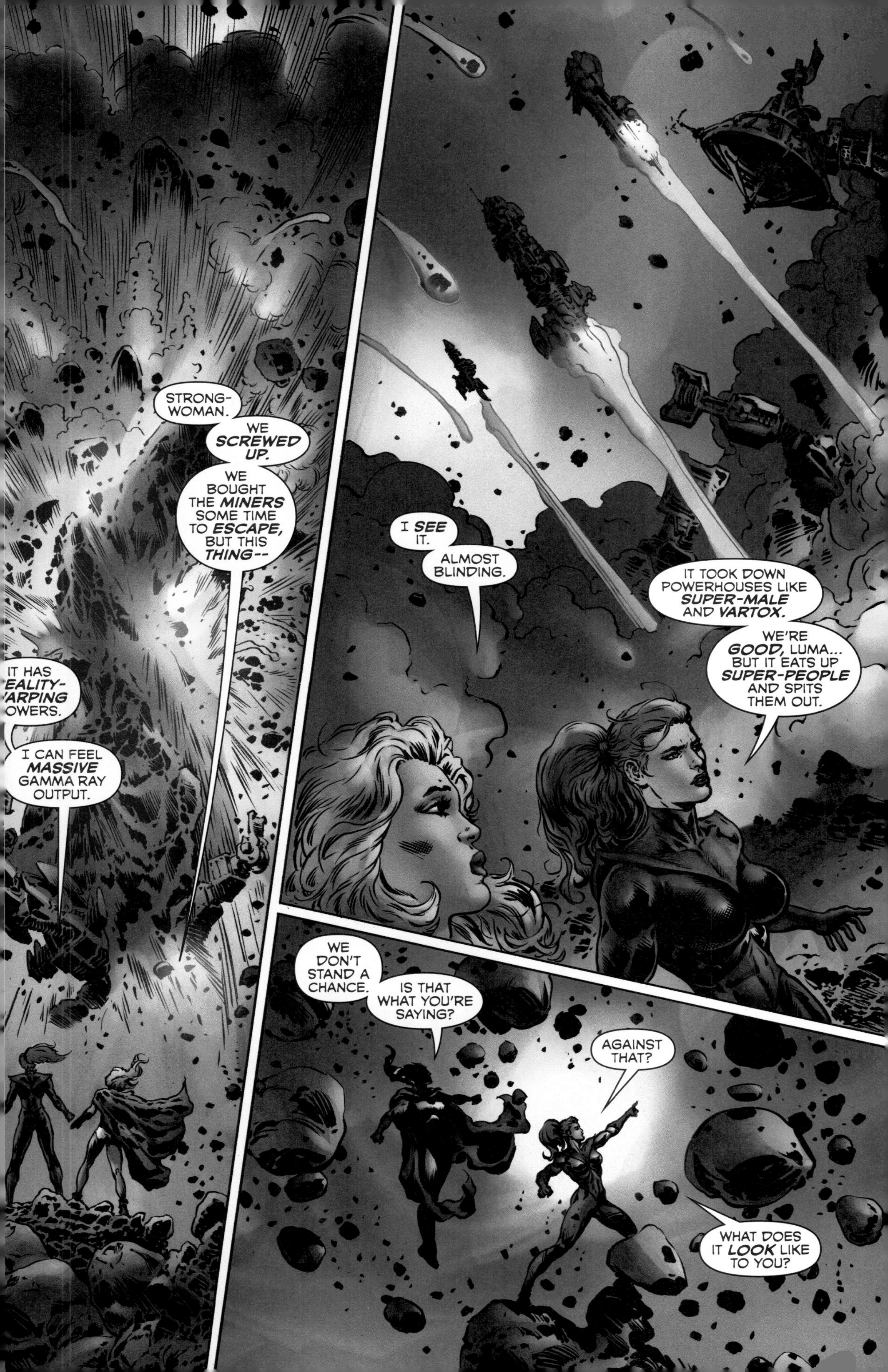
STRONG-WOMAN.
WE SCREWED UP.
WE BOUGHT THE MINERS SOME TIME TO ESCAPE, BUT THIS THING--
IT HAS REALITY-WARPING POWERS.
I CAN FEEL MASSIVE GAMMA RAY OUTPUT.
I SEE IT.
ALMOST BLINDING.
IT TOOK DOWN POWERHOUSES LIKE SUPER-MALE AND VARTOX.
WE'RE GOOD, LUMA... BUT IT EATS UP SUPER-PEOPLE AND SPITS THEM OUT.
WE DON'T STAND A CHANCE.
IS THAT WHAT YOU'RE SAYING?
AGAINST THAT?
WHAT DOES IT LOOK LIKE TO YOU?

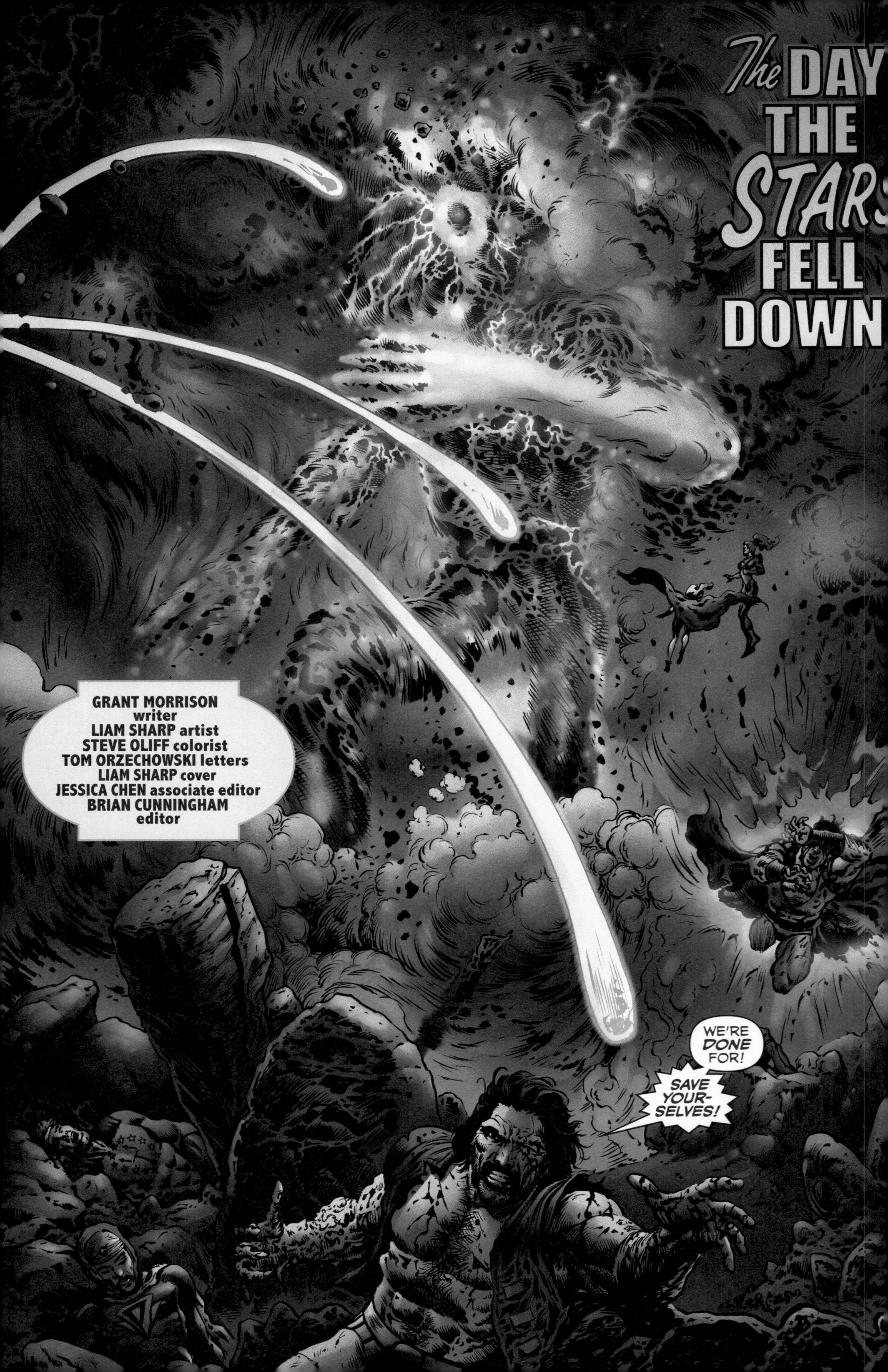
The DAY THE STARS FELL DOWN
GRANT MORRISON writer
LIAM SHARP artist
STEVE OLIFF colorist
TOM ORZECHOWSKI letters
LIAM SHARP cover
JESSICA CHEN associate editor
BRIAN CUNNINGHAM editor
WE'RE DONE FOR!
SAVE YOUR-SELVES!

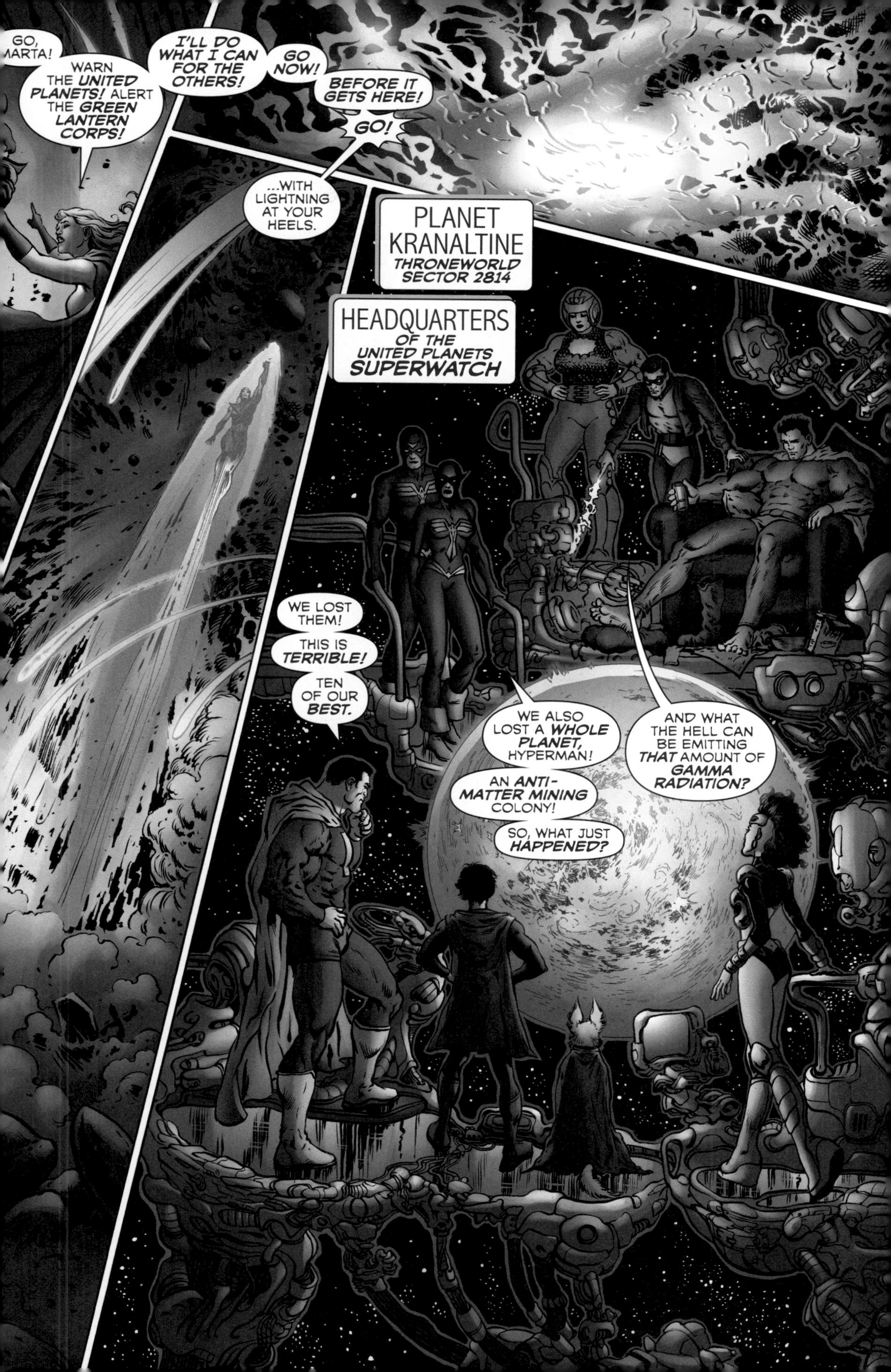
GO, MARTA!
WARN THE UNITED PLANETS! ALERT THE GREEN LANTERN CORPS!
I'LL DO WHAT I CAN FOR THE OTHERS!
GO NOW!
BEFORE IT GETS HERE!
GO!
...WITH LIGHTNING AT YOUR HEELS.
PLANET KRANALTINE
THRONEWORLD SECTOR 2814
HEADQUARTERS OF THE UNITED PLANETS SUPERWATCH
WE LOST THEM!
THIS IS TERRIBLE!
TEN OF OUR BEST.
WE ALSO LOST A WHOLE PLANET, HYPERMAN!
AN ANTI-MATTER MINING COLONY!
SO, WHAT JUST HAPPENED?
AND WHAT THE HELL CAN BE EMITTING THAT AMOUNT OF GAMMA RADIATION?

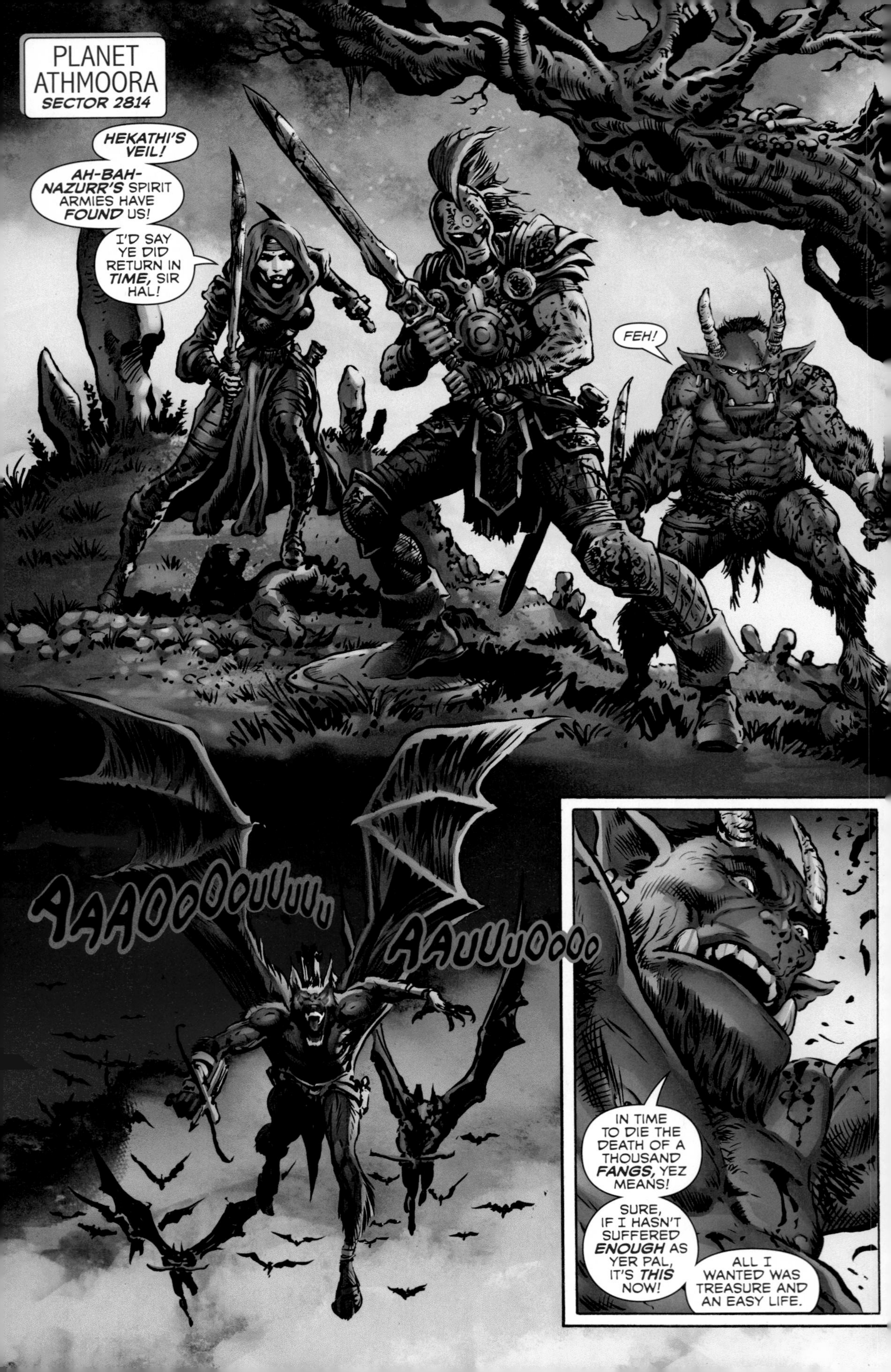
PLANET ATHMOORA SECTOR 2814
HEKATHI'S VEIL!
AH-BAH-NAZURR'S SPIRIT ARMIES HAVE FOUND US!
I'D SAY YE DID RETURN IN TIME, SIR HAL!
FEH!
AAAOOOOUUUUU
AAUUUOOOO
IN TIME TO DIE THE DEATH OF A THOUSAND FANGS, YEZ MEANS!
SURE, IF I HASN'T SUFFERED ENOUGH AS YER PAL, IT'S THIS NOW!
ALL I WANTED WAS TREASURE AND AN EASY LIFE.

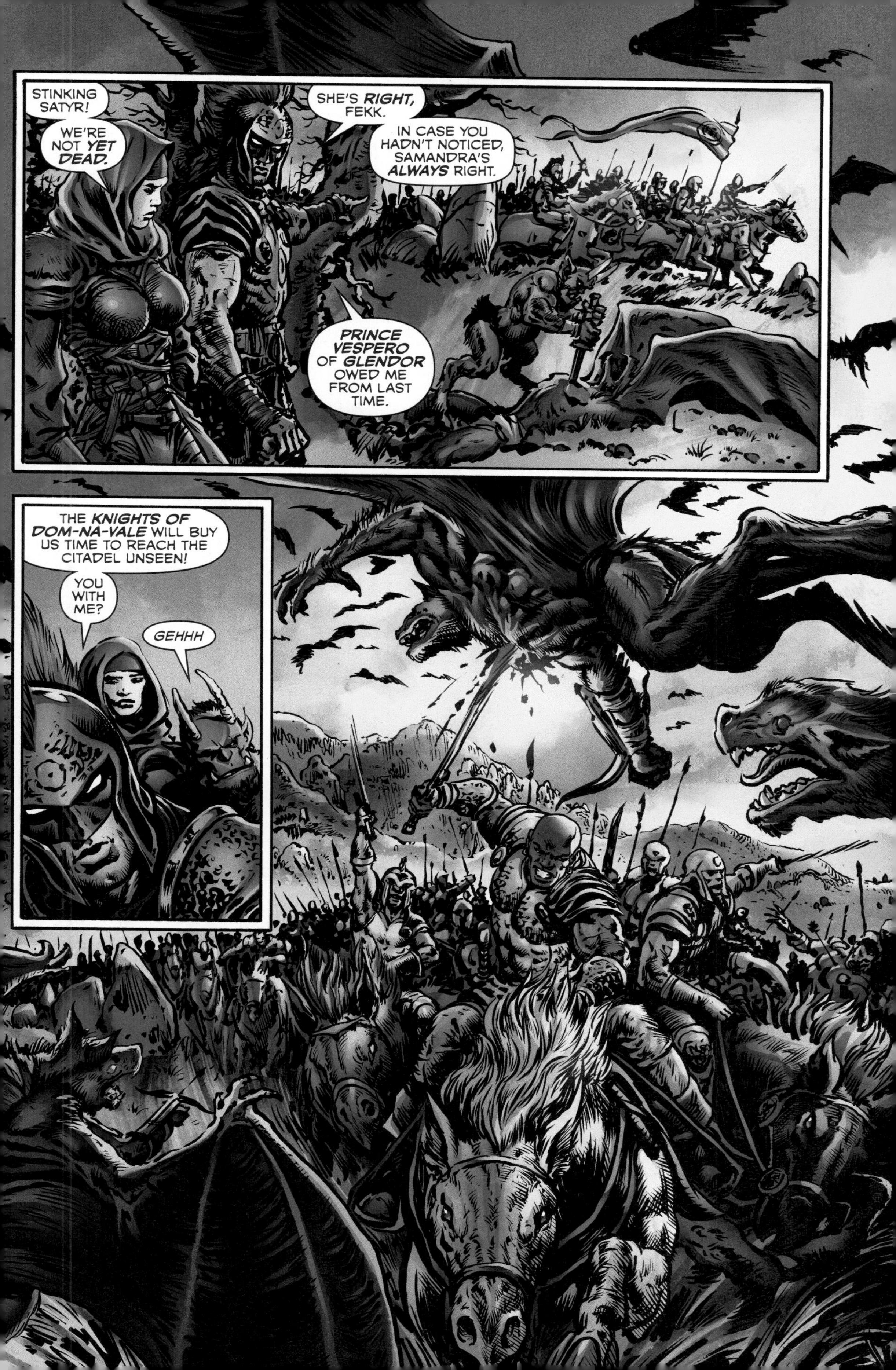
STINKING SATYR!
WE'RE NOT *YET DEAD.*
SHE'S *RIGHT,* FEKK.
IN CASE YOU HADN'T NOTICED, SAMANDRA'S *ALWAYS* RIGHT.
PRINCE VESPERO OF *GLENDOR* OWED ME FROM LAST TIME.
THE *KNIGHTS OF DOM-NA-VALE* WILL BUY US TIME TO REACH THE CITADEL UNSEEN!
YOU WITH ME?
GEHHH

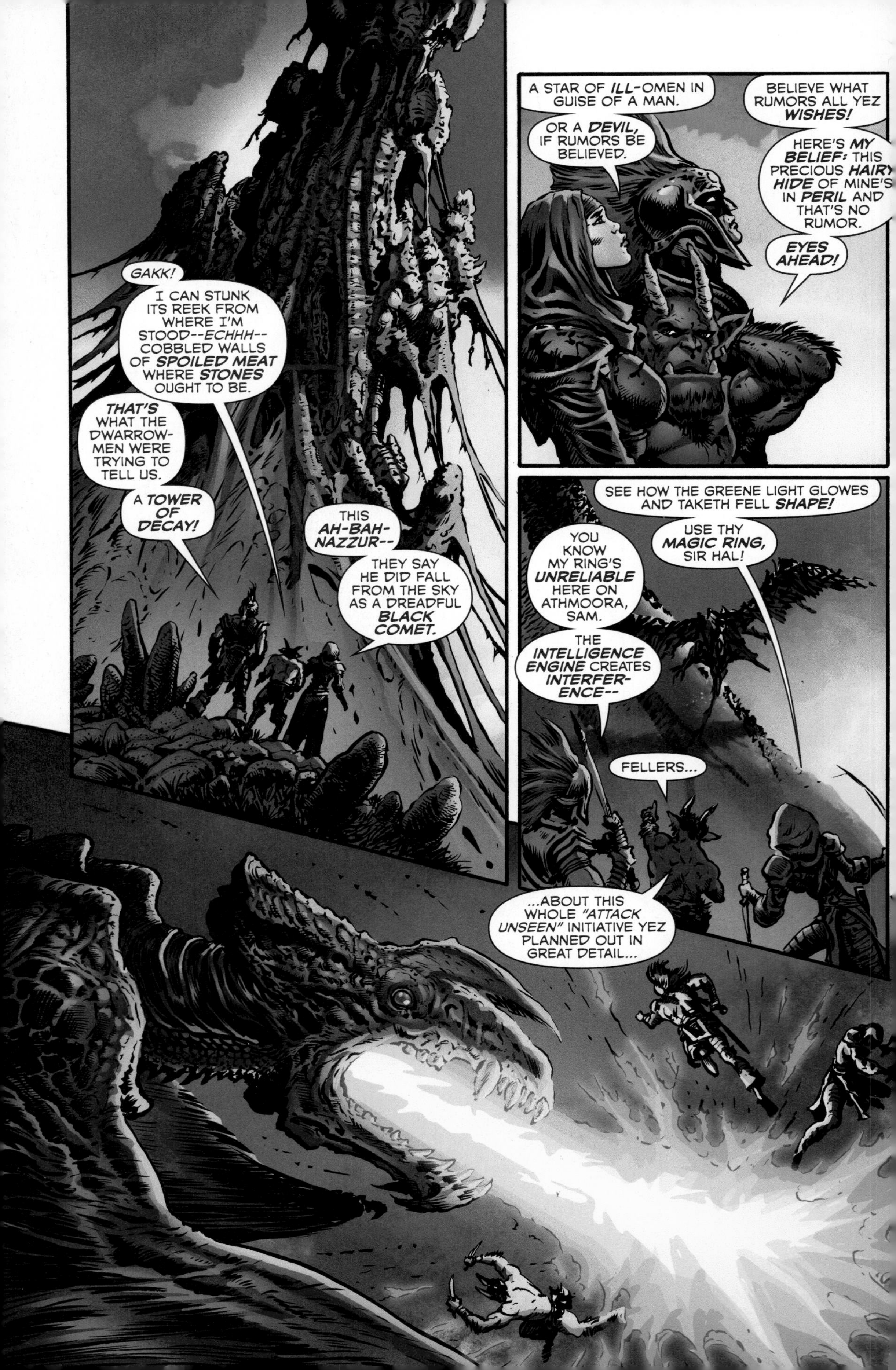
GAKK!
I CAN STUNK ITS REEK FROM WHERE I'M STOOD--ECHHH-- COBBLED WALLS OF SPOILED MEAT WHERE STONES OUGHT TO BE.
THAT'S WHAT THE DWARROW-MEN WERE TRYING TO TELL US.
A TOWER OF DECAY!
THIS AH-BAH-NAZZUR--
THEY SAY HE DID FALL FROM THE SKY AS A DREADFUL BLACK COMET.
A STAR OF ILL-OMEN IN GUISE OF A MAN.
OR A DEVIL, IF RUMORS BE BELIEVED.
BELIEVE WHAT RUMORS ALL YEZ WISHES!
HERE'S MY BELIEF: THIS PRECIOUS HAIRY HIDE OF MINE'S IN PERIL AND THAT'S NO RUMOR.
EYES AHEAD!
SEE HOW THE GREENE LIGHT GLOWES AND TAKETH FELL SHAPE!
USE THY MAGIC RING, SIR HAL!
YOU KNOW MY RING'S UNRELIABLE HERE ON ATHMOORA, SAM.
THE INTELLIGENCE ENGINE CREATES INTERFER-ENCE--
FELLERS...
...ABOUT THIS WHOLE "ATTACK UNSEEN" INITIATIVE YEZ PLANNED OUT IN GREAT DETAIL...

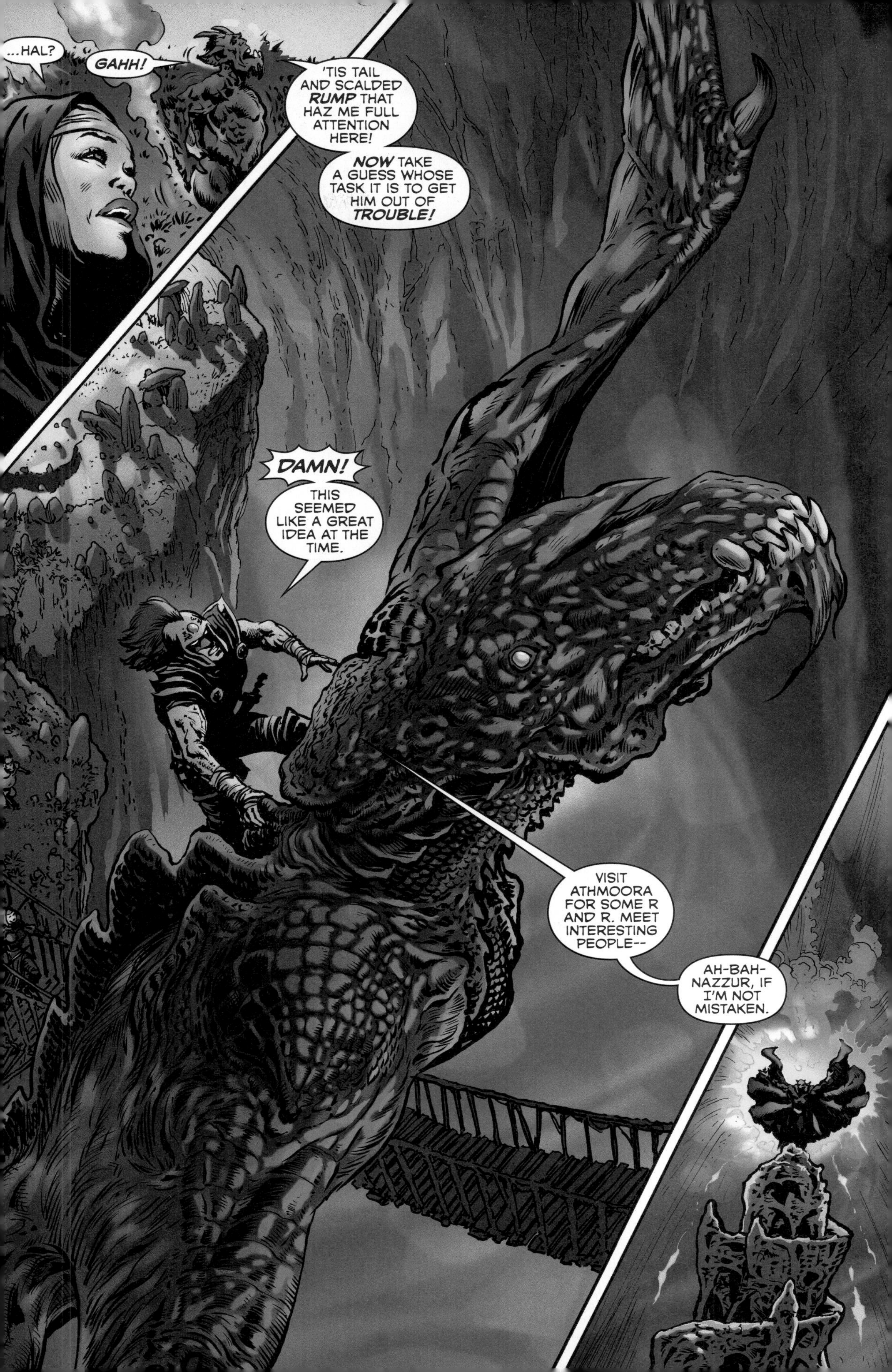
...HAL?
GAHH!
'TIS TAIL AND SCALDED RUMP THAT HAZ ME FULL ATTENTION HERE!
NOW TAKE A GUESS WHOSE TASK IT IS TO GET HIM OUT OF TROUBLE!
DAMN!
THIS SEEMED LIKE A GREAT IDEA AT THE TIME.
VISIT ATHMOORA FOR SOME R AND R. MEET INTERESTING PEOPLE--
AH-BAH-NAZZUR, IF I'M NOT MISTAKEN.

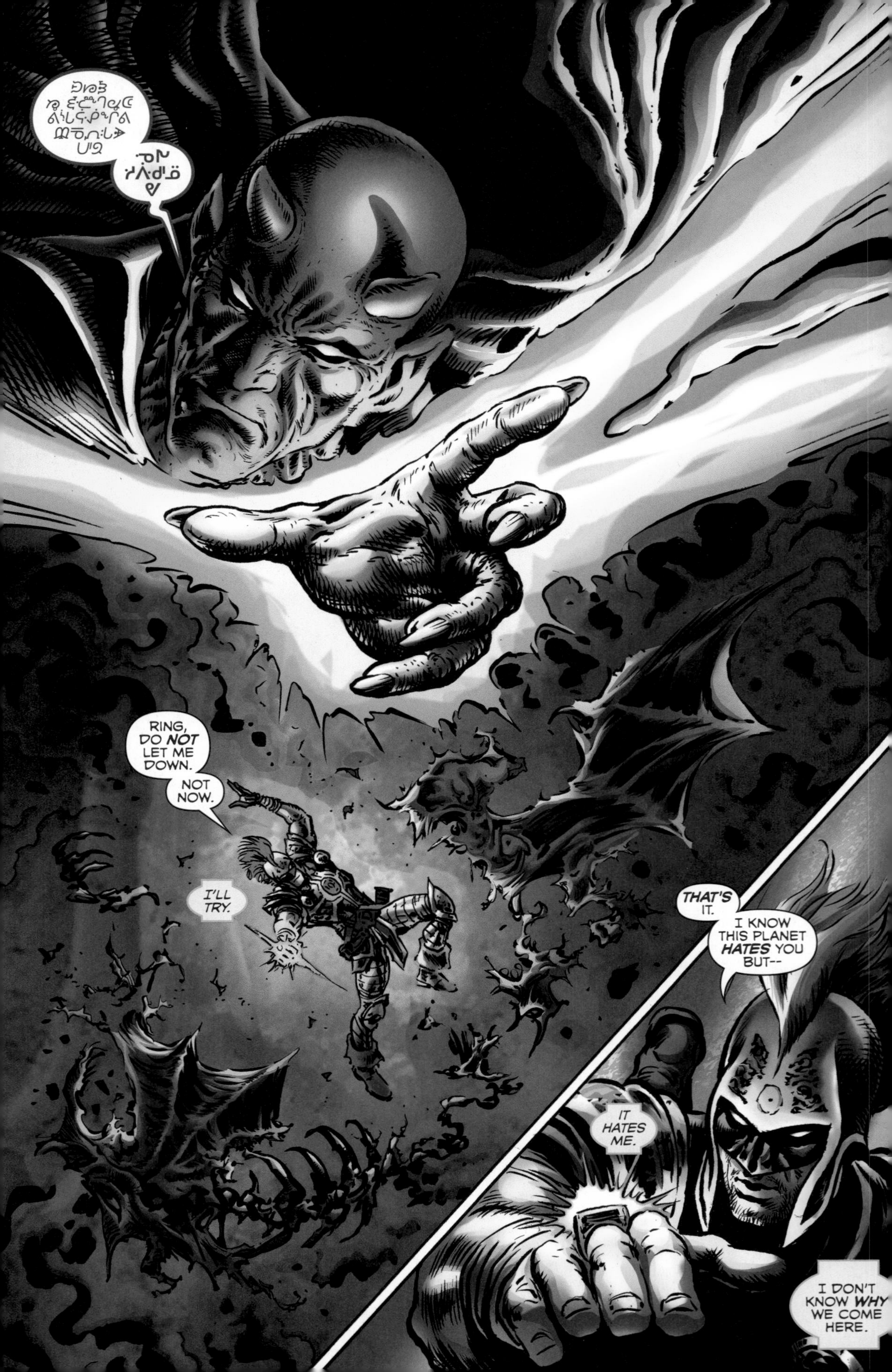
RING, DO **NOT** LET ME DOWN.
NOT NOW.
I'LL TRY.
THAT'S IT.
I KNOW THIS PLANET ***HATES*** YOU BUT--
IT HATES ME.
I DON'T KNOW ***WHY*** WE COME HERE.

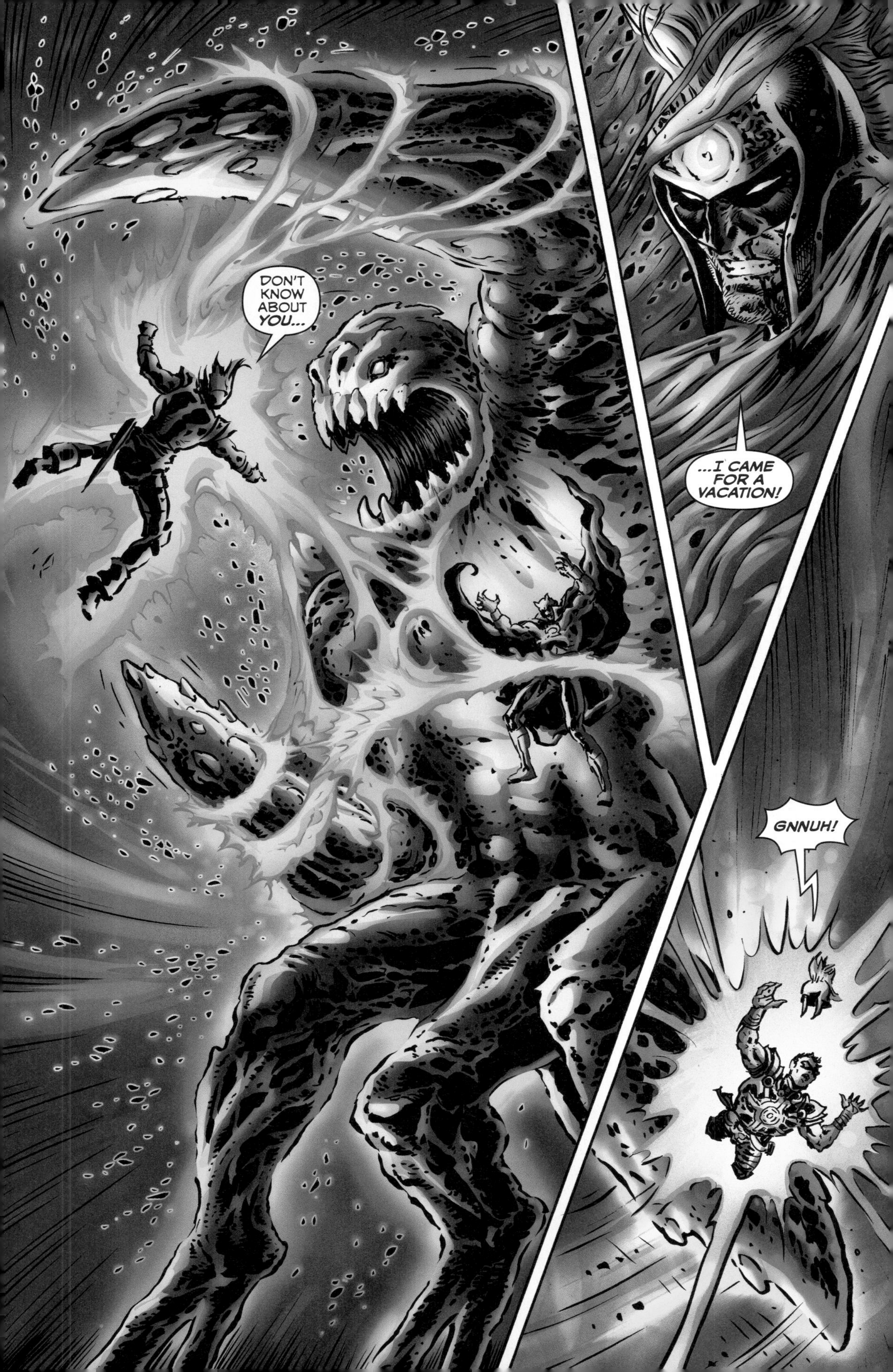
DON'T KNOW ABOUT YOU...
...I CAME FOR A VACATION!
GNNUH!

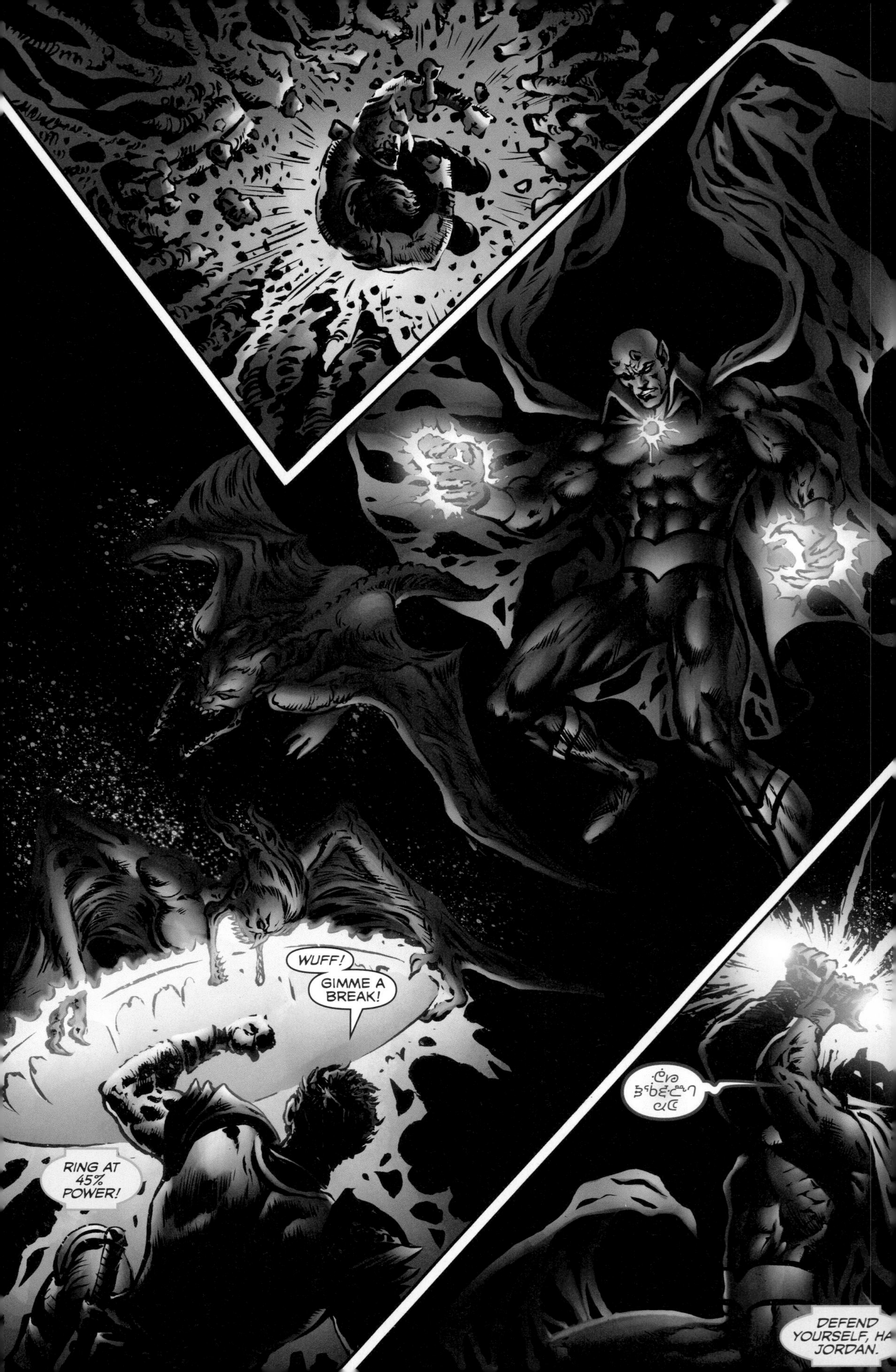
WUFF!
GIMME A BREAK!
RING AT 45% POWER!
DEFEND YOURSELF, HA
JORDAN.

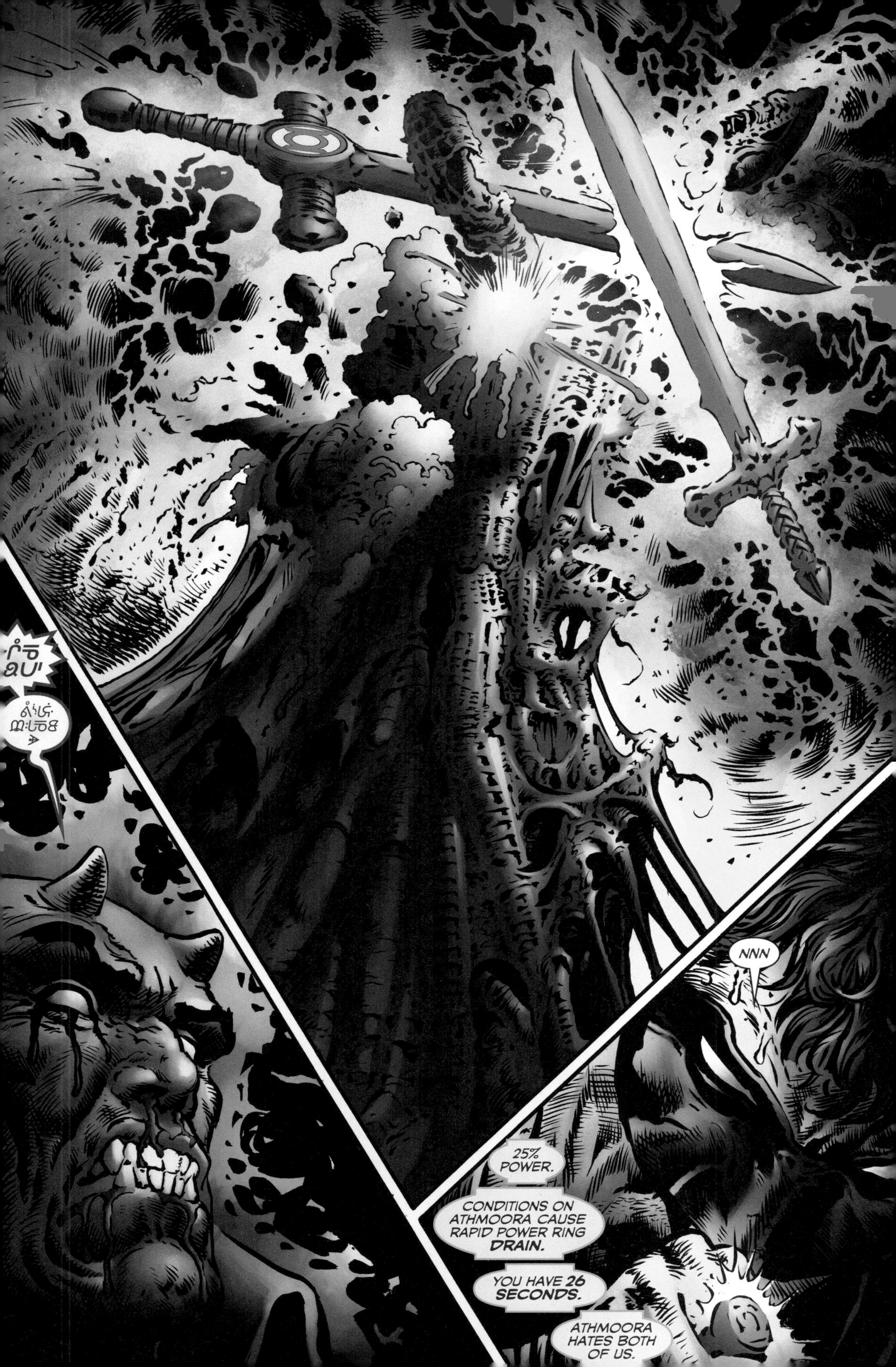
NNN
25% POWER.
CONDITIONS ON ATHMOORA CAUSE RAPID POWER RING DRAIN.
YOU HAVE 26 SECONDS.
ATHMOORA HATES BOTH OF US.

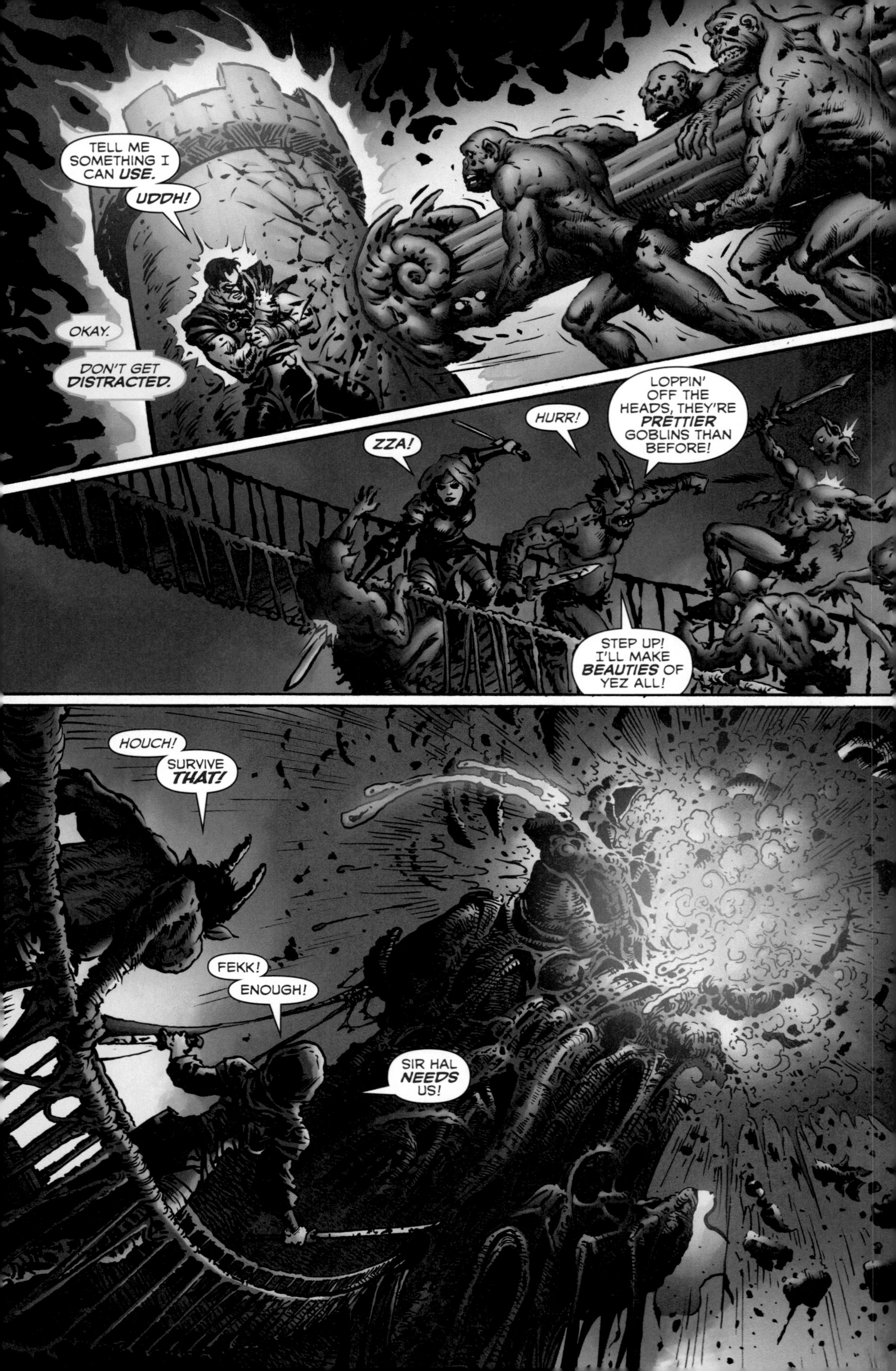
TELL ME SOMETHING I CAN USE.
UDDH!
OKAY.
DON'T GET DISTRACTED.
ZZA!
HURR!
LOPPIN' OFF THE HEADS, THEY'RE PRETTIER GOBLINS THAN BEFORE!
STEP UP! I'LL MAKE BEAUTIES OF YEZ ALL!
HOUCH!
SURVIVE THAT!
FEKK!
ENOUGH!
SIR HAL NEEDS US!

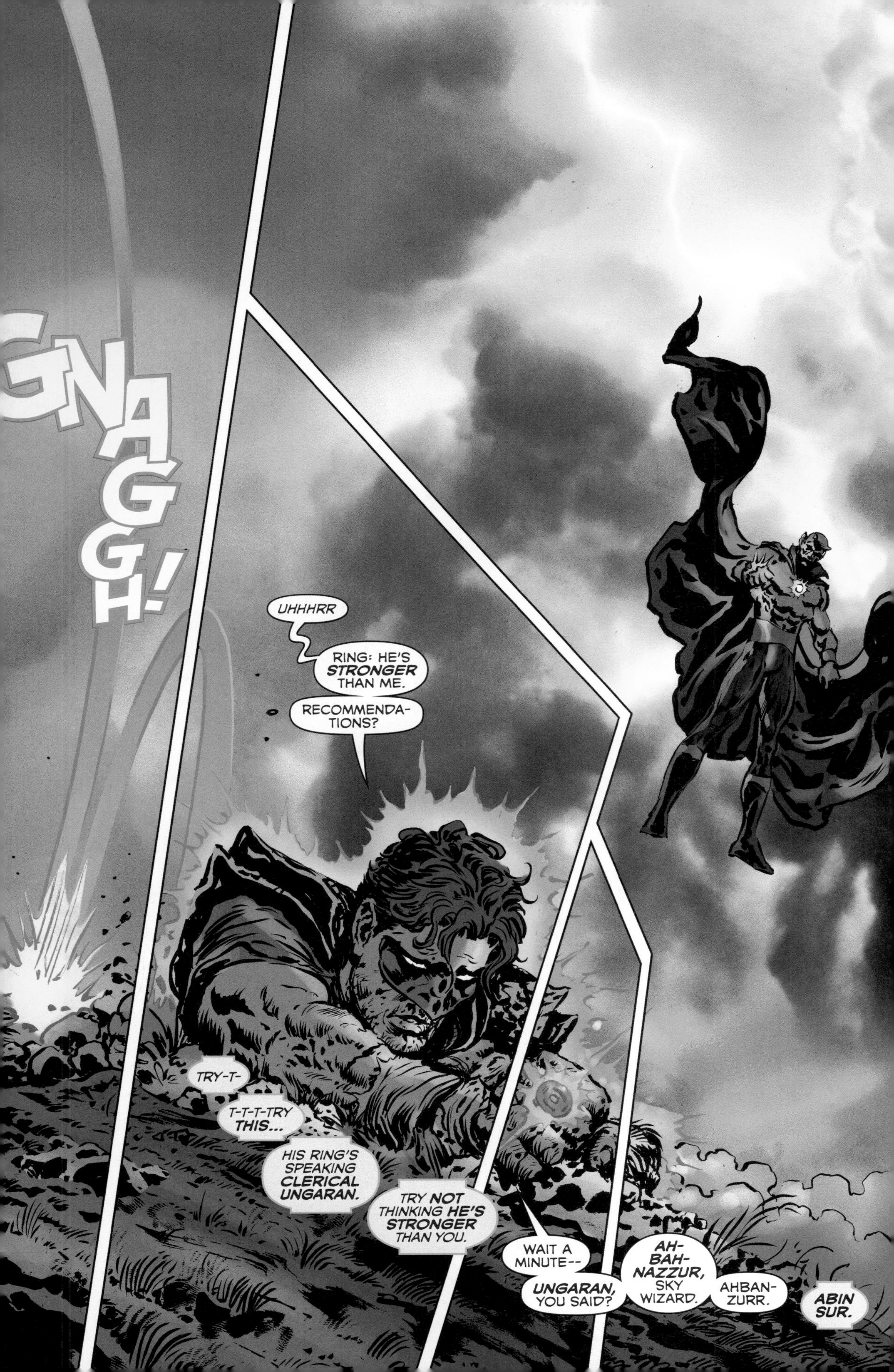
GNAGGH!
UHHHRR
RING: HE'S STRONGER THAN ME.
RECOMMENDATIONS?
TRY-T-
T-T-T-TRY THIS...
HIS RING'S SPEAKING CLERICAL UNGARAN.
TRY NOT THINKING HE'S STRONGER THAN YOU.
WAIT A MINUTE--
UNGARAN, YOU SAID?
AH-BAH-NAZZUR, SKY WIZARD.
AHBAN-ZURR.
ABIN SUR.

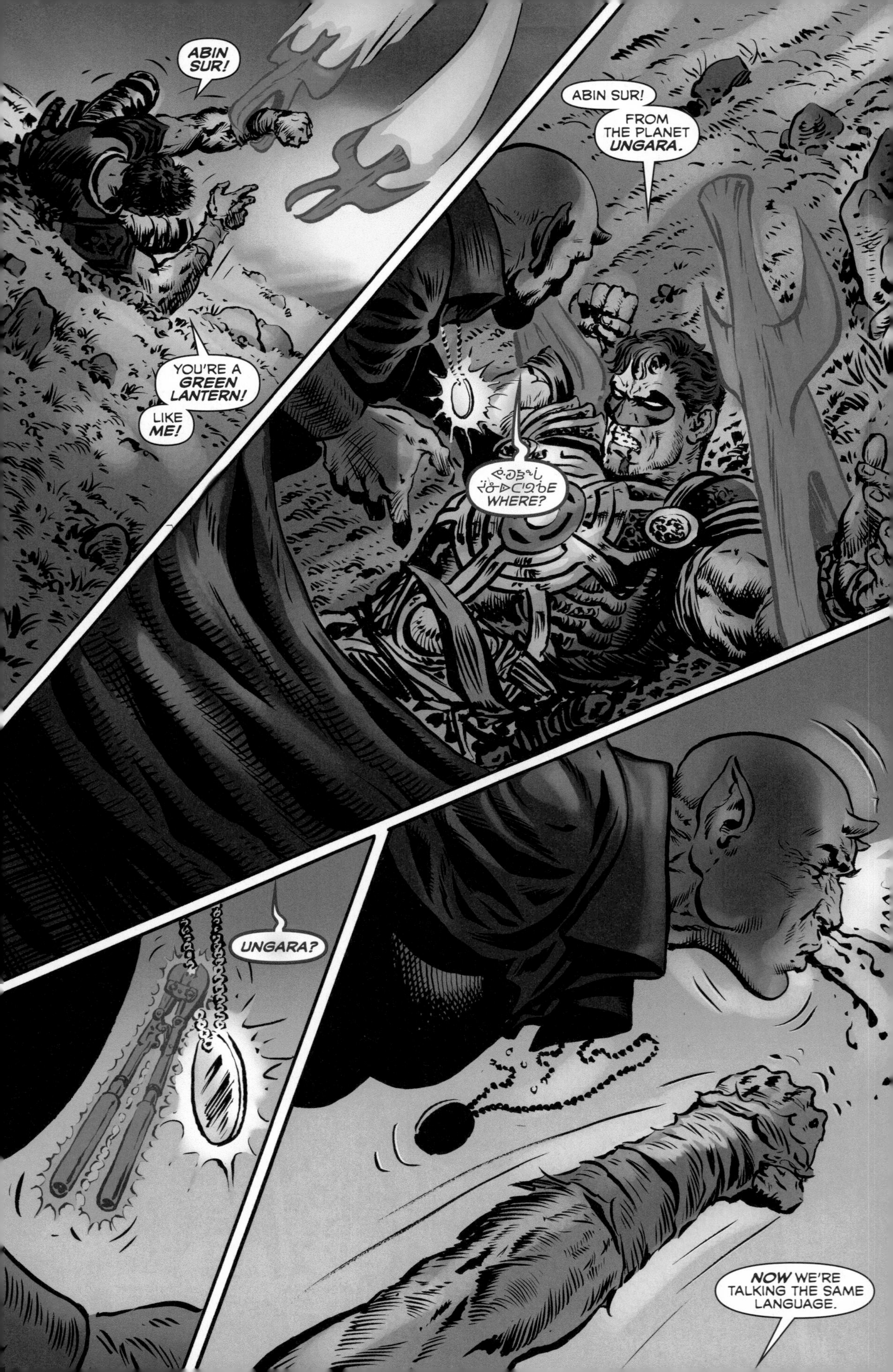
ABIN SUR!
YOU'RE A GREEN LANTERN!
LIKE ME!
ABIN SUR!
FROM THE PLANET UNGARA.
WHERE?
UNGARA?
NOW WE'RE TALKING THE SAME LANGUAGE.

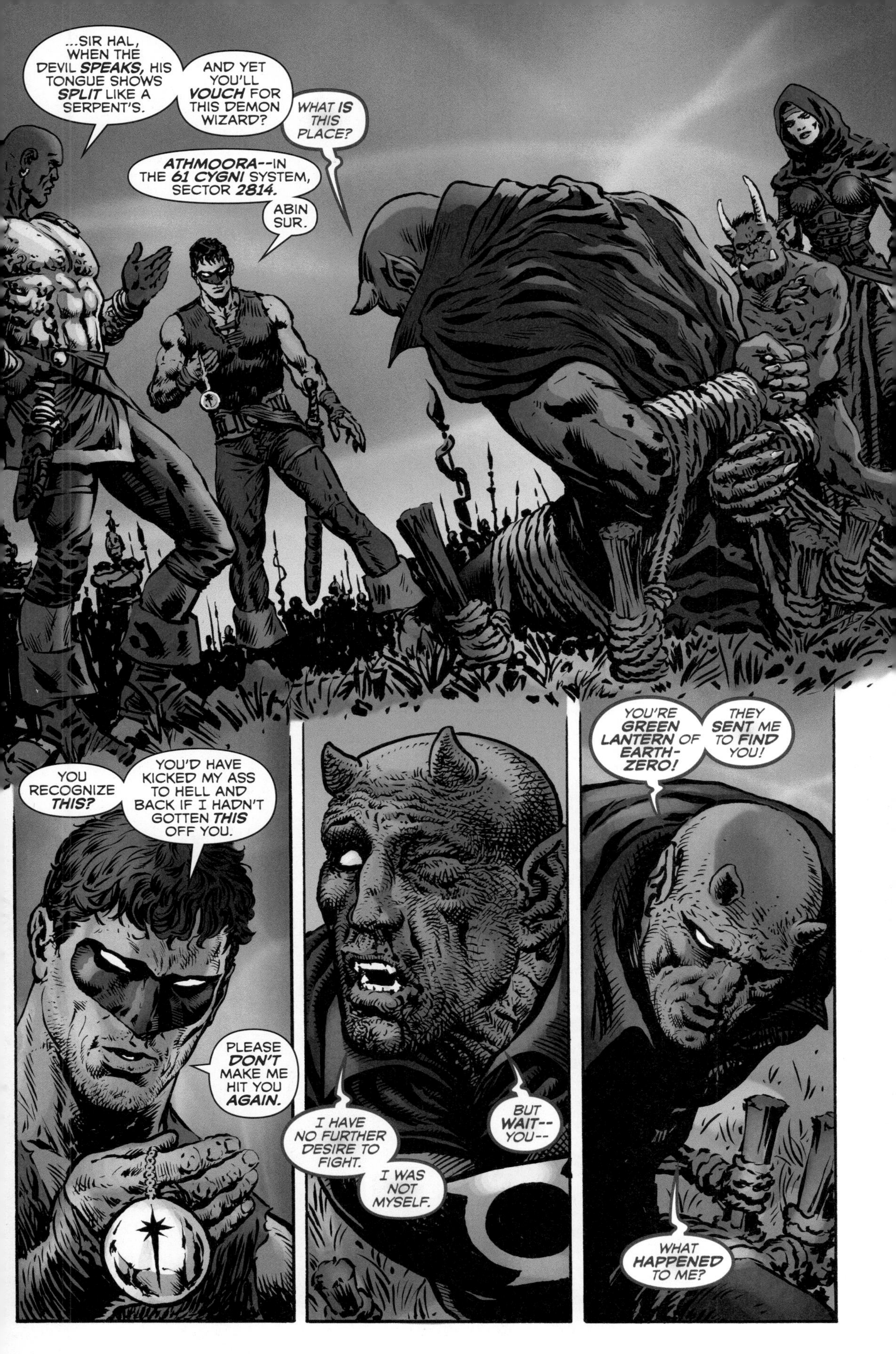
...SIR HAL, WHEN THE DEVIL SPEAKS, HIS TONGUE SHOWS SPLIT LIKE A SERPENT'S.
AND YET YOU'LL VOUCH FOR THIS DEMON WIZARD?
WHAT IS THIS PLACE?
ATHMOORA--IN THE 61 CYGNI SYSTEM, SECTOR 2814.
ABIN SUR.
YOU RECOGNIZE THIS?
YOU'D HAVE KICKED MY ASS TO HELL AND BACK IF I HADN'T GOTTEN THIS OFF YOU.
PLEASE DON'T MAKE ME HIT YOU AGAIN.
I HAVE NO FURTHER DESIRE TO FIGHT.
I WAS NOT MYSELF.
BUT WAIT-- YOU--
YOU'RE GREEN LANTERN OF EARTH-ZERO!
THEY SENT ME TO FIND YOU!
WHAT HAPPENED TO ME?

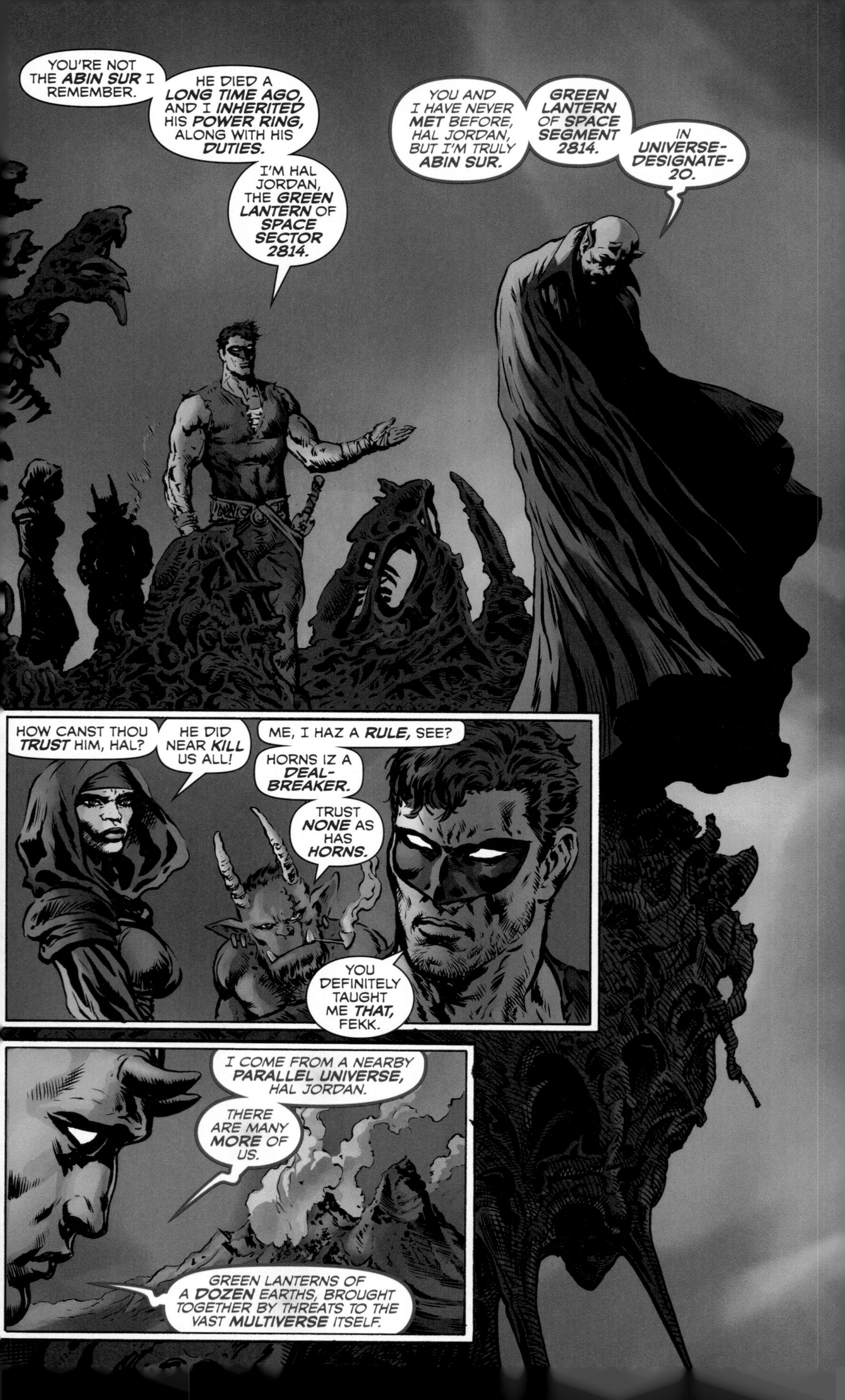
YOU'RE NOT THE ABIN SUR I REMEMBER.
HE DIED A LONG TIME AGO, AND I INHERITED HIS POWER RING, ALONG WITH HIS DUTIES.
I'M HAL JORDAN, THE GREEN LANTERN OF SPACE SECTOR 2814.
YOU AND I HAVE NEVER MET BEFORE, HAL JORDAN, BUT I'M TRULY ABIN SUR.
GREEN LANTERN OF SPACE SEGMENT 2814.
IN UNIVERSE-DESIGNATE-20.
HOW CANST THOU TRUST HIM, HAL?
HE DID NEAR KILL US ALL!
ME, I HAZ A RULE, SEE?
HORNS IZ A DEAL-BREAKER.
TRUST NONE AS HAS HORNS.
YOU DEFINITELY TAUGHT ME THAT, FEKK.
I COME FROM A NEARBY PARALLEL UNIVERSE, HAL JORDAN.
THERE ARE MANY MORE OF US.
GREEN LANTERNS OF A DOZEN EARTHS, BROUGHT TOGETHER BY THREATS TO THE VAST MULTIVERSE ITSELF.

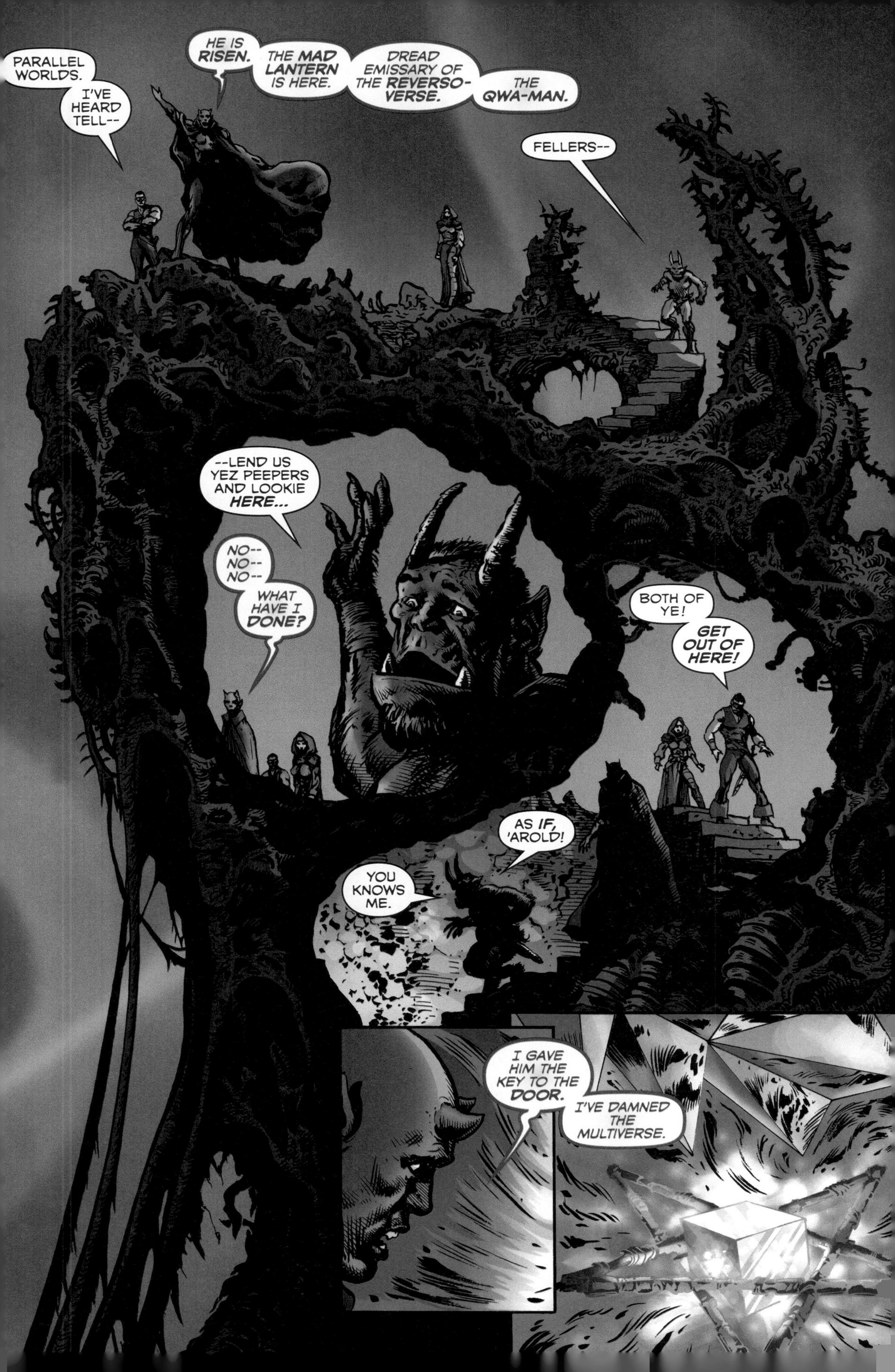

PARALLEL WORLDS.
I'VE HEARD TELL--
HE IS RISEN.
THE MAD LANTERN IS HERE.
DREAD EMISSARY OF THE REVERSO-VERSE.
THE QWA-MAN.
FELLERS--
--LEND US YEZ PEEPERS AND LOOKIE HERE...
NO-- NO-- NO--
WHAT HAVE I DONE?
BOTH OF YE!
GET OUT OF HERE!
AS IF, 'AROLD!
YOU KNOWS ME.
I GAVE HIM THE KEY TO THE DOOR.
I'VE DAMNED THE MULTIVERSE.

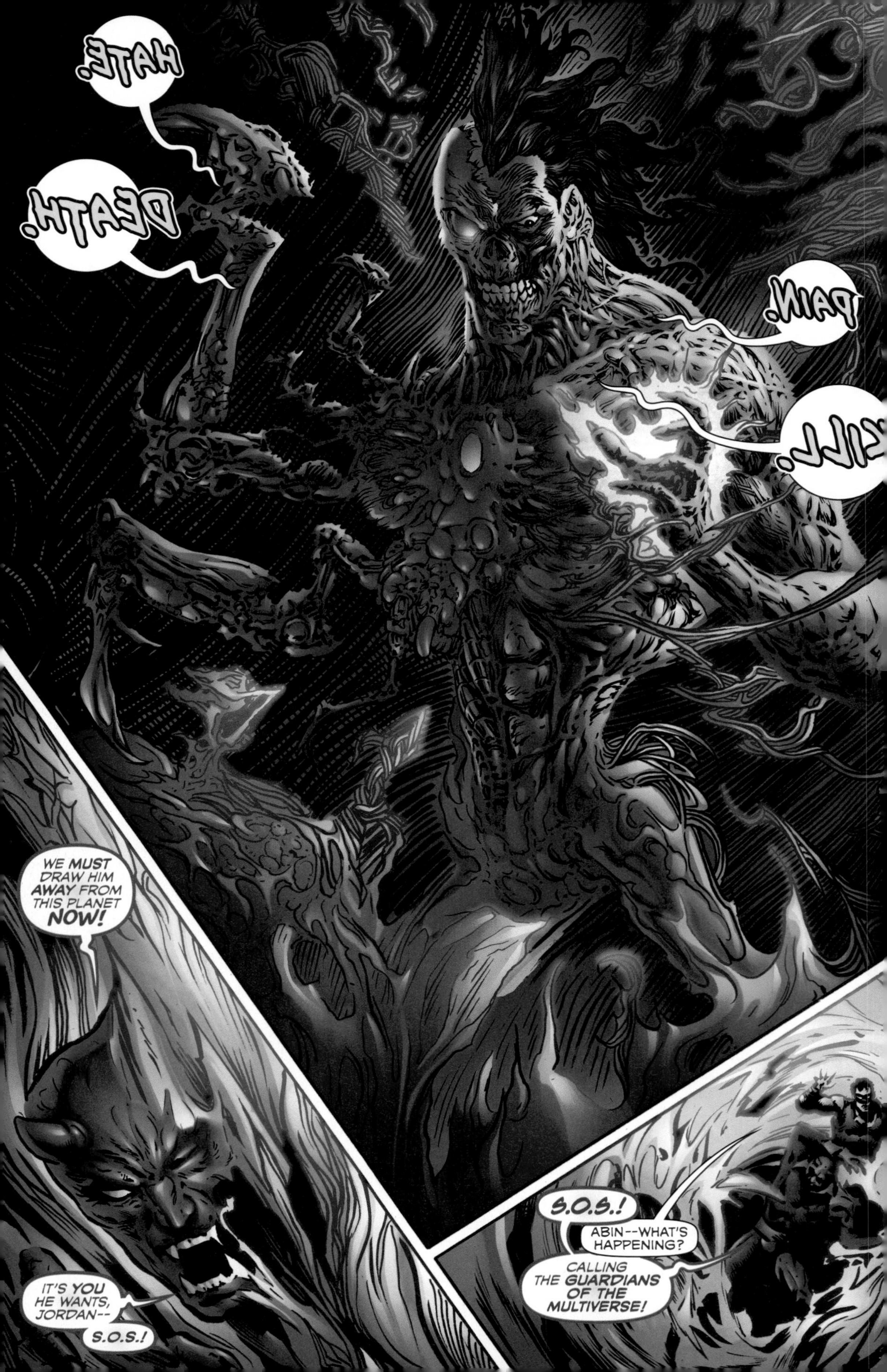
HATE.
DEATH.
PAIN.
WE MUST DRAW HIM AWAY FROM THIS PLANET NOW!
IT'S YOU HE WANTS, JORDAN--
S.O.S.!
S.O.S.!
ABIN--WHAT'S HAPPENING?
CALLING THE GUARDIANS OF THE MULTIVERSE!

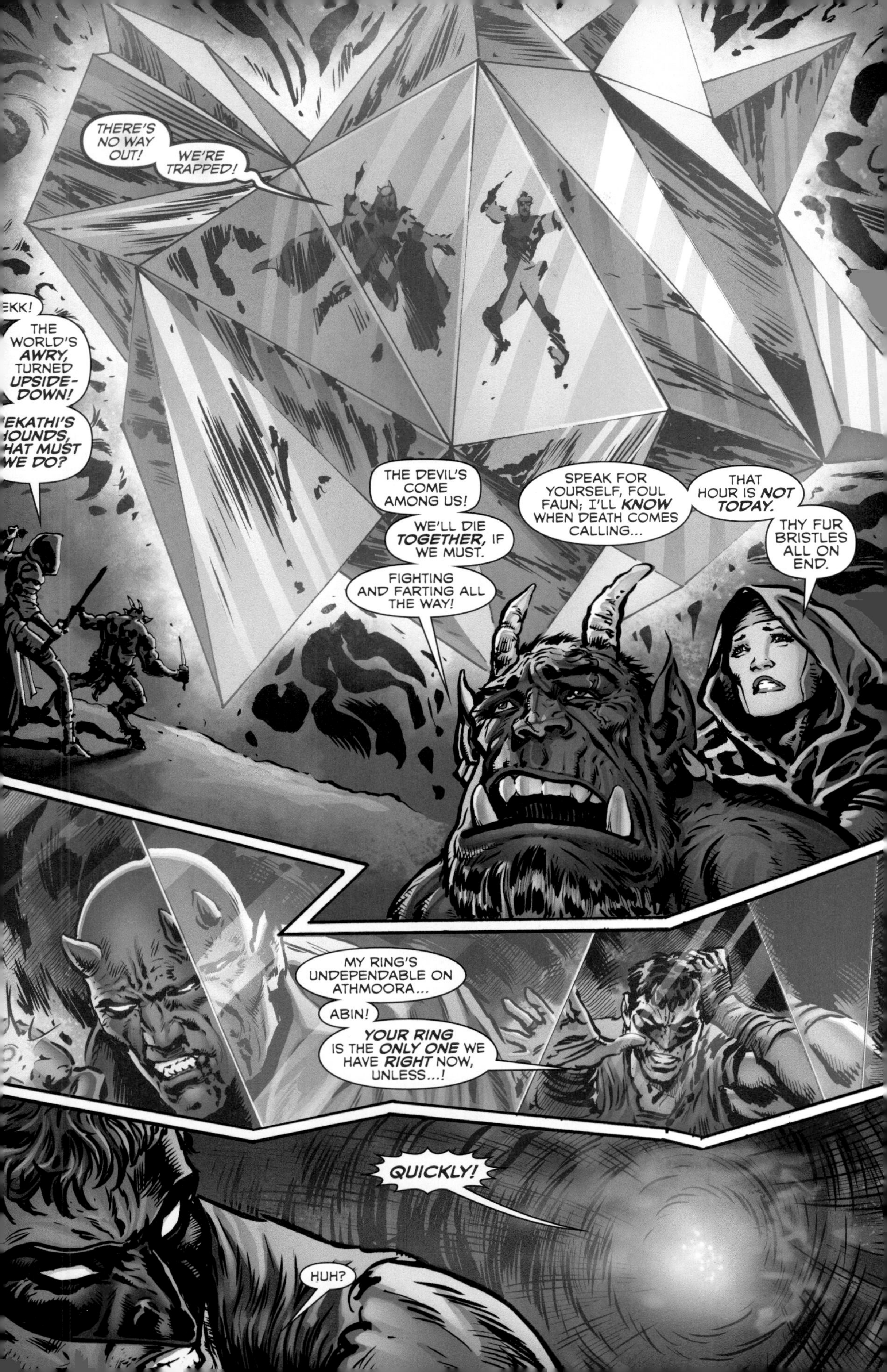

THERE'S NO WAY OUT!
WE'RE TRAPPED!
EKK!
THE WORLD'S AWRY, TURNED UPSIDE-DOWN!
EKATHI'S HOUNDS, HAT MUST WE DO?
THE DEVIL'S COME AMONG US!
WE'LL DIE TOGETHER, IF WE MUST.
FIGHTING AND FARTING ALL THE WAY!
SPEAK FOR YOURSELF, FOUL FAUN; I'LL KNOW WHEN DEATH COMES CALLING...
THAT HOUR IS NOT TODAY.
THY FUR BRISTLES ALL ON END.
MY RING'S UNDEPENDABLE ON ATHMOORA...
ABIN!
YOUR RING IS THE ONLY ONE WE HAVE RIGHT NOW, UNLESS...!
QUICKLY!
HUH?

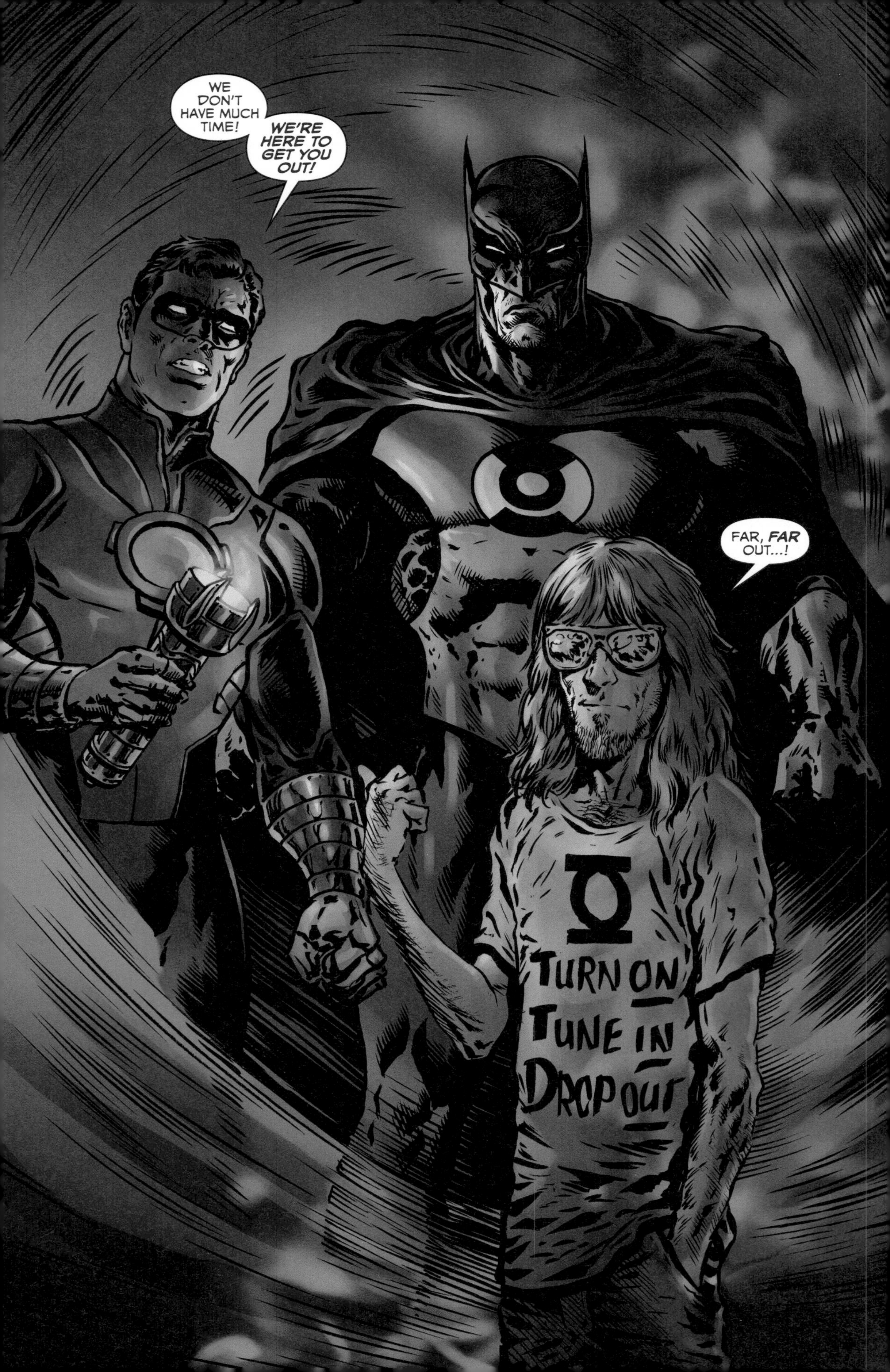
WE DON'T HAVE MUCH TIME!
WE'RE HERE TO GET YOU OUT!
FAR, FAR OUT...!
TURN ON TUNE IN DROP OUT

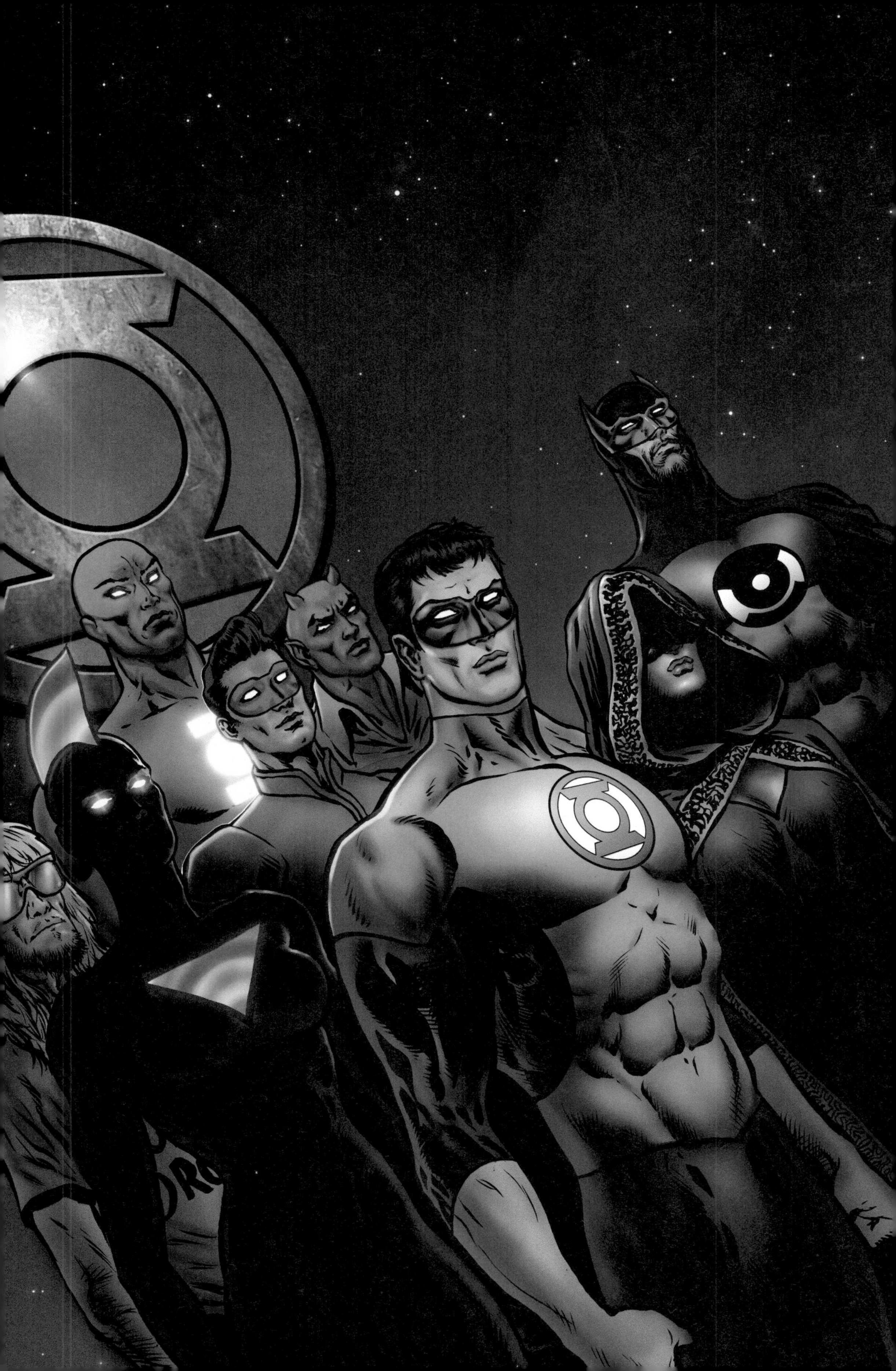

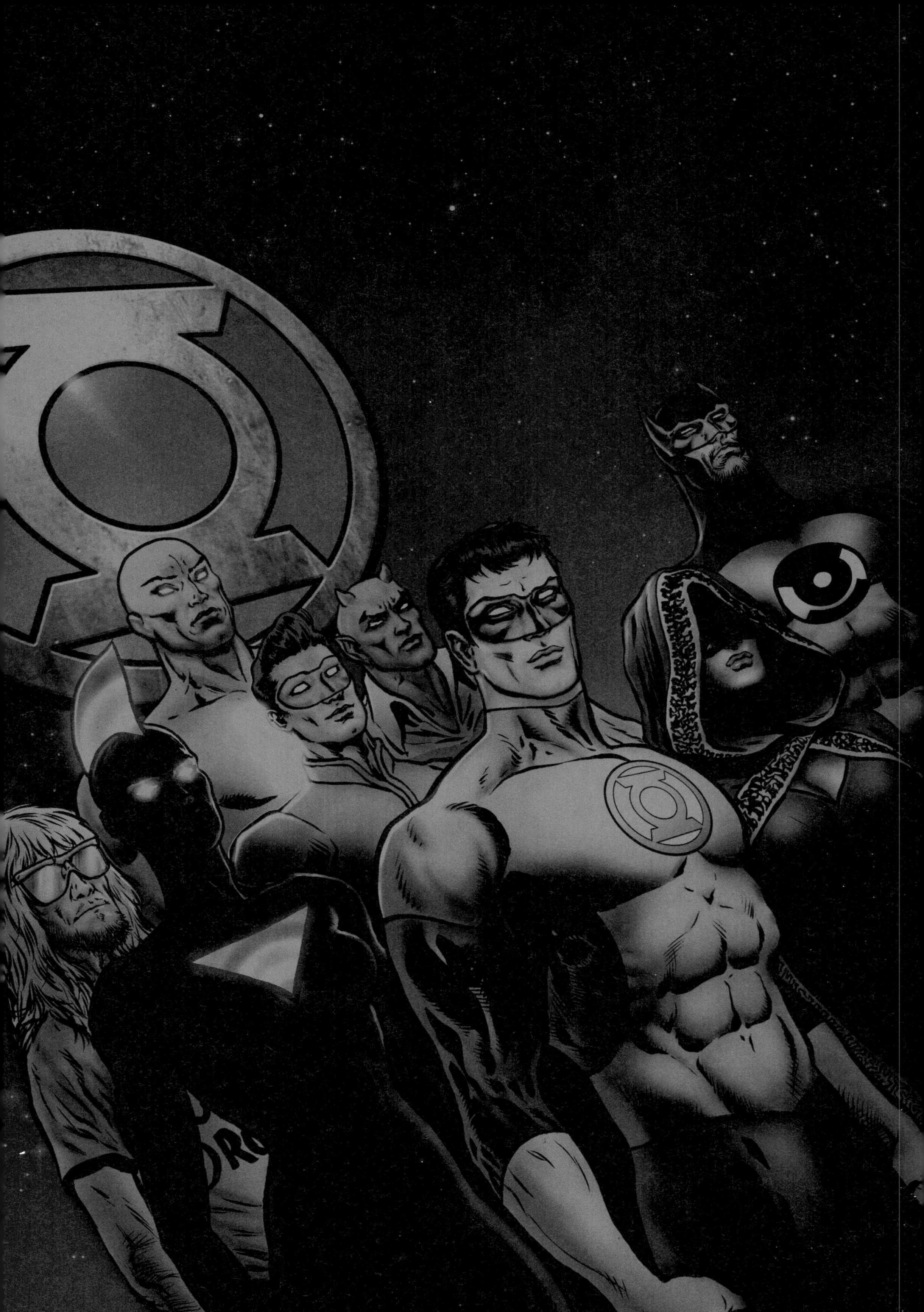

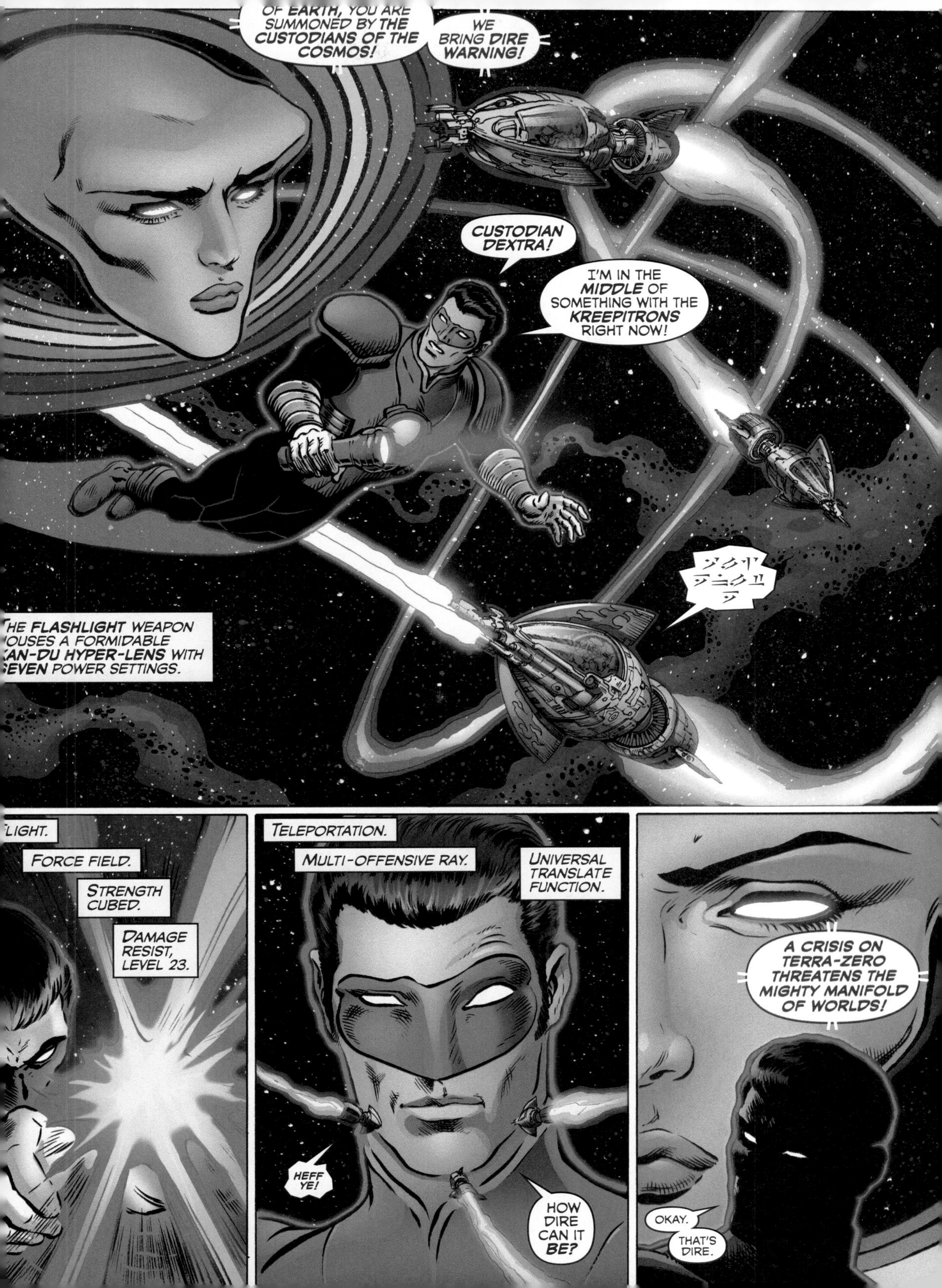
OF EARTH, YOU ARE SUMMONED BY THE CUSTODIANS OF THE COSMOS!
WE BRING DIRE WARNING!
CUSTODIAN DEXTRA!
I'M IN THE MIDDLE OF SOMETHING WITH THE KREEPITRONS RIGHT NOW!
THE FLASHLIGHT WEAPON HOUSES A FORMIDABLE KAN-DU HYPER-LENS WITH SEVEN POWER SETTINGS.
FLIGHT.
FORCE FIELD.
STRENGTH CUBED.
DAMAGE RESIST, LEVEL 23.
TELEPORTATION.
MULTI-OFFENSIVE RAY.
UNIVERSAL TRANSLATE FUNCTION.
HEFF YE!
HOW DIRE CAN IT BE?
A CRISIS ON TERRA-ZERO THREATENS THE MIGHTY MANIFOLD OF WORLDS!
OKAY.
THAT'S DIRE.

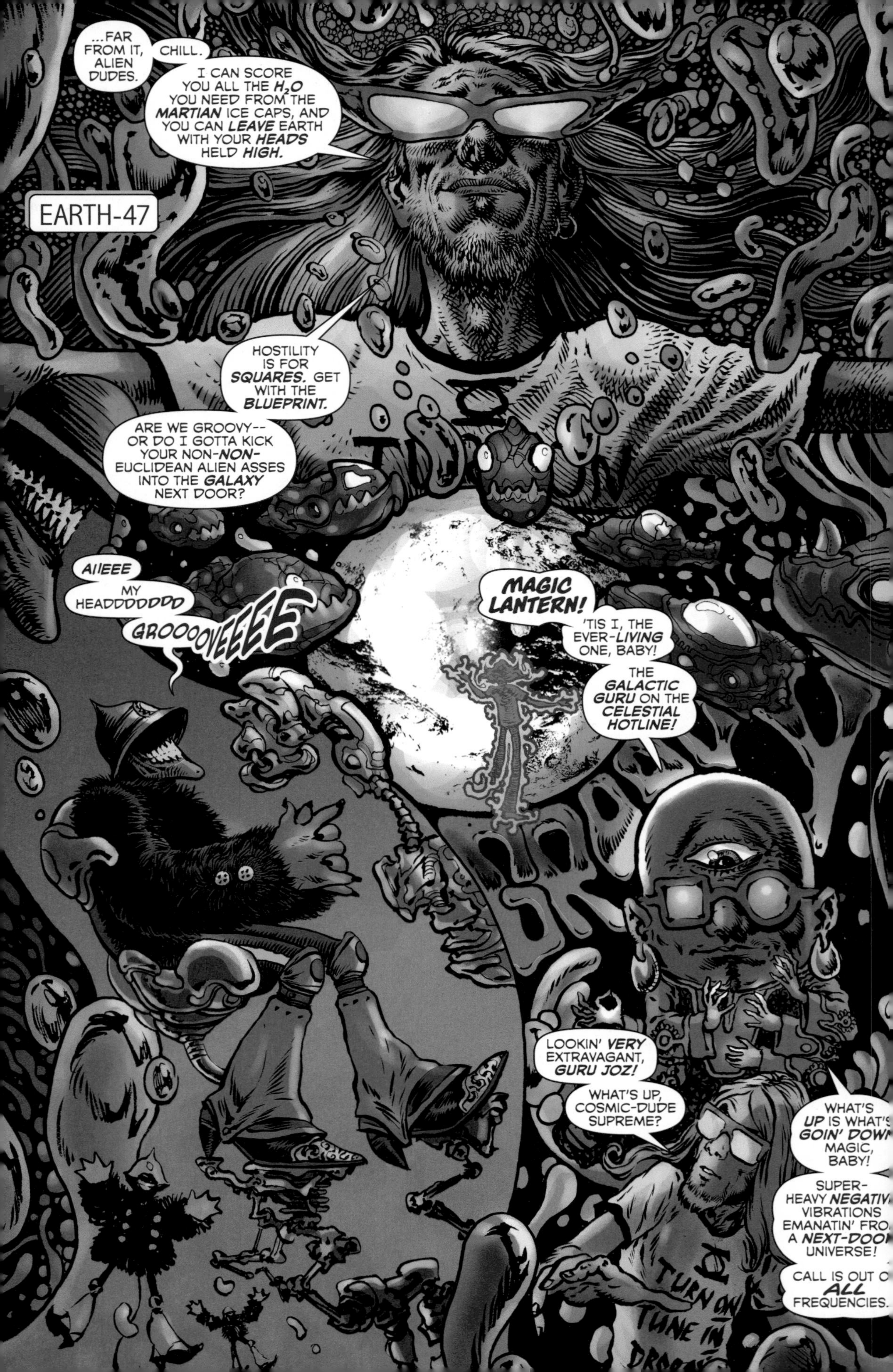

...FAR FROM IT, ALIEN DUDES.
CHILL.
I CAN SCORE YOU ALL THE H_2O YOU NEED FROM THE MARTIAN ICE CAPS, AND YOU CAN LEAVE EARTH WITH YOUR HEADS HELD HIGH.
EARTH-47
HOSTILITY IS FOR SQUARES. GET WITH THE BLUEPRINT.
ARE WE GROOVY-- OR DO I GOTTA KICK YOUR NON-NON-EUCLIDEAN ALIEN ASSES INTO THE GALAXY NEXT DOOR?
AIIEEE
MY HEADDDDDDD
GROOOOVEEEEE
MAGIC LANTERN!
'TIS I, THE EVER-LIVING ONE, BABY!
THE GALACTIC GURU ON THE CELESTIAL HOTLINE!
LOOKIN' VERY EXTRAVAGANT, GURU JOZ!
WHAT'S UP, COSMIC-DUDE SUPREME?
WHAT'S UP IS WHAT'S GOIN' DOWN MAGIC, BABY!
SUPER-HEAVY NEGATIV VIBRATIONS EMANATIN' FRO A NEXT-DOO UNIVERSE!
CALL IS OUT O ALL FREQUENCIES.
TURN ON TUNE IN

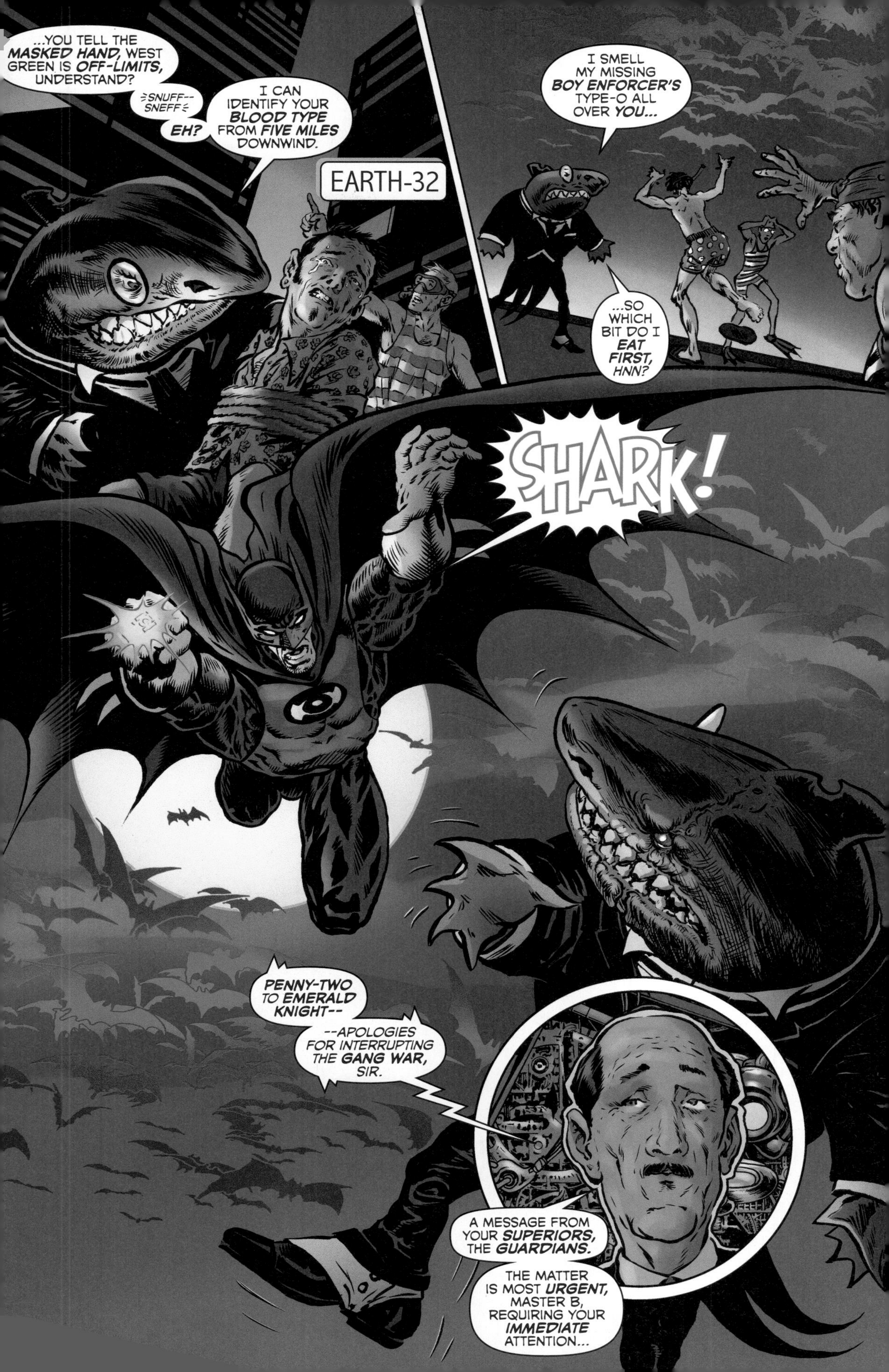

...YOU TELL THE MASKED HAND, WEST GREEN IS OFF-LIMITS, UNDERSTAND?
SNUFF-- SNEFF
EH?
I CAN IDENTIFY YOUR BLOOD TYPE FROM FIVE MILES DOWNWIND.
EARTH-32
I SMELL MY MISSING BOY ENFORCER'S TYPE-O ALL OVER YOU...
...SO WHICH BIT DO I EAT FIRST, HNN?
SHARK!
PENNY-TWO TO EMERALD KNIGHT--
--APOLOGIES FOR INTERRUPTING THE GANG WAR, SIR.
A MESSAGE FROM YOUR SUPERIORS, THE GUARDIANS.
THE MATTER IS MOST URGENT, MASTER B, REQUIRING YOUR IMMEDIATE ATTENTION...

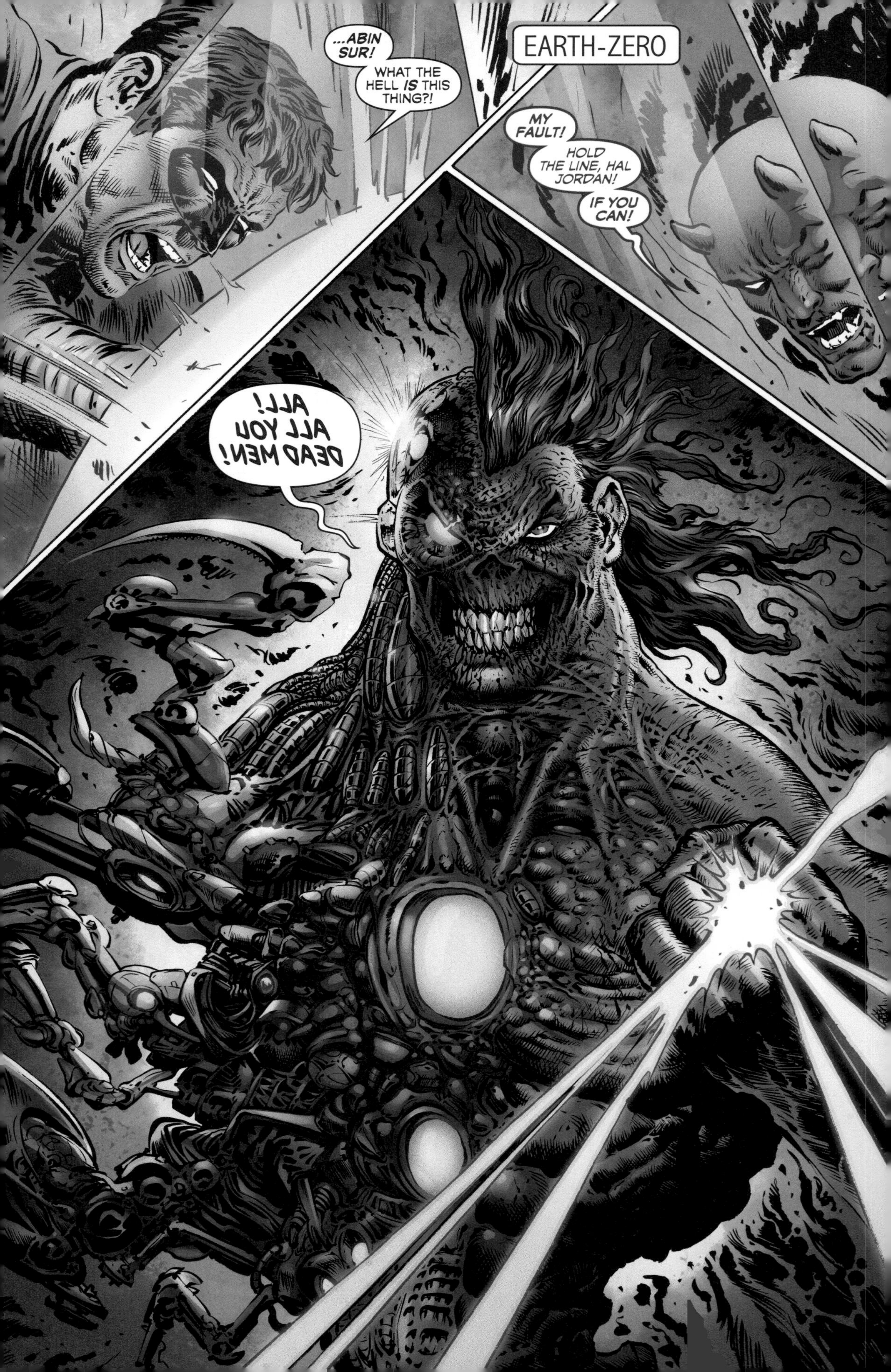
EARTH-ZERO
...ABIN SUR!
WHAT THE HELL IS THIS THING?!
MY FAULT!
HOLD THE LINE, HAL JORDAN!
IF YOU CAN!
ALL! ALL YOU DEAD MEN!

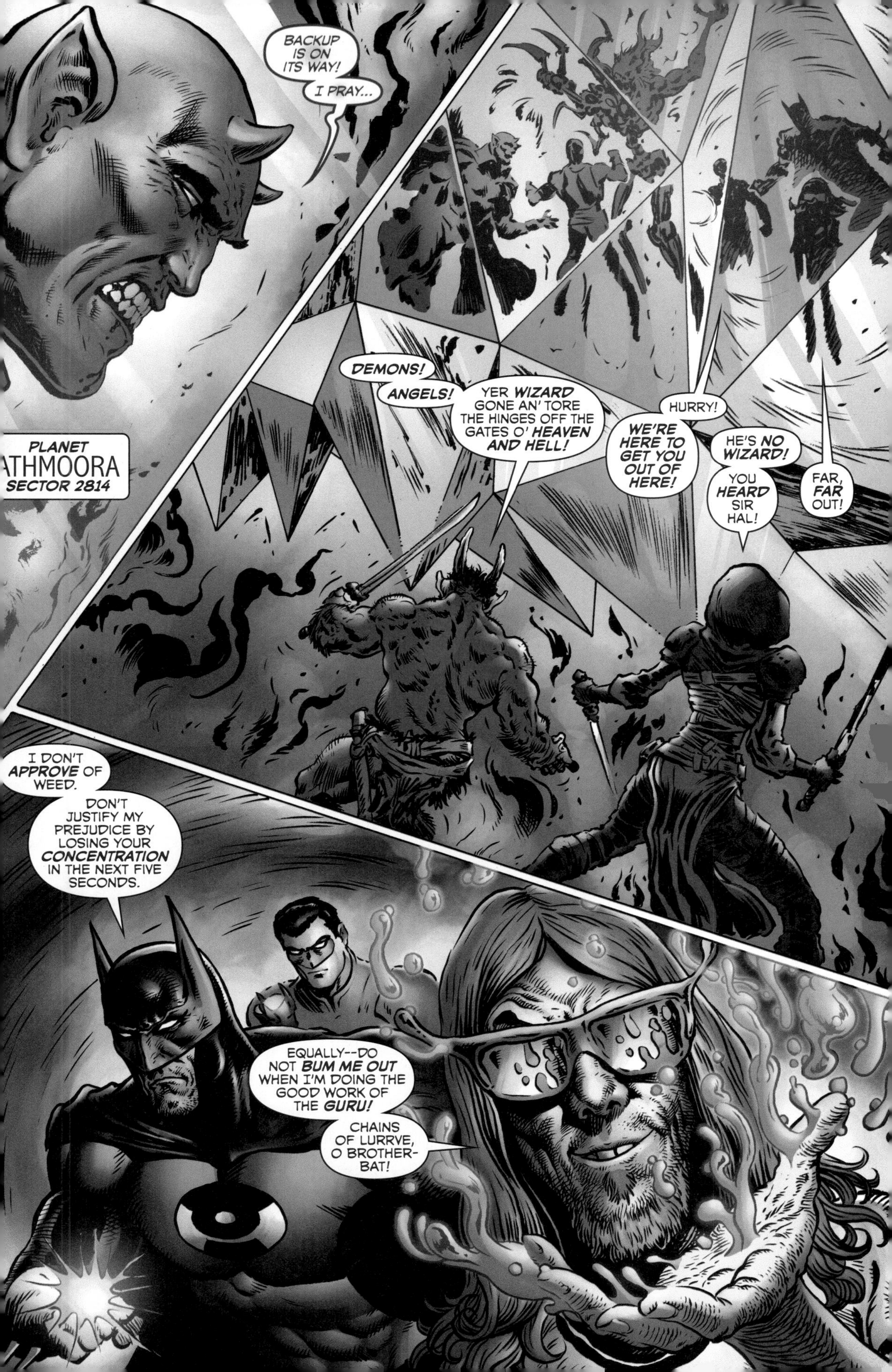
BACKUP IS ON ITS WAY!
I PRAY...
PLANET ATHMOORA SECTOR 2814
DEMONS!
ANGELS!
YER WIZARD GONE AN' TORE THE HINGES OFF THE GATES O' HEAVEN AND HELL!
HURRY!
WE'RE HERE TO GET YOU OUT OF HERE!
HE'S NO WIZARD!
YOU HEARD SIR HAL!
FAR, FAR OUT!
I DON'T APPROVE OF WEED.
DON'T JUSTIFY MY PREJUDICE BY LOSING YOUR CONCENTRATION IN THE NEXT FIVE SECONDS.
EQUALLY--DO NOT BUM ME OUT WHEN I'M DOING THE GOOD WORK OF THE GURU!
CHAINS OF LURRVE, O BROTHER-BAT!

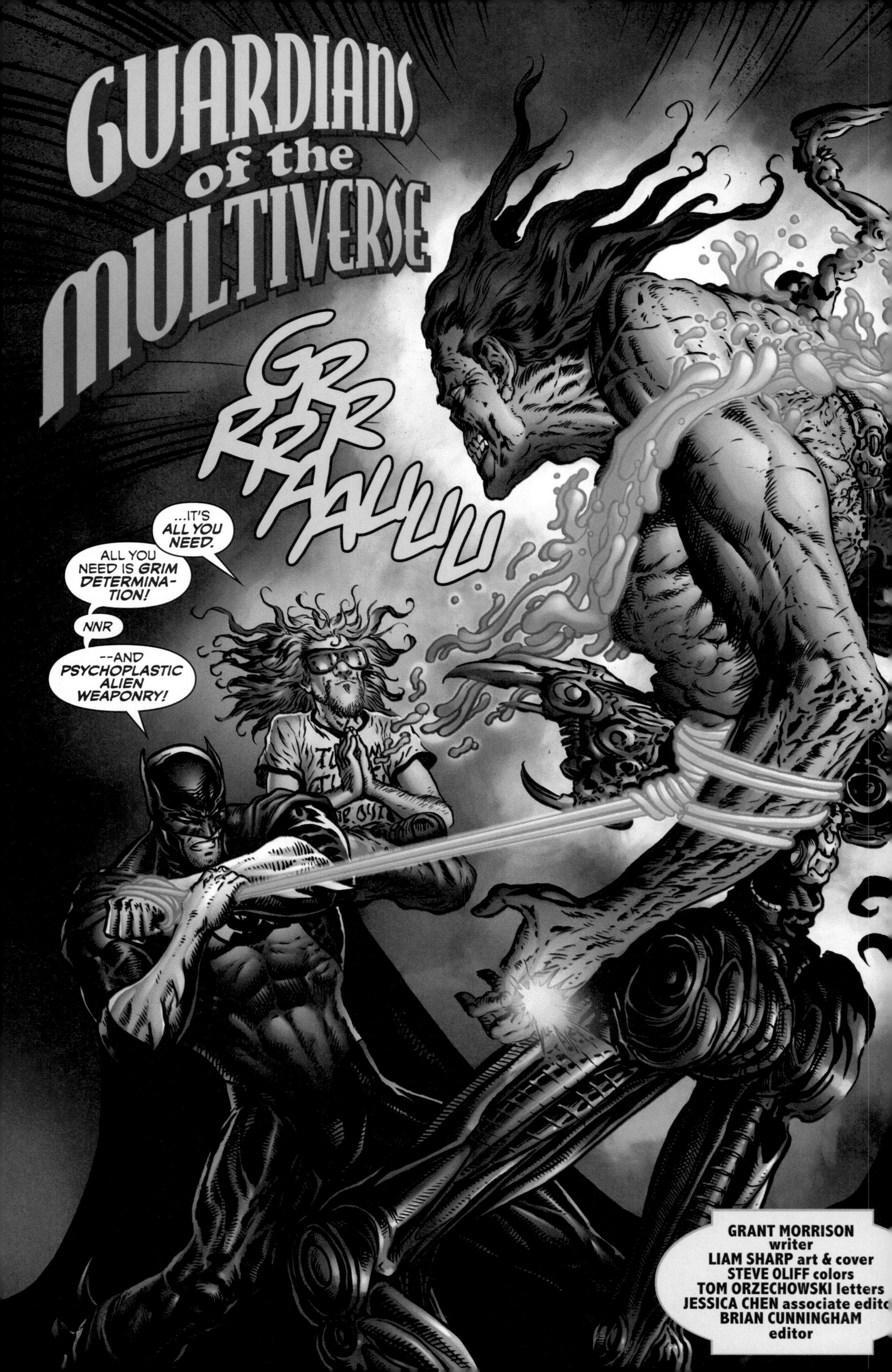
GUARDIANS of the MULTIVERSE
GRRRAUUUU
...IT'S ALL YOU NEED.
ALL YOU NEED IS GRIM DETERMINATION!
NNR
--AND PSYCHOPLASTIC ALIEN WEAPONRY!
GRANT MORRISON writer
LIAM SHARP art & cover
STEVE OLIFF colors
TOM ORZECHOWSKI letters
JESSICA CHEN associate edito
BRIAN CUNNINGHAM editor

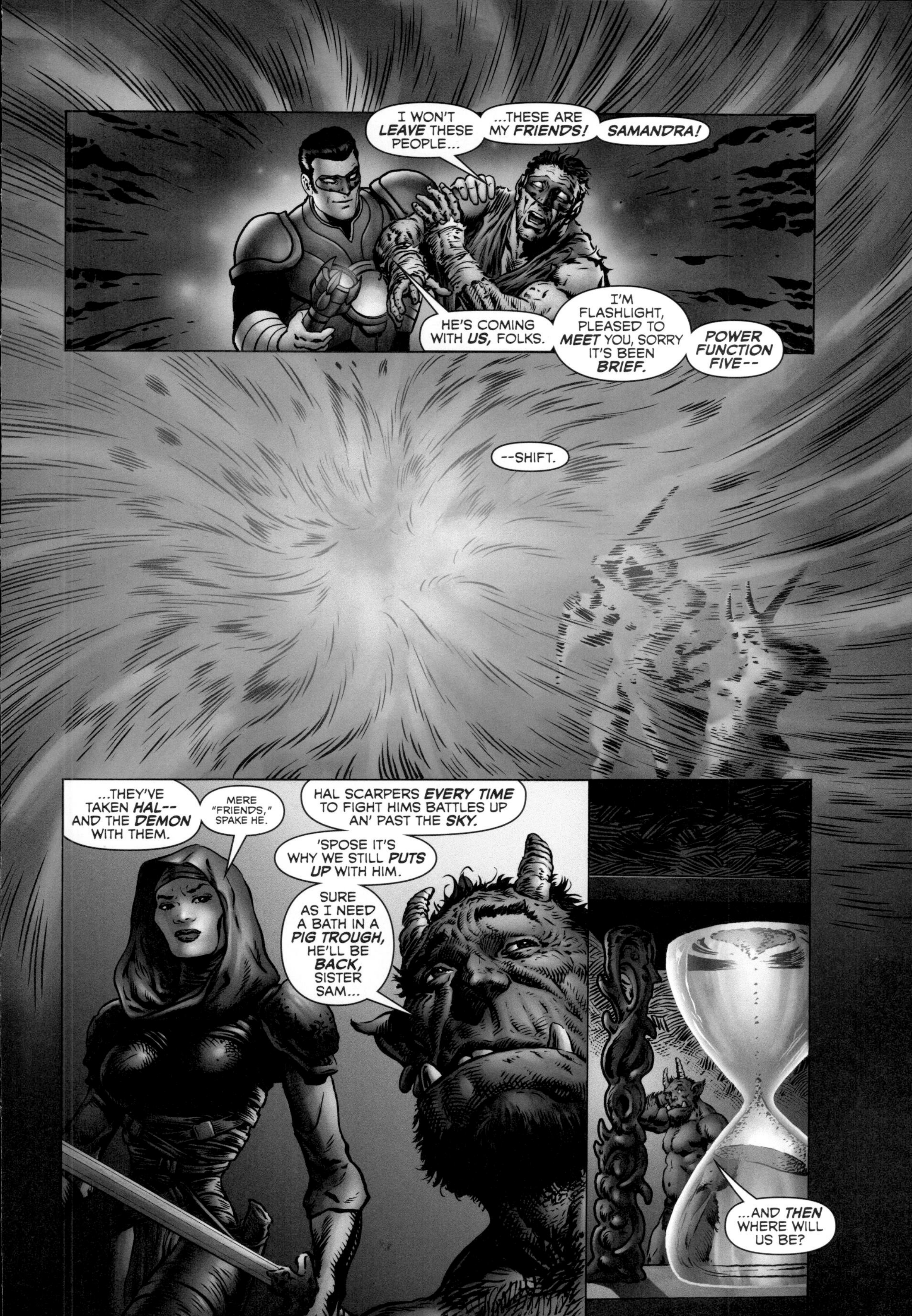
I WON'T *LEAVE* THESE PEOPLE...
...THESE ARE MY *FRIENDS!*
SAMANDRA!
HE'S COMING WITH *US,* FOLKS.
I'M FLASHLIGHT, PLEASED TO *MEET* YOU, SORRY IT'S BEEN *BRIEF.*
POWER FUNCTION FIVE--
--SHIFT.
...THEY'VE TAKEN *HAL--* AND THE *DEMON* WITH THEM.
MERE "FRIENDS," SPAKE HE.
HAL SCARPERS *EVERY TIME* TO FIGHT HIMS BATTLES UP AN' PAST THE *SKY.*
'SPOSE IT'S WHY WE STILL *PUTS UP* WITH HIM.
SURE AS I NEED A BATH IN A *PIG TROUGH,* HE'LL BE *BACK,* SISTER SAM...
...AND *THEN* WHERE WILL US BE?

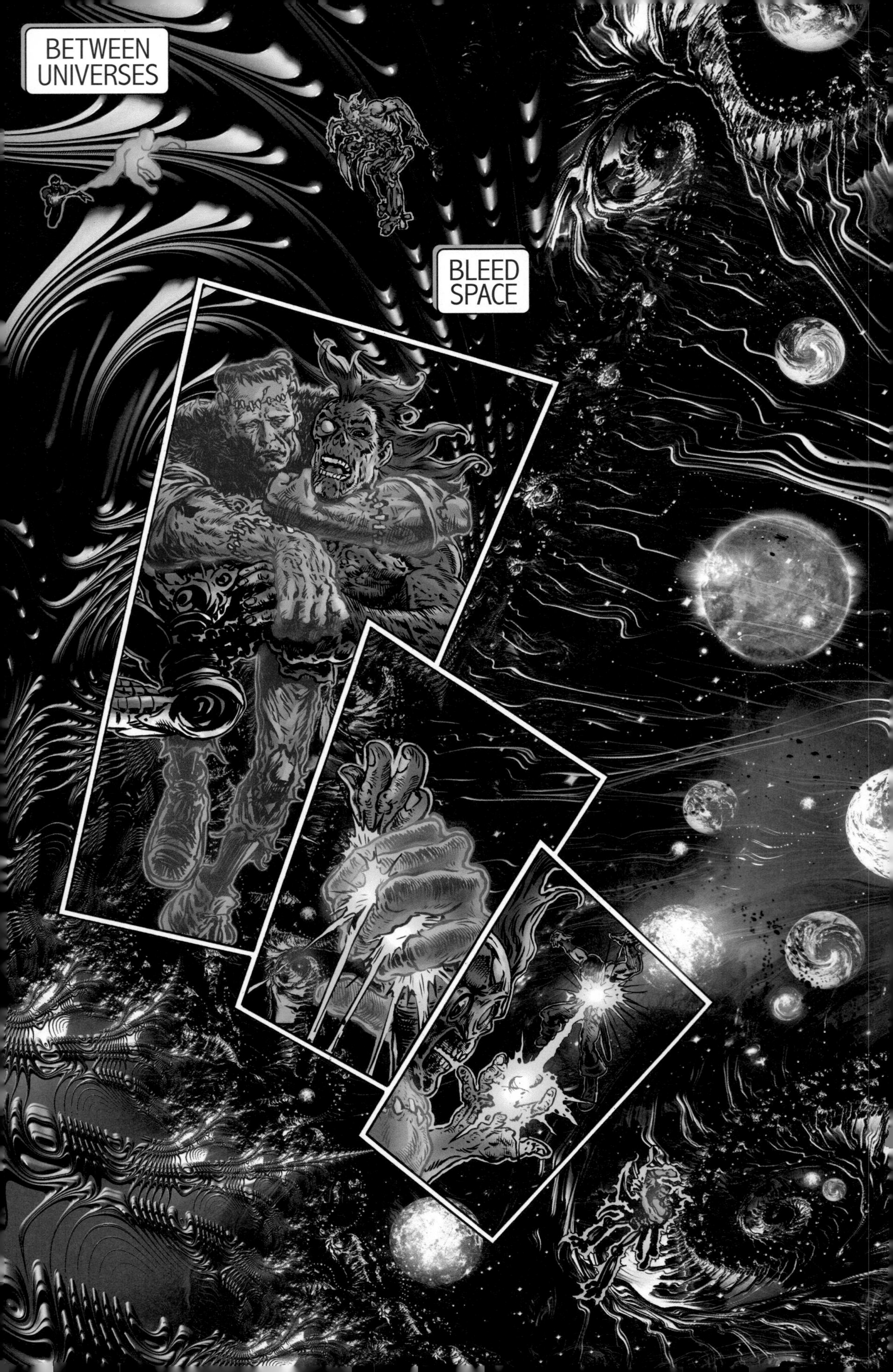
BETWEEN UNIVERSES
BLEED SPACE

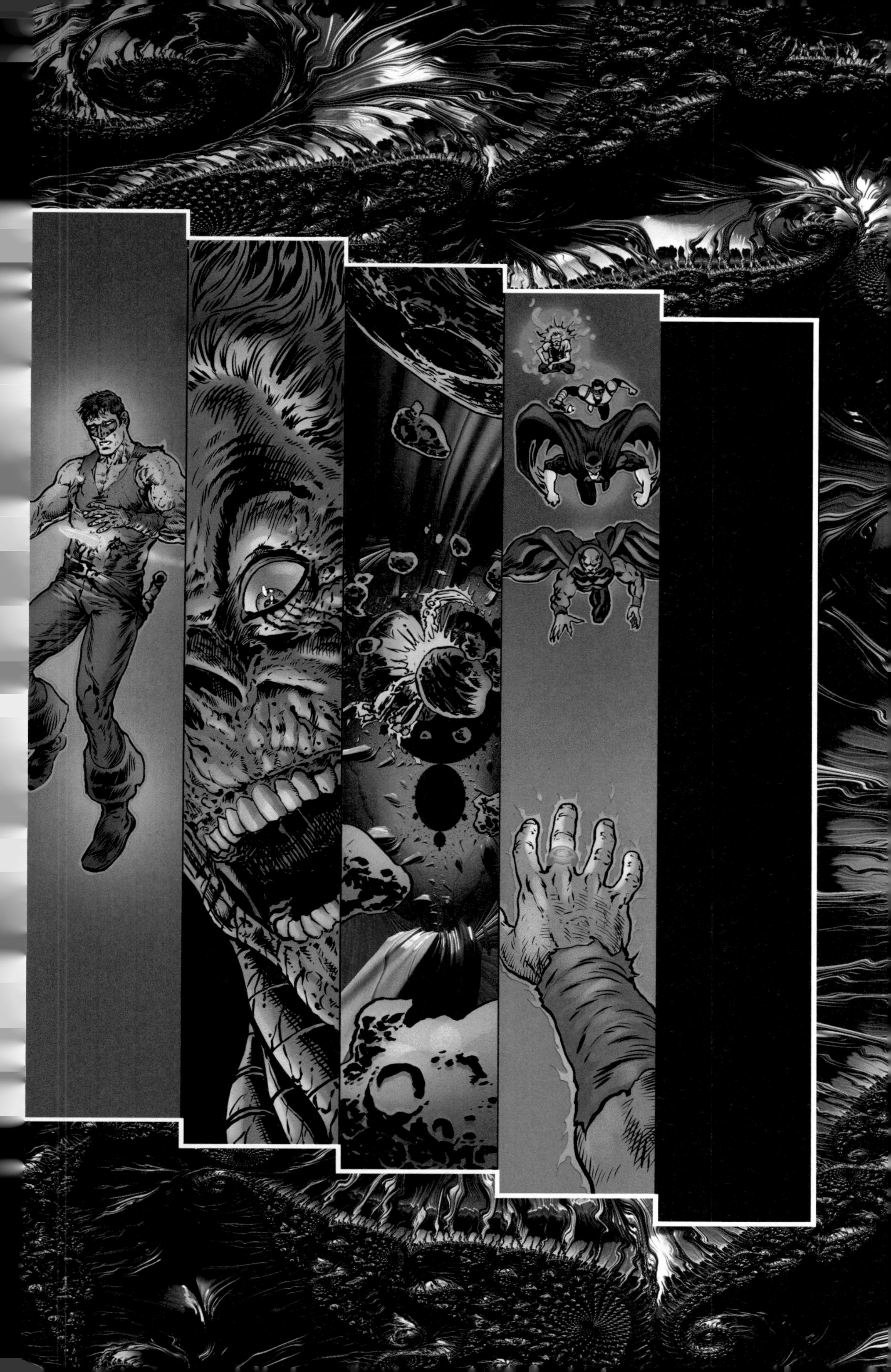

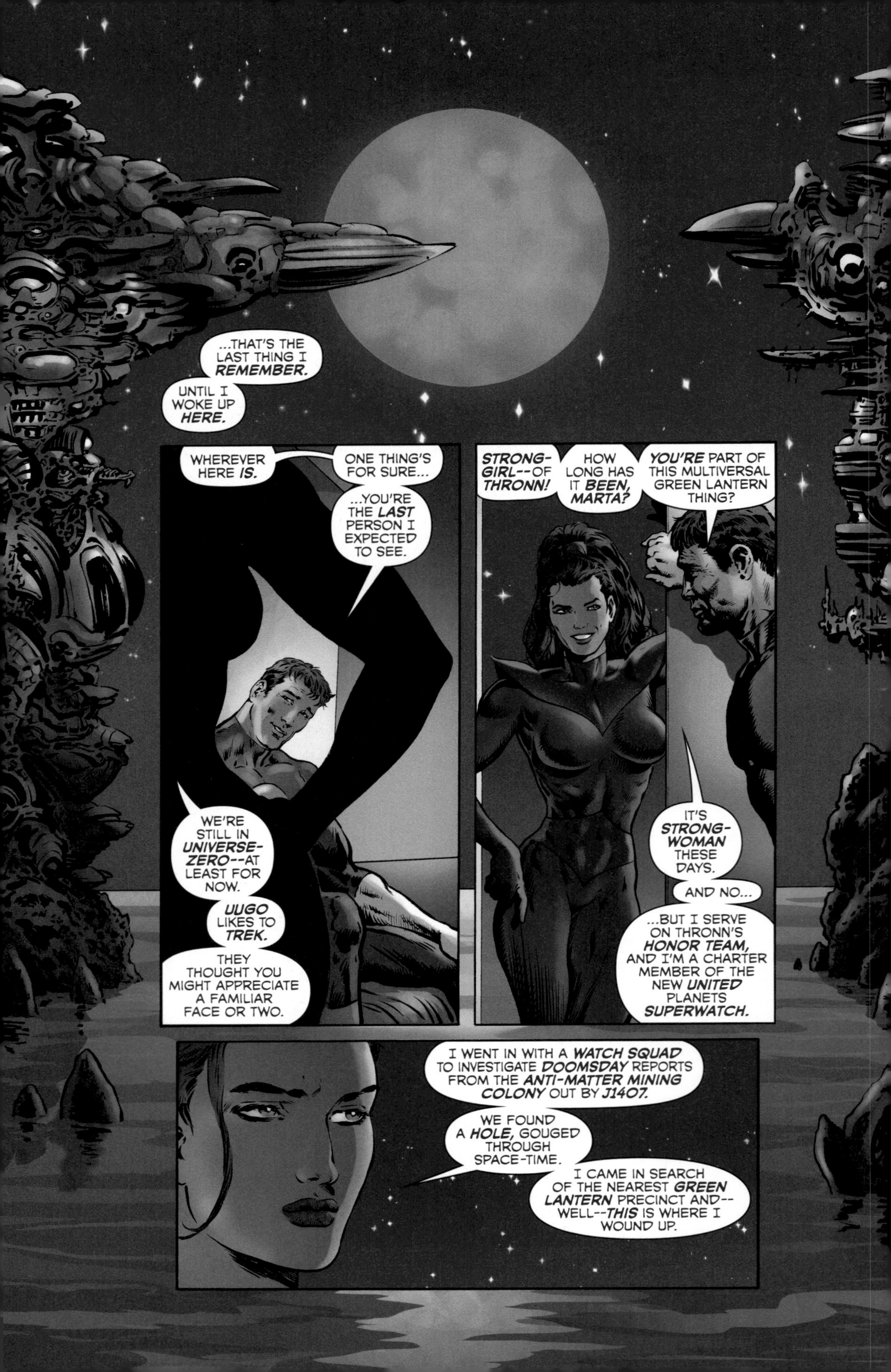

...THAT'S THE LAST THING I REMEMBER.
UNTIL I WOKE UP HERE.
WHEREVER HERE IS.
ONE THING'S FOR SURE...
...YOU'RE THE LAST PERSON I EXPECTED TO SEE.
WE'RE STILL IN UNIVERSE-ZERO--AT LEAST FOR NOW.
UUGO LIKES TO TREK.
THEY THOUGHT YOU MIGHT APPRECIATE A FAMILIAR FACE OR TWO.
STRONG-GIRL--OF THRONN!
HOW LONG HAS IT BEEN, MARTA?
YOU'RE PART OF THIS MULTIVERSAL GREEN LANTERN THING?
IT'S STRONG-WOMAN THESE DAYS.
AND NO...
...BUT I SERVE ON THRONN'S HONOR TEAM, AND I'M A CHARTER MEMBER OF THE NEW UNITED PLANETS SUPERWATCH.
I WENT IN WITH A WATCH SQUAD TO INVESTIGATE DOOMSDAY REPORTS FROM THE ANTI-MATTER MINING COLONY OUT BY J1407.
WE FOUND A HOLE, GOUGED THROUGH SPACE-TIME.
I CAME IN SEARCH OF THE NEAREST GREEN LANTERN PRECINCT AND--WELL--THIS IS WHERE I WOUND UP.

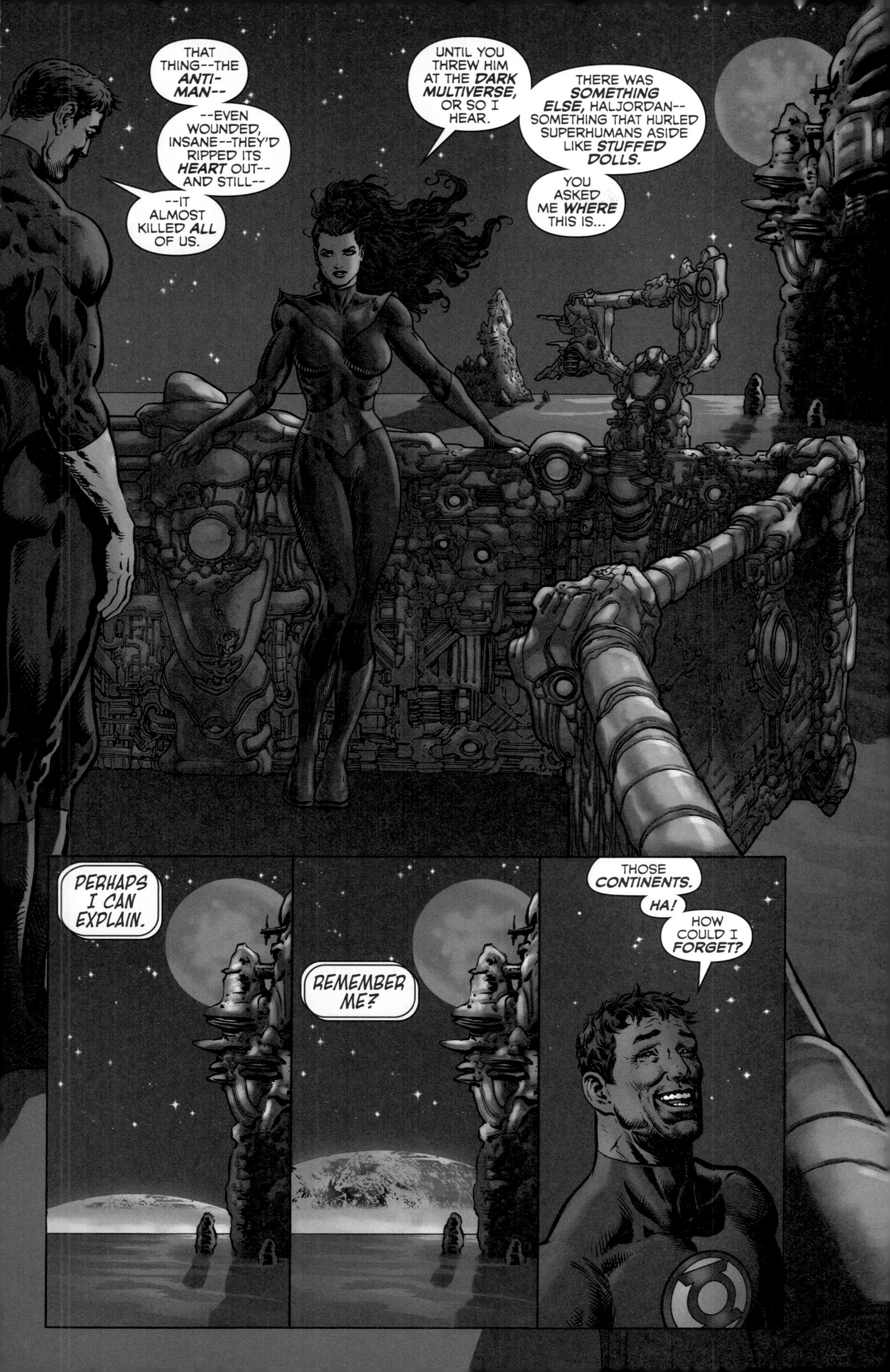
THAT THING--THE ANTI-MAN--
--EVEN WOUNDED, INSANE--THEY'D RIPPED ITS HEART OUT--AND STILL--
--IT ALMOST KILLED ALL OF US.
UNTIL YOU THREW HIM AT THE DARK MULTIVERSE, OR SO I HEAR.
THERE WAS SOMETHING ELSE, HALJORDAN--SOMETHING THAT HURLED SUPERHUMANS ASIDE LIKE STUFFED DOLLS.
YOU ASKED ME WHERE THIS IS...
PERHAPS I CAN EXPLAIN.
REMEMBER ME?
THOSE CONTINENTS.
HA!
HOW COULD I FORGET?

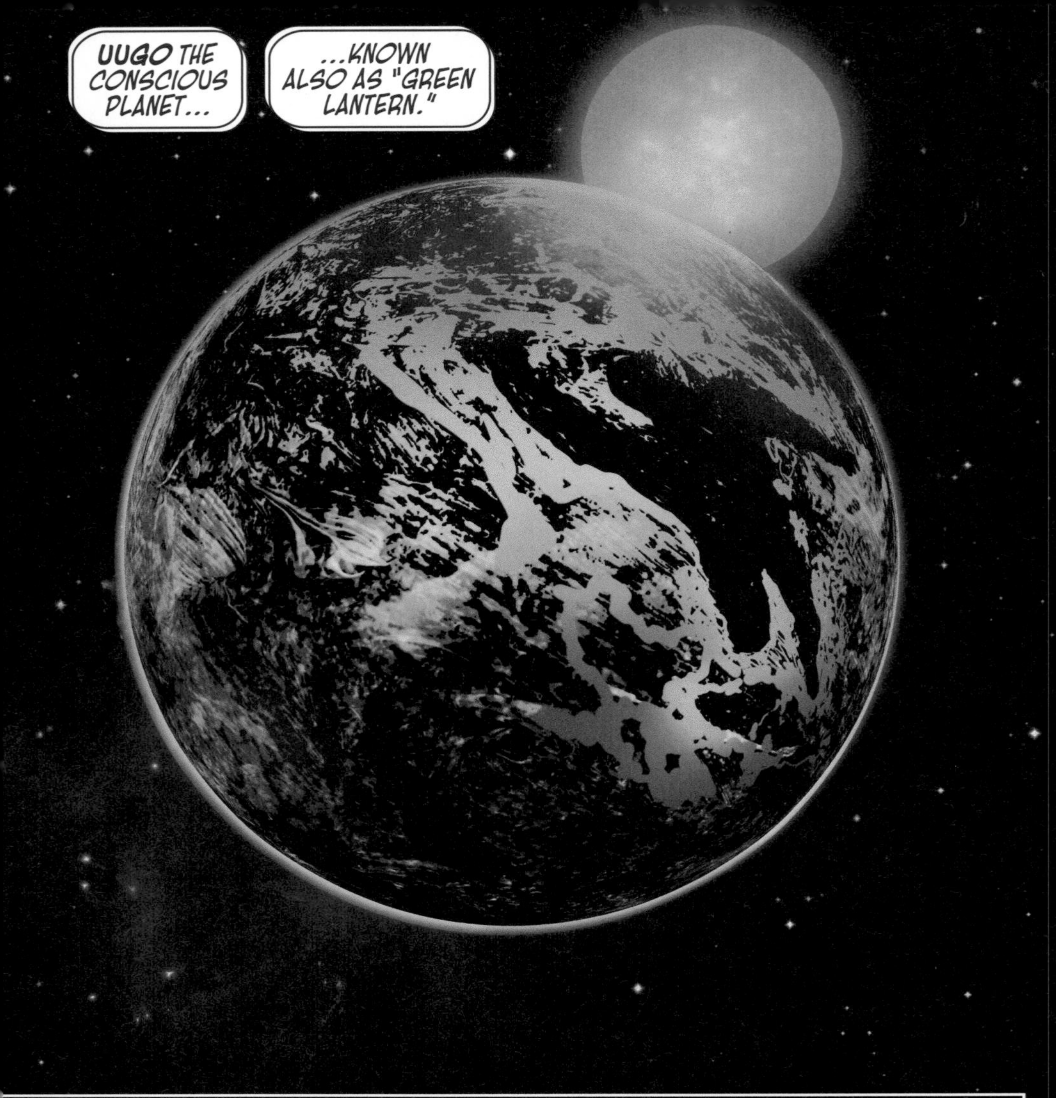
UUGO THE CONSCIOUS PLANET...
...KNOWN ALSO AS "GREEN LANTERN."

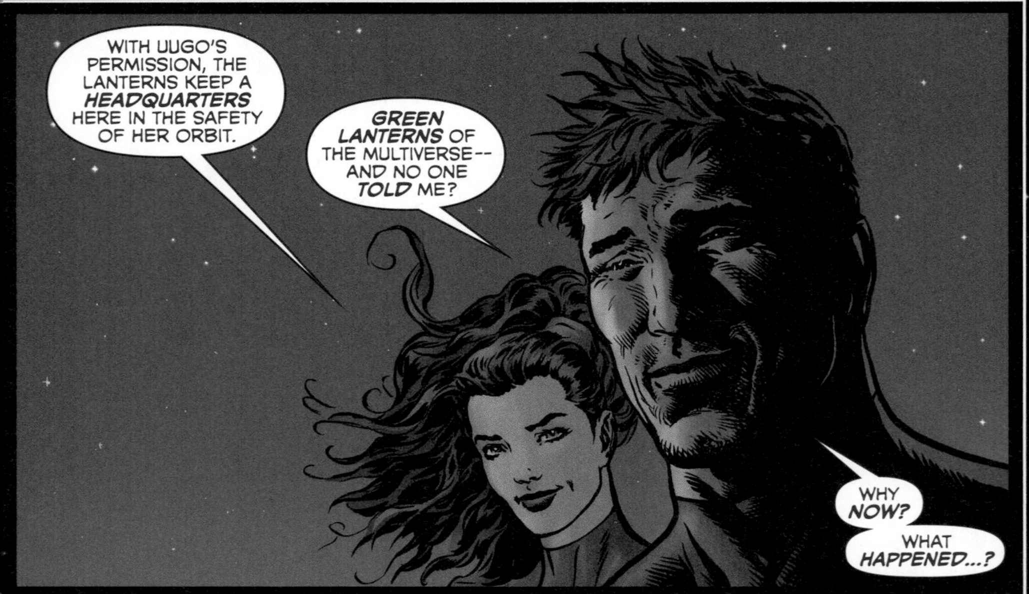
WITH UUGO'S PERMISSION, THE LANTERNS KEEP A HEADQUARTERS HERE IN THE SAFETY OF HER ORBIT.
GREEN LANTERNS OF THE MULTIVERSE--AND NO ONE TOLD ME?
WHY NOW?
WHAT HAPPENED...?

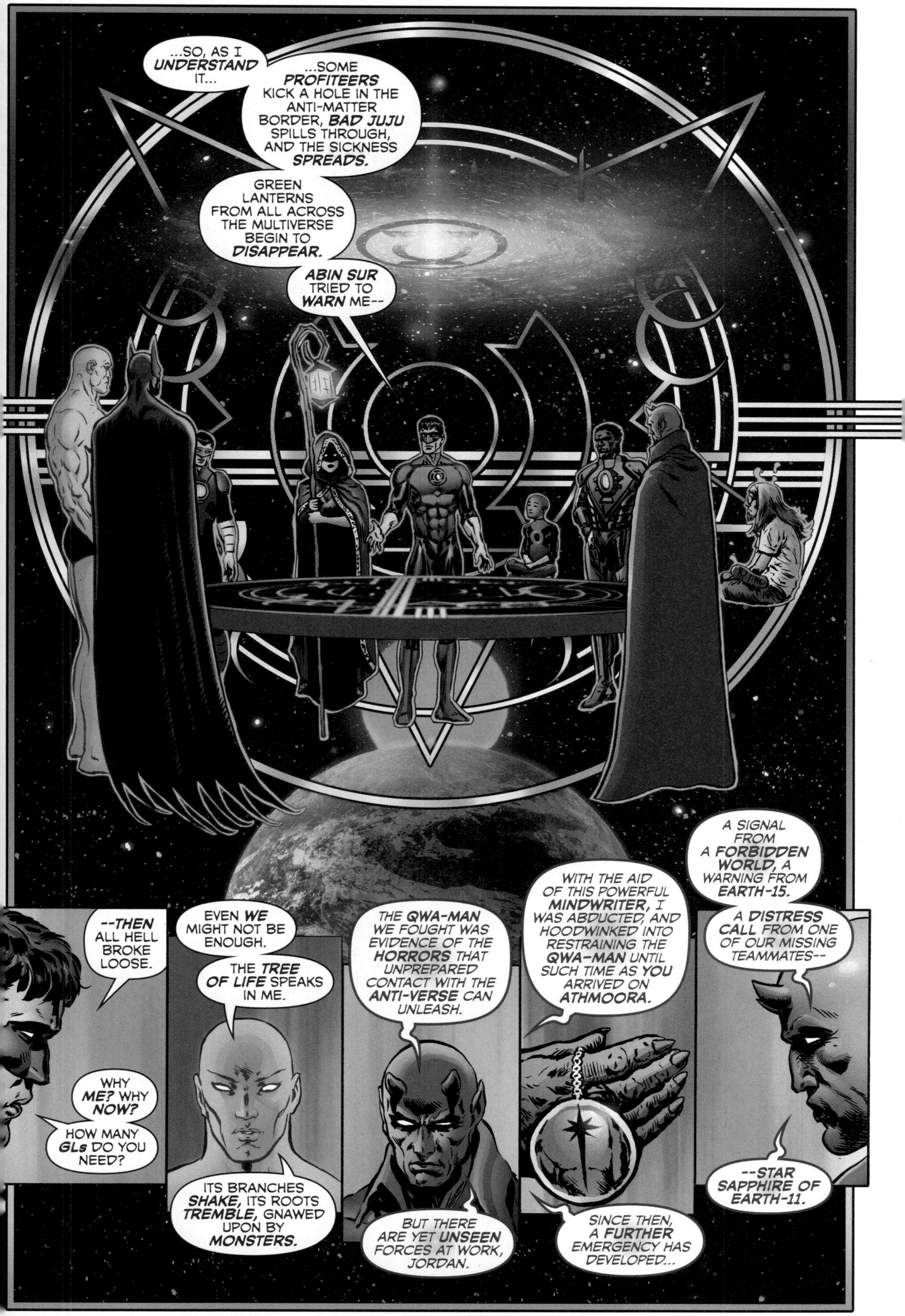

...SO, AS I UNDERSTAND IT...
...SOME PROFITEERS KICK A HOLE IN THE ANTI-MATTER BORDER, BAD JUJU SPILLS THROUGH, AND THE SICKNESS SPREADS.
GREEN LANTERNS FROM ALL ACROSS THE MULTIVERSE BEGIN TO DISAPPEAR.
ABIN SUR TRIED TO WARN ME--
--THEN ALL HELL BROKE LOOSE.
WHY ME? WHY NOW?
HOW MANY GLs DO YOU NEED?
EVEN WE MIGHT NOT BE ENOUGH.
THE TREE OF LIFE SPEAKS IN ME.
ITS BRANCHES SHAKE, ITS ROOTS TREMBLE, GNAWED UPON BY MONSTERS.
THE QWA-MAN WE FOUGHT WAS EVIDENCE OF THE HORRORS THAT UNPREPARED CONTACT WITH THE ANTI-VERSE CAN UNLEASH.
BUT THERE ARE YET UNSEEN FORCES AT WORK, JORDAN.
WITH THE AID OF THIS POWERFUL MINDWRITER, I WAS ABDUCTED, AND HOODWINKED INTO RESTRAINING THE QWA-MAN UNTIL SUCH TIME AS YOU ARRIVED ON ATHMOORA.
SINCE THEN, A FURTHER EMERGENCY HAS DEVELOPED...
A SIGNAL FROM A FORBIDDEN WORLD, A WARNING FROM EARTH-15.
A DISTRESS CALL FROM ONE OF OUR MISSING TEAMMATES--
--STAR SAPPHIRE OF EARTH-11.

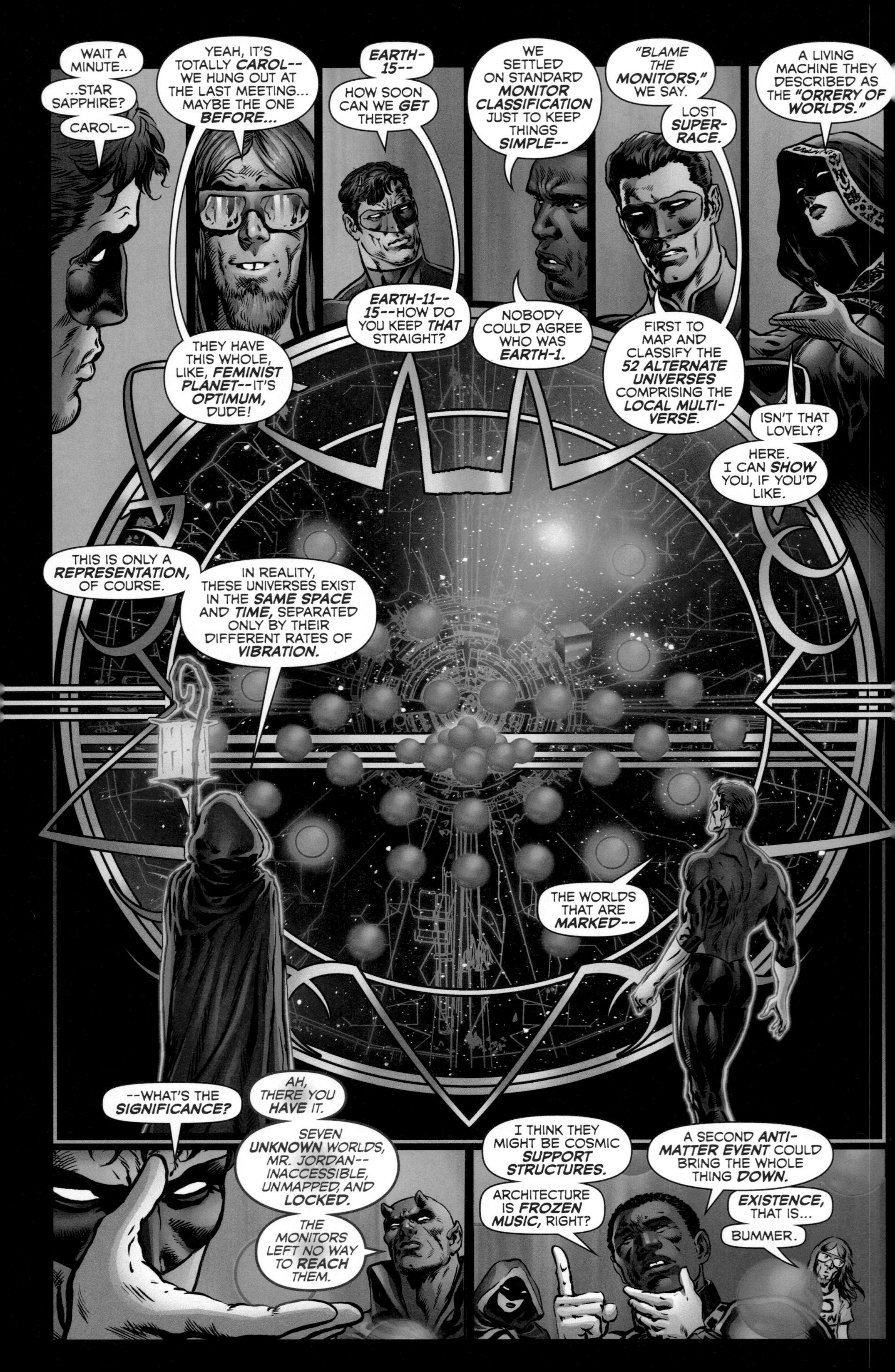
WAIT A MINUTE...
...STAR SAPPHIRE?
CAROL--
YEAH, IT'S TOTALLY CAROL-- WE HUNG OUT AT THE LAST MEETING... MAYBE THE ONE BEFORE...
THEY HAVE THIS WHOLE, LIKE, FEMINIST PLANET--IT'S OPTIMUM, DUDE!
EARTH-15--
HOW SOON CAN WE GET THERE?
EARTH-11--15--HOW DO YOU KEEP THAT STRAIGHT?
WE SETTLED ON STANDARD MONITOR CLASSIFICATION JUST TO KEEP THINGS SIMPLE--
NOBODY COULD AGREE WHO WAS EARTH-1.
"BLAME THE MONITORS," WE SAY.
LOST SUPER-RACE.
FIRST TO MAP AND CLASSIFY THE 52 ALTERNATE UNIVERSES COMPRISING THE LOCAL MULTI-VERSE.
A LIVING MACHINE THEY DESCRIBED AS THE "ORRERY OF WORLDS."
ISN'T THAT LOVELY?
HERE. I CAN SHOW YOU, IF YOU'D LIKE.
THIS IS ONLY A REPRESENTATION, OF COURSE.
IN REALITY, THESE UNIVERSES EXIST IN THE SAME SPACE AND TIME, SEPARATED ONLY BY THEIR DIFFERENT RATES OF VIBRATION.
THE WORLDS THAT ARE MARKED--
--WHAT'S THE SIGNIFICANCE?
AH, THERE YOU HAVE IT.
SEVEN UNKNOWN WORLDS, MR. JORDAN-- INACCESSIBLE, UNMAPPED, AND LOCKED.
THE MONITORS LEFT NO WAY TO REACH THEM.
I THINK THEY MIGHT BE COSMIC SUPPORT STRUCTURES.
ARCHITECTURE IS FROZEN MUSIC, RIGHT?
A SECOND ANTI-MATTER EVENT COULD BRING THE WHOLE THING DOWN.
EXISTENCE, THAT IS...
BUMMER.

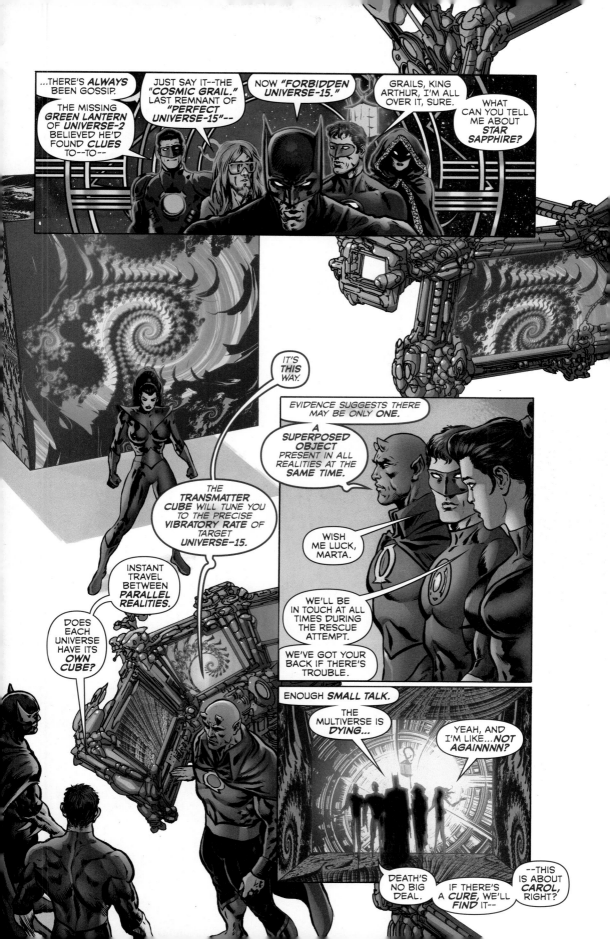

...THERE'S *ALWAYS* BEEN GOSSIP.

THE MISSING *GREEN LANTERN* OF *UNIVERSE-2* BELIEVED HE'D FOUND *CLUES* TO--TO--

JUST SAY IT--THE *"COSMIC GRAIL."* LAST REMNANT OF *"PERFECT UNIVERSE-15"*--

NOW *"FORBIDDEN UNIVERSE-15."*

GRAILS, KING ARTHUR, I'M ALL OVER IT, SURE.

WHAT CAN YOU TELL ME ABOUT *STAR SAPPHIRE?*

IT'S *THIS WAY.*

EVIDENCE SUGGESTS THERE MAY BE ONLY *ONE.*

A *SUPERPOSED OBJECT* PRESENT IN ALL REALITIES AT THE *SAME TIME.*

THE *TRANSMATTER CUBE* WILL TUNE YOU TO THE PRECISE *VIBRATORY RATE* OF TARGET *UNIVERSE-15.*

WISH ME LUCK, MARTA.

WE'LL BE IN TOUCH AT ALL TIMES DURING THE RESCUE ATTEMPT.

WE'VE GOT YOUR BACK IF THERE'S TROUBLE.

INSTANT TRAVEL BETWEEN *PARALLEL REALITIES.*

DOES EACH UNIVERSE HAVE ITS *OWN* CUBE?

ENOUGH *SMALL TALK.*

THE MULTIVERSE IS *DYING...*

YEAH, AND I'M LIKE...*NOT AGAINNNN?*

DEATH'S NO BIG DEAL.

IF THERE'S A *CURE,* WE'LL *FIND* IT--

--THIS IS ABOUT *CAROL,* RIGHT?

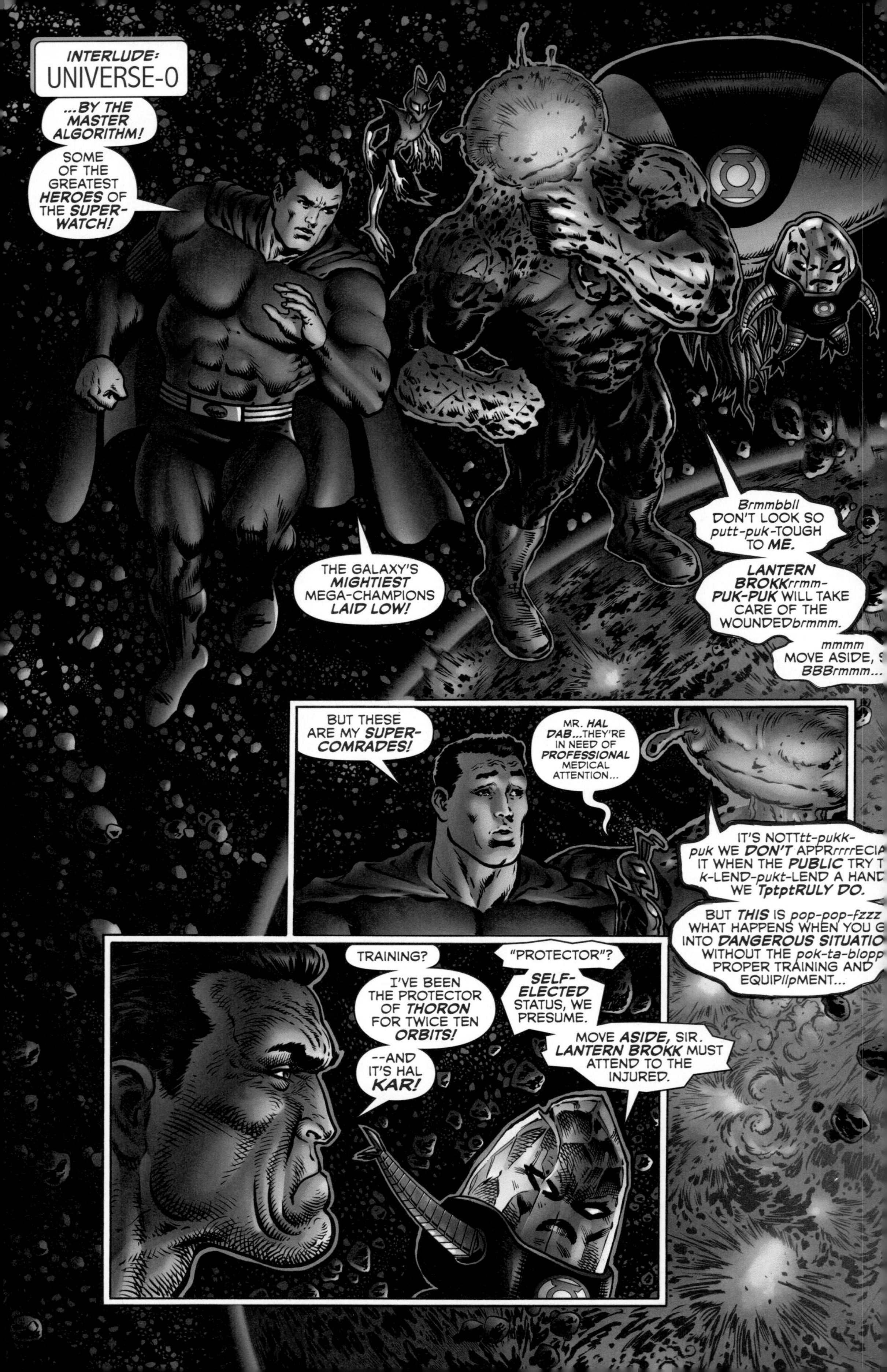
INTERLUDE:
UNIVERSE-0
...BY THE MASTER ALGORITHM!
SOME OF THE GREATEST HEROES OF THE SUPER-WATCH!
THE GALAXY'S MIGHTIEST MEGA-CHAMPIONS LAID LOW!
Brmmbbll DON'T LOOK SO putt-puk-TOUGH TO ME.
LANTERN BROKKrrmm-PUK-PUK WILL TAKE CARE OF THE WOUNDEDbrmmm.
mmmm MOVE ASIDE, BBBrmmm...
BUT THESE ARE MY SUPER-COMRADES!
MR. HAL DAB...THEY'RE IN NEED OF PROFESSIONAL MEDICAL ATTENTION...
IT'S NOTTtt-pukk-puk WE DON'T APPRrrrrECIA IT WHEN THE PUBLIC TRY T k-LEND-pukt-LEND A HAND WE TptptRULY DO.
BUT THIS IS pop-pop-fzzz WHAT HAPPENS WHEN YOU INTO DANGEROUS SITUATIO WITHOUT THE pok-ta-blopp PROPER TRAINING AND EQUIPllpMENT...
TRAINING?
I'VE BEEN THE PROTECTOR OF THORON FOR TWICE TEN ORBITS!
--AND IT'S HAL KAR!
"PROTECTOR"?
SELF-ELECTED STATUS, WE PRESUME.
MOVE ASIDE, SIR. LANTERN BROKK MUST ATTEND TO THE INJURED.

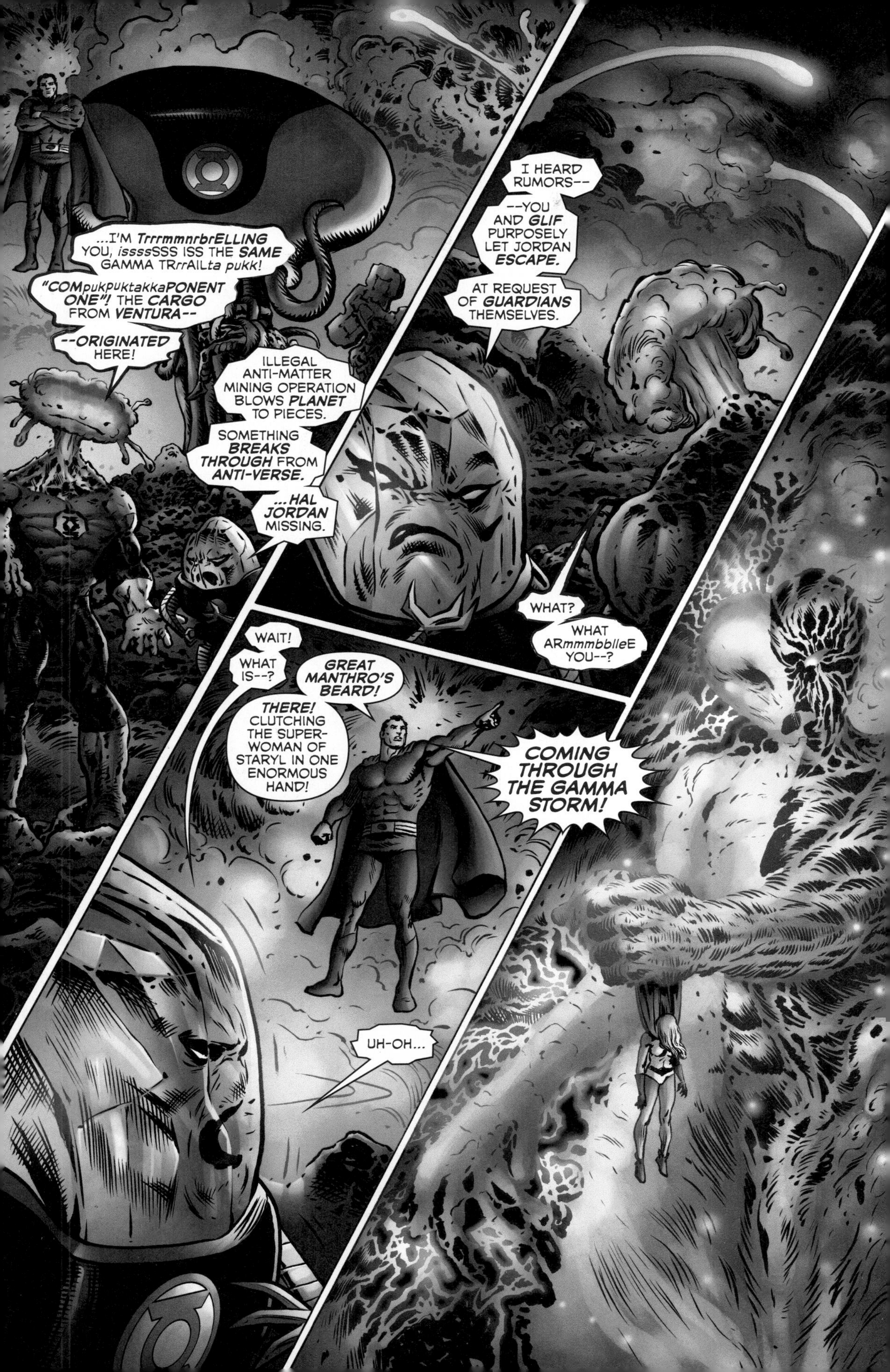
...I'M TrrrmmnrbrELLING YOU, issssSSS ISS THE SAME GAMMA TRrrAILta pukk!
"COMpukpuktakkaPONENT ONE"! THE CARGO FROM VENTURA--
--ORIGINATED HERE!
ILLEGAL ANTI-MATTER MINING OPERATION BLOWS PLANET TO PIECES.
SOMETHING BREAKS THROUGH FROM ANTI-VERSE.
...HAL JORDAN MISSING.
I HEARD RUMORS--
--YOU AND GLIF PURPOSELY LET JORDAN ESCAPE.
AT REQUEST OF GUARDIANS THEMSELVES.
WHAT?
WHAT ARmmmbblleE YOU--?
WAIT!
WHAT IS--?
GREAT MANTHRO'S BEARD!
THERE! CLUTCHING THE SUPER-WOMAN OF STARYL IN ONE ENORMOUS HAND!
COMING THROUGH THE GAMMA STORM!
UH-OH...

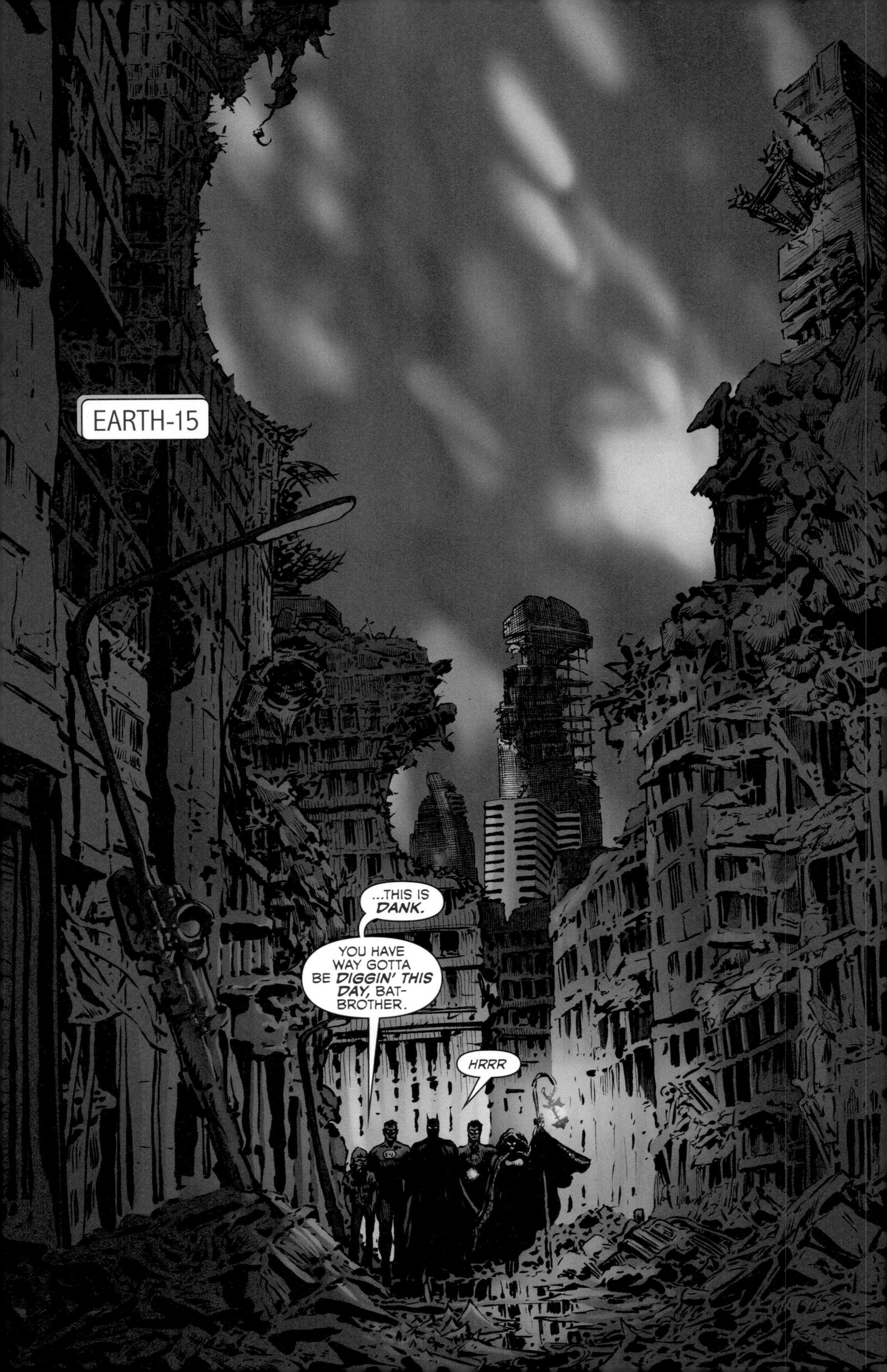
EARTH-15
...THIS IS DANK.
YOU HAVE WAY GOTTA BE DIGGIN' THIS DAY, BAT-BROTHER.
HRRR

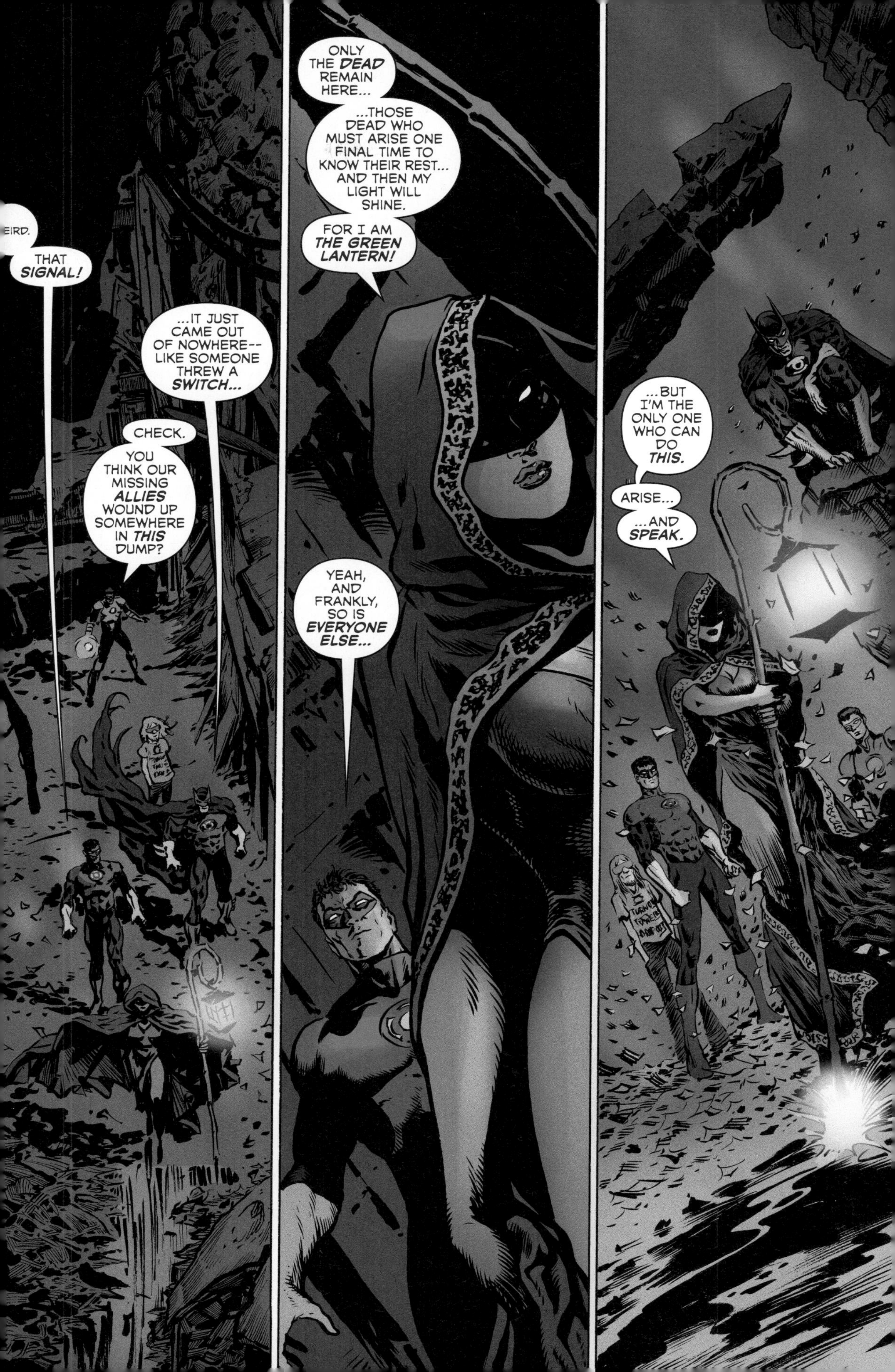
EIRD.
THAT SIGNAL!
...IT JUST CAME OUT OF NOWHERE-- LIKE SOMEONE THREW A SWITCH...
CHECK.
YOU THINK OUR MISSING ALLIES WOUND UP SOMEWHERE IN THIS DUMP?
ONLY THE DEAD REMAIN HERE...
...THOSE DEAD WHO MUST ARISE ONE FINAL TIME TO KNOW THEIR REST... AND THEN MY LIGHT WILL SHINE.
FOR I AM THE GREEN LANTERN!
YEAH, AND FRANKLY, SO IS EVERYONE ELSE...
...BUT I'M THE ONLY ONE WHO CAN DO THIS.
ARISE...
...AND SPEAK.

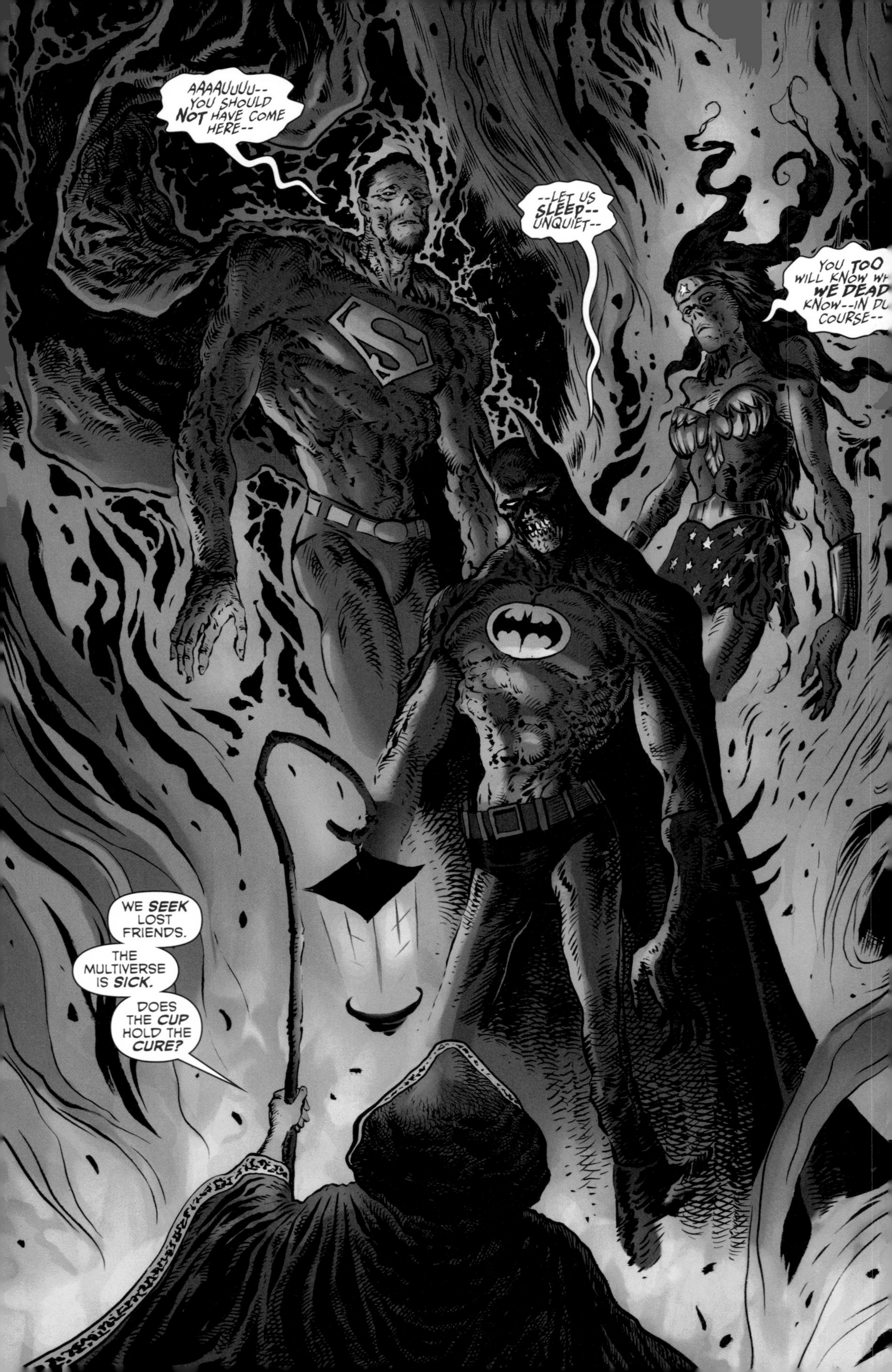
AAAAUUUU--YOU SHOULD NOT HAVE COME HERE--
--LET US SLEEP--UNQUIET--
YOU TOO WILL KNOW WH WE DEAD KNOW--IN DU COURSE--
WE SEEK LOST FRIENDS.
THE MULTIVERSE IS SICK.
DOES THE CUP HOLD THE CURE?

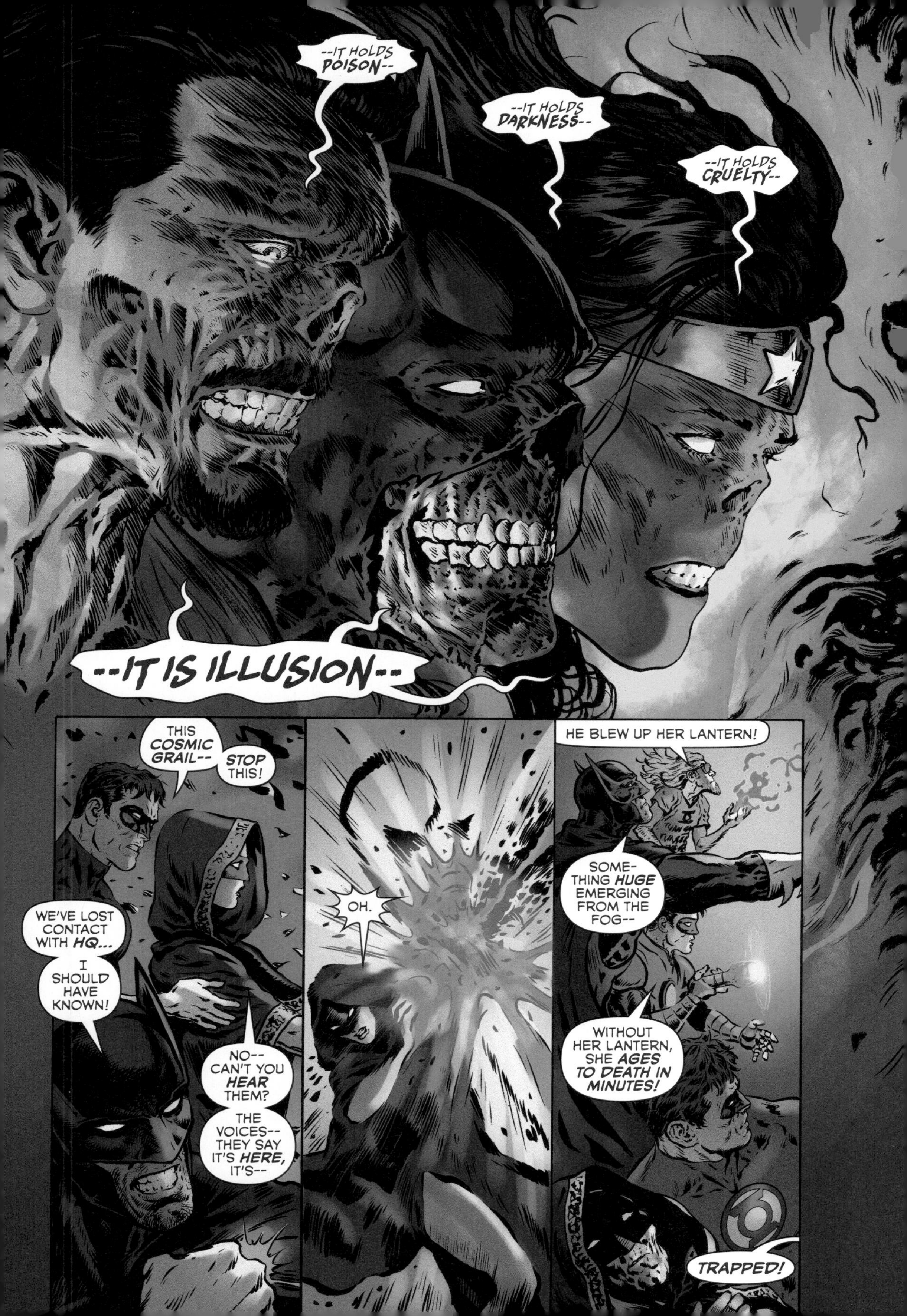
--IT HOLDS POISON--
--IT HOLDS DARKNESS--
--IT HOLDS CRUELTY--
--IT IS ILLUSION--
THIS COSMIC GRAIL--
STOP THIS!
WE'VE LOST CONTACT WITH HQ...
I SHOULD HAVE KNOWN!
NO-- CAN'T YOU HEAR THEM?
THE VOICES-- THEY SAY IT'S HERE, IT'S--
OH.
HE BLEW UP HER LANTERN!
SOME-THING HUGE EMERGING FROM THE FOG--
WITHOUT HER LANTERN, SHE AGES TO DEATH IN MINUTES!
TRAPPED!

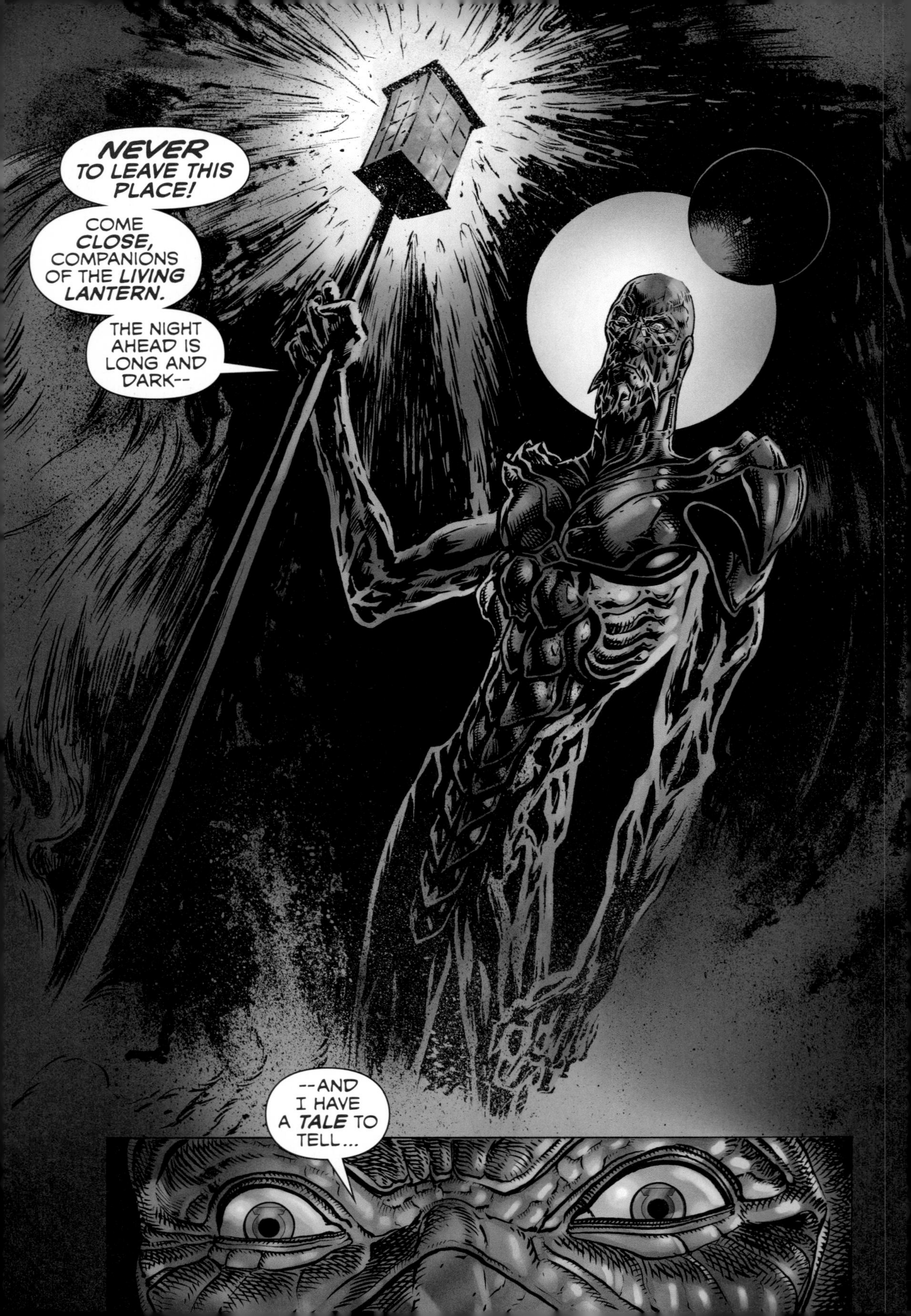
NEVER TO LEAVE THIS PLACE!
COME CLOSE, COMPANIONS OF THE LIVING LANTERN.
THE NIGHT AHEAD IS LONG AND DARK--
--AND I HAVE A TALE TO TELL...

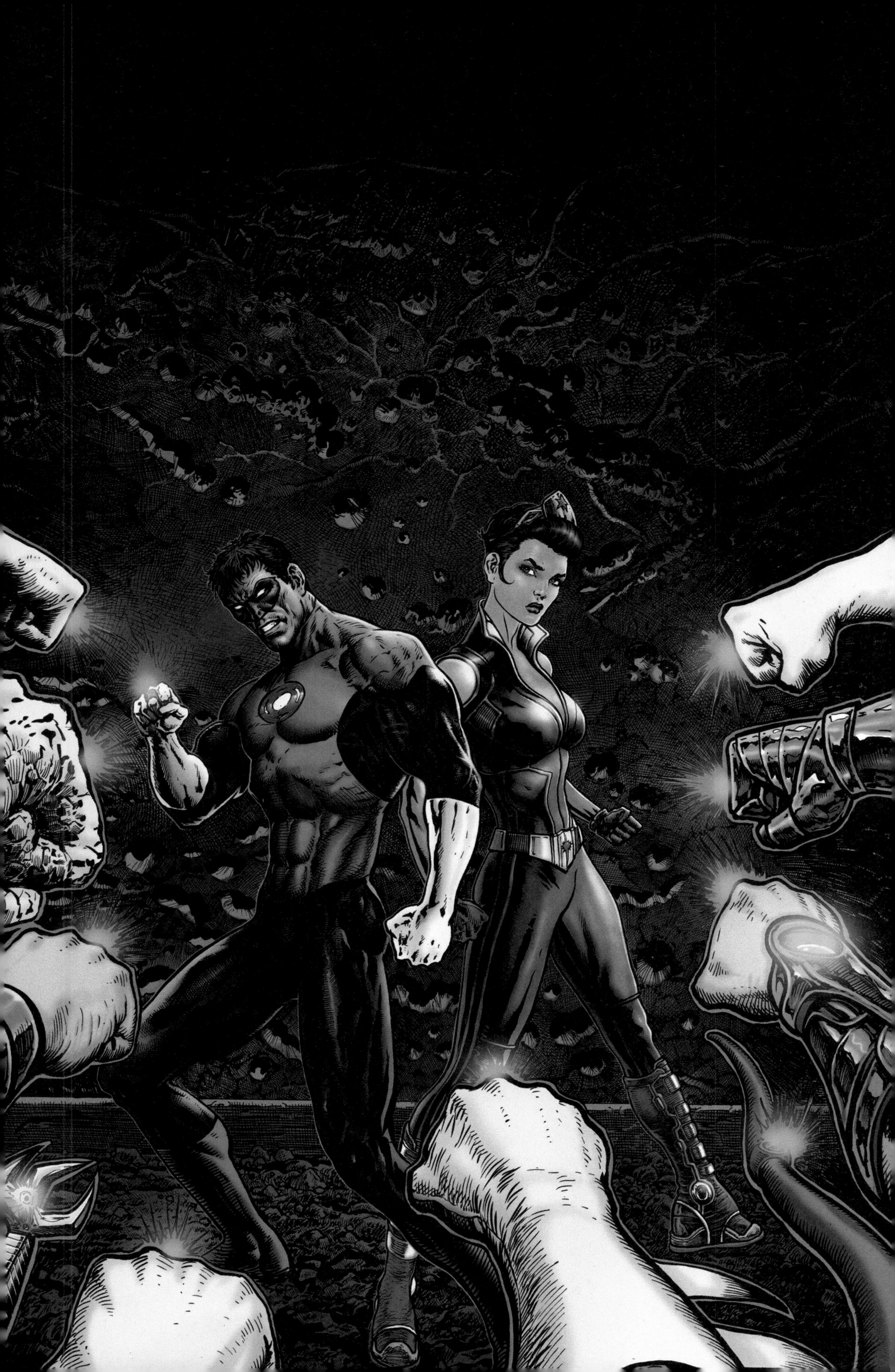

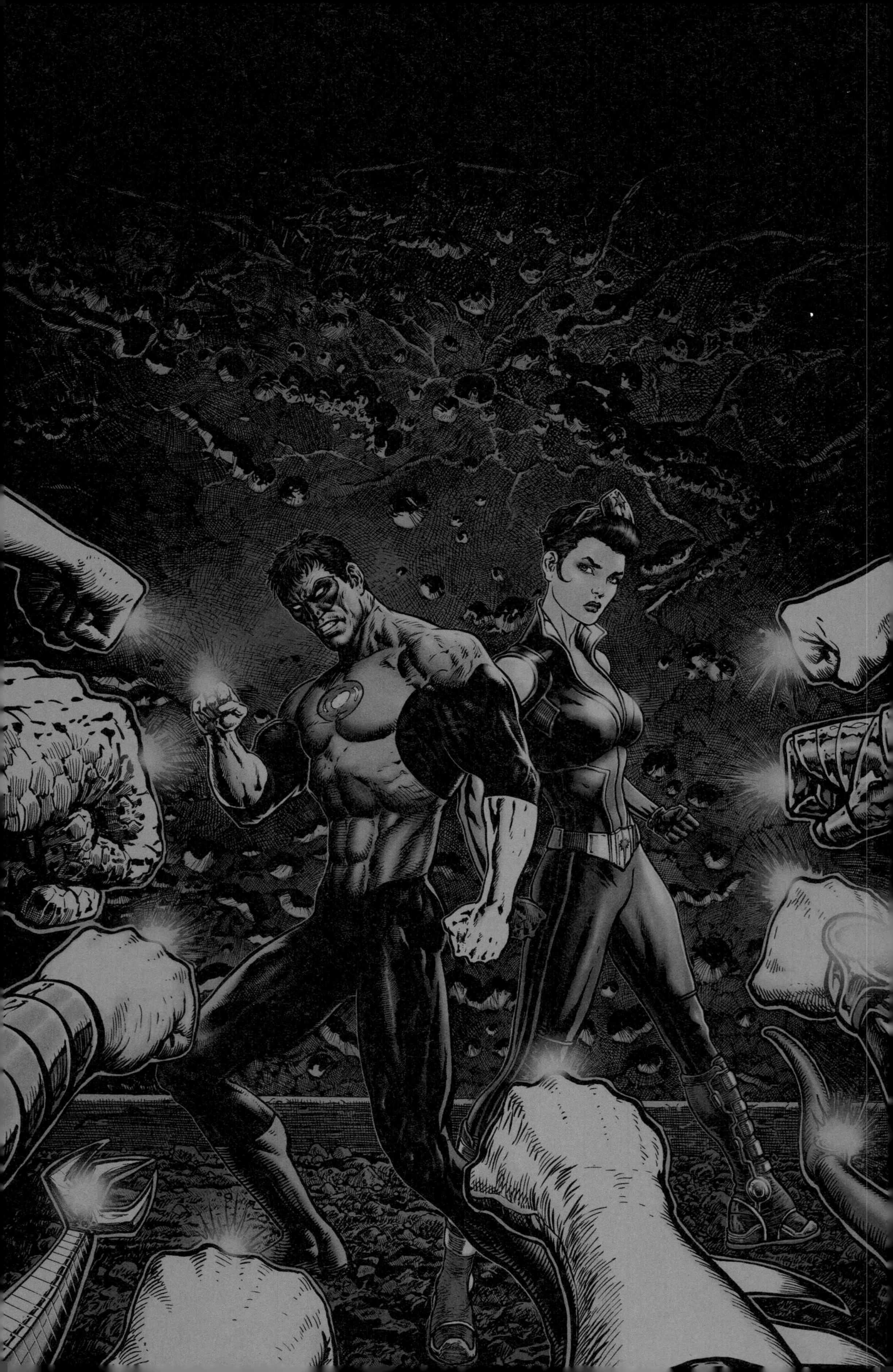

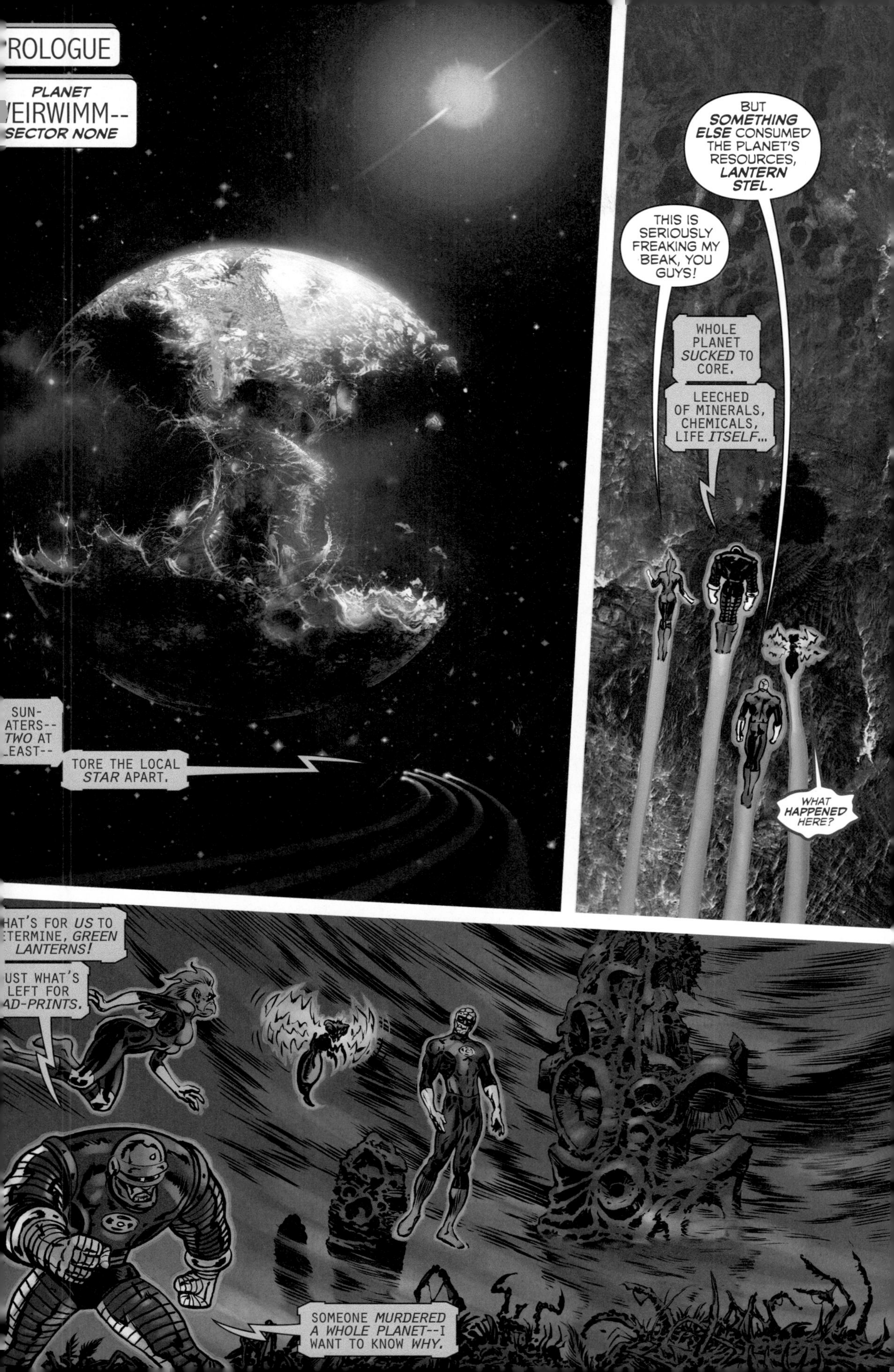

ROLOGUE
PLANET
VEIRWIMM--
SECTOR NONE
SUN-
ATERS--
TWO AT
LEAST--
TORE THE LOCAL
STAR APART.
BUT
SOMETHING
ELSE CONSUMED
THE PLANET'S
RESOURCES,
LANTERN
STEL.
THIS IS
SERIOUSLY
FREAKING MY
BEAK, YOU
GUYS!
WHOLE
PLANET
SUCKED TO
CORE.
LEECHED
OF MINERALS,
CHEMICALS,
LIFE ITSELF...
WHAT
HAPPENED
HERE?
HAT'S FOR US TO
ETERMINE, GREEN
LANTERNS!
UST WHAT'S
LEFT FOR
AD-PRINTS.
SOMEONE MURDERED
A WHOLE PLANET--I
WANT TO KNOW WHY.

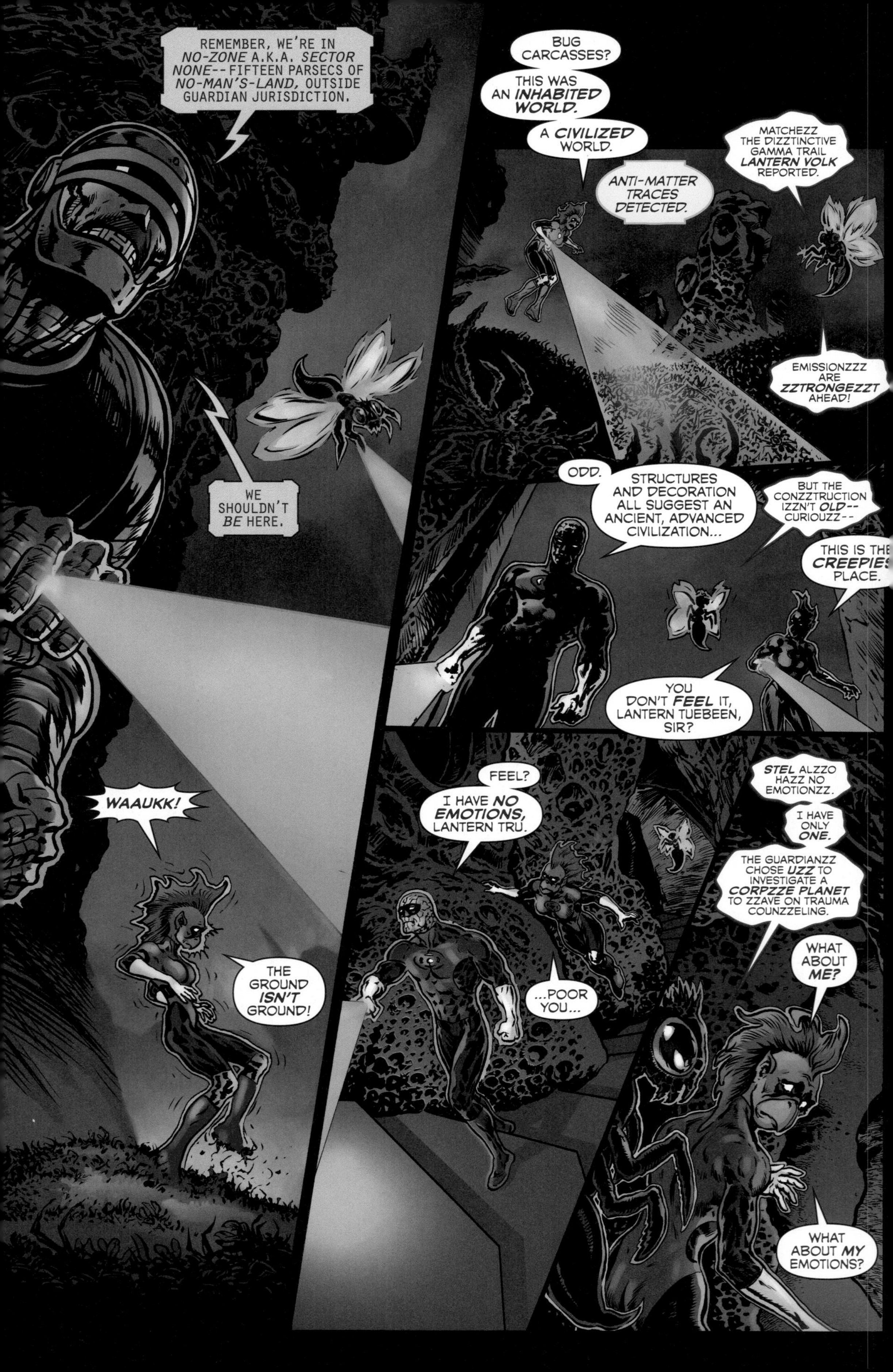

REMEMBER, WE'RE IN NO-ZONE A.K.A. SECTOR NONE--FIFTEEN PARSECS OF NO-MAN'S-LAND, OUTSIDE GUARDIAN JURISDICTION.
WE SHOULDN'T BE HERE.
BUG CARCASSES?
THIS WAS AN INHABITED WORLD.
A CIVILIZED WORLD.
ANTI-MATTER TRACES DETECTED.
MATCHEZZ THE DIZZTINCTIVE GAMMA TRAIL LANTERN VOLK REPORTED.
EMISSIONZZZ ARE ZZTRONGEZZT AHEAD!
ODD.
STRUCTURES AND DECORATION ALL SUGGEST AN ANCIENT, ADVANCED CIVILIZATION...
BUT THE CONZZTRUCTION IZZN'T OLD-- CURIOUZZ--
THIS IS THE CREEPIES PLACE.
YOU DON'T FEEL IT, LANTERN TUEBEEN, SIR?
WAAUKK!
THE GROUND ISN'T GROUND!
FEEL?
I HAVE NO EMOTIONS, LANTERN TRU.
...POOR YOU...
STEL ALZZO HAZZ NO EMOTIONZZ.
I HAVE ONLY ONE.
THE GUARDIANZZ CHOSE UZZ TO INVESTIGATE A CORPZZE PLANET TO ZZAVE ON TRAUMA COUNZZELING.
WHAT ABOUT ME?
WHAT ABOUT MY EMOTIONS?

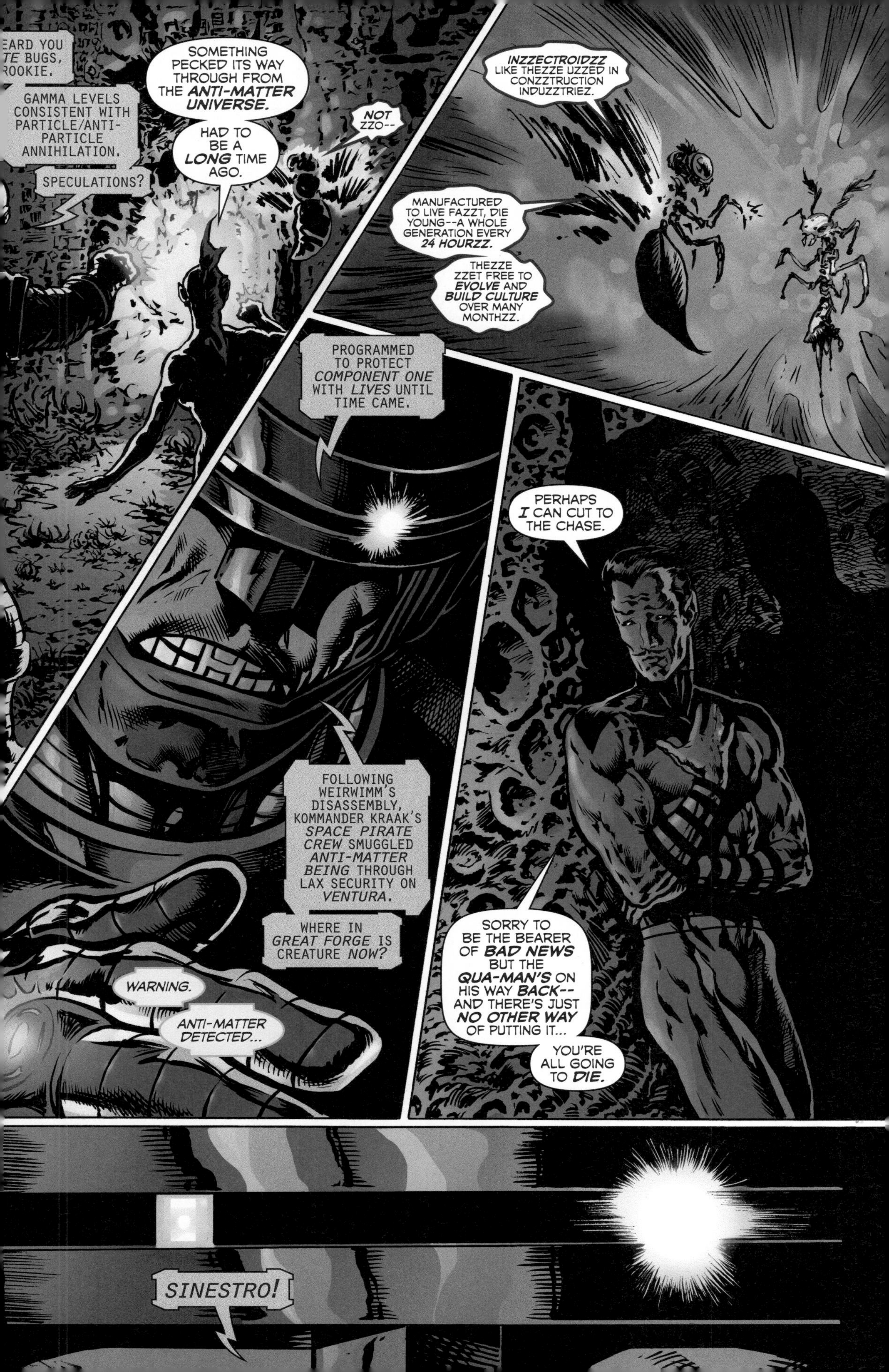
EARD YOU
TE BUGS,
ROOKIE.
GAMMA LEVELS CONSISTENT WITH PARTICLE/ANTI-PARTICLE ANNIHILATION.
SPECULATIONS?
SOMETHING PECKED ITS WAY THROUGH FROM THE ANTI-MATTER UNIVERSE.
HAD TO BE A LONG TIME AGO.
NOT ZZO--
INZZECTROIDZZ LIKE THEZZE UZZED IN CONZZTRUCTION INDUZZTRIEZ.
MANUFACTURED TO LIVE FAZZT, DIE YOUNG--A WHOLE GENERATION EVERY 24 HOURZZ.
THEZZE ZZET FREE TO EVOLVE AND BUILD CULTURE OVER MANY MONTHZZ.
PROGRAMMED TO PROTECT COMPONENT ONE WITH LIVES UNTIL TIME CAME.
FOLLOWING WEIRWIMM'S DISASSEMBLY, KOMMANDER KRAAK'S SPACE PIRATE CREW SMUGGLED ANTI-MATTER BEING THROUGH LAX SECURITY ON VENTURA.
WHERE IN GREAT FORGE IS CREATURE NOW?
WARNING.
ANTI-MATTER DETECTED...
PERHAPS I CAN CUT TO THE CHASE.
SORRY TO BE THE BEARER OF BAD NEWS BUT THE QUA-MAN'S ON HIS WAY BACK--AND THERE'S JUST NO OTHER WAY OF PUTTING IT...
YOU'RE ALL GOING TO DIE.
SINESTRO!

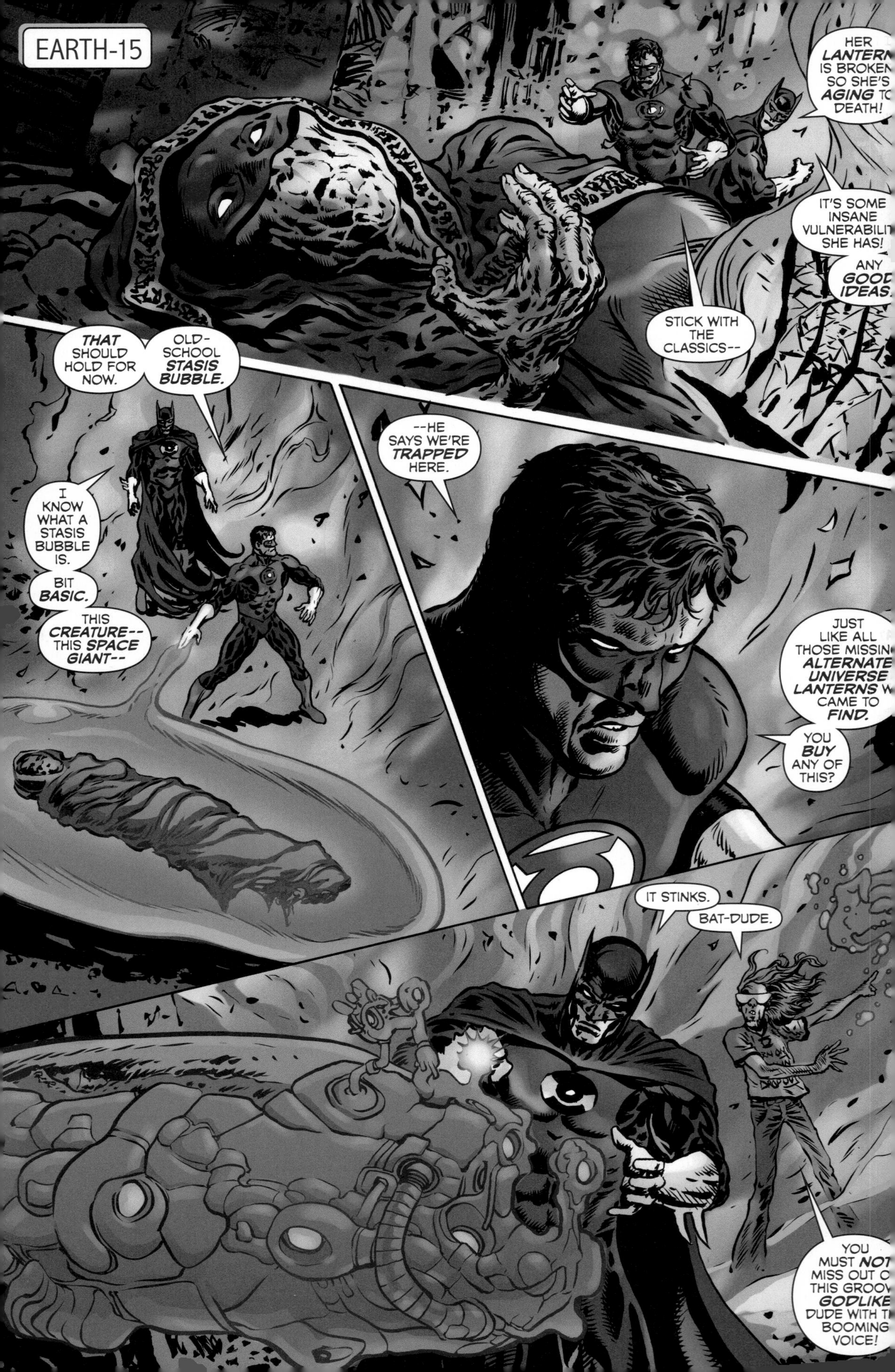
EARTH-15
HER LANTERN IS BROKEN SO SHE'S AGING TO DEATH!
IT'S SOME INSANE VULNERABILITY SHE HAS!
ANY GOOD IDEAS?
STICK WITH THE CLASSICS--
THAT SHOULD HOLD FOR NOW.
OLD-SCHOOL STASIS BUBBLE.
I KNOW WHAT A STASIS BUBBLE IS.
BIT BASIC.
THIS CREATURE-- THIS SPACE GIANT--
--HE SAYS WE'RE TRAPPED HERE.
JUST LIKE ALL THOSE MISSING ALTERNATE UNIVERSE LANTERNS WE CAME TO FIND.
YOU BUY ANY OF THIS?
IT STINKS.
BAT-DUDE.
YOU MUST NOT MISS OUT ON THIS GROOVY GODLIKE DUDE WITH THE BOOMING VOICE!

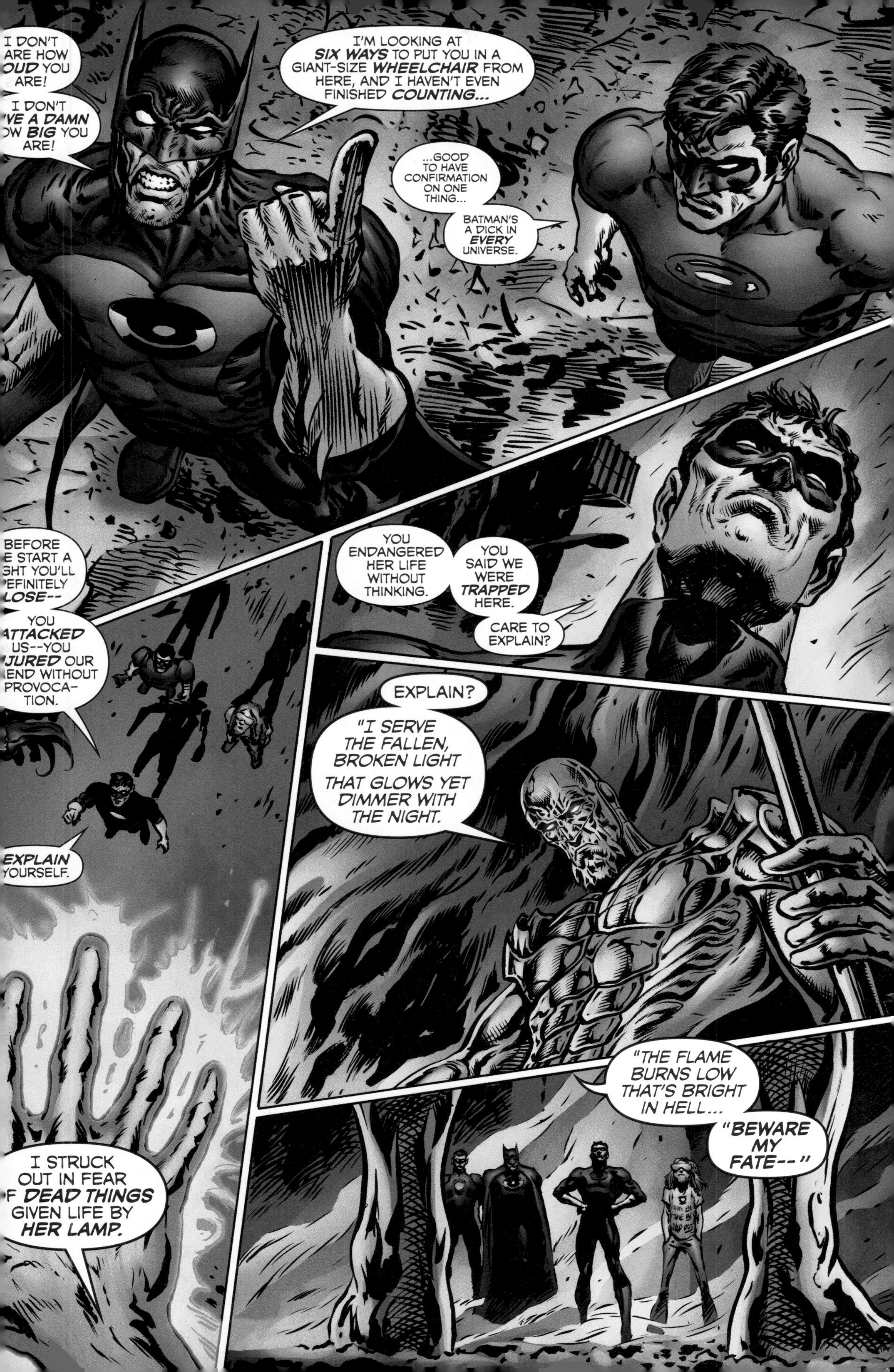
I DON'T ARE HOW OUD YOU ARE!
I DON'T VE A DAMN OW BIG YOU ARE!
I'M LOOKING AT SIX WAYS TO PUT YOU IN A GIANT-SIZE WHEELCHAIR FROM HERE, AND I HAVEN'T EVEN FINISHED COUNTING...
...GOOD TO HAVE CONFIRMATION ON ONE THING...
BATMAN'S A DICK IN EVERY UNIVERSE.
BEFORE E START A GHT YOU'LL EFINITELY LOSE--
YOU ATTACKED US--YOU JURED OUR IEND WITHOUT PROVOCA-TION.
EXPLAIN YOURSELF.
YOU ENDANGERED HER LIFE WITHOUT THINKING.
YOU SAID WE WERE TRAPPED HERE.
CARE TO EXPLAIN?
EXPLAIN?
"I SERVE THE FALLEN, BROKEN LIGHT
THAT GLOWS YET DIMMER WITH THE NIGHT.
"THE FLAME BURNS LOW THAT'S BRIGHT IN HELL...
"BEWARE MY FATE--"
I STRUCK OUT IN FEAR F DEAD THINGS GIVEN LIFE BY HER LAMP.

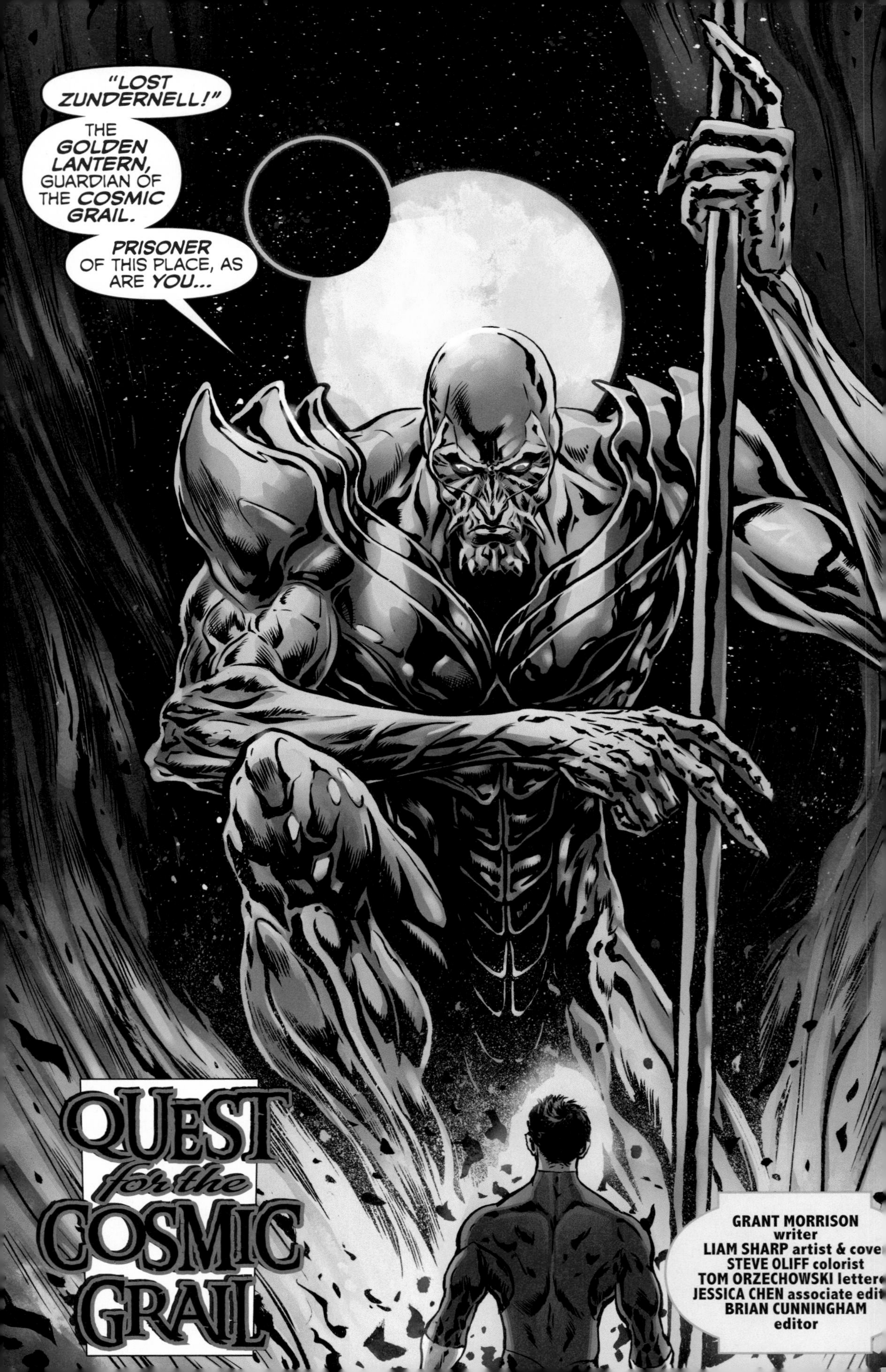
"LOST ZUNDERNELL!"
THE GOLDEN LANTERN, GUARDIAN OF THE COSMIC GRAIL.
PRISONER OF THIS PLACE, AS ARE YOU...
QUEST for the COSMIC GRAIL
GRANT MORRISON writer
LIAM SHARP artist & cove
STEVE OLIFF colorist
TOM ORZECHOWSKI letter
JESSICA CHEN associate edi
BRIAN CUNNINGHAM editor

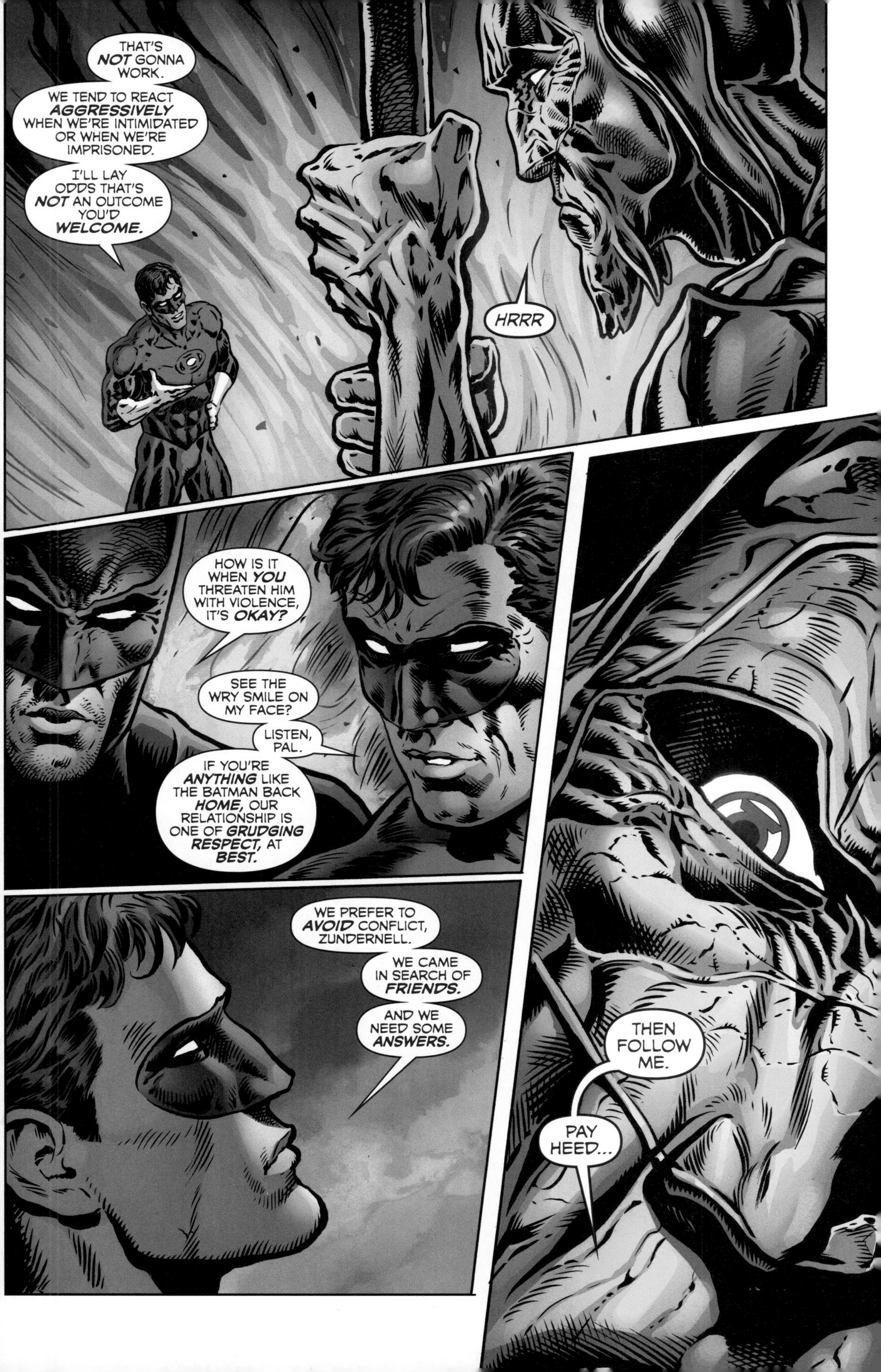
THAT'S NOT GONNA WORK.
WE TEND TO REACT AGGRESSIVELY WHEN WE'RE INTIMIDATED OR WHEN WE'RE IMPRISONED.
I'LL LAY ODDS THAT'S NOT AN OUTCOME YOU'D WELCOME.
HRRR
HOW IS IT WHEN YOU THREATEN HIM WITH VIOLENCE, IT'S OKAY?
SEE THE WRY SMILE ON MY FACE?
LISTEN, PAL.
IF YOU'RE ANYTHING LIKE THE BATMAN BACK HOME, OUR RELATIONSHIP IS ONE OF GRUDGING RESPECT, AT BEST.
WE PREFER TO AVOID CONFLICT, ZUNDERNELL.
WE CAME IN SEARCH OF FRIENDS.
AND WE NEED SOME ANSWERS.
THEN FOLLOW ME.
PAY HEED...

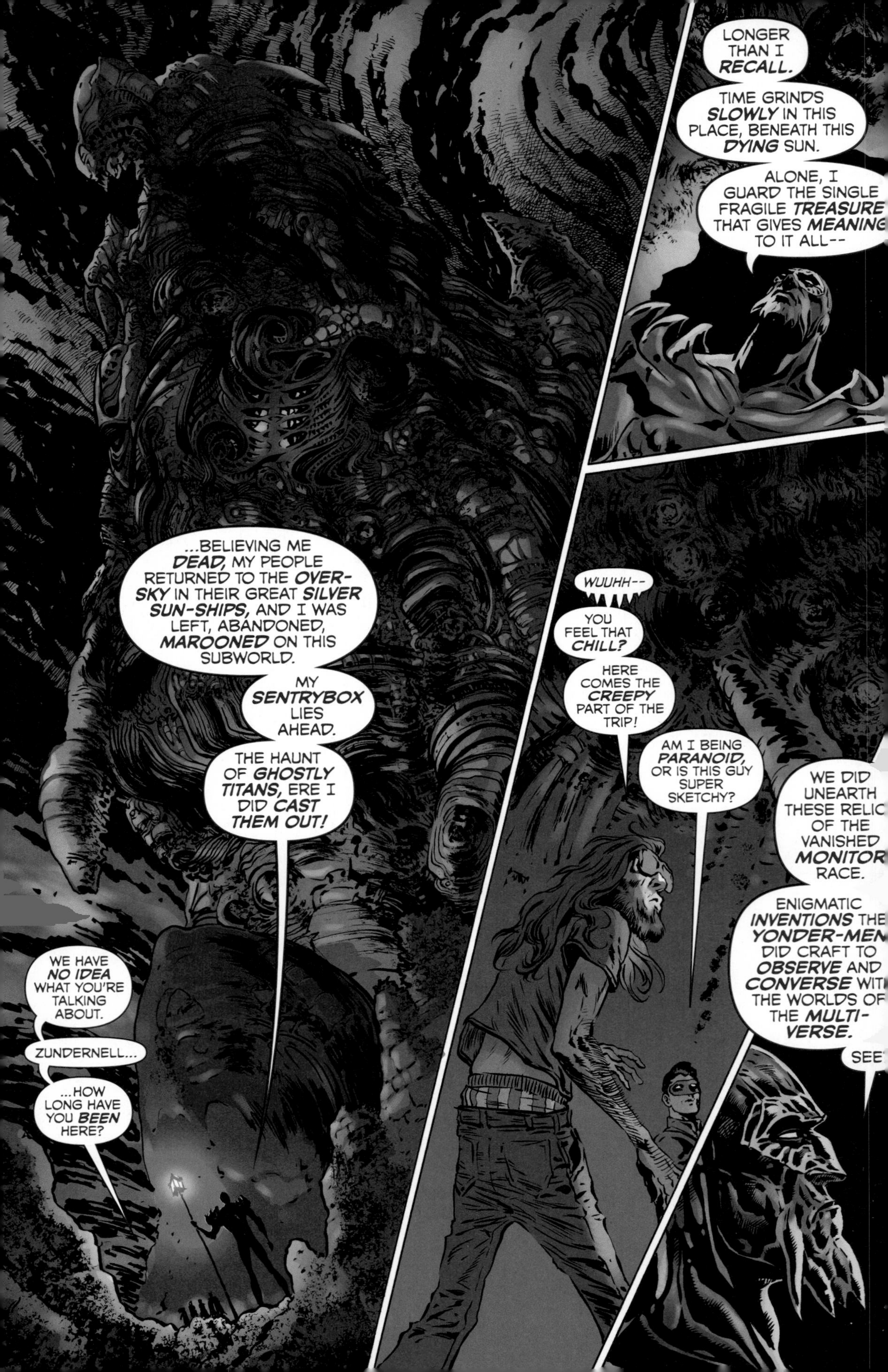

LONGER THAN I RECALL.
TIME GRINDS SLOWLY IN THIS PLACE, BENEATH THIS DYING SUN.
ALONE, I GUARD THE SINGLE FRAGILE TREASURE THAT GIVES MEANING TO IT ALL--
...BELIEVING ME DEAD, MY PEOPLE RETURNED TO THE OVER-SKY IN THEIR GREAT SILVER SUN-SHIPS, AND I WAS LEFT, ABANDONED, MAROONED ON THIS SUBWORLD.
MY SENTRYBOX LIES AHEAD.
THE HAUNT OF GHOSTLY TITANS, ERE I DID CAST THEM OUT!
WE HAVE NO IDEA WHAT YOU'RE TALKING ABOUT.
ZUNDERNELL...
...HOW LONG HAVE YOU BEEN HERE?
WUUHH--
YOU FEEL THAT CHILL?
HERE COMES THE CREEPY PART OF THE TRIP!
AM I BEING PARANOID, OR IS THIS GUY SUPER SKETCHY?
WE DID UNEARTH THESE RELIC OF THE VANISHED MONITOR RACE.
ENIGMATIC INVENTIONS THE YONDER-MEN DID CRAFT TO OBSERVE AND CONVERSE WIT THE WORLDS OF THE MULTI-VERSE.
SEE

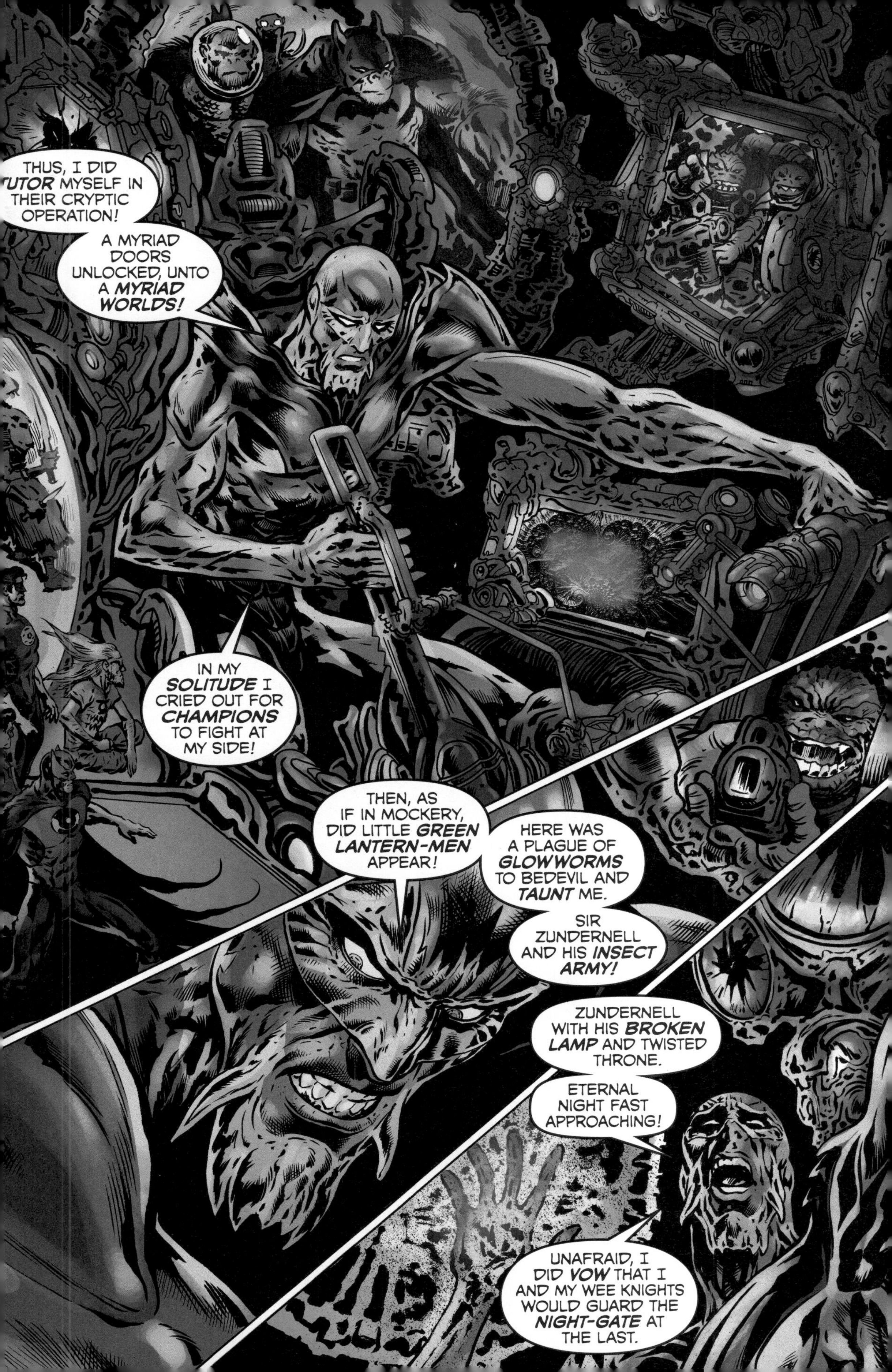
THUS, I DID TUTOR MYSELF IN THEIR CRYPTIC OPERATION!
A MYRIAD DOORS UNLOCKED, UNTO A MYRIAD WORLDS!
IN MY SOLITUDE I CRIED OUT FOR CHAMPIONS TO FIGHT AT MY SIDE!
THEN, AS IF IN MOCKERY, DID LITTLE GREEN LANTERN-MEN APPEAR!
HERE WAS A PLAGUE OF GLOWWORMS TO BEDEVIL AND TAUNT ME.
SIR ZUNDERNELL AND HIS INSECT ARMY!
ZUNDERNELL WITH HIS BROKEN LAMP AND TWISTED THRONE.
ETERNAL NIGHT FAST APPROACHING!
UNAFRAID, I DID VOW THAT I AND MY WEE KNIGHTS WOULD GUARD THE NIGHT-GATE AT THE LAST.

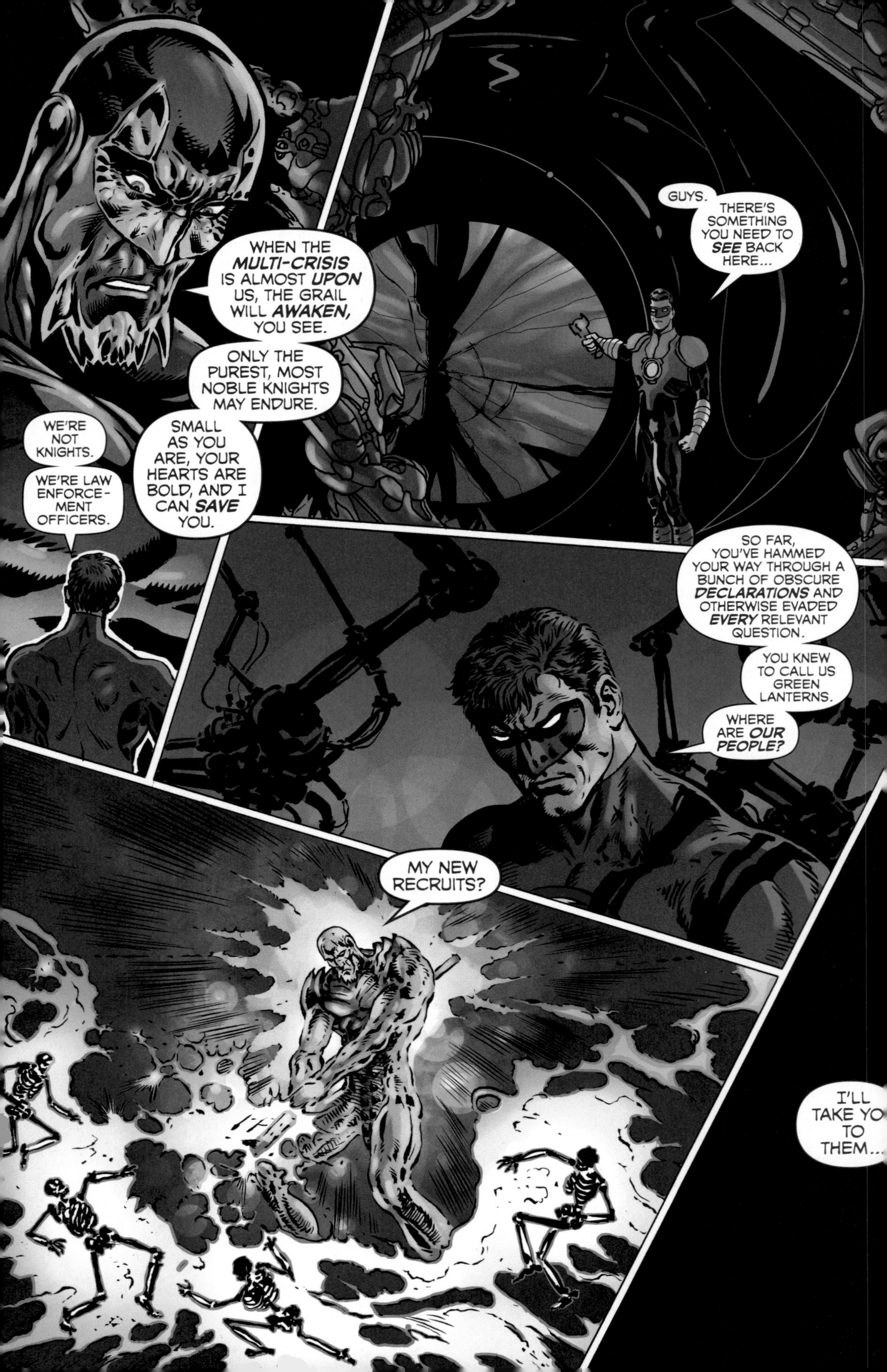
WHEN THE MULTI-CRISIS IS ALMOST UPON US, THE GRAIL WILL AWAKEN, YOU SEE.
ONLY THE PUREST, MOST NOBLE KNIGHTS MAY ENDURE.
SMALL AS YOU ARE, YOUR HEARTS ARE BOLD, AND I CAN SAVE YOU.
WE'RE NOT KNIGHTS.
WE'RE LAW ENFORCE-MENT OFFICERS.
GUYS.
THERE'S SOMETHING YOU NEED TO SEE BACK HERE...
SO FAR, YOU'VE HAMMED YOUR WAY THROUGH A BUNCH OF OBSCURE DECLARATIONS AND OTHERWISE EVADED EVERY RELEVANT QUESTION.
YOU KNEW TO CALL US GREEN LANTERNS.
WHERE ARE OUR PEOPLE?
MY NEW RECRUITS?
I'LL TAKE YO TO THEM...

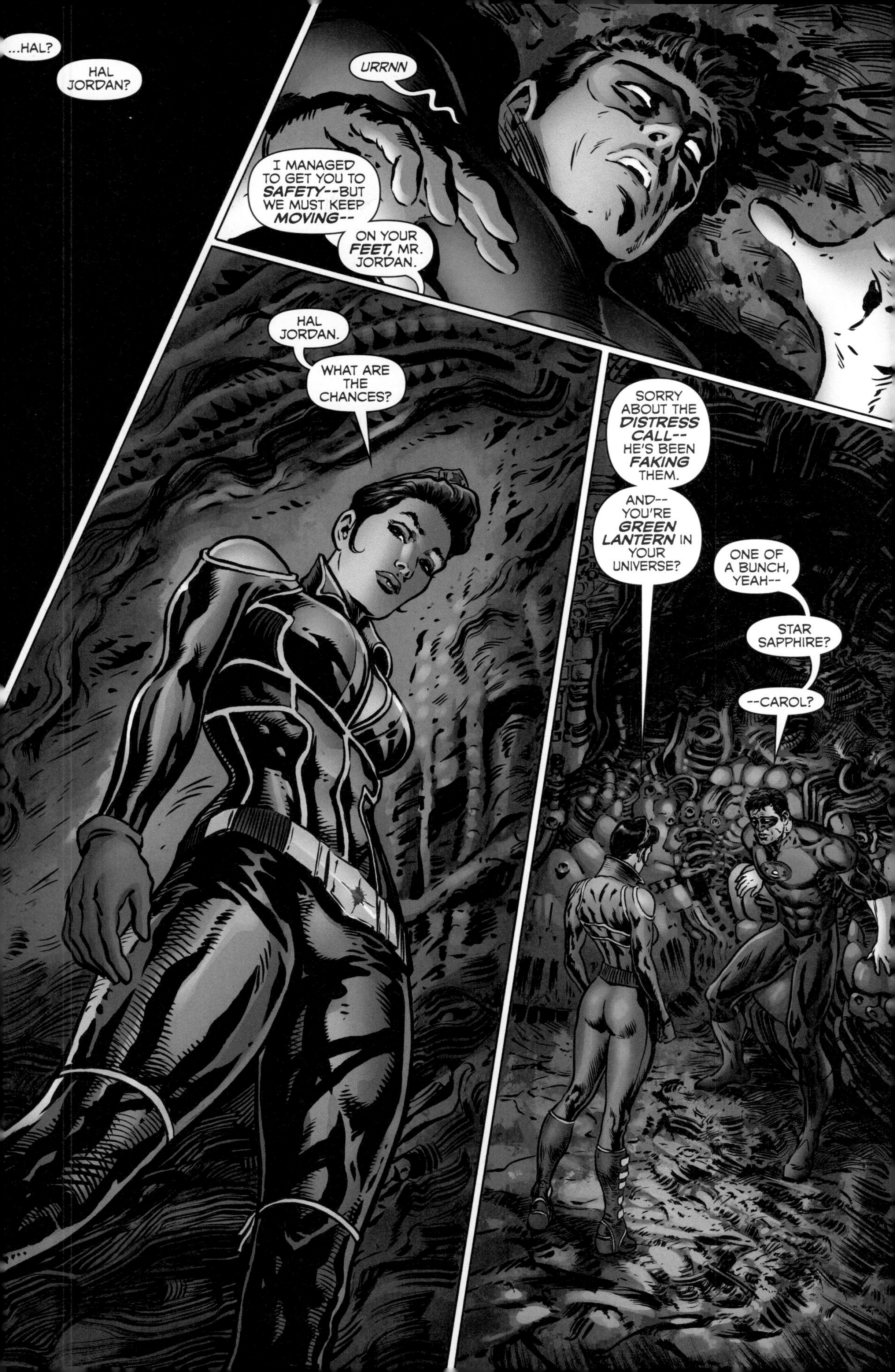
...HAL?
HAL JORDAN?
URRNN
I MANAGED TO GET YOU TO **SAFETY**--BUT WE MUST KEEP **MOVING**--
ON YOUR **FEET,** MR. JORDAN.
HAL JORDAN.
WHAT ARE THE CHANCES?
SORRY ABOUT THE **DISTRESS CALL**-- HE'S BEEN **FAKING** THEM.
AND-- YOU'RE **GREEN LANTERN** IN YOUR UNIVERSE?
ONE OF A BUNCH, YEAH--
STAR SAPPHIRE?
--CAROL?

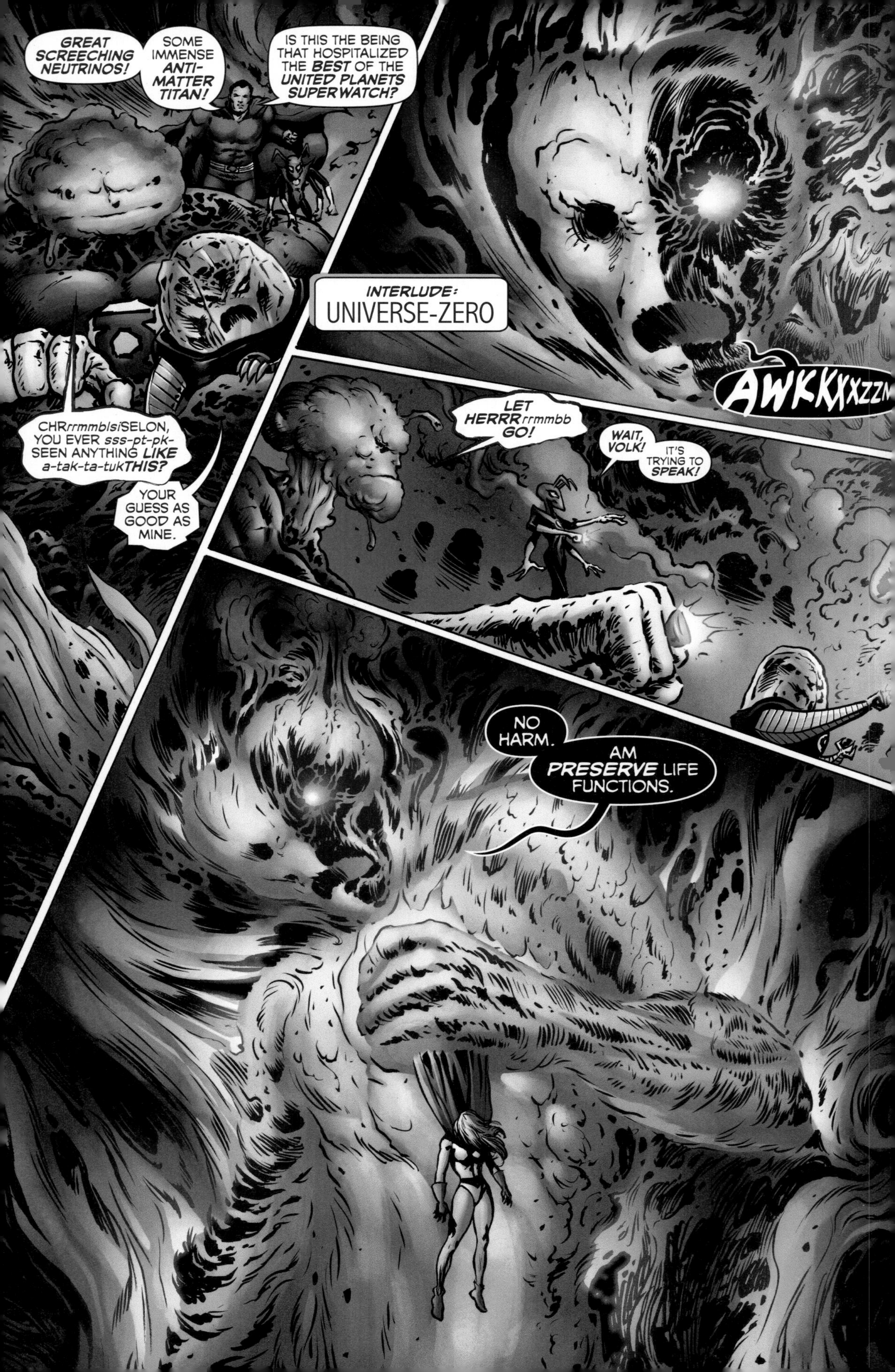
GREAT SCREECHING NEUTRINOS!
SOME IMMENSE ANTI-MATTER TITAN!
IS THIS THE BEING THAT HOSPITALIZED THE BEST OF THE UNITED PLANETS SUPERWATCH?
CHRrrmmblsiSELON, YOU EVER sss-pt-pk-SEEN ANYTHING LIKE a-tak-ta-tukTHIS?
YOUR GUESS AS GOOD AS MINE.
INTERLUDE:
UNIVERSE-ZERO
AWKKXXZZN
LET HERRRrrmmbb GO!
WAIT, VOLK!
IT'S TRYING TO SPEAK!
NO HARM.
AM PRESERVE LIFE FUNCTIONS.

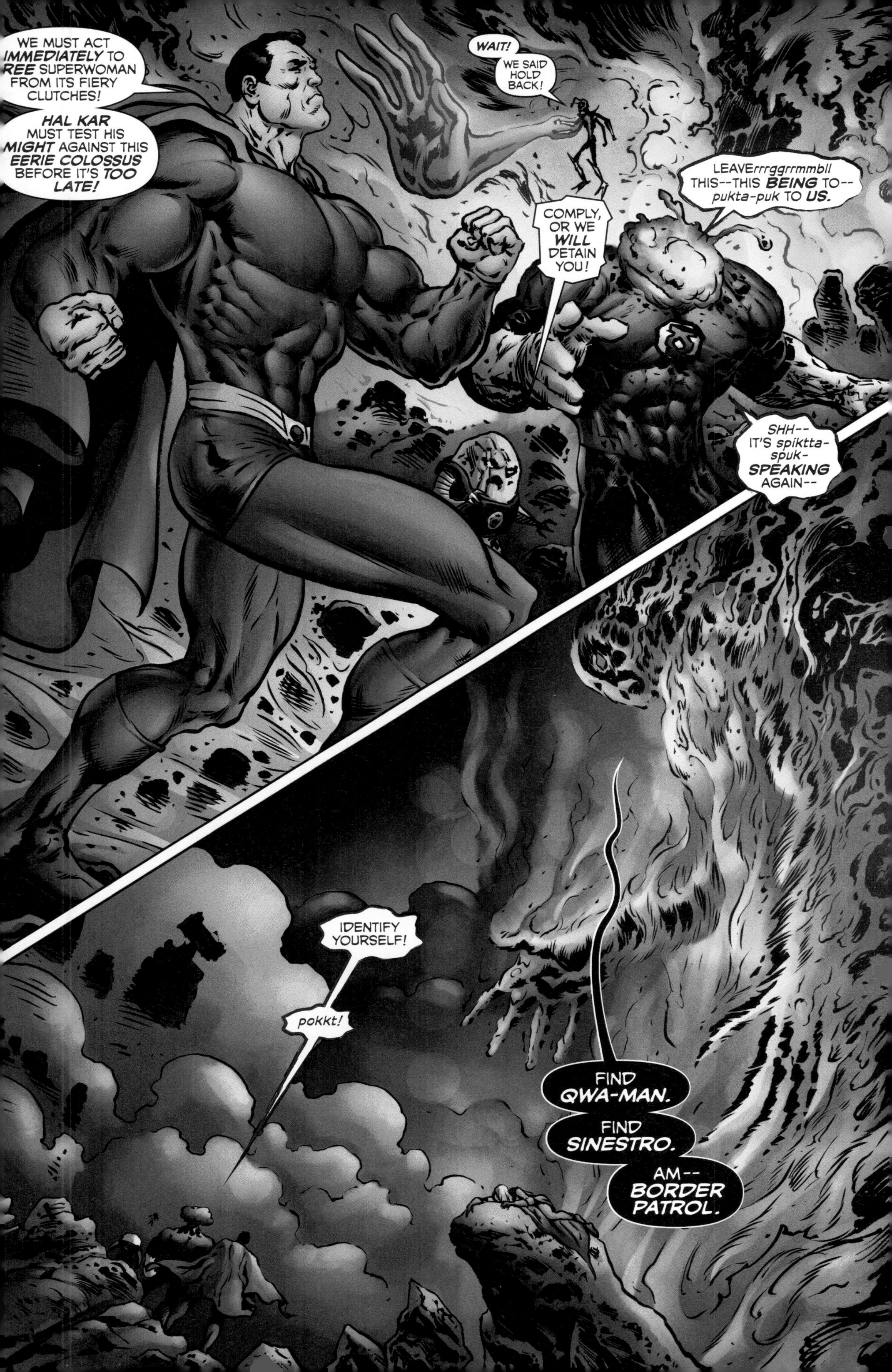
WE MUST ACT IMMEDIATELY TO REE SUPERWOMAN FROM ITS FIERY CLUTCHES!
HAL KAR MUST TEST HIS MIGHT AGAINST THIS EERIE COLOSSUS BEFORE IT'S TOO LATE!
WAIT!
WE SAID HOLD BACK!
LEAVErrrggrrmmbll THIS--THIS BEING TO-- pukta-puk TO US.
COMPLY, OR WE WILL DETAIN YOU!
SHH-- IT'S spiktta-spuk-SPEAKING AGAIN--
IDENTIFY YOURSELF!
pokkt!
FIND QWA-MAN.
FIND SINESTRO.
AM-- BORDER PATROL.

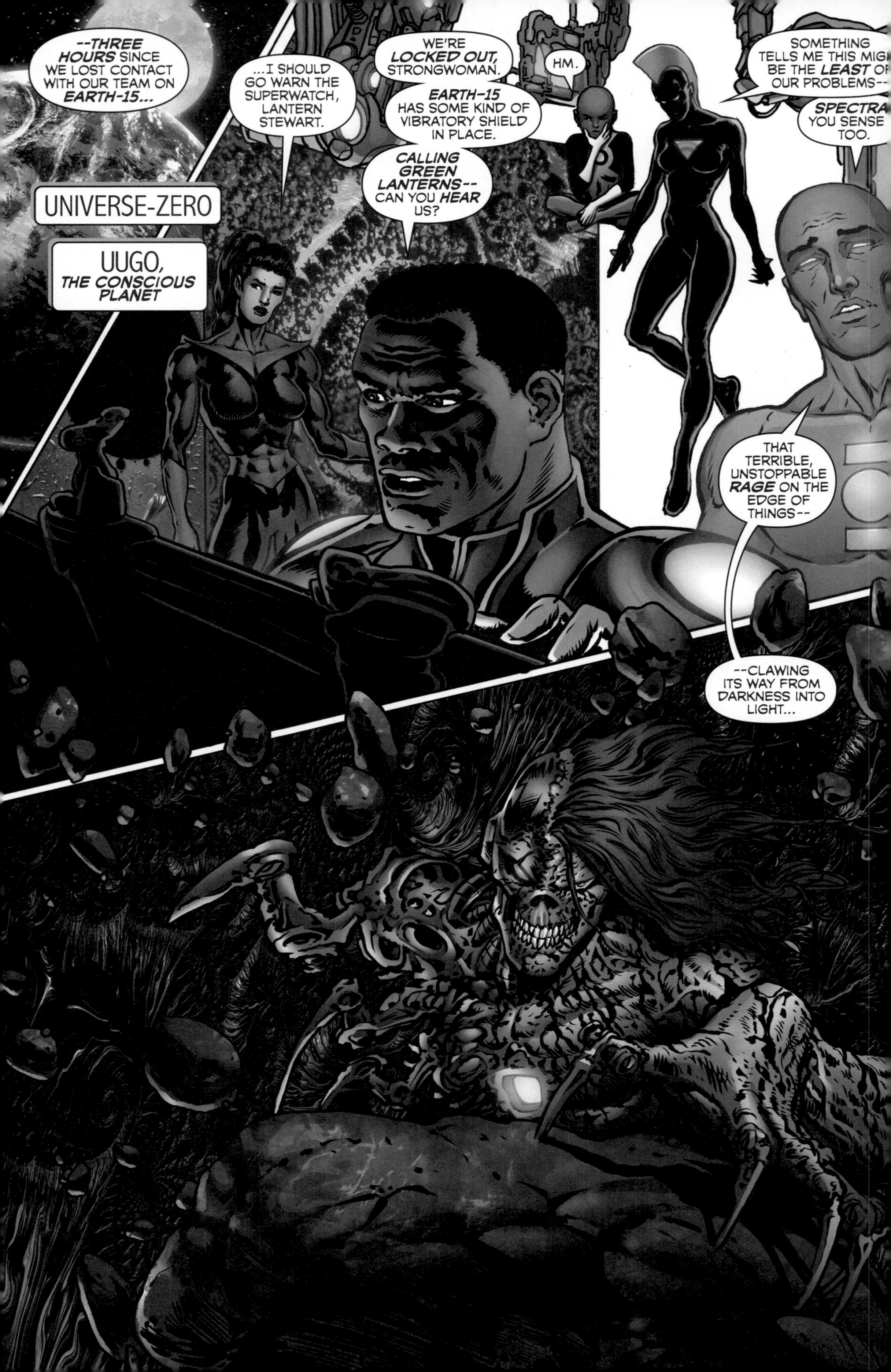
--THREE HOURS SINCE WE LOST CONTACT WITH OUR TEAM ON EARTH-15...
UNIVERSE-ZERO
UUGO, THE CONSCIOUS PLANET
...I SHOULD GO WARN THE SUPERWATCH, LANTERN STEWART.
WE'RE LOCKED OUT, STRONGWOMAN.
EARTH-15 HAS SOME KIND OF VIBRATORY SHIELD IN PLACE.
CALLING GREEN LANTERNS-- CAN YOU HEAR US?
HM.
SOMETHING TELLS ME THIS MIGH BE THE LEAST OF OUR PROBLEMS--
SPECTRA YOU SENSE TOO.
THAT TERRIBLE, UNSTOPPABLE RAGE ON THE EDGE OF THINGS--
--CLAWING ITS WAY FROM DARKNESS INTO LIGHT...

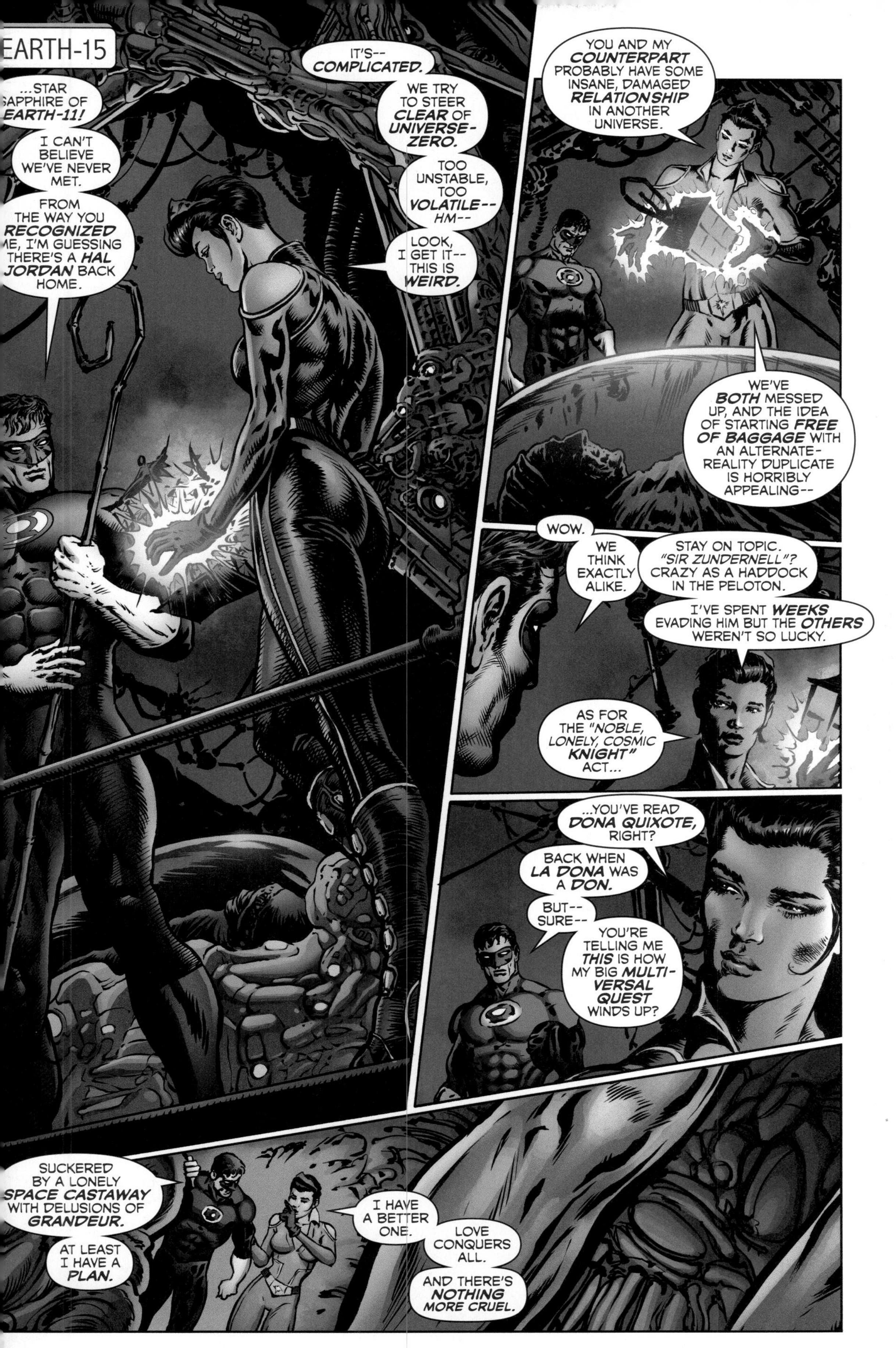
EARTH-15
...STAR SAPPHIRE OF EARTH-11!
I CAN'T BELIEVE WE'VE NEVER MET.
FROM THE WAY YOU RECOGNIZED ME, I'M GUESSING THERE'S A HAL JORDAN BACK HOME.
IT'S-- COMPLICATED.
WE TRY TO STEER CLEAR OF UNIVERSE-ZERO.
TOO UNSTABLE, TOO VOLATILE-- HM--
LOOK, I GET IT-- THIS IS WEIRD.
YOU AND MY COUNTERPART PROBABLY HAVE SOME INSANE, DAMAGED RELATIONSHIP IN ANOTHER UNIVERSE.
WE'VE BOTH MESSED UP, AND THE IDEA OF STARTING FREE OF BAGGAGE WITH AN ALTERNATE-REALITY DUPLICATE IS HORRIBLY APPEALING--
WOW.
WE THINK EXACTLY ALIKE.
STAY ON TOPIC. "SIR ZUNDERNELL"? CRAZY AS A HADDOCK IN THE PELOTON.
I'VE SPENT WEEKS EVADING HIM BUT THE OTHERS WEREN'T SO LUCKY.
AS FOR THE "NOBLE, LONELY, COSMIC KNIGHT" ACT...
...YOU'VE READ DONA QUIXOTE, RIGHT?
BACK WHEN LA DONA WAS A DON.
BUT-- SURE--
YOU'RE TELLING ME THIS IS HOW MY BIG MULTI-VERSAL QUEST WINDS UP?
SUCKERED BY A LONELY SPACE CASTAWAY WITH DELUSIONS OF GRANDEUR.
AT LEAST I HAVE A PLAN.
I HAVE A BETTER ONE.
LOVE CONQUERS ALL.
AND THERE'S NOTHING MORE CRUEL.

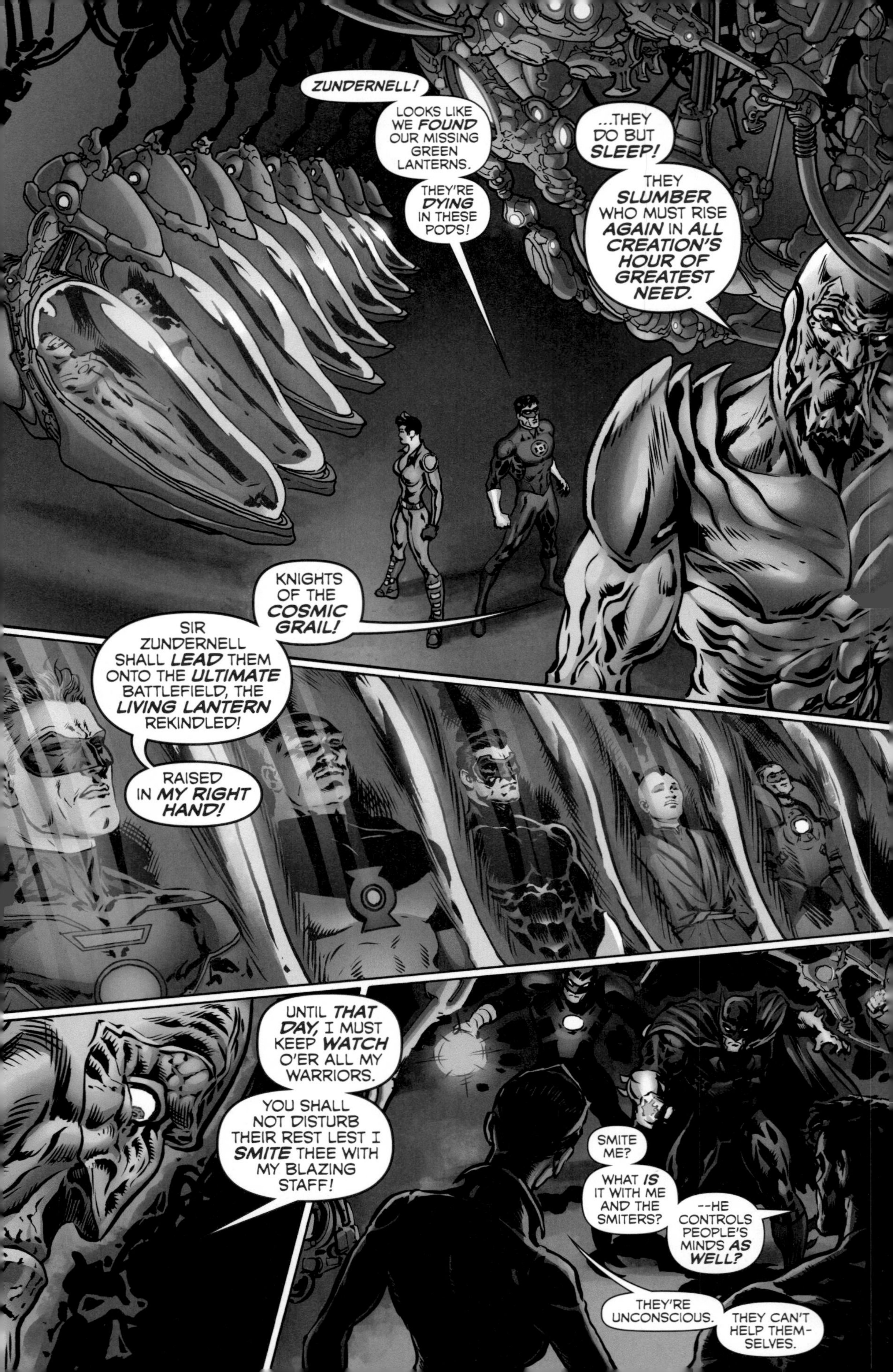
ZUNDERNELL!
LOOKS LIKE WE FOUND OUR MISSING GREEN LANTERNS.
THEY'RE DYING IN THESE PODS!
...THEY DO BUT SLEEP!
THEY SLUMBER WHO MUST RISE AGAIN IN ALL CREATION'S HOUR OF GREATEST NEED.
KNIGHTS OF THE COSMIC GRAIL!
SIR ZUNDERNELL SHALL LEAD THEM ONTO THE ULTIMATE BATTLEFIELD, THE LIVING LANTERN REKINDLED!
RAISED IN MY RIGHT HAND!
UNTIL THAT DAY, I MUST KEEP WATCH O'ER ALL MY WARRIORS.
YOU SHALL NOT DISTURB THEIR REST LEST I SMITE THEE WITH MY BLAZING STAFF!
SMITE ME?
WHAT IS IT WITH ME AND THE SMITERS?
--HE CONTROLS PEOPLE'S MINDS AS WELL?
THEY'RE UNCONSCIOUS.
THEY CAN'T HELP THEM-SELVES.

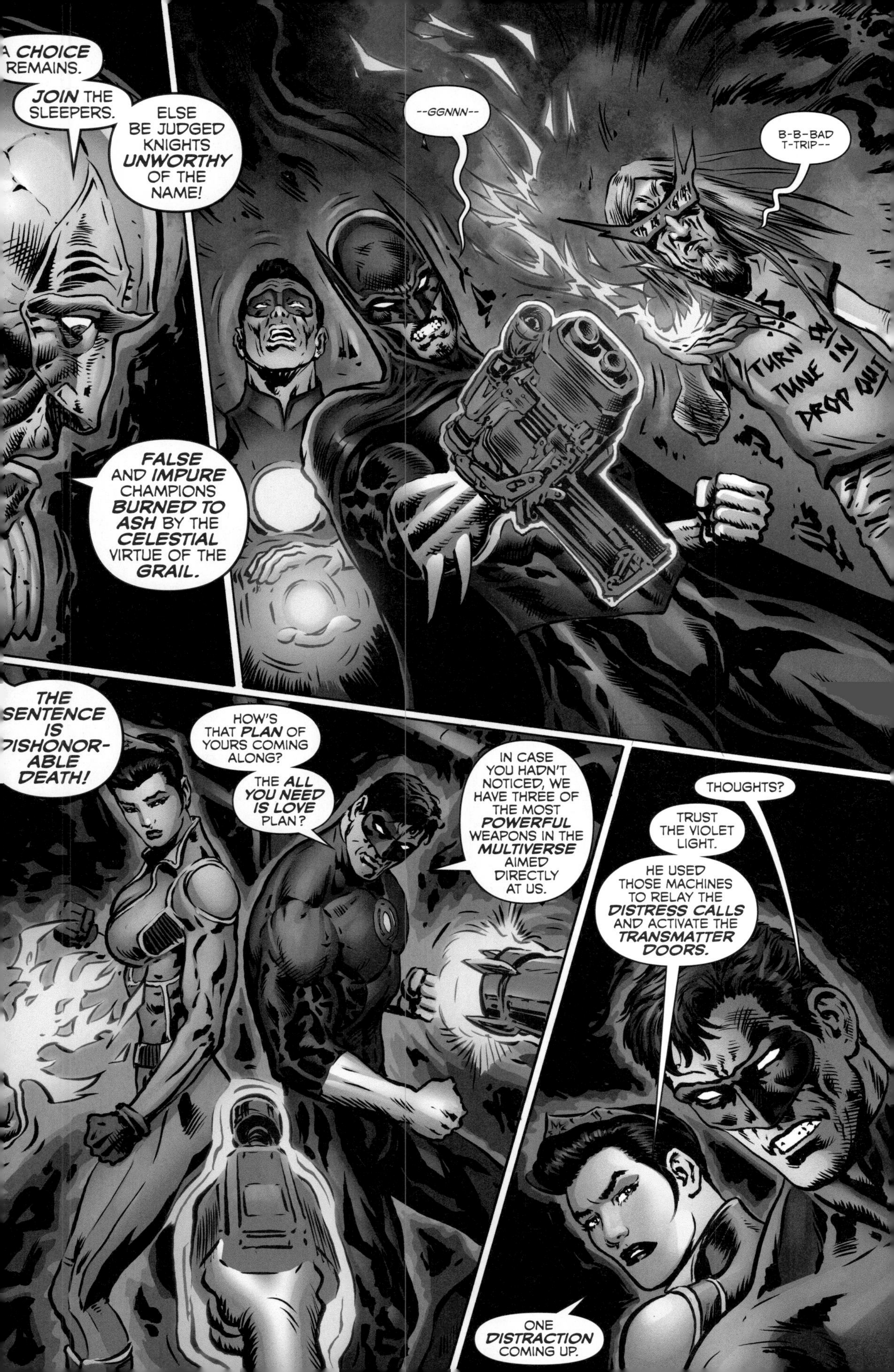
A CHOICE REMAINS.
JOIN THE SLEEPERS.
ELSE BE JUDGED KNIGHTS UNWORTHY OF THE NAME!
--GGNNN--
B-B-BAD T-TRIP--
TURN ON TUNE IN DROP OUT
FALSE AND IMPURE CHAMPIONS BURNED TO ASH BY THE CELESTIAL VIRTUE OF THE GRAIL.
THE SENTENCE IS DISHONOR-ABLE DEATH!
HOW'S THAT PLAN OF YOURS COMING ALONG?
THE ALL YOU NEED IS LOVE PLAN?
IN CASE YOU HADN'T NOTICED, WE HAVE THREE OF THE MOST POWERFUL WEAPONS IN THE MULTIVERSE AIMED DIRECTLY AT US.
THOUGHTS?
TRUST THE VIOLET LIGHT.
HE USED THOSE MACHINES TO RELAY THE DISTRESS CALLS AND ACTIVATE THE TRANSMATTER DOORS.
ONE DISTRACTION COMING UP.

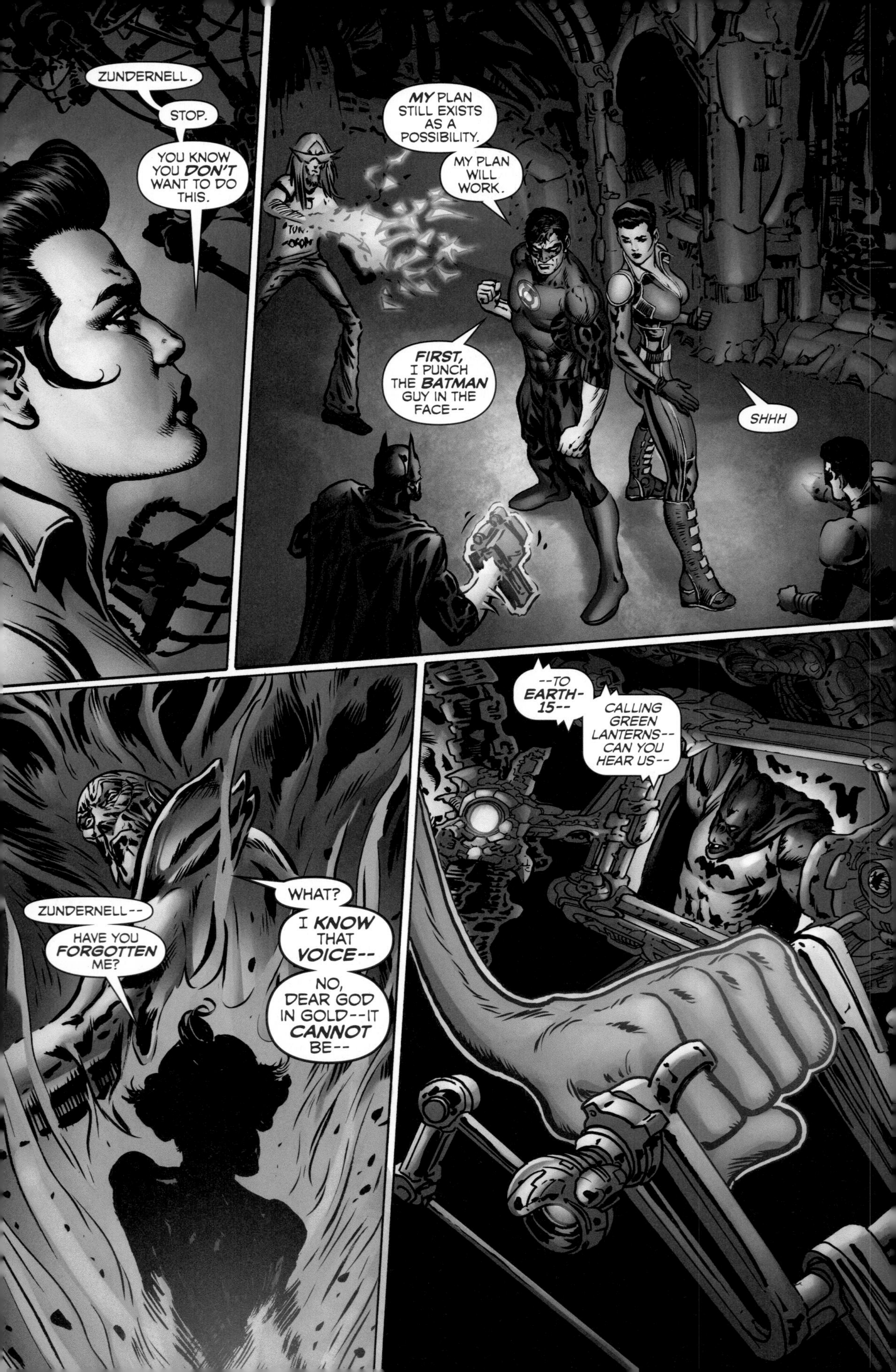
ZUNDERNELL.
STOP.
YOU KNOW YOU DON'T WANT TO DO THIS.
MY PLAN STILL EXISTS AS A POSSIBILITY.
MY PLAN WILL WORK.
FIRST, I PUNCH THE BATMAN GUY IN THE FACE--
SHHH
ZUNDERNELL--
HAVE YOU FORGOTTEN ME?
WHAT?
I KNOW THAT VOICE--
NO, DEAR GOD IN GOLD--IT CANNOT BE--
--TO EARTH-15--
CALLING GREEN LANTERNS-- CAN YOU HEAR US--

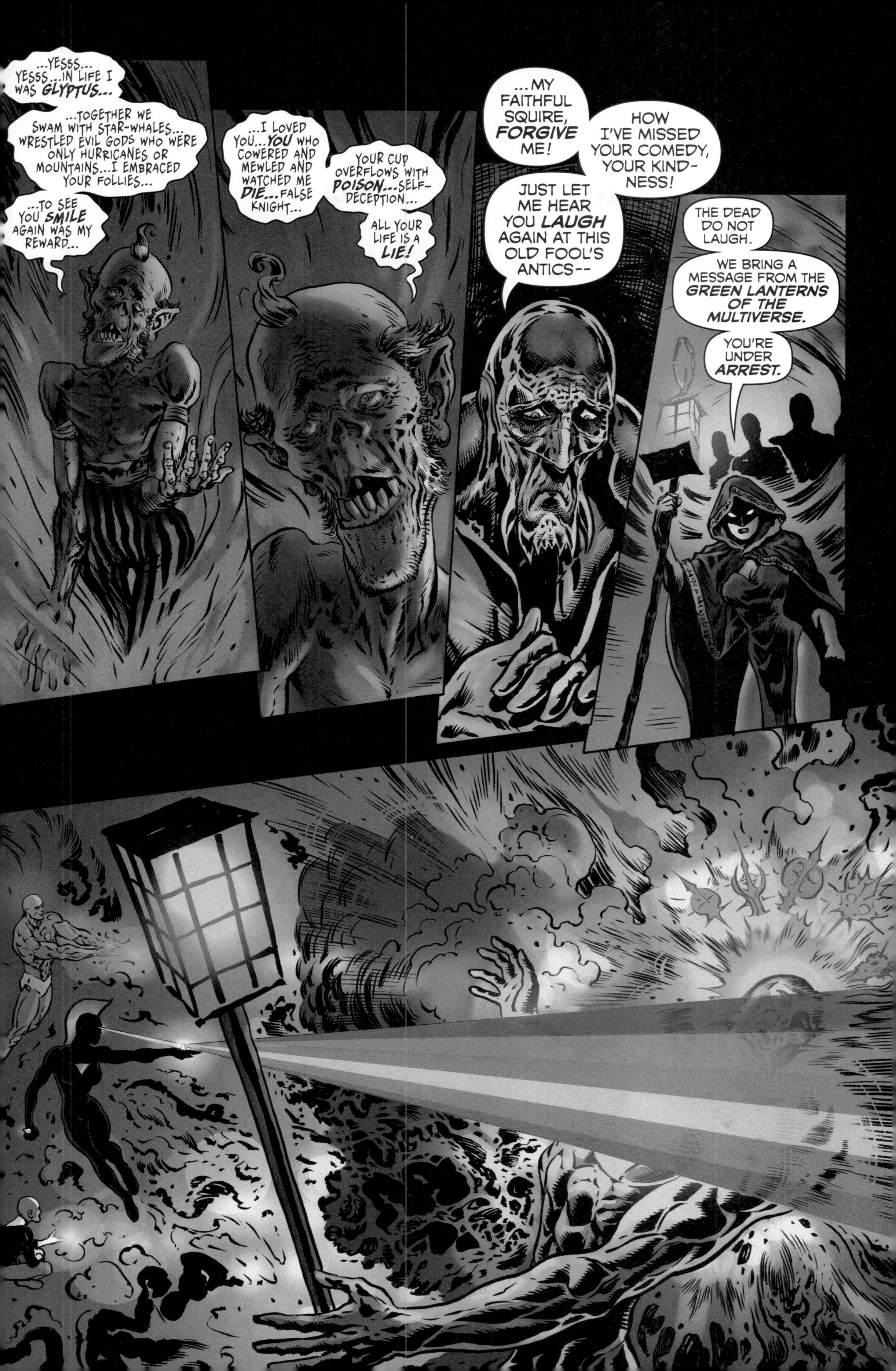
...YESSS... YESSS...IN LIFE I WAS GLYPTUS...
...TOGETHER WE SWAM WITH STAR-WHALES... WRESTLED EVIL GODS WHO WERE ONLY HURRICANES OR MOUNTAINS...I EMBRACED YOUR FOLLIES...
...TO SEE YOU SMILE AGAIN WAS MY REWARD...
...I LOVED YOU...YOU WHO COWERED AND MEWLED AND WATCHED ME DIE...FALSE KNIGHT...
YOUR CUP OVERFLOWS WITH POISON...SELF-DECEPTION...
ALL YOUR LIFE IS A LIE!
...MY FAITHFUL SQUIRE, FORGIVE ME!
HOW I'VE MISSED YOUR COMEDY, YOUR KIND-NESS!
JUST LET ME HEAR YOU LAUGH AGAIN AT THIS OLD FOOL'S ANTICS--
THE DEAD DO NOT LAUGH.
WE BRING A MESSAGE FROM THE GREEN LANTERNS OF THE MULTIVERSE.
YOU'RE UNDER ARREST.

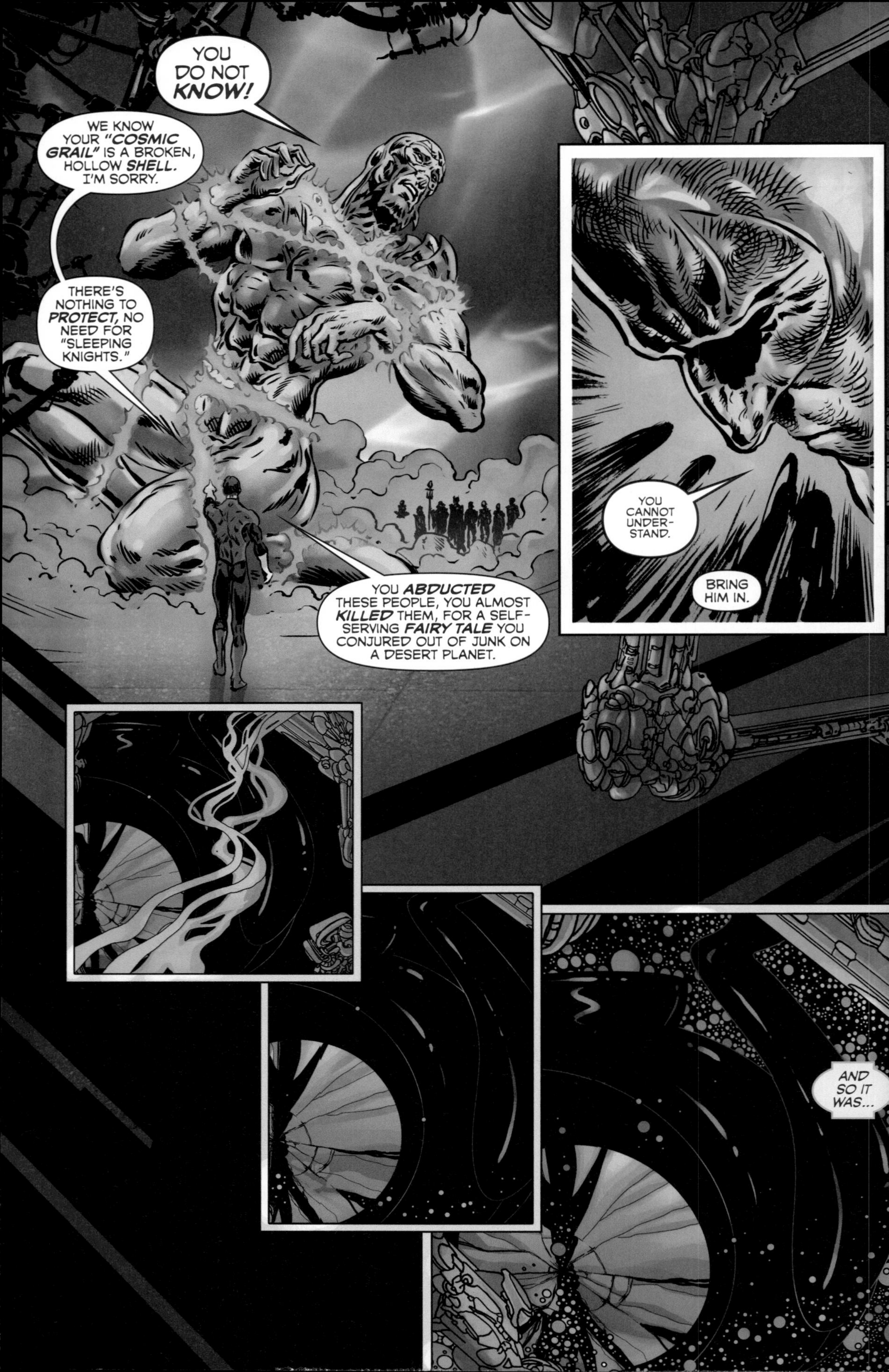

YOU DO NOT KNOW!
WE KNOW YOUR "COSMIC GRAIL" IS A BROKEN, HOLLOW SHELL. I'M SORRY.
THERE'S NOTHING TO PROTECT, NO NEED FOR "SLEEPING KNIGHTS."
YOU ABDUCTED THESE PEOPLE, YOU ALMOST KILLED THEM, FOR A SELF-SERVING FAIRY TALE YOU CONJURED OUT OF JUNK ON A DESERT PLANET.
YOU CANNOT UNDER-STAND.
BRING HIM IN.
AND SO IT WAS...

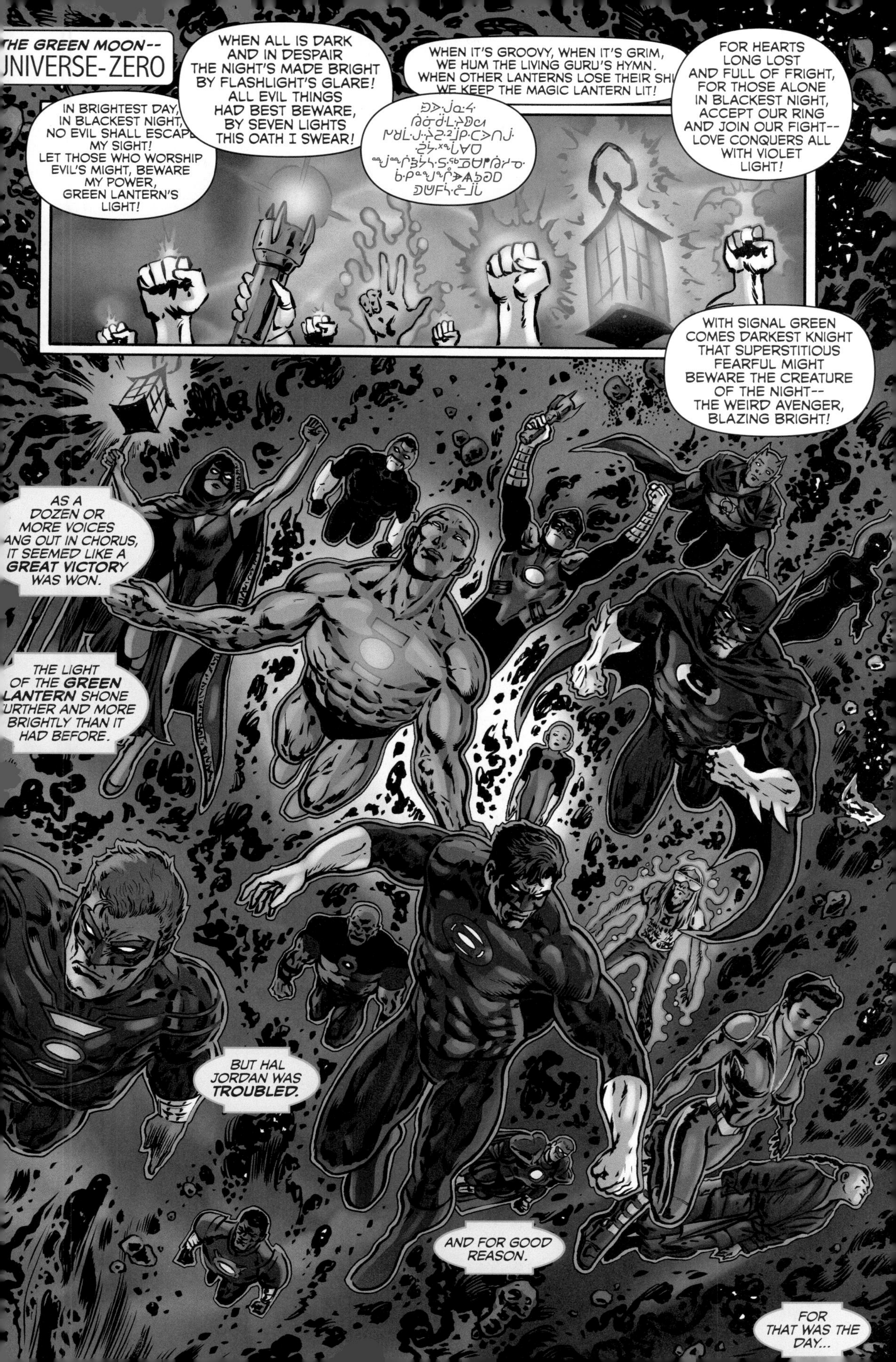

THE GREEN MOON-- UNIVERSE-ZERO
IN BRIGHTEST DAY, IN BLACKEST NIGHT, NO EVIL SHALL ESCAP MY SIGHT! LET THOSE WHO WORSHIP EVIL'S MIGHT, BEWARE MY POWER, GREEN LANTERN'S LIGHT!
WHEN ALL IS DARK AND IN DESPAIR THE NIGHT'S MADE BRIGHT BY FLASHLIGHT'S GLARE! ALL EVIL THINGS HAD BEST BEWARE, BY SEVEN LIGHTS THIS OATH I SWEAR!
WHEN IT'S GROOVY, WHEN IT'S GRIM, WE HUM THE LIVING GURU'S HYMN. WHEN OTHER LANTERNS LOSE THEIR SHI WE KEEP THE MAGIC LANTERN LIT!
FOR HEARTS LONG LOST AND FULL OF FRIGHT, FOR THOSE ALONE IN BLACKEST NIGHT, ACCEPT OUR RING AND JOIN OUR FIGHT-- LOVE CONQUERS ALL WITH VIOLET LIGHT!
WITH SIGNAL GREEN COMES DARKEST KNIGHT THAT SUPERSTITIOUS FEARFUL MIGHT BEWARE THE CREATURE OF THE NIGHT-- THE WEIRD AVENGER, BLAZING BRIGHT!
AS A DOZEN OR MORE VOICES ANG OUT IN CHORUS, IT SEEMED LIKE A GREAT VICTORY WAS WON.
THE LIGHT OF THE GREEN LANTERN SHONE URTHER AND MORE BRIGHTLY THAN IT HAD BEFORE.
BUT HAL JORDAN WAS TROUBLED.
AND FOR GOOD REASON.
FOR THAT WAS THE DAY...

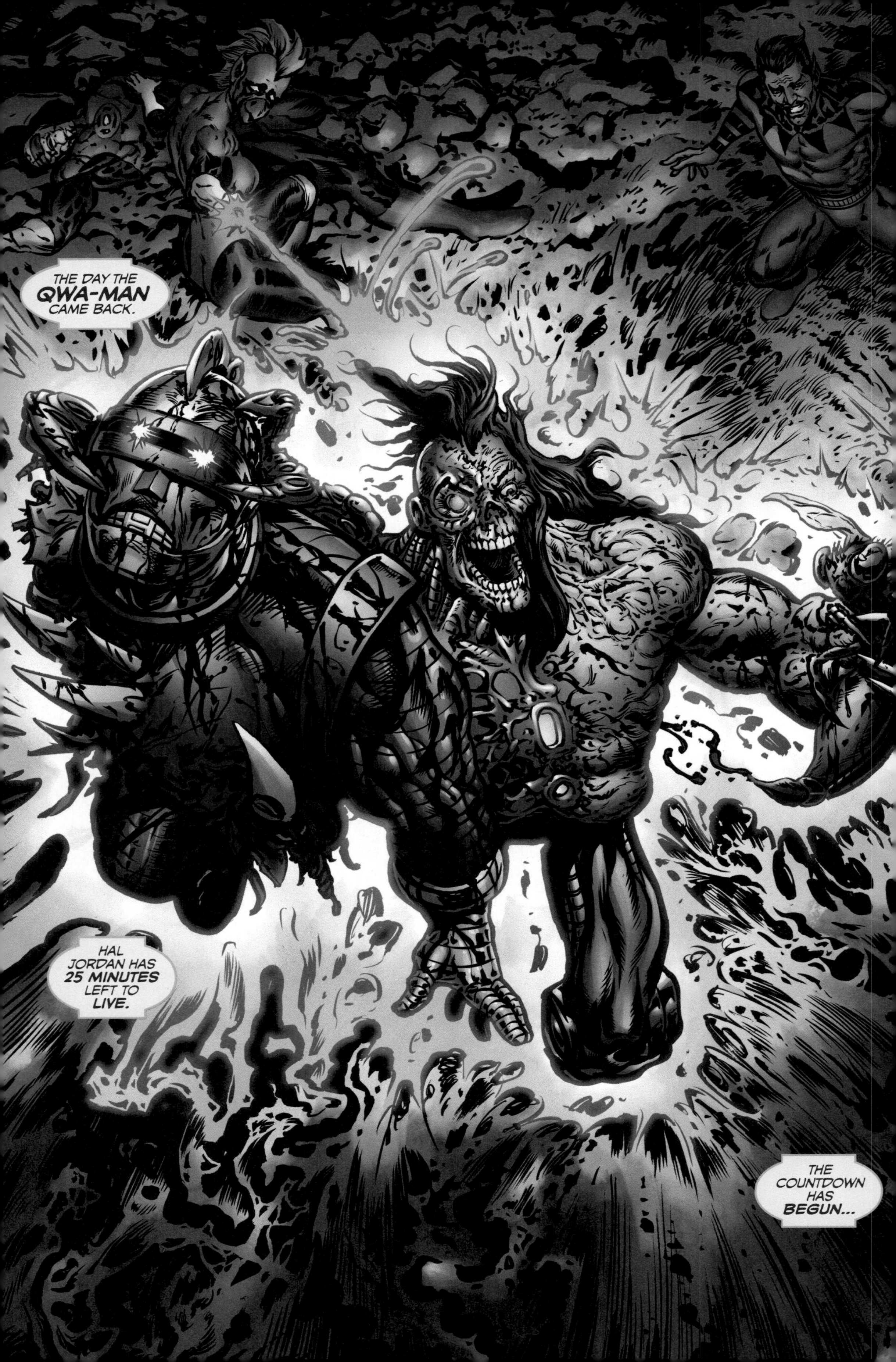
THE DAY THE QWA-MAN CAME BACK.
HAL JORDAN HAS 25 MINUTES LEFT TO LIVE.
THE COUNTDOWN HAS BEGUN...

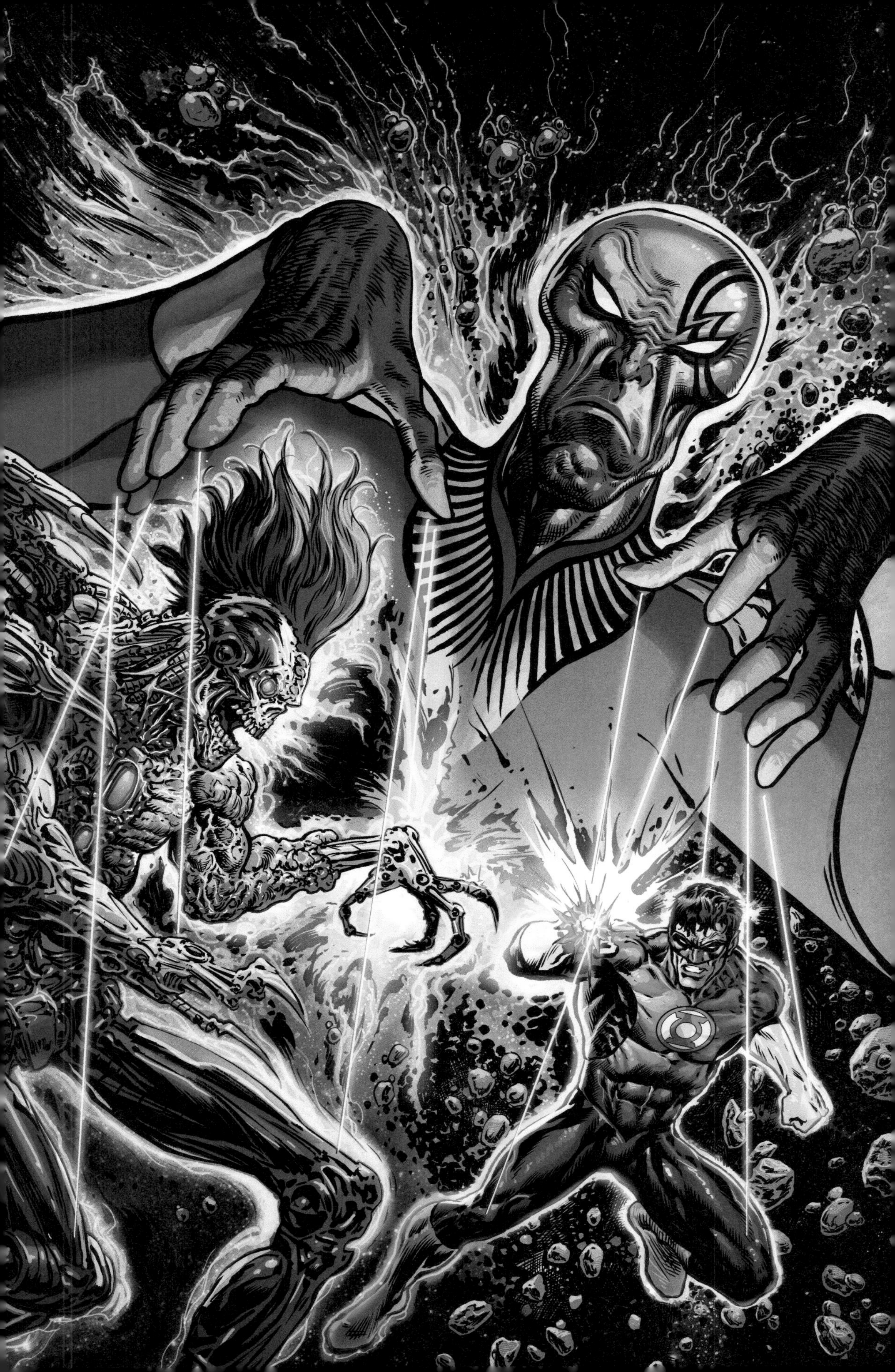

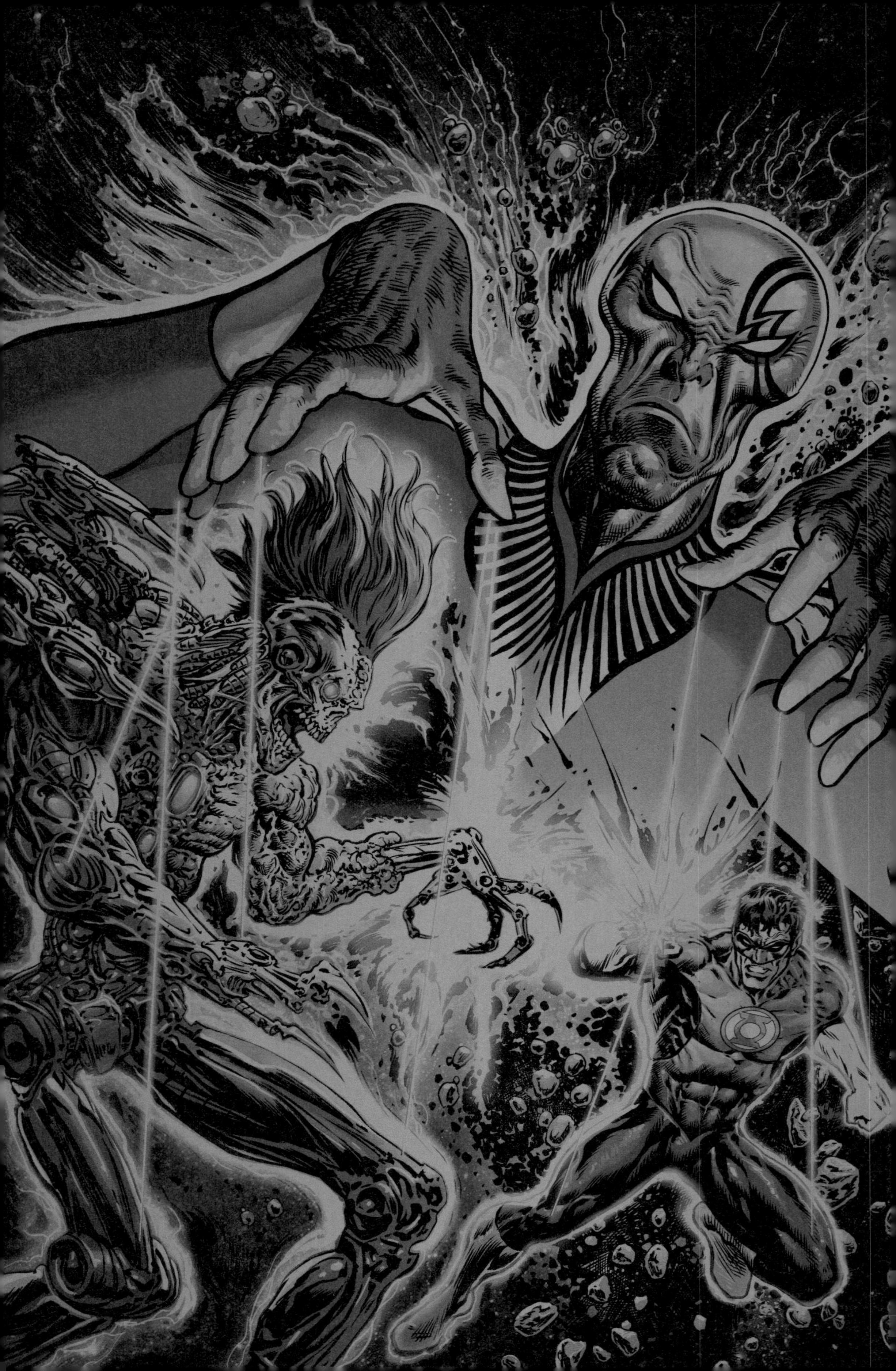

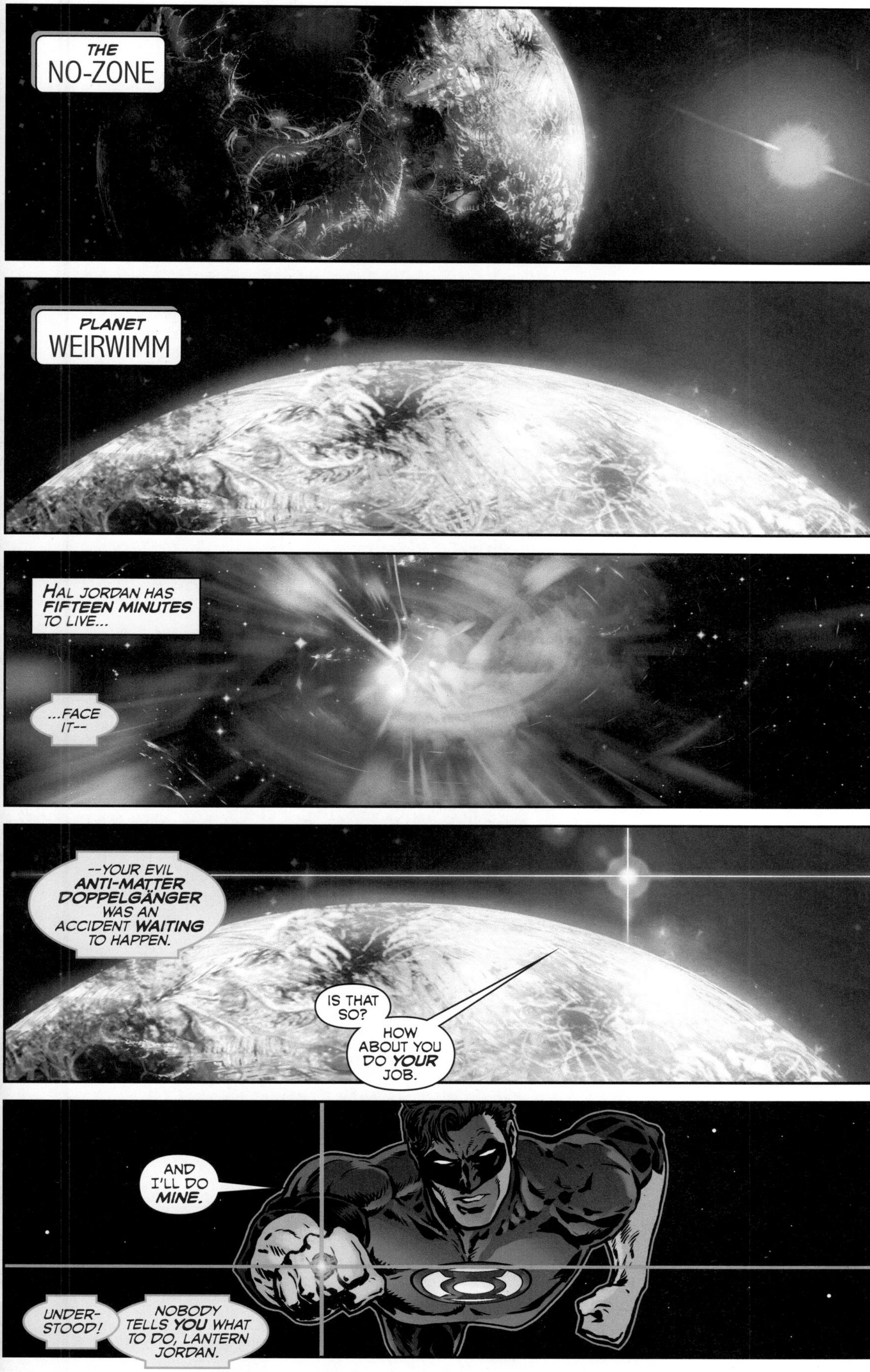
THE NO-ZONE
PLANET WEIRWIMM
HAL JORDAN HAS FIFTEEN MINUTES TO LIVE...
...FACE IT--
--YOUR EVIL ANTI-MATTER DOPPELGÄNGER WAS AN ACCIDENT WAITING TO HAPPEN.
IS THAT SO?
HOW ABOUT YOU DO YOUR JOB.
AND I'LL DO MINE.
UNDER-STOOD!
NOBODY TELLS YOU WHAT TO DO, LANTERN JORDAN.

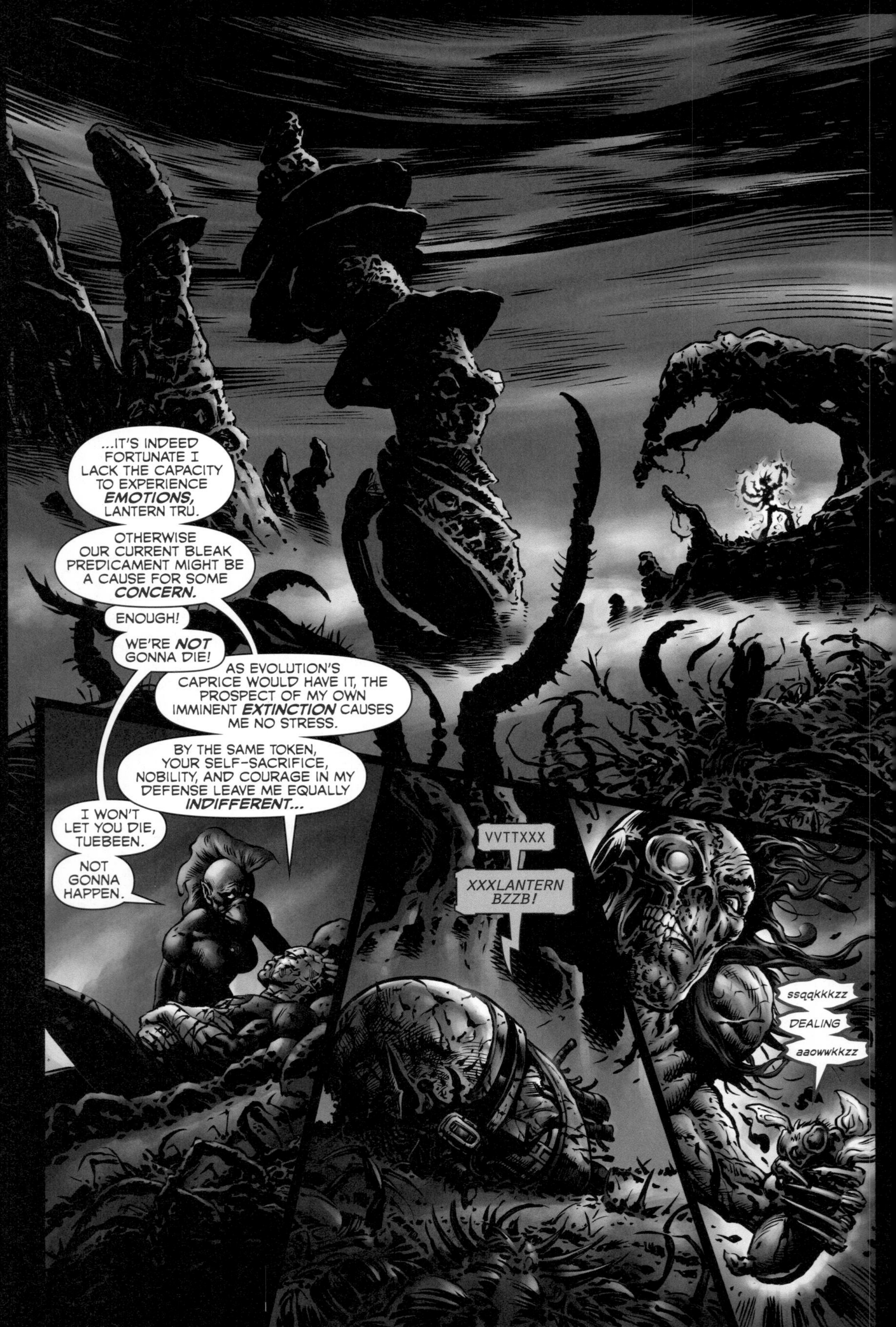
...IT'S INDEED FORTUNATE I LACK THE CAPACITY TO EXPERIENCE *EMOTIONS,* LANTERN TRU.
OTHERWISE OUR CURRENT BLEAK PREDICAMENT MIGHT BE A CAUSE FOR SOME *CONCERN.*
ENOUGH!
WE'RE *NOT* GONNA DIE!
AS EVOLUTION'S CAPRICE WOULD HAVE IT, THE PROSPECT OF MY OWN IMMINENT *EXTINCTION* CAUSES ME NO STRESS.
BY THE SAME TOKEN, YOUR SELF-SACRIFICE, NOBILITY, AND COURAGE IN MY DEFENSE LEAVE ME EQUALLY *INDIFFERENT...*
I WON'T LET YOU DIE, TUEBEEN.
NOT GONNA HAPPEN.
VVTTXXX
XXXLANTERN BZZB!
ssqqkkkzz
DEALING
aaowwkkzz

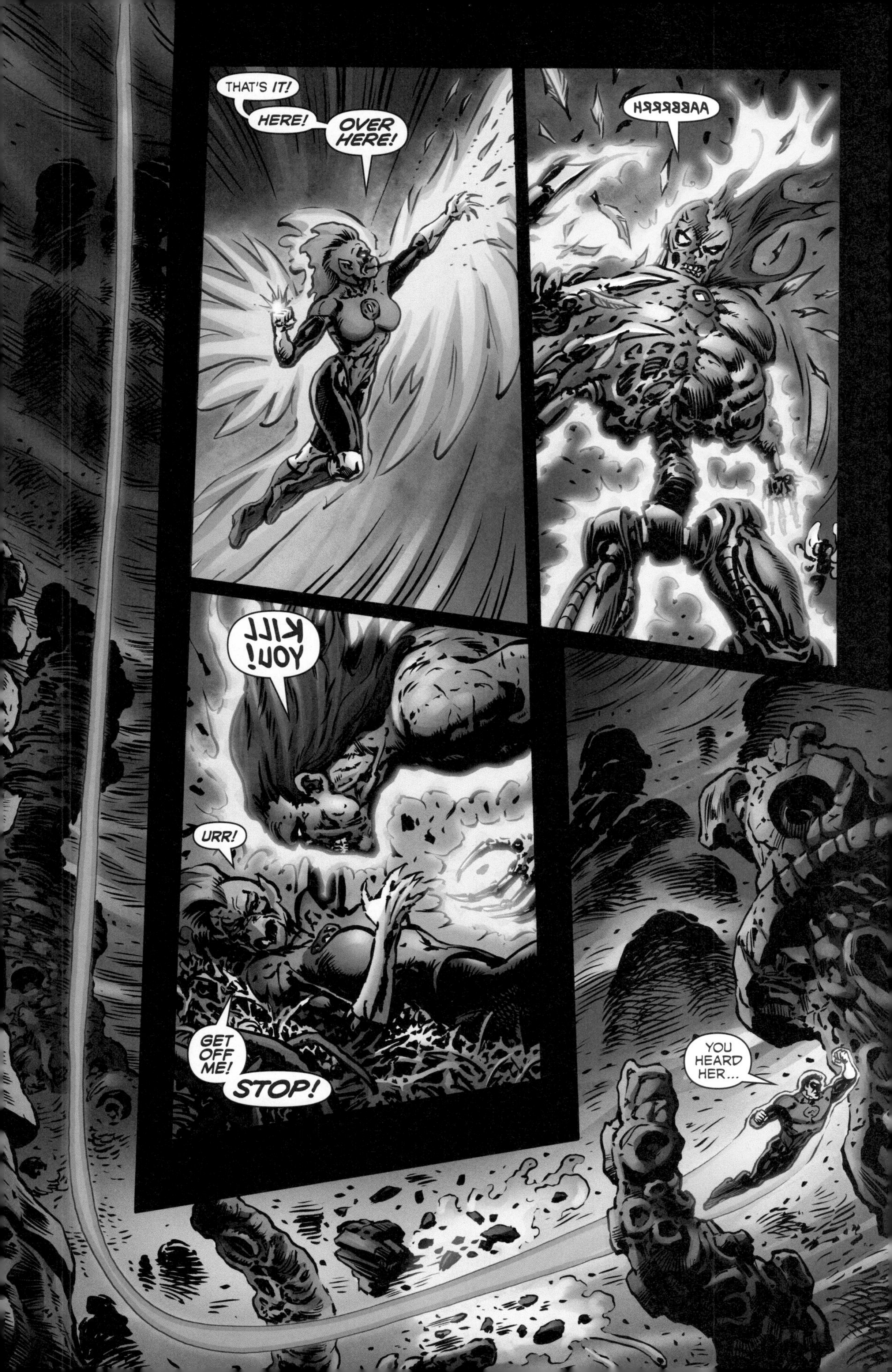
THAT'S *IT!*
HERE!
OVER HERE!
AABBRRRH
KILL YOU!
URR!
GET OFF ME!
STOP!
YOU HEARD HER...

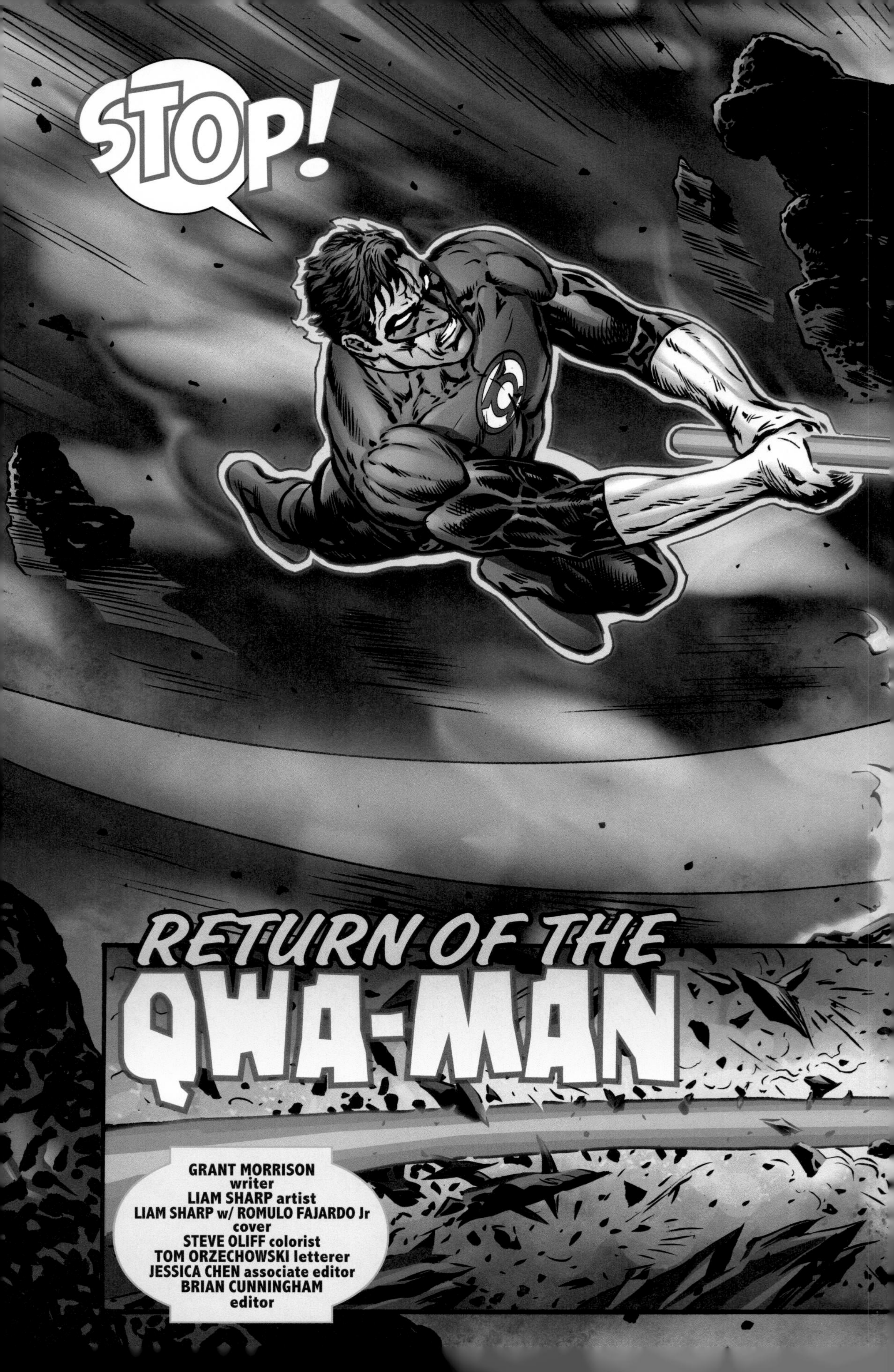
STOP!
RETURN OF THE
QWA-MAN
GRANT MORRISON writer
LIAM SHARP artist
LIAM SHARP w/ ROMULO FAJARDO Jr cover
STEVE OLIFF colorist
TOM ORZECHOWSKI letterer
JESSICA CHEN associate editor
BRIAN CUNNINGHAM editor

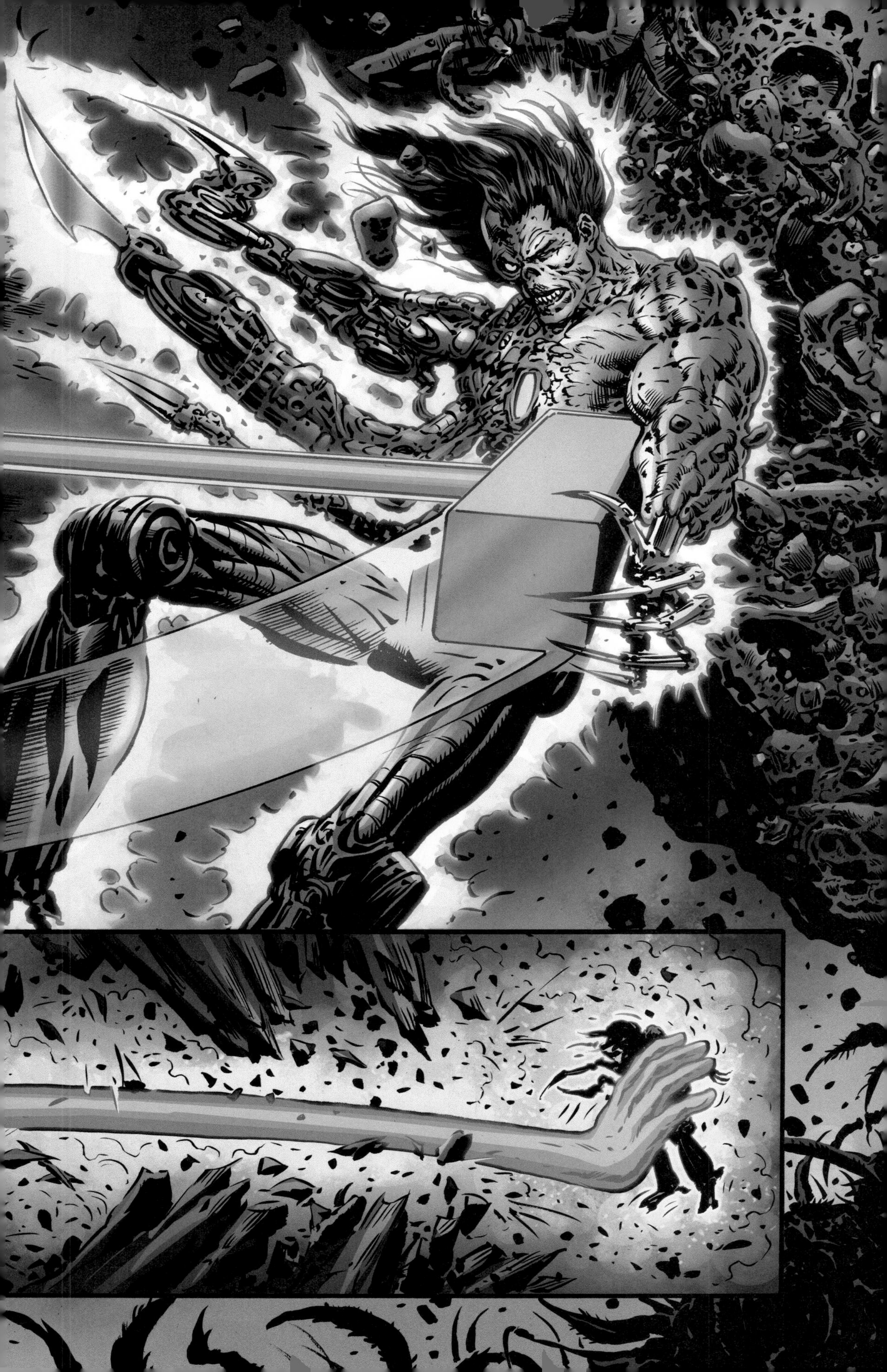

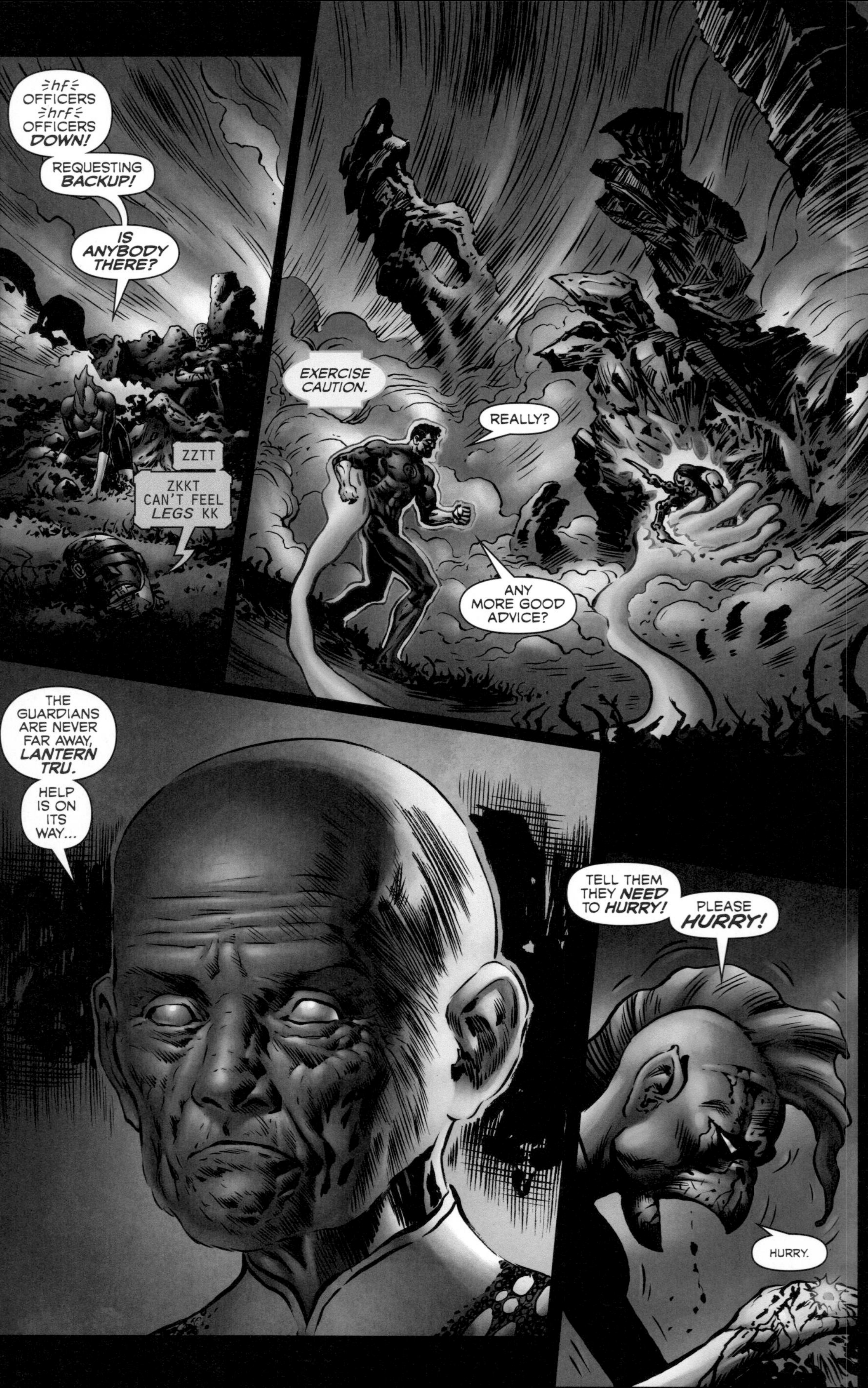
hf
OFFICERS
hrf
OFFICERS
DOWN!
REQUESTING BACKUP!
IS ANYBODY THERE?
ZZTT
ZKKT CAN'T FEEL LEGS KK
EXERCISE CAUTION.
REALLY?
ANY MORE GOOD ADVICE?
THE GUARDIANS ARE NEVER FAR AWAY, LANTERN TRU.
HELP IS ON ITS WAY...
TELL THEM THEY NEED TO HURRY!
PLEASE HURRY!
HURRY.

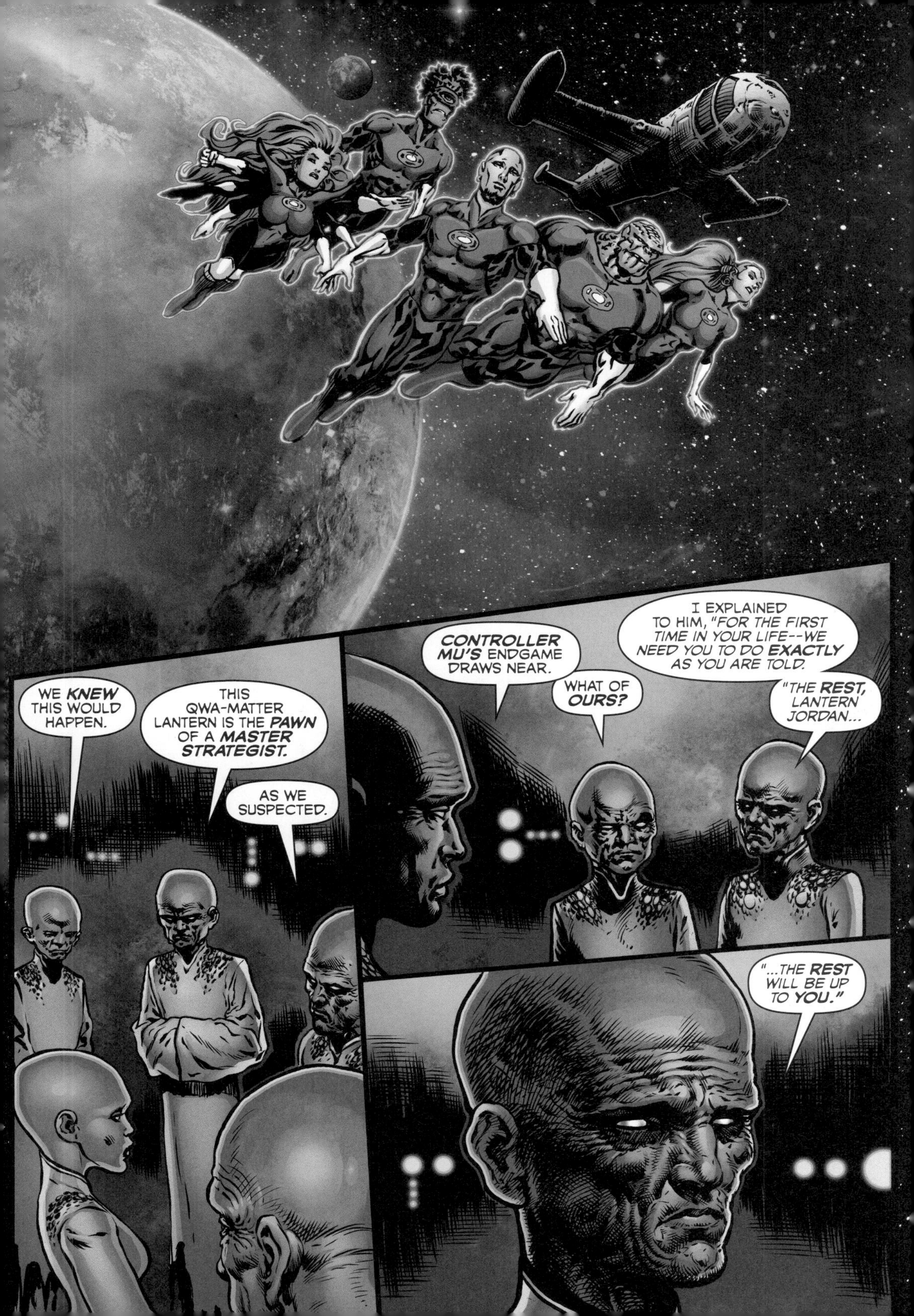
WE KNEW THIS WOULD HAPPEN.
THIS QWA-MATTER LANTERN IS THE PAWN OF A MASTER STRATEGIST.
AS WE SUSPECTED.
CONTROLLER MU'S ENDGAME DRAWS NEAR.
WHAT OF OURS?
I EXPLAINED TO HIM, "FOR THE FIRST TIME IN YOUR LIFE--WE NEED YOU TO DO EXACTLY AS YOU ARE TOLD.
"THE REST, LANTERN JORDAN...
"...THE REST WILL BE UP TO YOU."

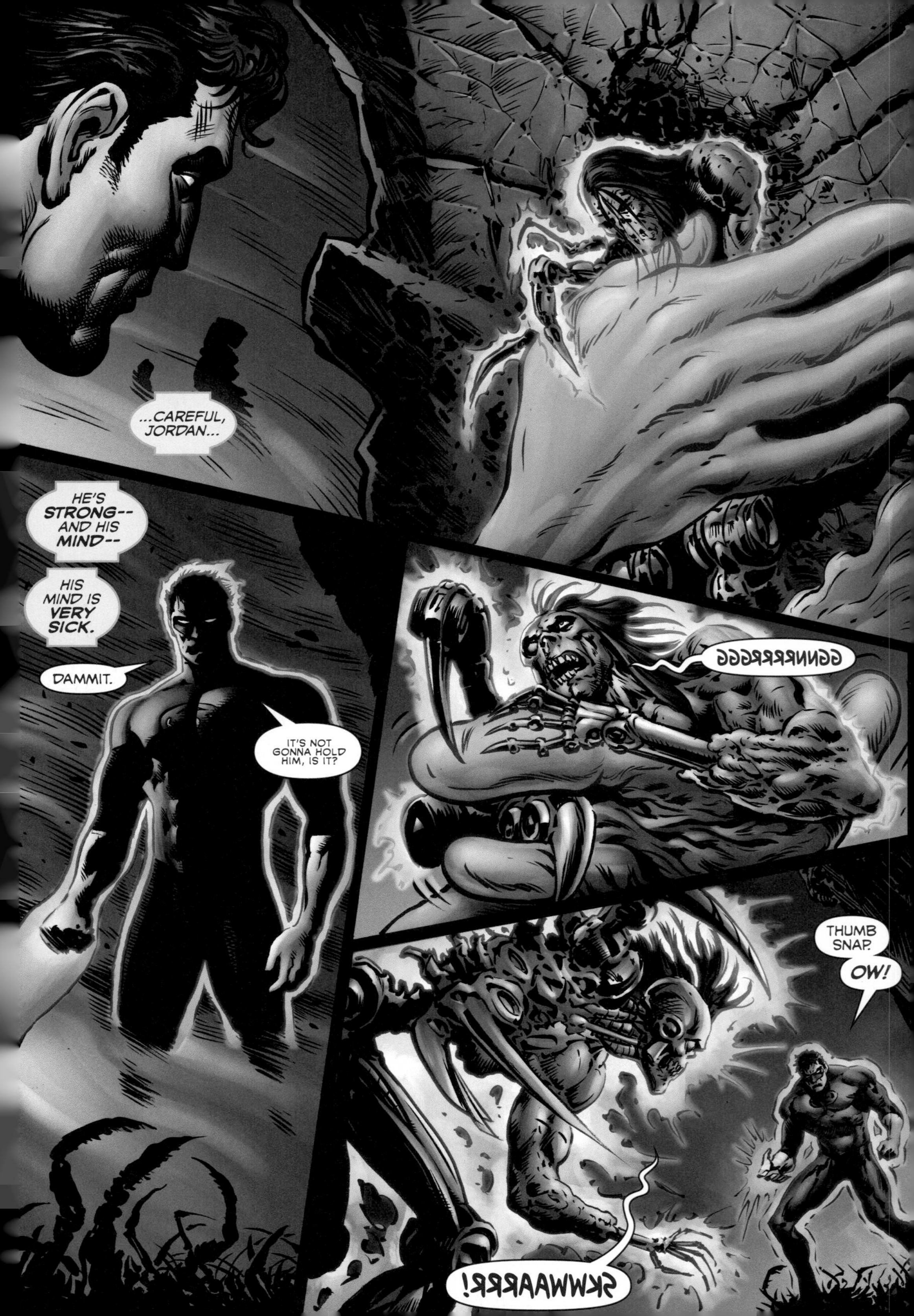
...CAREFUL, JORDAN...
HE'S STRONG-- AND HIS MIND--
HIS MIND IS VERY SICK.
DAMMIT.
IT'S NOT GONNA HOLD HIM, IS IT?
GGNNRRRGGG
THUMB SNAP.
OW!
SKWWARRR!

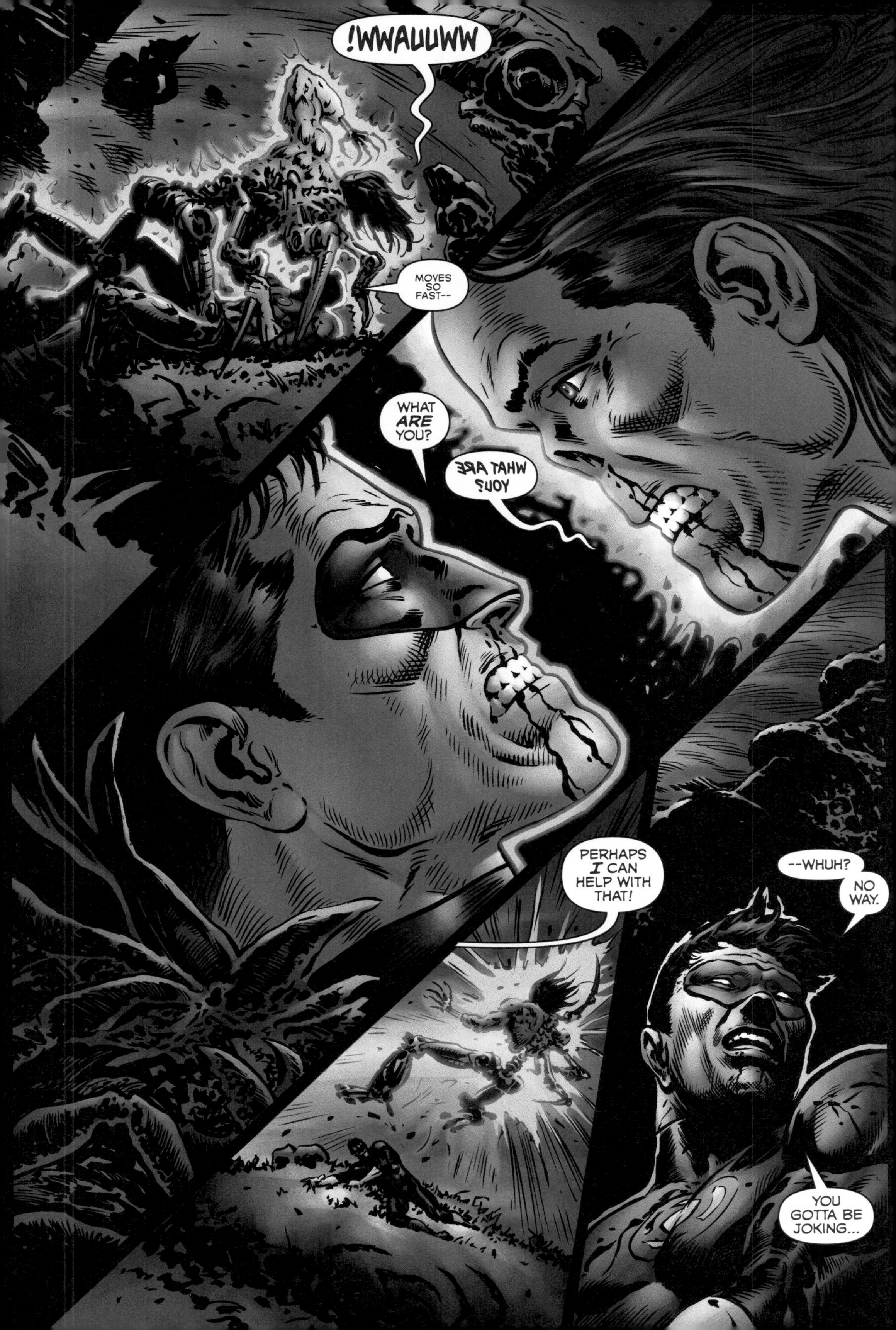
!WWAUUWW
MOVES SO FAST--
WHAT ARE YOU?
WHAT ARE YOU?
PERHAPS I CAN HELP WITH THAT!
--WHUH?
NO WAY.
YOU GOTTA BE JOKING...

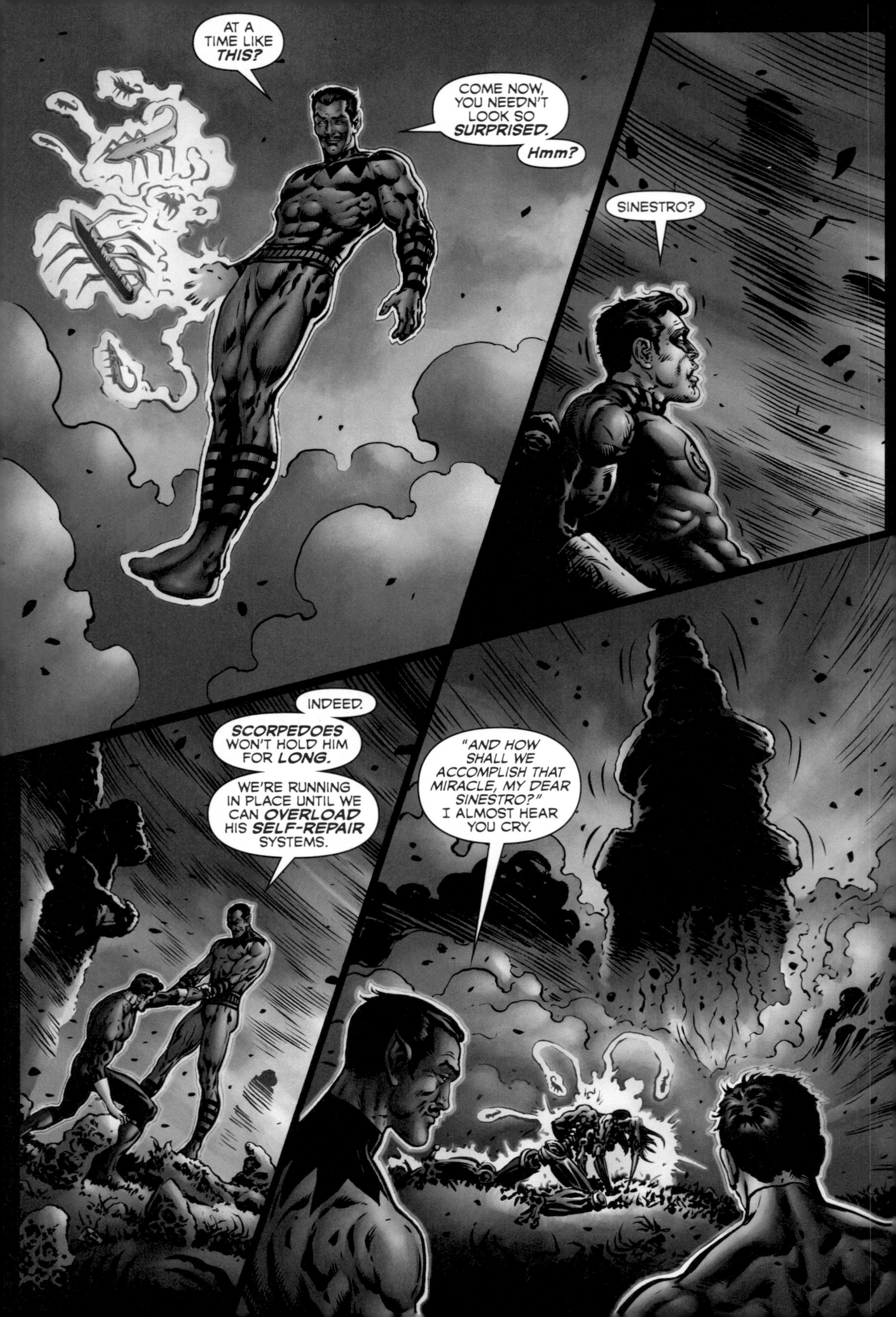
AT A TIME LIKE THIS?
COME NOW, YOU NEEDN'T LOOK SO SURPRISED.
Hmm?
SINESTRO?
INDEED.
SCORPEDOES WON'T HOLD HIM FOR LONG.
WE'RE RUNNING IN PLACE UNTIL WE CAN OVERLOAD HIS SELF-REPAIR SYSTEMS.
"AND HOW SHALL WE ACCOMPLISH THAT MIRACLE, MY DEAR SINESTRO?" I ALMOST HEAR YOU CRY.

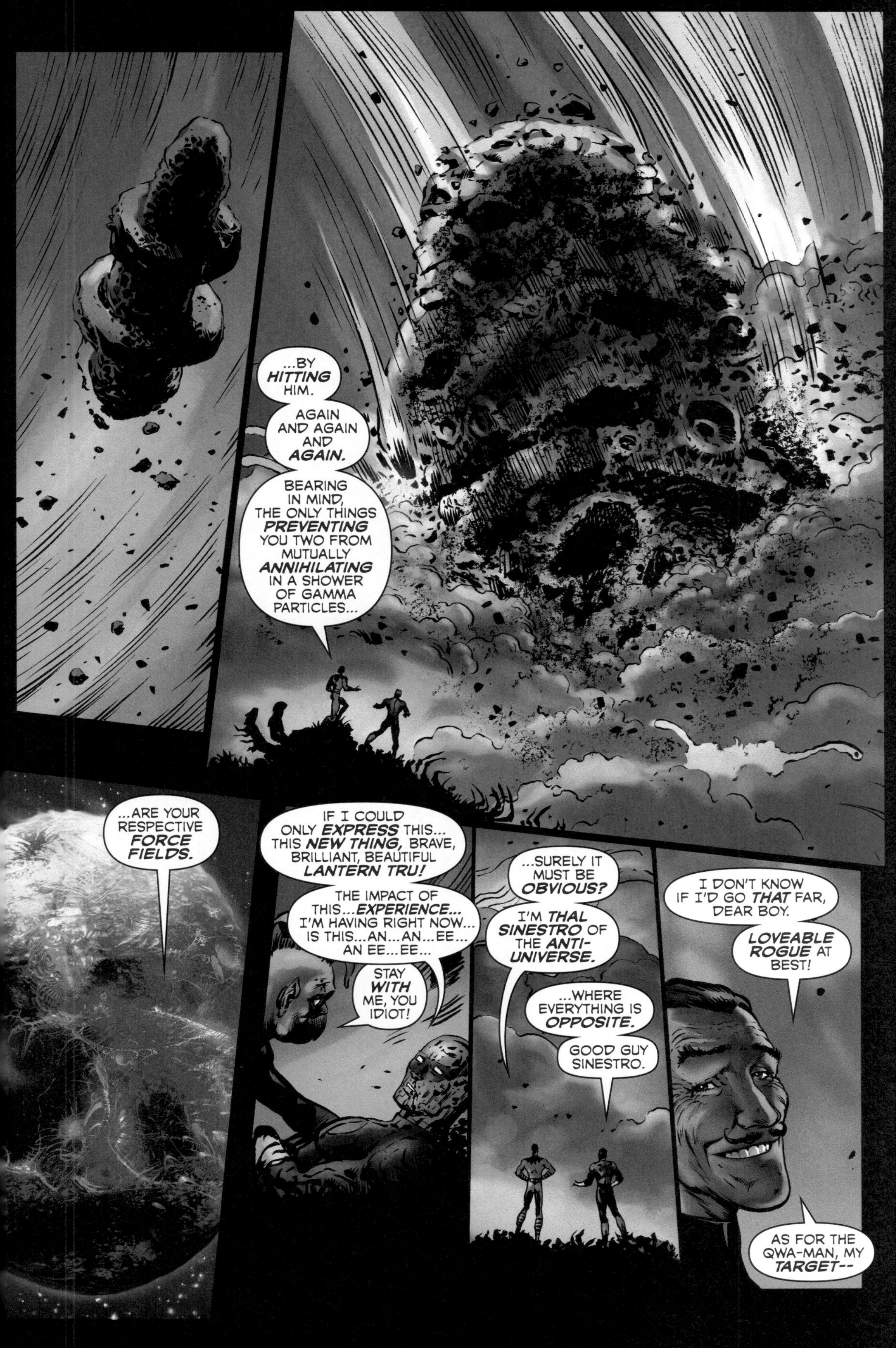
...BY HITTING HIM.
AGAIN AND AGAIN AND AGAIN.
BEARING IN MIND, THE ONLY THINGS PREVENTING YOU TWO FROM MUTUALLY ANNIHILATING IN A SHOWER OF GAMMA PARTICLES...
...ARE YOUR RESPECTIVE FORCE FIELDS.
IF I COULD ONLY EXPRESS THIS... THIS NEW THING, BRAVE, BRILLIANT, BEAUTIFUL LANTERN TRU!
THE IMPACT OF THIS...EXPERIENCE... I'M HAVING RIGHT NOW... IS THIS...AN...AN...EE... AN EE...EE...
STAY WITH ME, YOU IDIOT!
...SURELY IT MUST BE OBVIOUS?
I'M THAL SINESTRO OF THE ANTI-UNIVERSE.
...WHERE EVERYTHING IS OPPOSITE.
GOOD GUY SINESTRO.
I DON'T KNOW IF I'D GO THAT FAR, DEAR BOY.
LOVEABLE ROGUE AT BEST!
AS FOR THE QWA-MAN, MY TARGET--

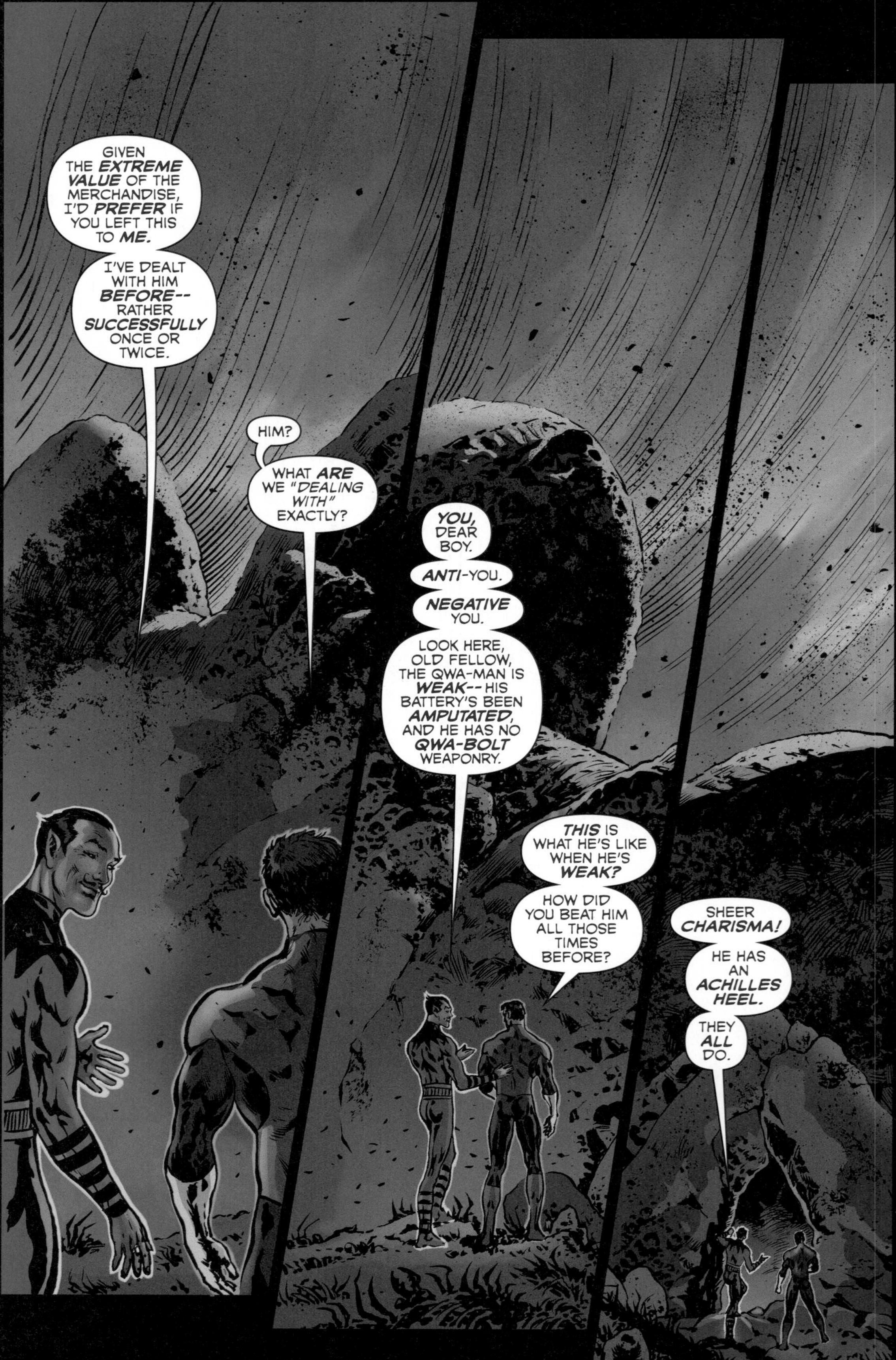
GIVEN THE EXTREME VALUE OF THE MERCHANDISE, I'D PREFER IF YOU LEFT THIS TO ME.
I'VE DEALT WITH HIM BEFORE-- RATHER SUCCESSFULLY ONCE OR TWICE.
HIM?
WHAT ARE WE "DEALING WITH" EXACTLY?
YOU, DEAR BOY.
ANTI-YOU.
NEGATIVE YOU.
LOOK HERE, OLD FELLOW, THE QWA-MAN IS WEAK-- HIS BATTERY'S BEEN AMPUTATED, AND HE HAS NO QWA-BOLT WEAPONRY.
THIS IS WHAT HE'S LIKE WHEN HE'S WEAK?
HOW DID YOU BEAT HIM ALL THOSE TIMES BEFORE?
SHEER CHARISMA!
HE HAS AN ACHILLES HEEL.
THEY ALL DO.

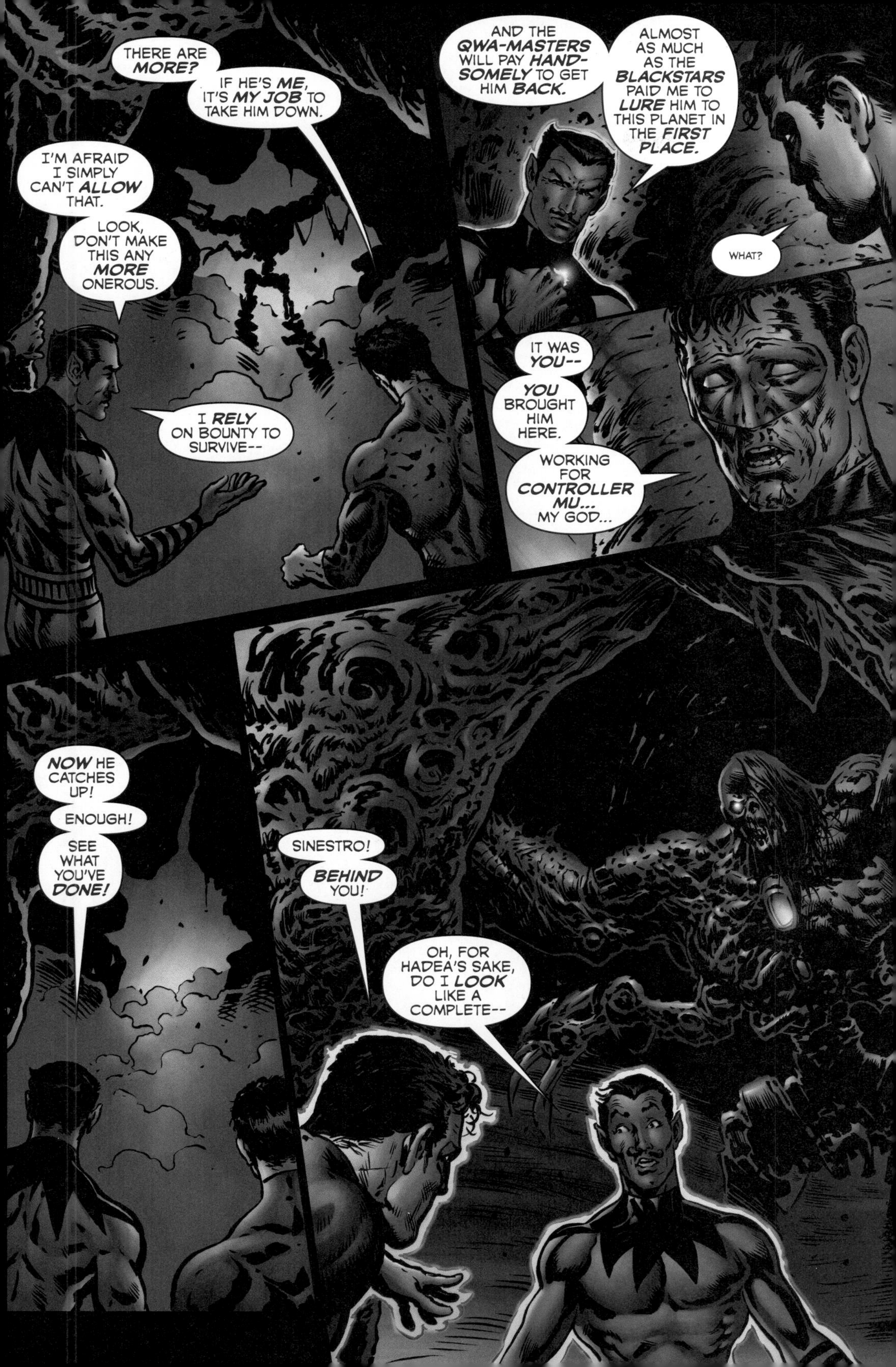
THERE ARE MORE?
IF HE'S ME, IT'S MY JOB TO TAKE HIM DOWN.
I'M AFRAID I SIMPLY CAN'T ALLOW THAT.
LOOK, DON'T MAKE THIS ANY MORE ONEROUS.
I RELY ON BOUNTY TO SURVIVE--
AND THE QWA-MASTERS WILL PAY HANDSOMELY TO GET HIM BACK.
ALMOST AS MUCH AS THE BLACKSTARS PAID ME TO LURE HIM TO THIS PLANET IN THE FIRST PLACE.
WHAT?
IT WAS YOU--
YOU BROUGHT HIM HERE.
WORKING FOR CONTROLLER MU... MY GOD...
NOW HE CATCHES UP!
ENOUGH!
SEE WHAT YOU'VE DONE!
SINESTRO!
BEHIND YOU!
OH, FOR HADEA'S SAKE, DO I LOOK LIKE A COMPLETE--

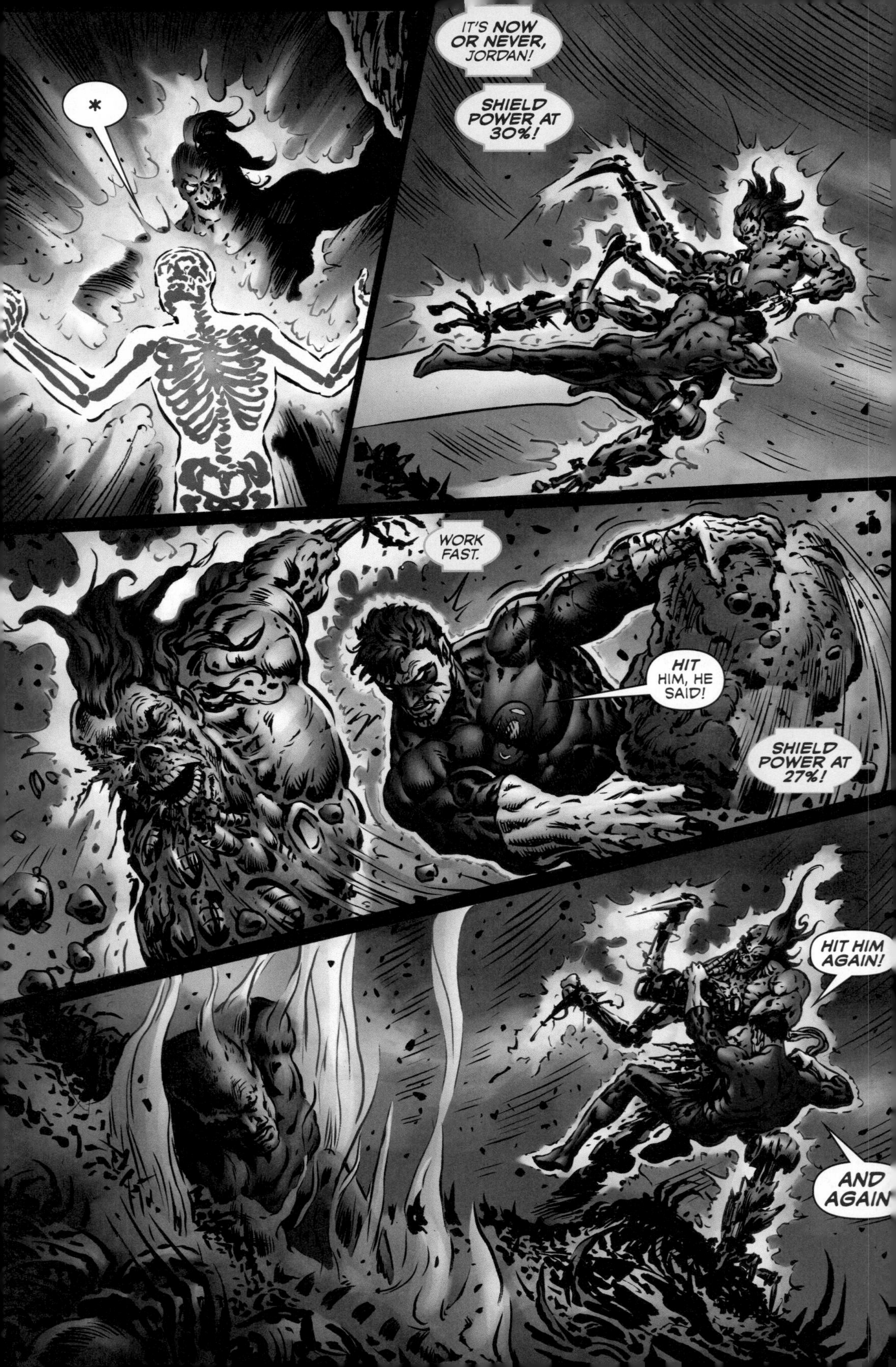
*
IT'S NOW OR NEVER, JORDAN!
SHIELD POWER AT 30%!
WORK FAST.
HIT HIM, HE SAID!
SHIELD POWER AT 27%!
HIT HIM AGAIN!
AND AGAIN

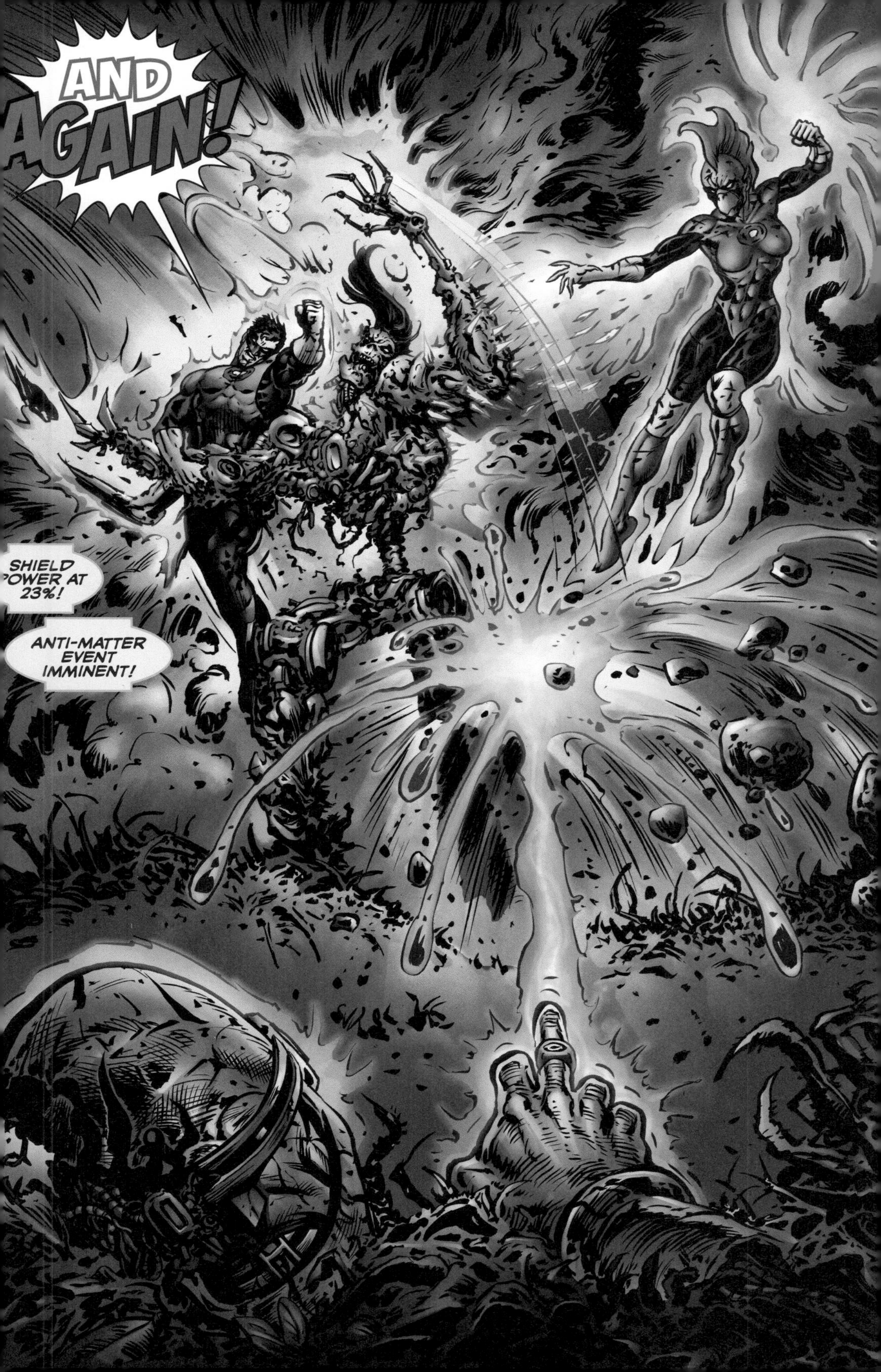
AND AGAIN!
SHIELD POWER AT 23%!
ANTI-MATTER EVENT IMMINENT!

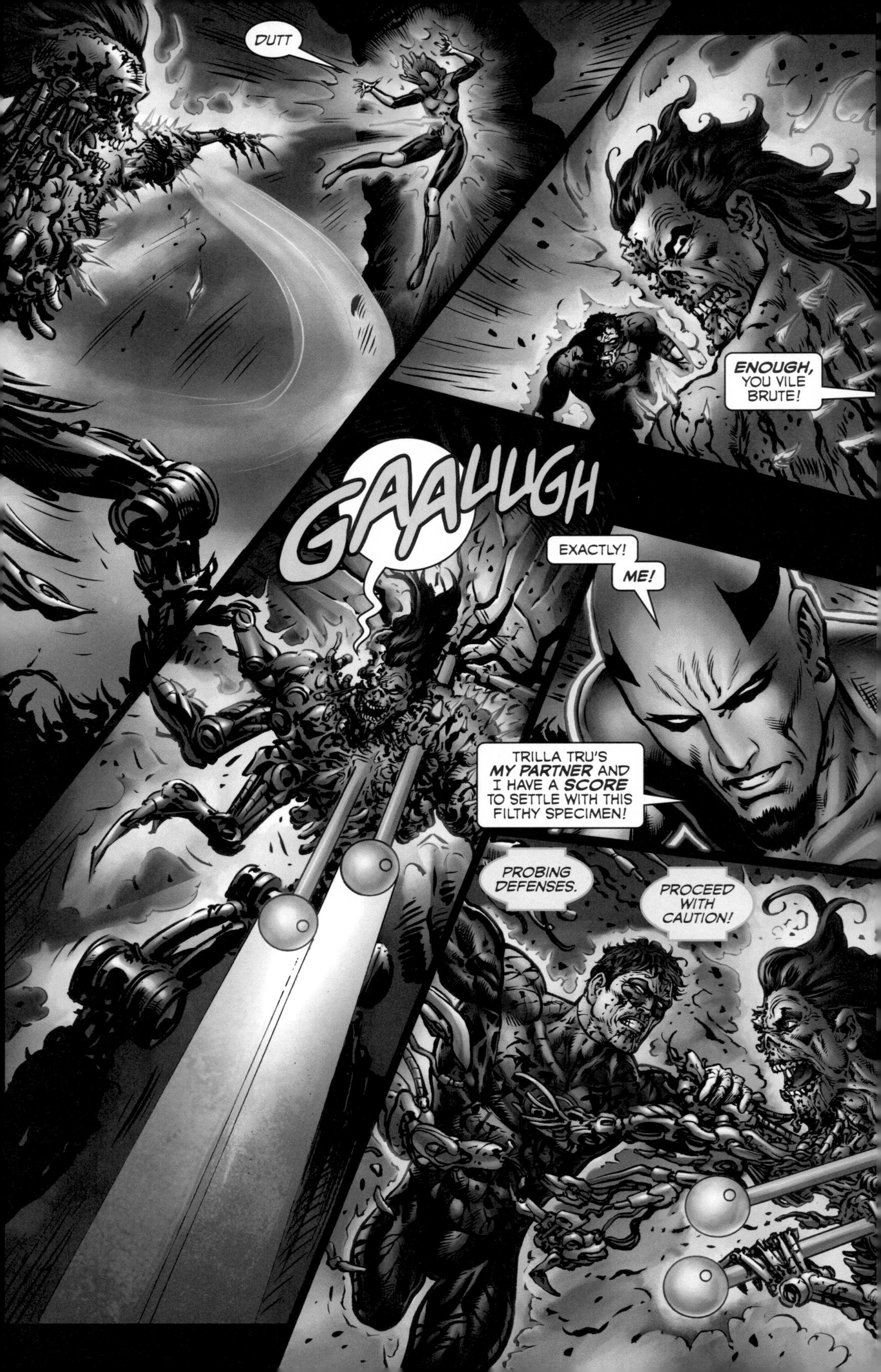
DUTT
ENOUGH, YOU VILE BRUTE!
GAAUGH
EXACTLY! ME!
TRILLA TRU'S MY PARTNER AND I HAVE A SCORE TO SETTLE WITH THIS FILTHY SPECIMEN!
PROBING DEFENSES.
PROCEED WITH CAUTION!

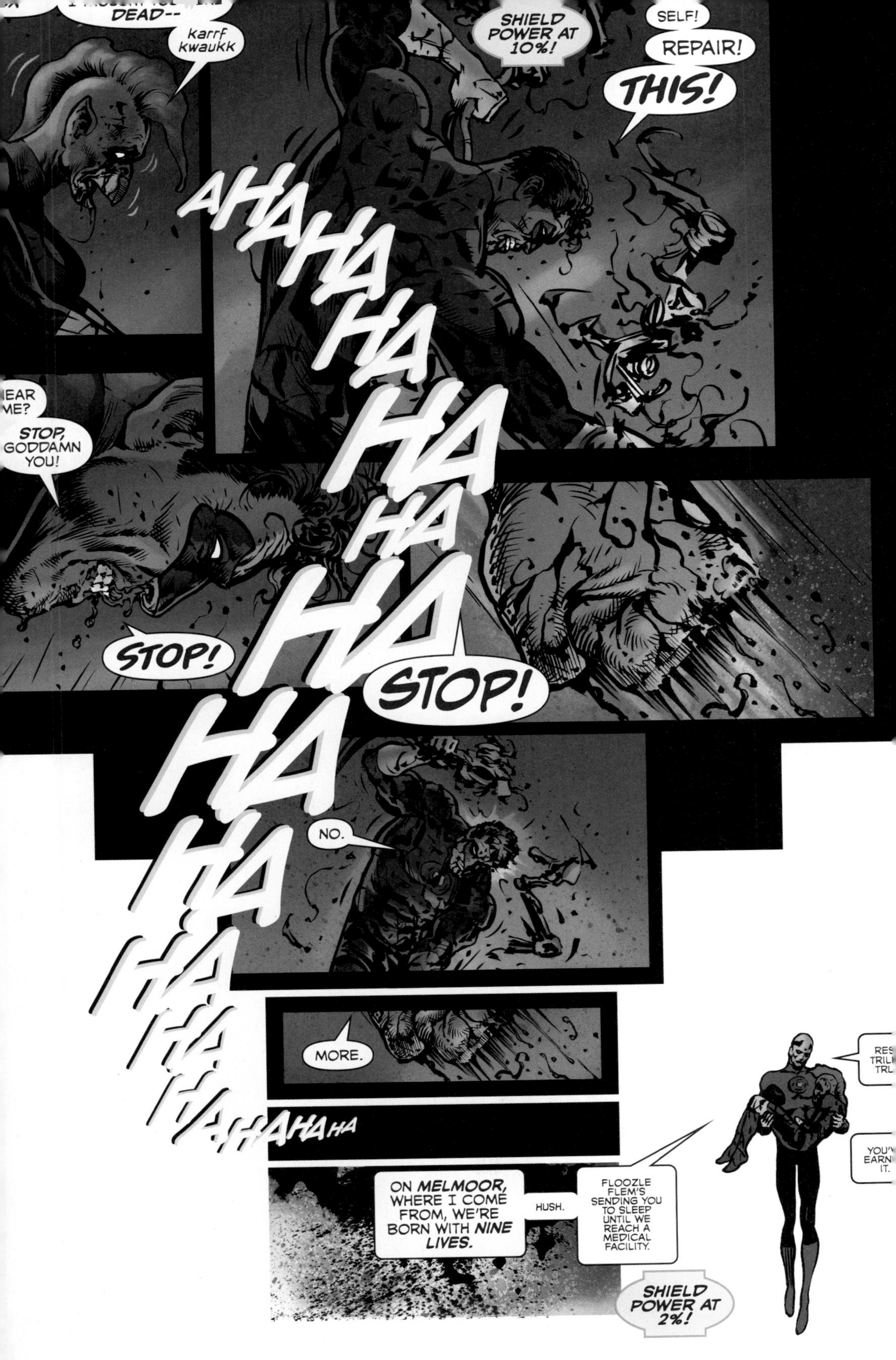
DEAD--
karrf kwaukk
SHIELD POWER AT 10%!
SELF!
REPAIR!
THIS!
AHAHAHAHAHAHAHAHAHAHAHAHAHAHAHAHA
STOP, GODDAMN YOU!
STOP!
STOP!
NO.
MORE.
ON MELMOOR, WHERE I COME FROM, WE'RE BORN WITH NINE LIVES.
HUSH.
FLOOZLE FLEM'S SENDING YOU TO SLEEP UNTIL WE REACH A MEDICAL FACILITY.
SHIELD POWER AT 2%!

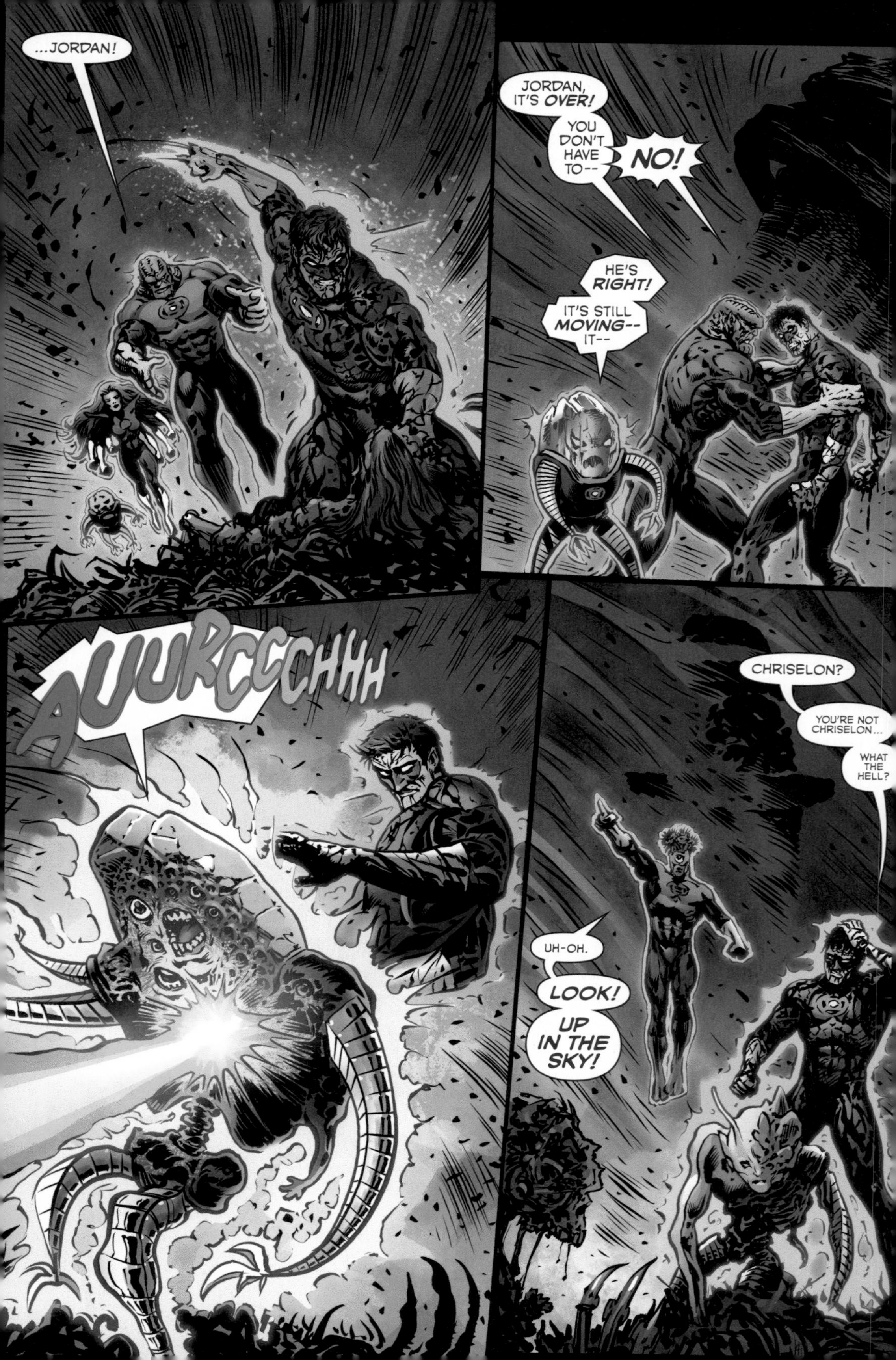
...JORDAN!
JORDAN, IT'S OVER!
YOU DON'T HAVE TO--
NO!
HE'S RIGHT!
IT'S STILL MOVING-- IT--
AUURCCCHHH
CHRISELON?
YOU'RE NOT CHRISELON...
WHAT THE HELL?
UH-OH.
LOOK!
UP IN THE SKY!

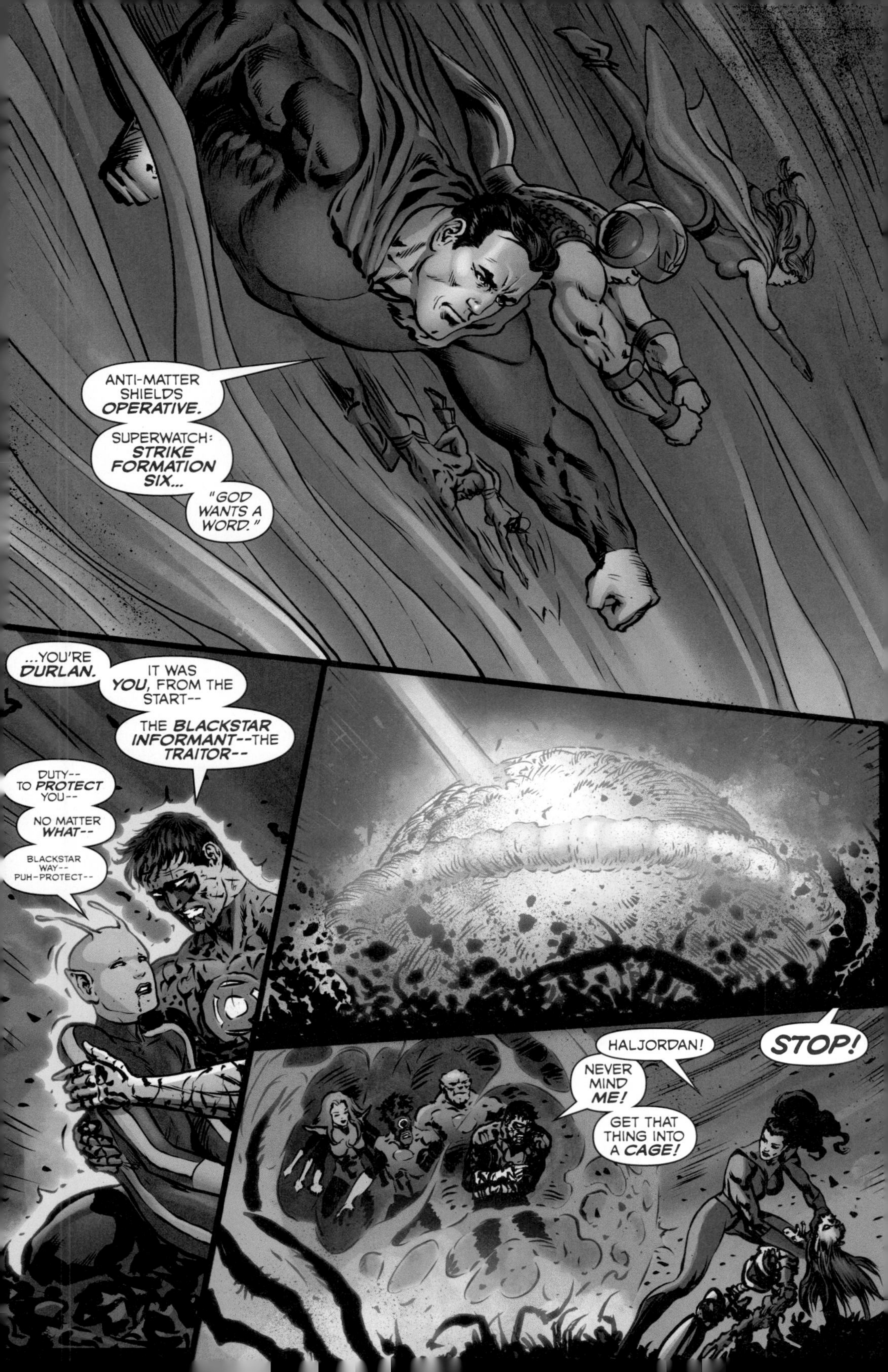
ANTI-MATTER SHIELDS OPERATIVE.
SUPERWATCH: STRIKE FORMATION SIX...
"GOD WANTS A WORD."
...YOU'RE DURLAN.
IT WAS YOU, FROM THE START--
THE BLACKSTAR INFORMANT--THE TRAITOR--
DUTY-- TO PROTECT YOU--
NO MATTER WHAT--
BLACKSTAR WAY-- PUH-PROTECT--
HALJORDAN!
NEVER MIND ME!
GET THAT THING INTO A CAGE!
STOP!

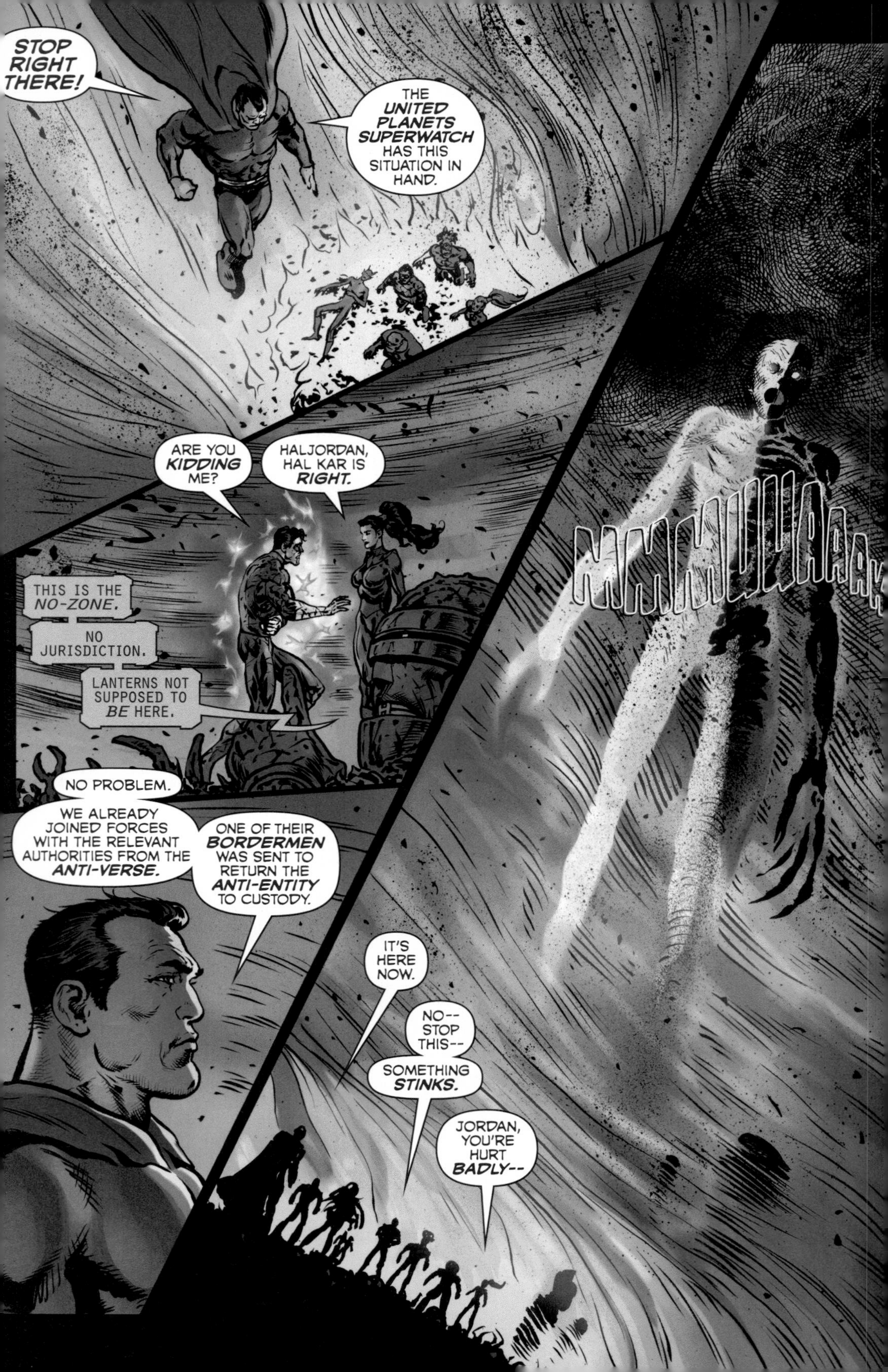
STOP RIGHT THERE!
THE UNITED PLANETS SUPERWATCH HAS THIS SITUATION IN HAND.
ARE YOU KIDDING ME?
HALJORDAN, HAL KAR IS RIGHT.
THIS IS THE NO-ZONE.
NO JURISDICTION.
LANTERNS NOT SUPPOSED TO BE HERE.
NO PROBLEM.
WE ALREADY JOINED FORCES WITH THE RELEVANT AUTHORITIES FROM THE ANTI-VERSE.
ONE OF THEIR BORDERMEN WAS SENT TO RETURN THE ANTI-ENTITY TO CUSTODY.
MMMMUUWAAAA
IT'S HERE NOW.
NO-- STOP THIS--
SOMETHING STINKS.
JORDAN, YOU'RE HURT BADLY--

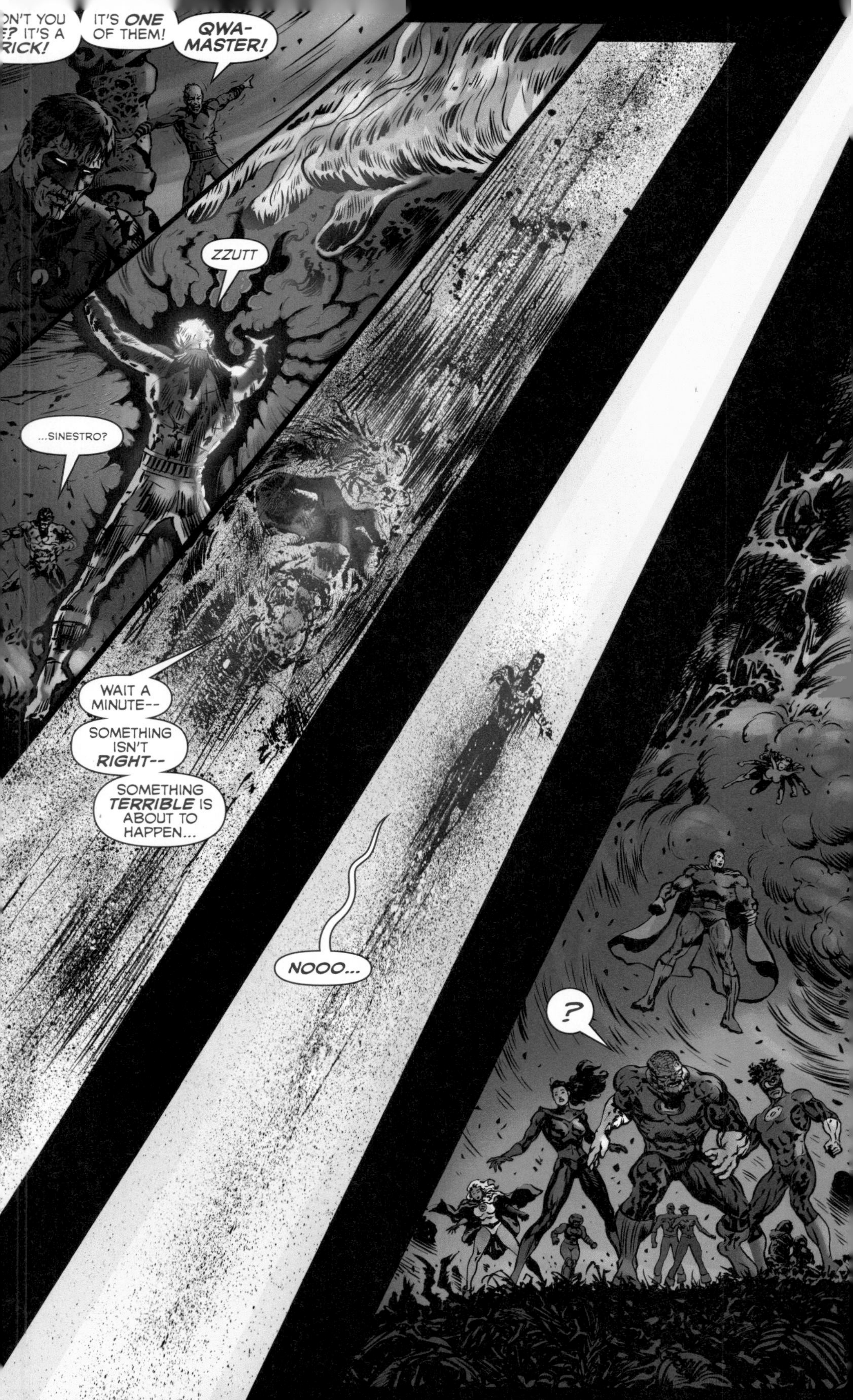
IT'S ONE OF THEM!
QWA-MASTER!
ZZUTT
...SINESTRO?
WAIT A MINUTE--
SOMETHING ISN'T RIGHT--
SOMETHING TERRIBLE IS ABOUT TO HAPPEN...
NOOO...
?

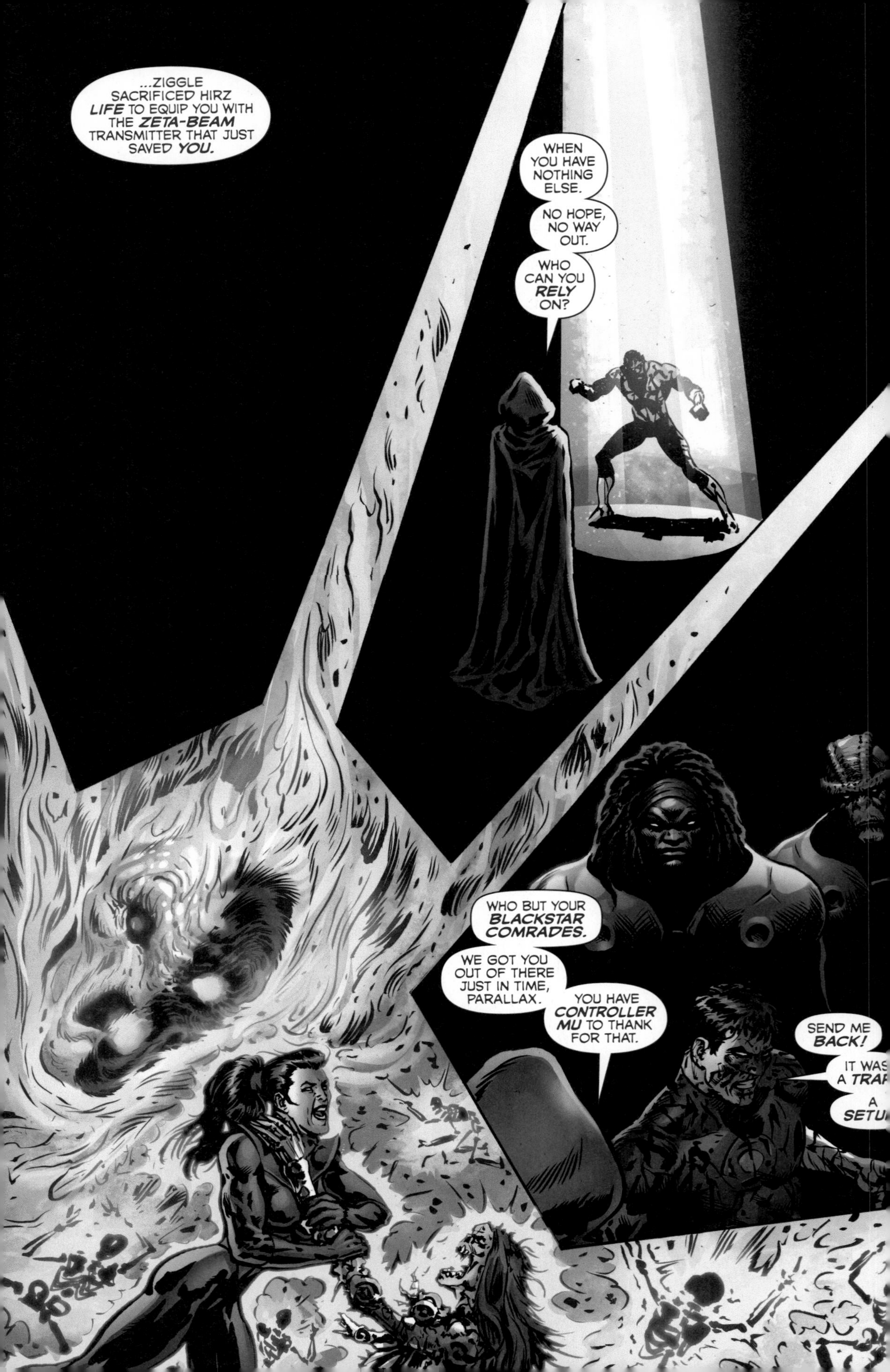
...ZIGGLE SACRIFICED HIRZ LIFE TO EQUIP YOU WITH THE ZETA-BEAM TRANSMITTER THAT JUST SAVED YOU.
WHEN YOU HAVE NOTHING ELSE.
NO HOPE, NO WAY OUT.
WHO CAN YOU RELY ON?
WHO BUT YOUR BLACKSTAR COMRADES.
WE GOT YOU OUT OF THERE JUST IN TIME, PARALLAX.
YOU HAVE CONTROLLER MU TO THANK FOR THAT.
SEND ME BACK!

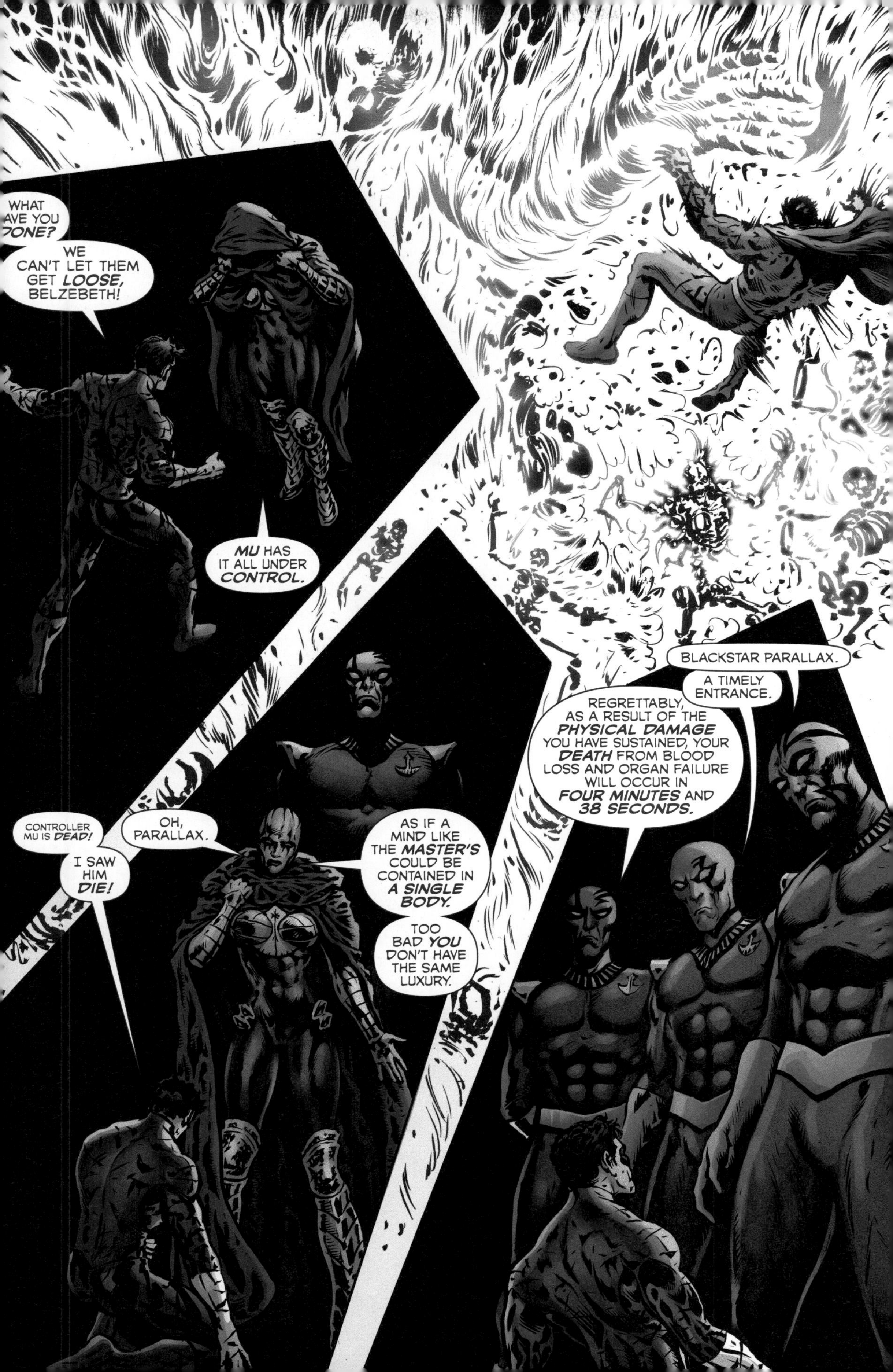
WHAT HAVE YOU DONE?
WE CAN'T LET THEM GET LOOSE, BELZEBETH!
MU HAS IT ALL UNDER CONTROL.
CONTROLLER MU IS DEAD!
I SAW HIM DIE!
OH, PARALLAX.
AS IF A MIND LIKE THE MASTER'S COULD BE CONTAINED IN A SINGLE BODY.
TOO BAD YOU DON'T HAVE THE SAME LUXURY.
BLACKSTAR PARALLAX.
A TIMELY ENTRANCE.
REGRETTABLY, AS A RESULT OF THE PHYSICAL DAMAGE YOU HAVE SUSTAINED, YOUR DEATH FROM BLOOD LOSS AND ORGAN FAILURE WILL OCCUR IN FOUR MINUTES AND 38 SECONDS.

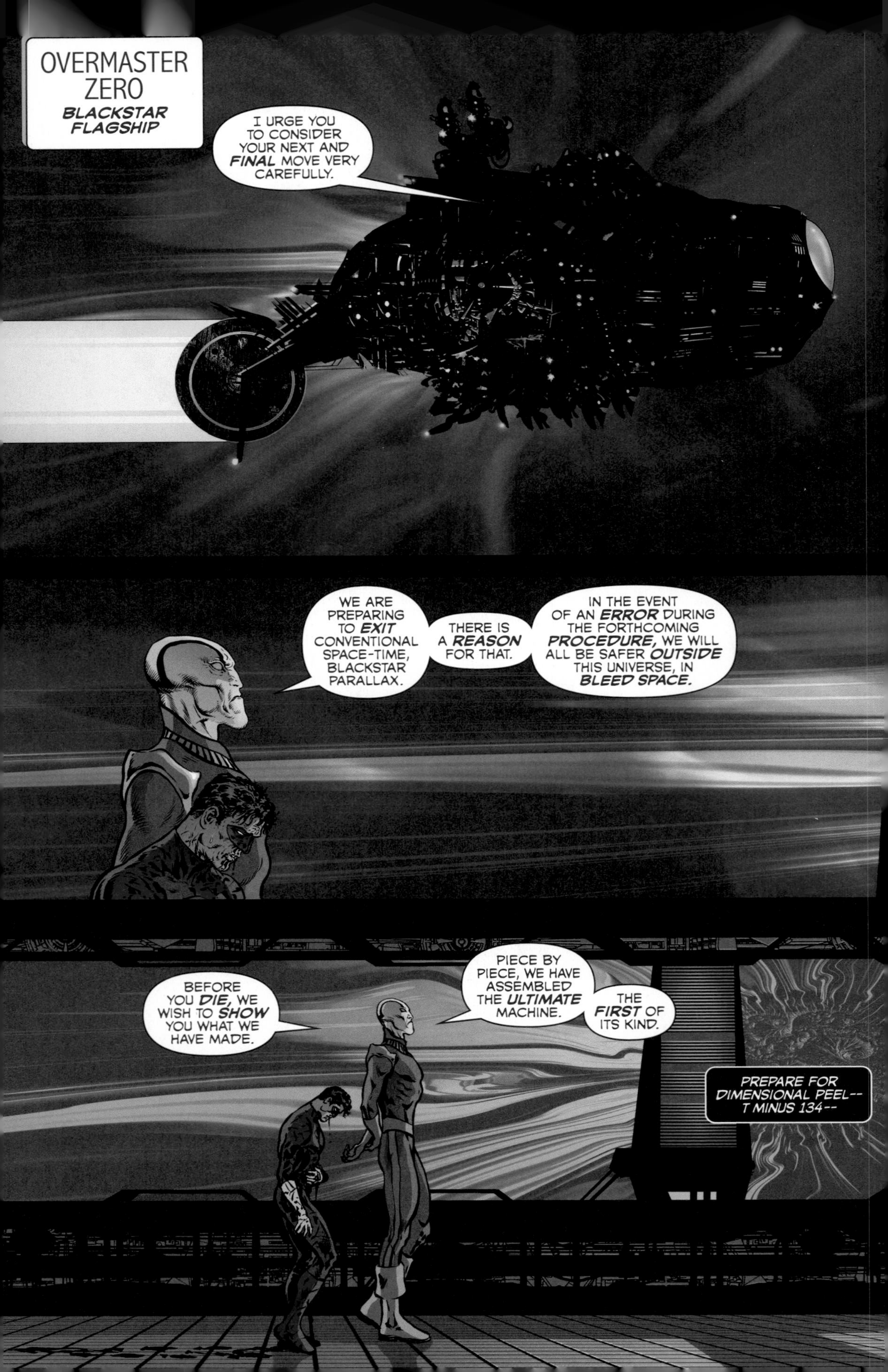
OVERMASTER ZERO
BLACKSTAR FLAGSHIP
I URGE YOU TO CONSIDER YOUR NEXT AND FINAL MOVE VERY CAREFULLY.
WE ARE PREPARING TO EXIT CONVENTIONAL SPACE-TIME, BLACKSTAR PARALLAX.
THERE IS A REASON FOR THAT.
IN THE EVENT OF AN ERROR DURING THE FORTHCOMING PROCEDURE, WE WILL ALL BE SAFER OUTSIDE THIS UNIVERSE, IN BLEED SPACE.
BEFORE YOU DIE, WE WISH TO SHOW YOU WHAT WE HAVE MADE.
PIECE BY PIECE, WE HAVE ASSEMBLED THE ULTIMATE MACHINE.
THE FIRST OF ITS KIND.
PREPARE FOR DIMENSIONAL PEEL-- T MINUS 134--

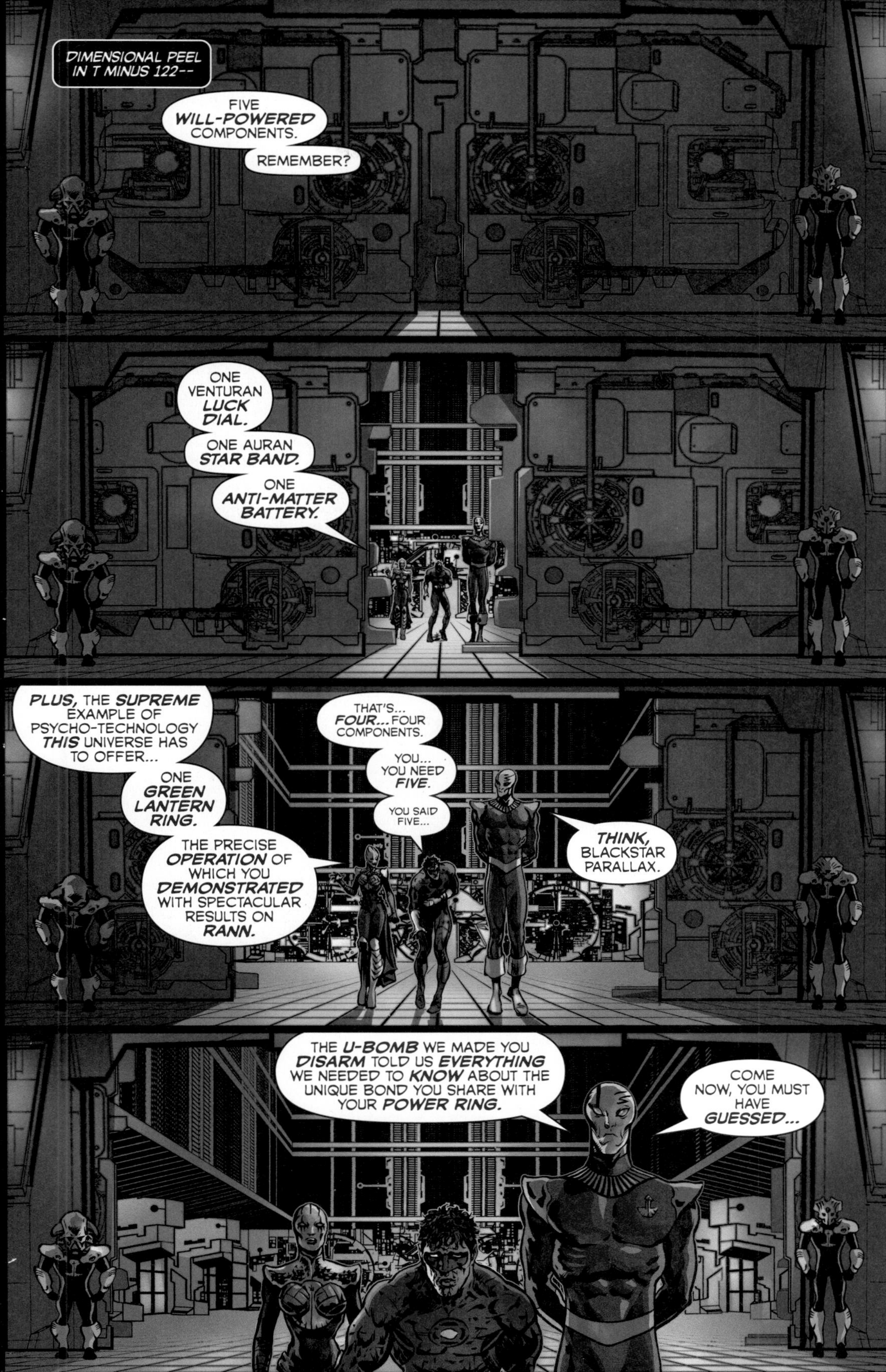
DIMENSIONAL PEEL IN T MINUS 122--
FIVE WILL-POWERED COMPONENTS.
REMEMBER?
ONE VENTURAN LUCK DIAL.
ONE AURAN STAR BAND.
ONE ANTI-MATTER BATTERY.
PLUS, THE SUPREME EXAMPLE OF PSYCHO-TECHNOLOGY THIS UNIVERSE HAS TO OFFER...
ONE GREEN LANTERN RING.
THE PRECISE OPERATION OF WHICH YOU DEMONSTRATED WITH SPECTACULAR RESULTS ON RANN.
THAT'S... FOUR... FOUR COMPONENTS.
YOU... YOU NEED FIVE.
YOU SAID FIVE...
THINK, BLACKSTAR PARALLAX.
THE U-BOMB WE MADE YOU DISARM TOLD US EVERYTHING WE NEEDED TO KNOW ABOUT THE UNIQUE BOND YOU SHARE WITH YOUR POWER RING.
COME NOW, YOU MUST HAVE GUESSED...

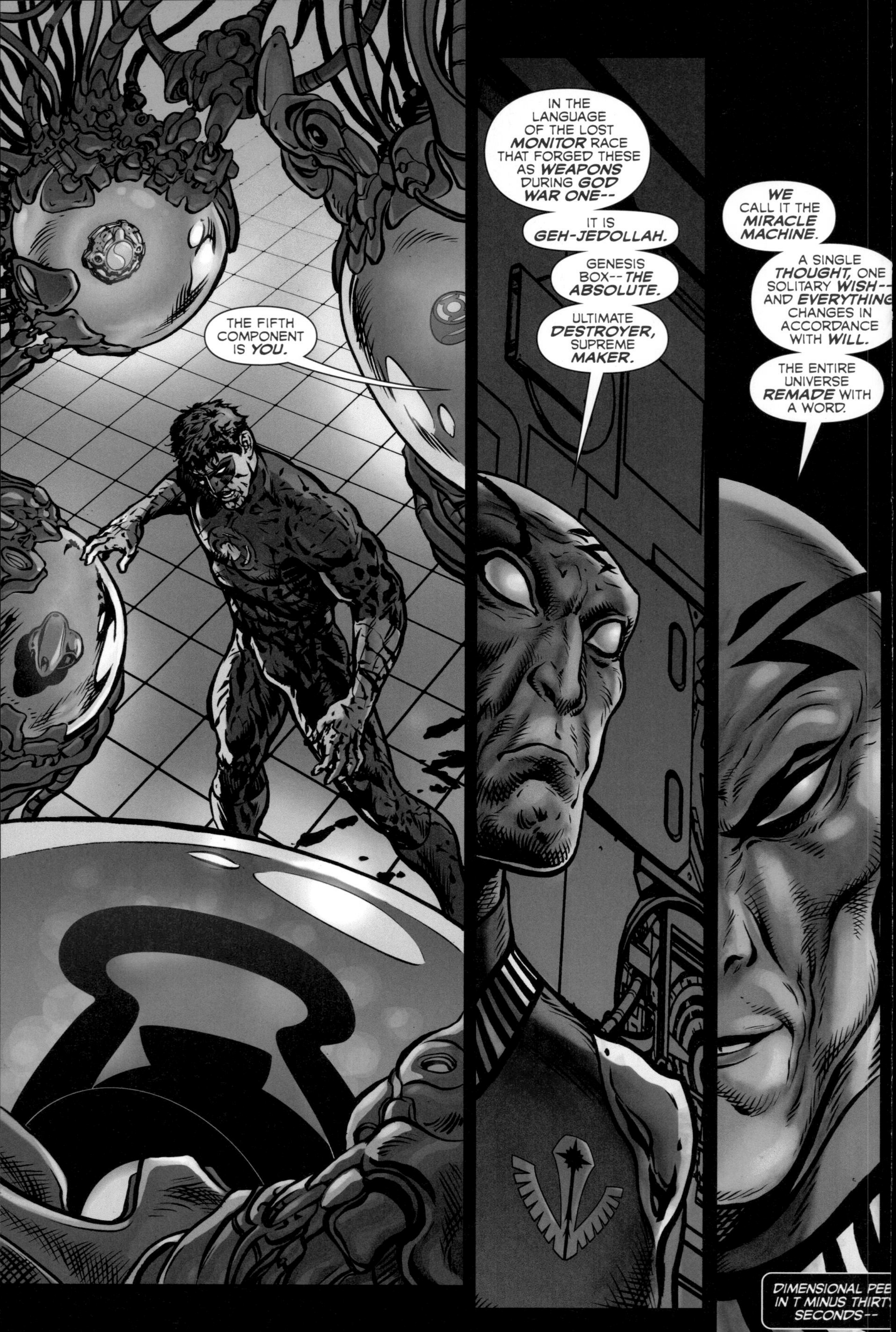
THE FIFTH COMPONENT IS YOU.
IN THE LANGUAGE OF THE LOST MONITOR RACE THAT FORGED THESE AS WEAPONS DURING GOD WAR ONE--
IT IS GEH-JEDOLLAH.
GENESIS BOX-- THE ABSOLUTE.
ULTIMATE DESTROYER, SUPREME MAKER.
WE CALL IT THE MIRACLE MACHINE.
A SINGLE THOUGHT, ONE SOLITARY WISH-- AND EVERYTHING CHANGES IN ACCORDANCE WITH WILL.
THE ENTIRE UNIVERSE REMADE WITH A WORD.
DIMENSIONAL PEE IN T MINUS THIRT SECONDS--

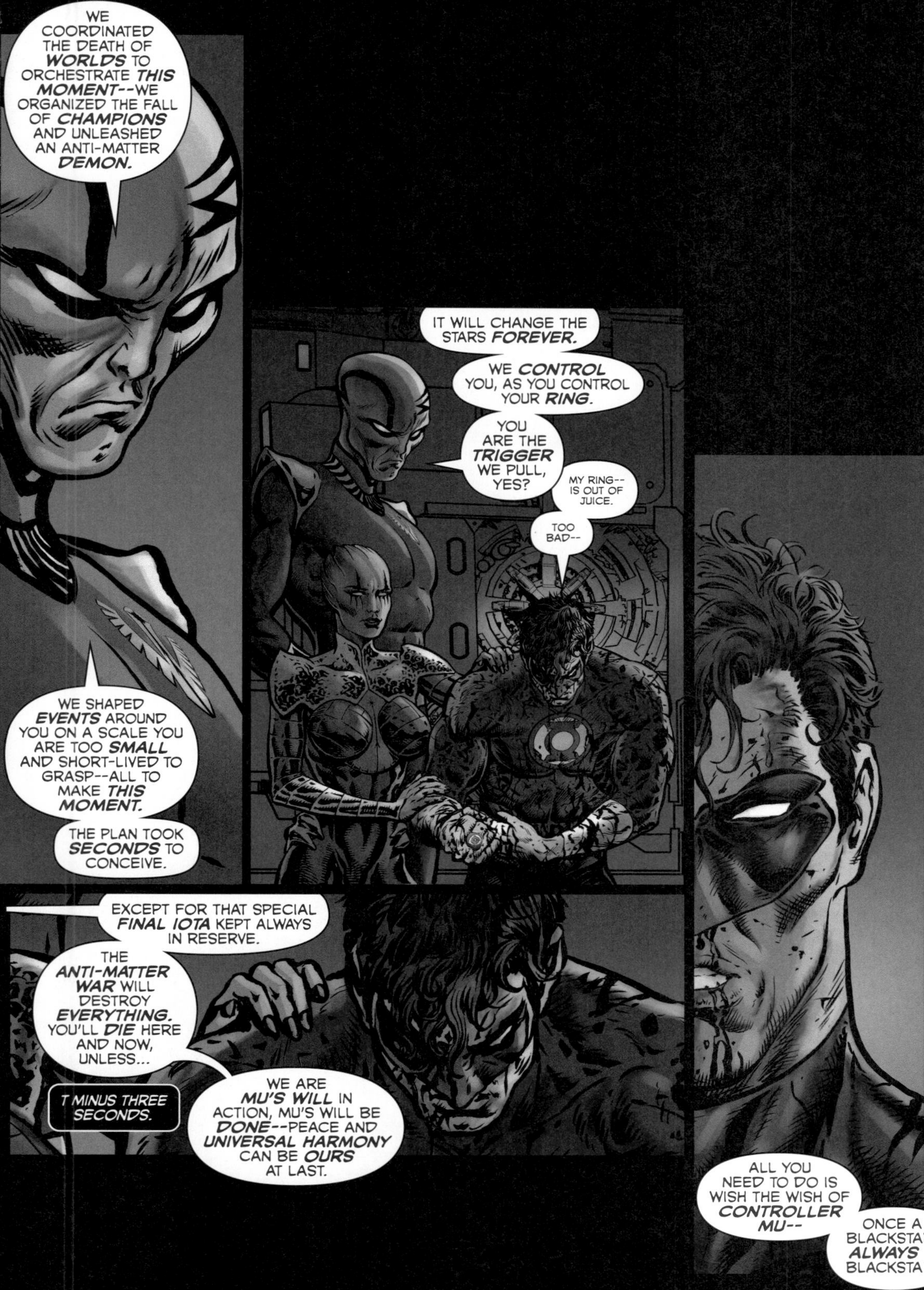
WE COORDINATED THE DEATH OF WORLDS TO ORCHESTRATE THIS MOMENT--WE ORGANIZED THE FALL OF CHAMPIONS AND UNLEASHED AN ANTI-MATTER DEMON.
WE SHAPED EVENTS AROUND YOU ON A SCALE YOU ARE TOO SMALL AND SHORT-LIVED TO GRASP--ALL TO MAKE THIS MOMENT.
THE PLAN TOOK SECONDS TO CONCEIVE.
IT WILL CHANGE THE STARS FOREVER.
WE CONTROL YOU, AS YOU CONTROL YOUR RING.
YOU ARE THE TRIGGER WE PULL, YES?
MY RING-- IS OUT OF JUICE.
TOO BAD--
EXCEPT FOR THAT SPECIAL FINAL IOTA KEPT ALWAYS IN RESERVE.
THE ANTI-MATTER WAR WILL DESTROY EVERYTHING. YOU'LL DIE HERE AND NOW, UNLESS...
T MINUS THREE SECONDS.
WE ARE MU'S WILL IN ACTION, MU'S WILL BE DONE--PEACE AND UNIVERSAL HARMONY CAN BE OURS AT LAST.
ALL YOU NEED TO DO IS WISH THE WISH OF CONTROLLER MU--

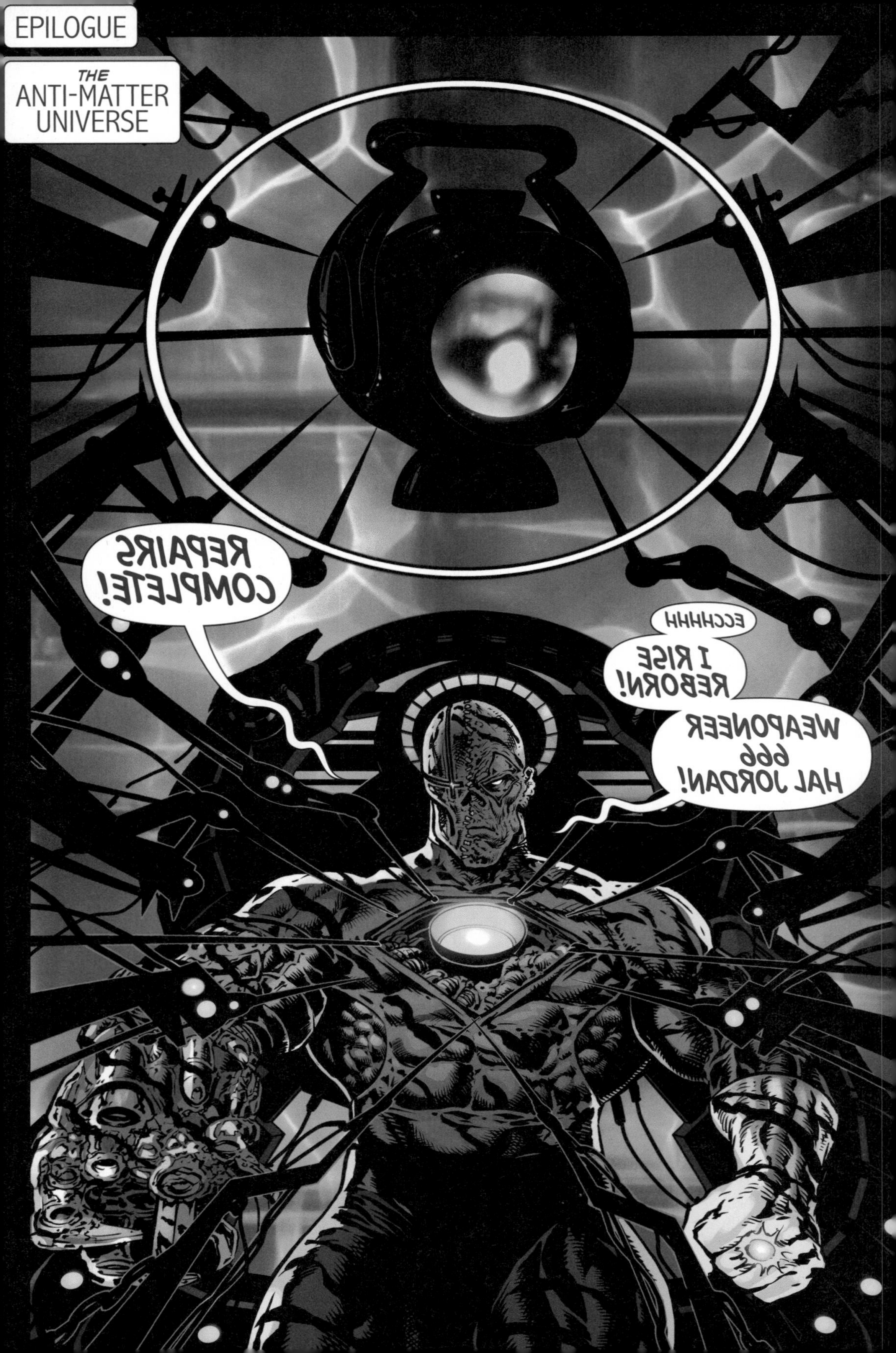
EPILOGUE
THE ANTI-MATTER UNIVERSE
REPAIRS COMPLETE!
ECCHHHH
I RISE REBORN!
WEAPONEER 666 HAL JORDAN!

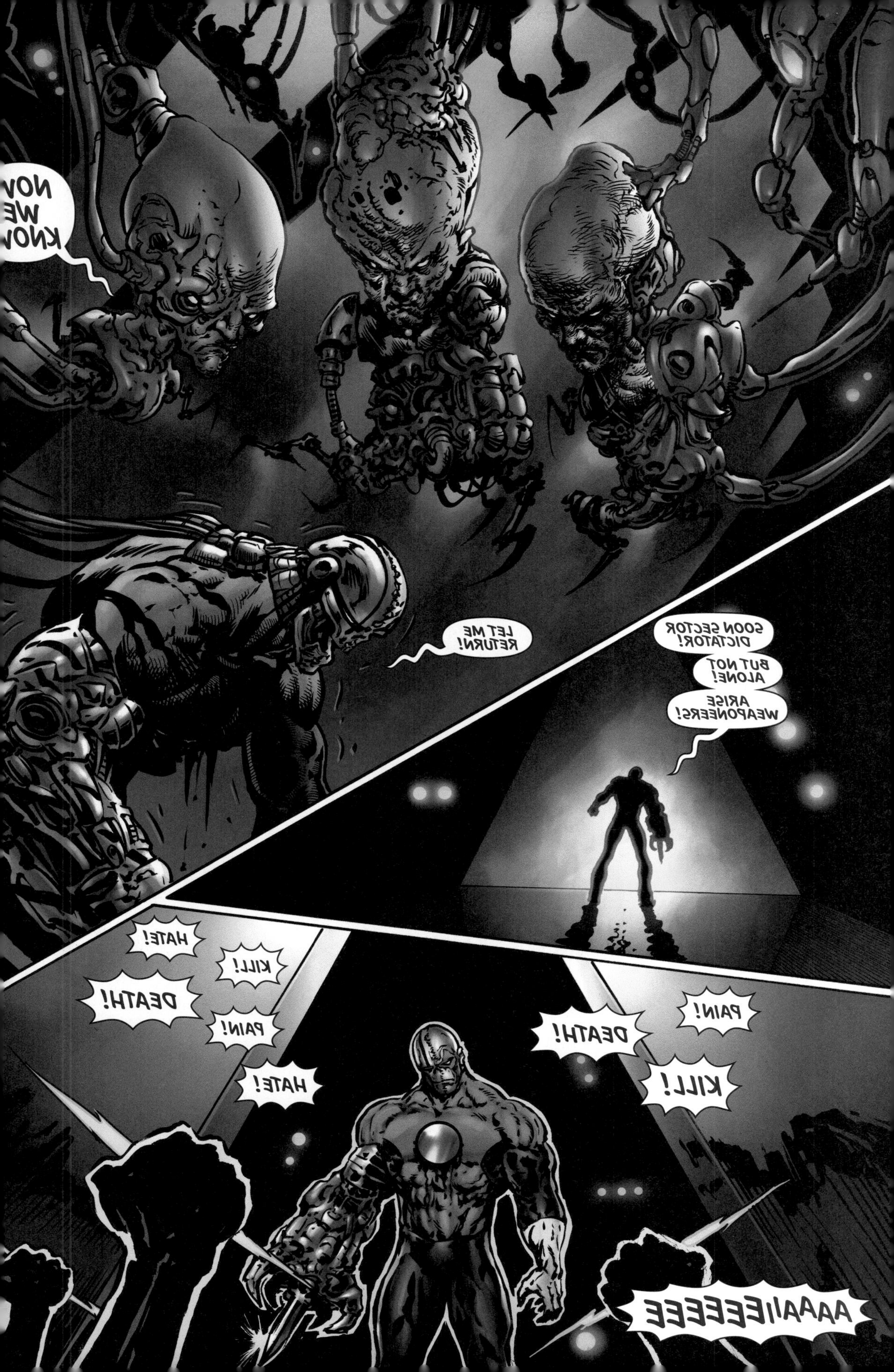
NOW WE KNOW
LET ME RETURN!
SOON SECTOR DICTATOR!
BUT NOT ALONE!
ARISE WEAPONEERS!
HATE!
KILL!
DEATH!
PAIN!
HATE!
PAIN!
DEATH!
KILL!
AAAAIIEEEEE

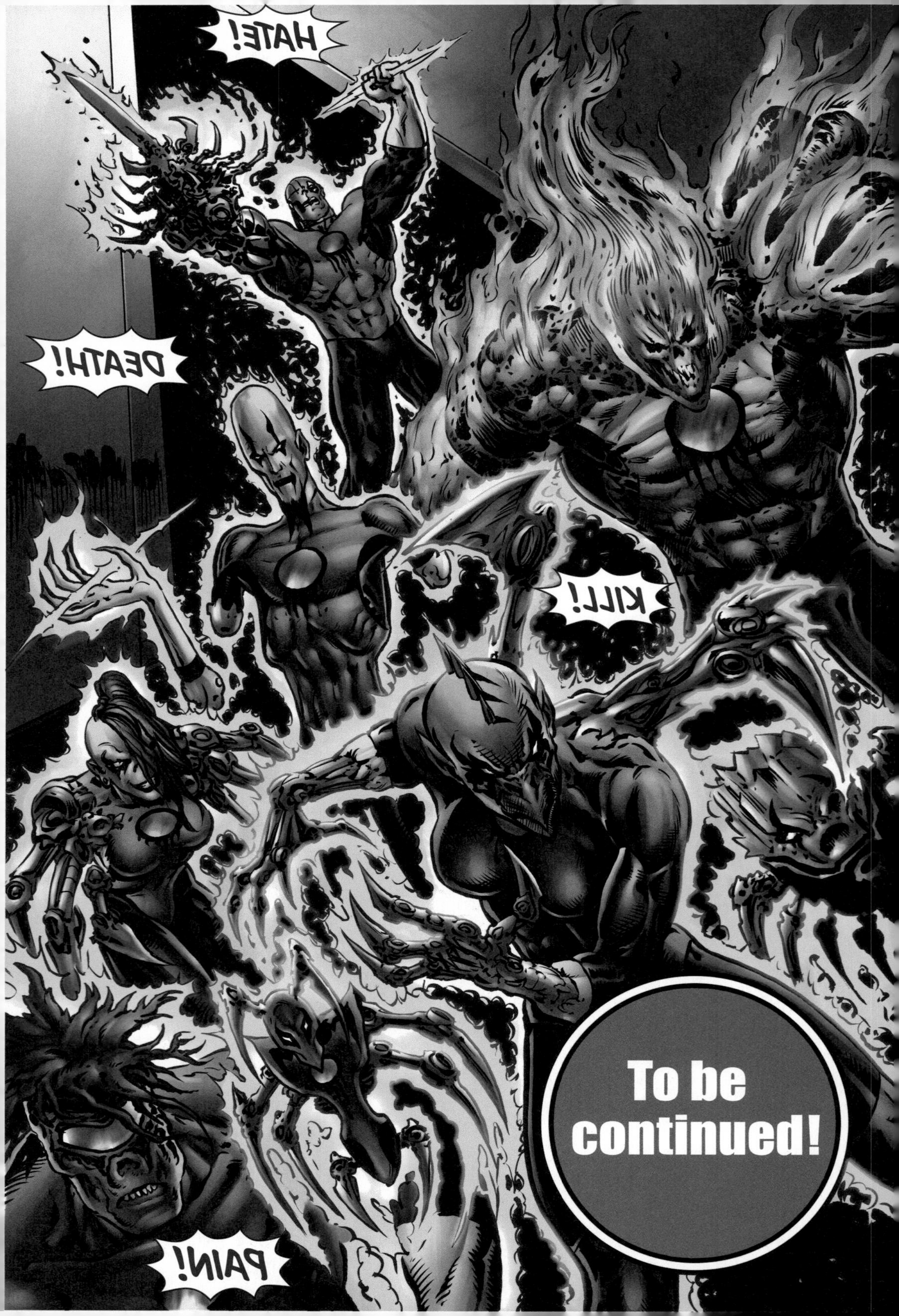
HATE!
DEATH!
KILL!
PAIN!
To be continued!

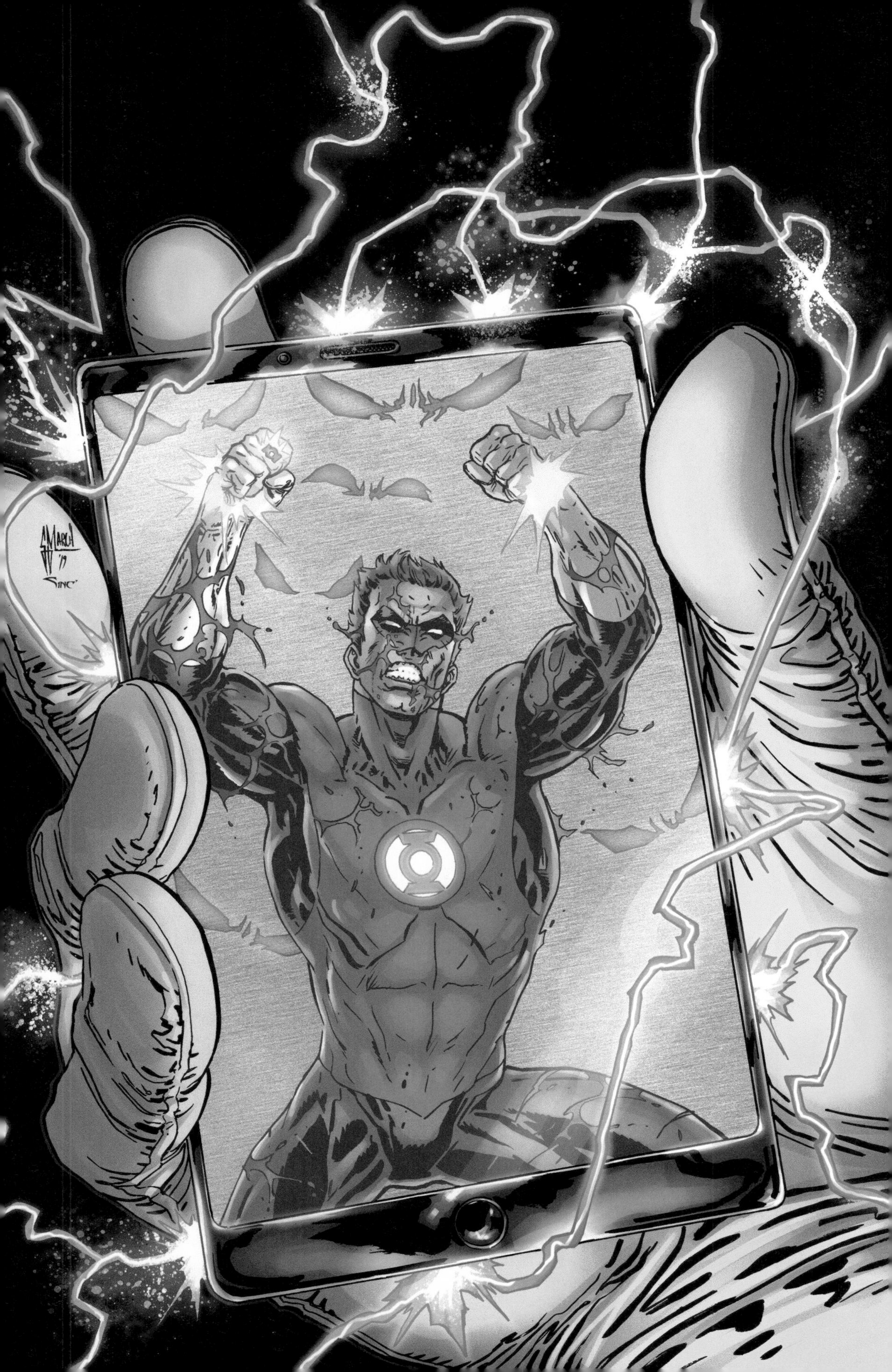

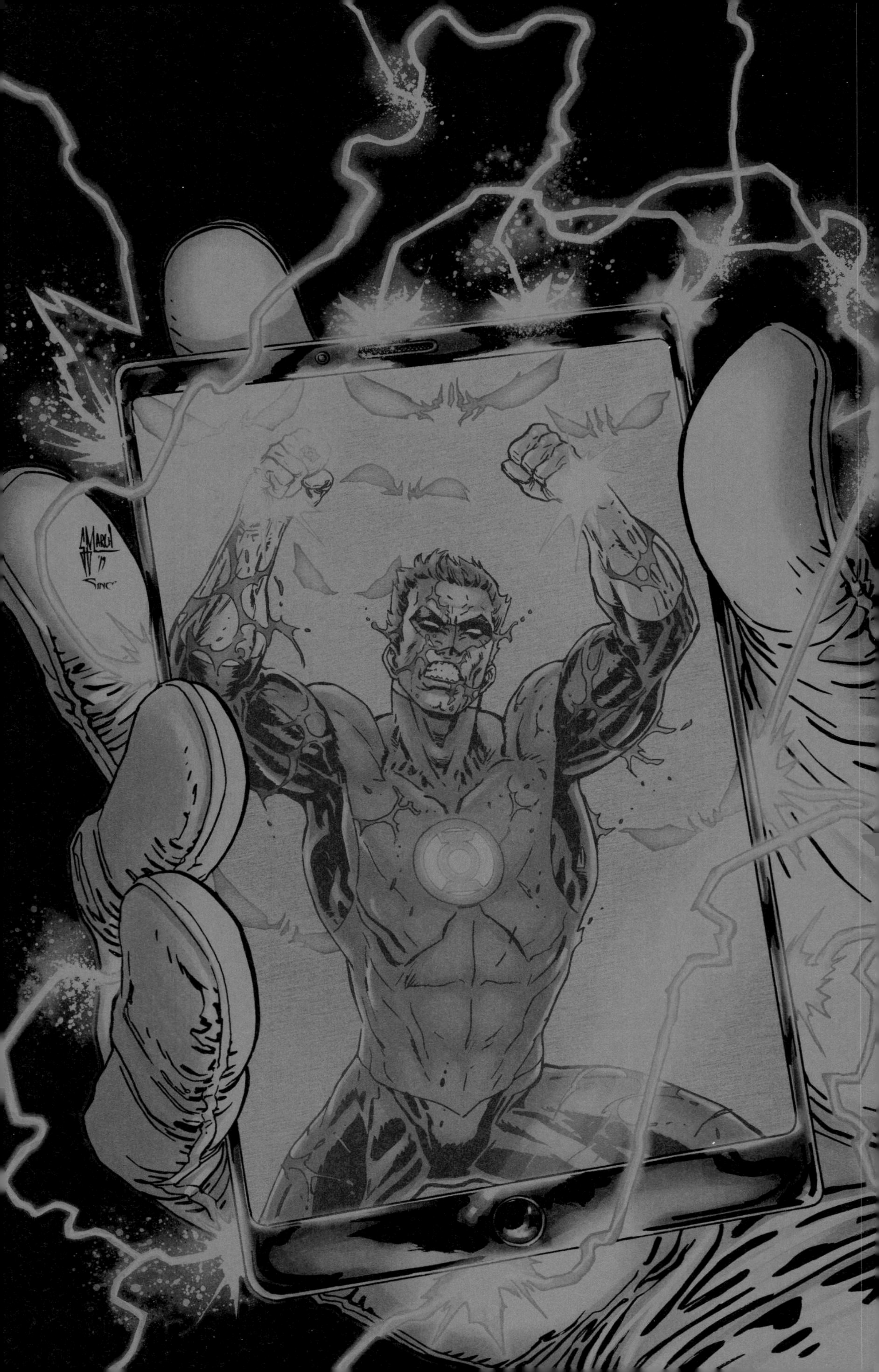

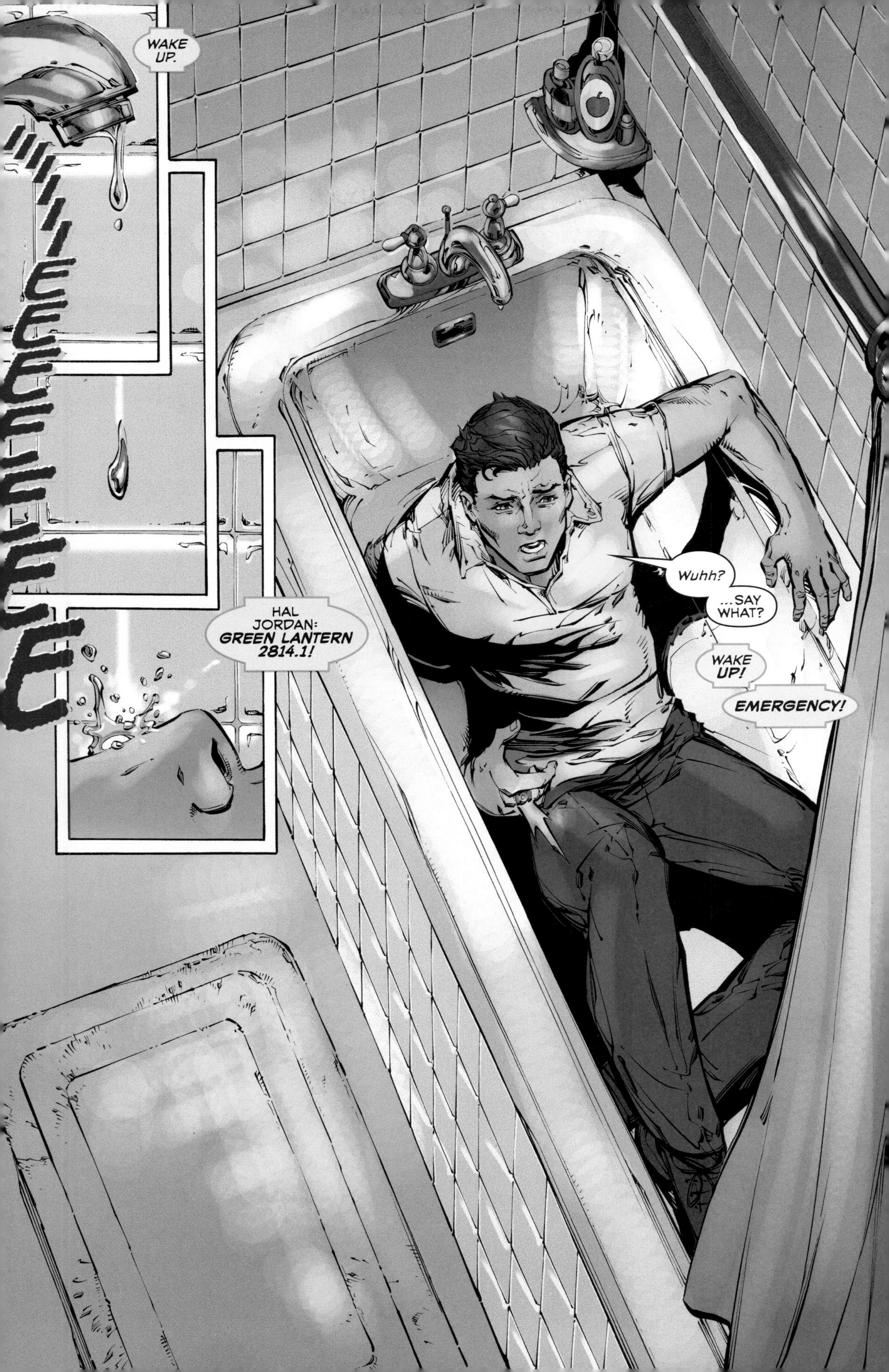
WAKE UP.
IIIIEEEEEEEEEE
HAL JORDAN: GREEN LANTERN 2814.1!
Wuhh?
...SAY WHAT?
WAKE UP!
EMERGENCY!

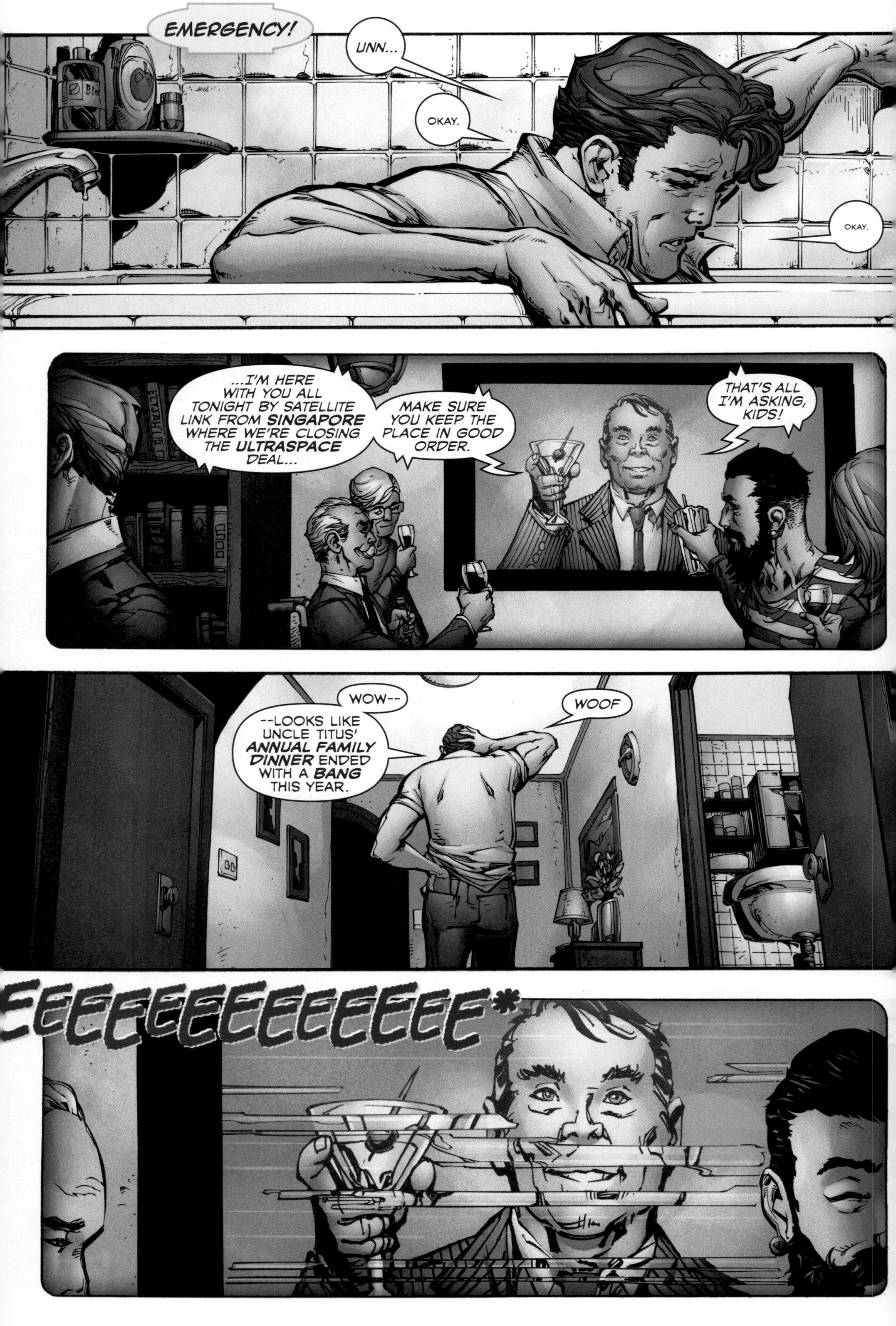
EMERGENCY!
UNN...
OKAY.
OKAY.
...I'M HERE WITH YOU ALL TONIGHT BY SATELLITE LINK FROM SINGAPORE WHERE WE'RE CLOSING THE ULTRASPACE DEAL...
MAKE SURE YOU KEEP THE PLACE IN GOOD ORDER.
THAT'S ALL I'M ASKING, KIDS!
WOW--
--LOOKS LIKE UNCLE TITUS' ANNUAL FAMILY DINNER ENDED WITH A BANG THIS YEAR.
WOOF
EEEEEEEEEEEEE*

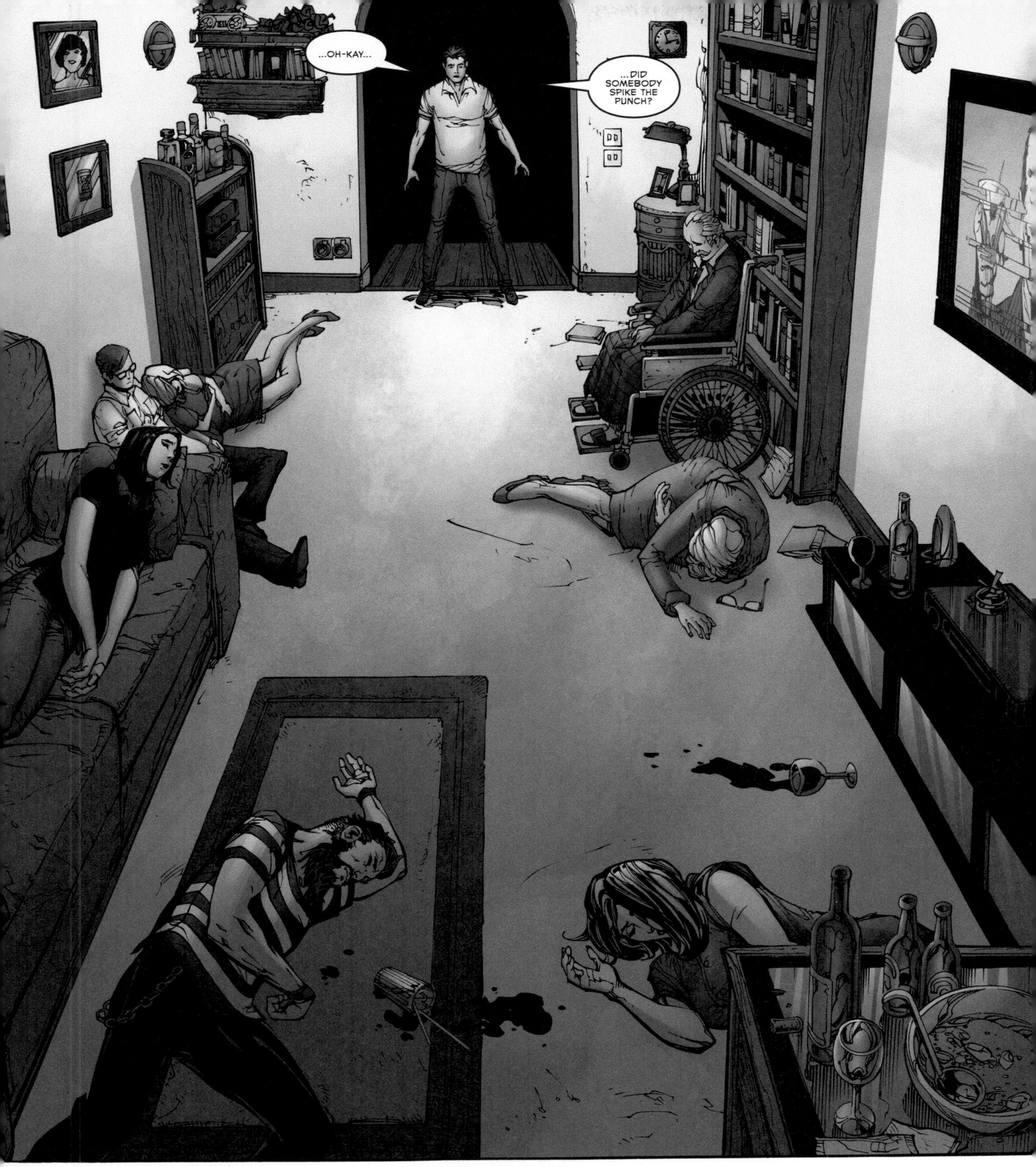
...OH-KAY...
...DID SOMEBODY SPIKE THE PUNCH?

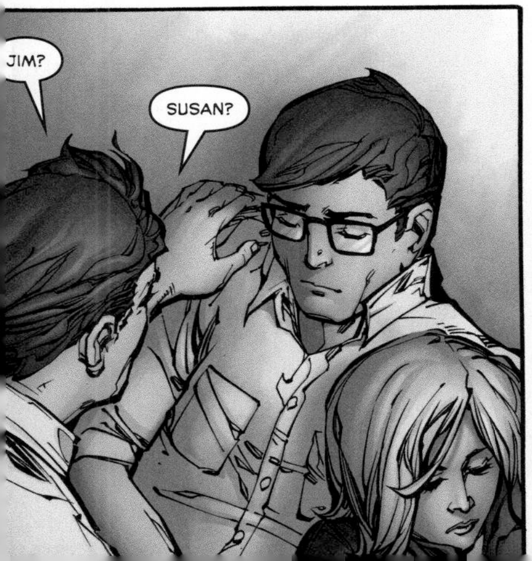
JIM?
SUSAN?

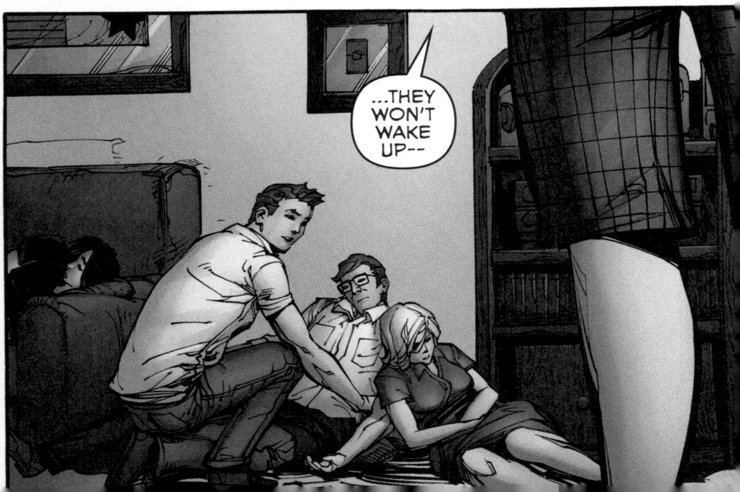
...THEY WON'T WAKE UP--

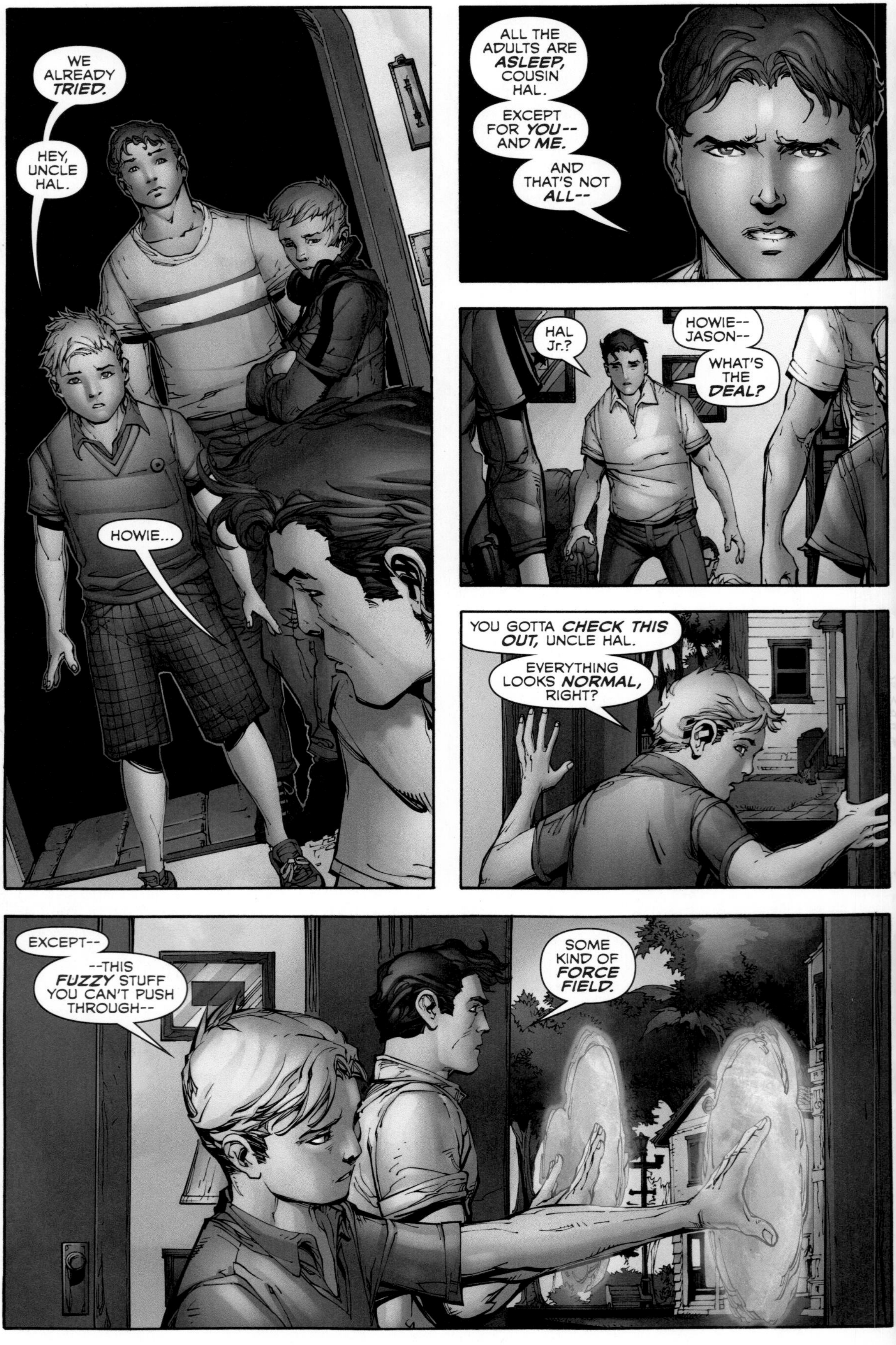
WE ALREADY TRIED.
HEY, UNCLE HAL.
HOWIE...
ALL THE ADULTS ARE ASLEEP, COUSIN HAL.
EXCEPT FOR YOU--AND ME.
AND THAT'S NOT ALL--
HAL Jr.?
HOWIE--JASON--
WHAT'S THE DEAL?
YOU GOTTA CHECK THIS OUT, UNCLE HAL.
EVERYTHING LOOKS NORMAL, RIGHT?
EXCEPT--
--THIS FUZZY STUFF YOU CAN'T PUSH THROUGH--
SOME KIND OF FORCE FIELD.

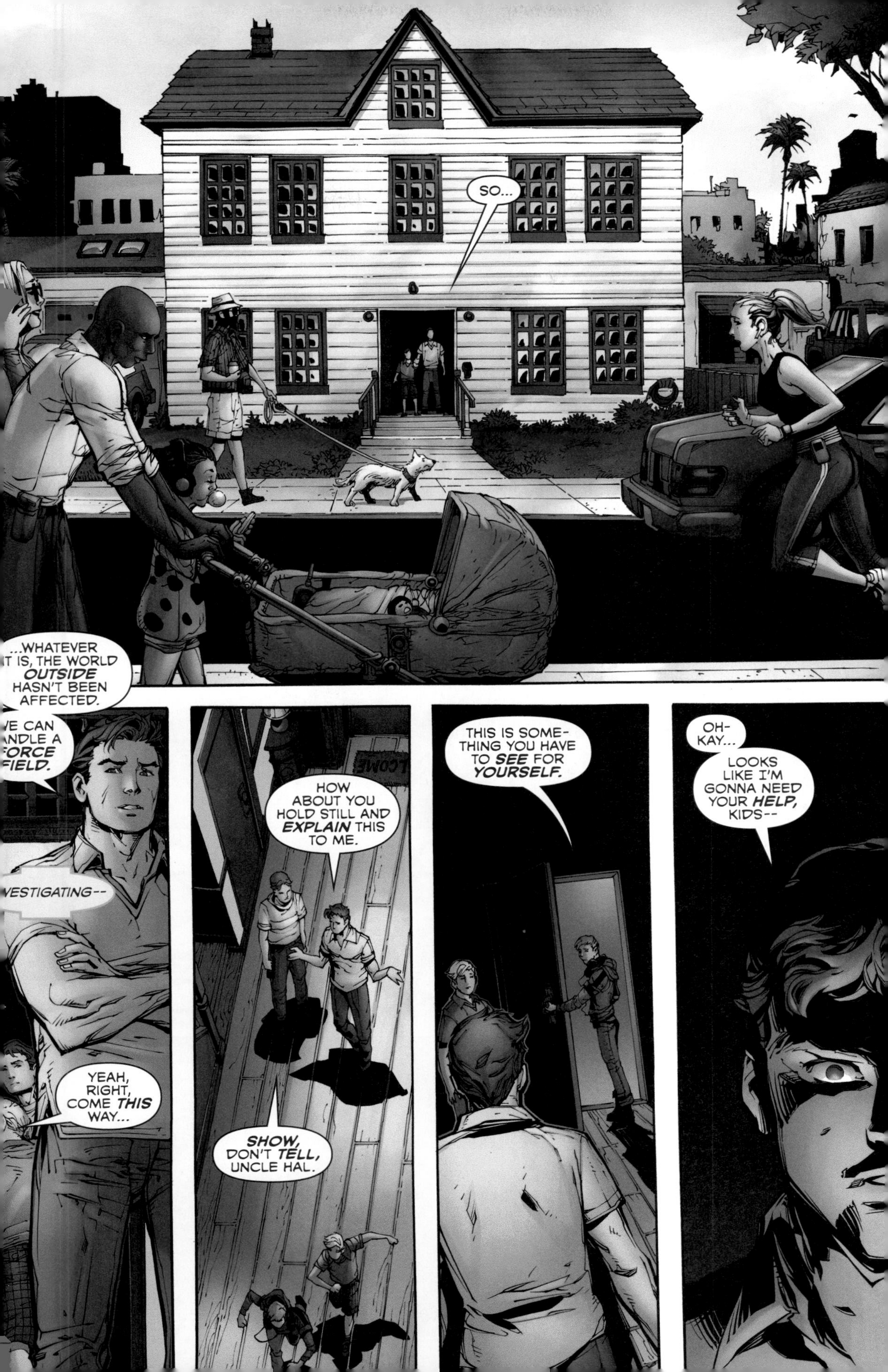
SO...
...WHATEVER IT IS, THE WORLD OUTSIDE HASN'T BEEN AFFECTED.
WE CAN HANDLE A FORCE FIELD.
VESTIGATING--
YEAH, RIGHT, COME THIS WAY...
HOW ABOUT YOU HOLD STILL AND EXPLAIN THIS TO ME.
SHOW, DON'T TELL, UNCLE HAL.
THIS IS SOMETHING YOU HAVE TO SEE FOR YOURSELF.
OH-KAY...
LOOKS LIKE I'M GONNA NEED YOUR HELP, KIDS--

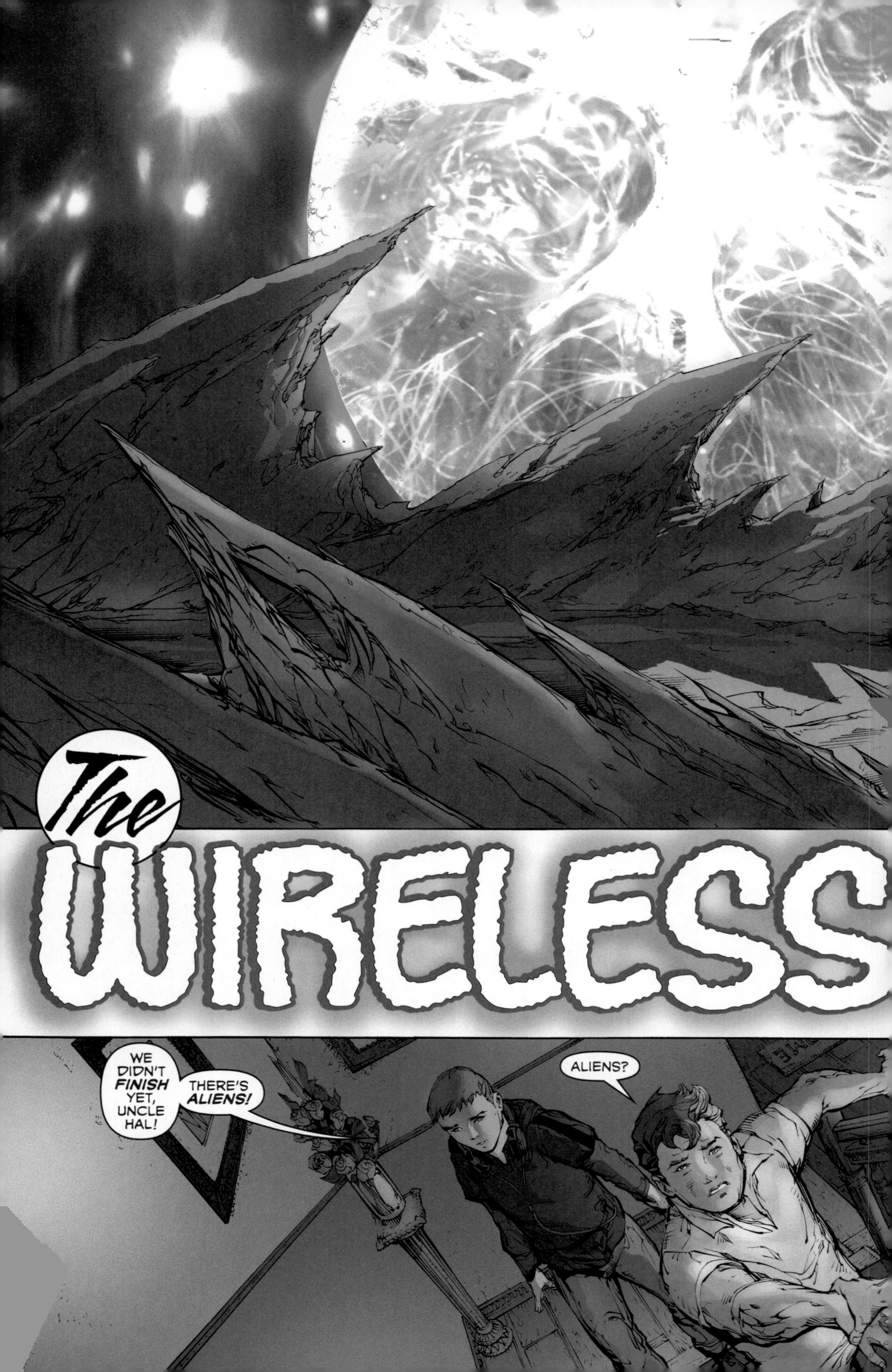

The WIRELESS
WE DIDN'T FINISH YET, UNCLE HAL!
THERE'S ALIENS!
ALIENS?

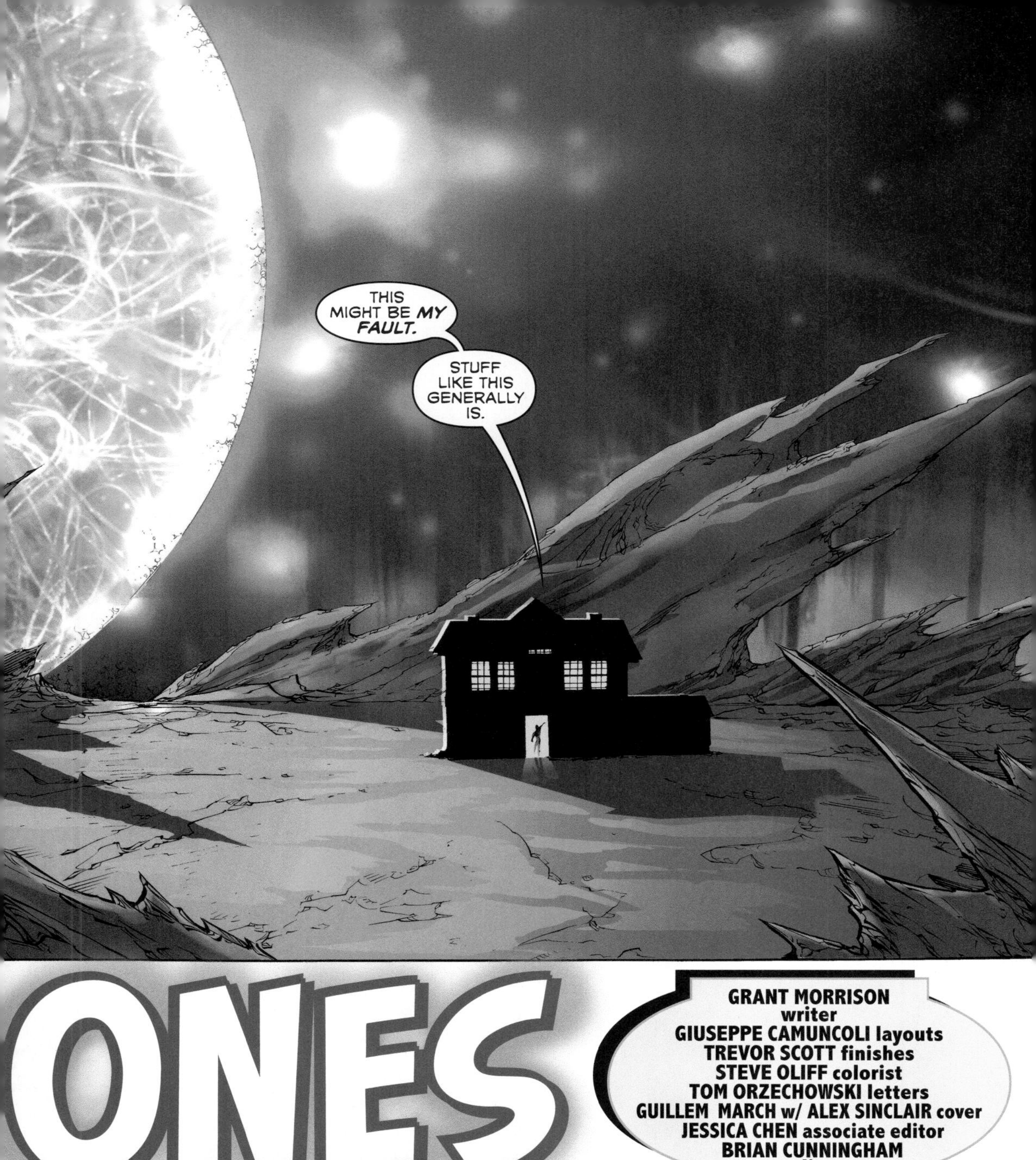
THIS MIGHT BE *MY FAULT.*
STUFF LIKE THIS GENERALLY IS.

ONES

GRANT MORRISON writer
GIUSEPPE CAMUNCOLI layouts
TREVOR SCOTT finishes
STEVE OLIFF colorist
TOM ORZECHOWSKI letters
GUILLEM MARCH w/ ALEX SINCLAIR cover
JESSICA CHEN associate editor
BRIAN CUNNINGHAM editor

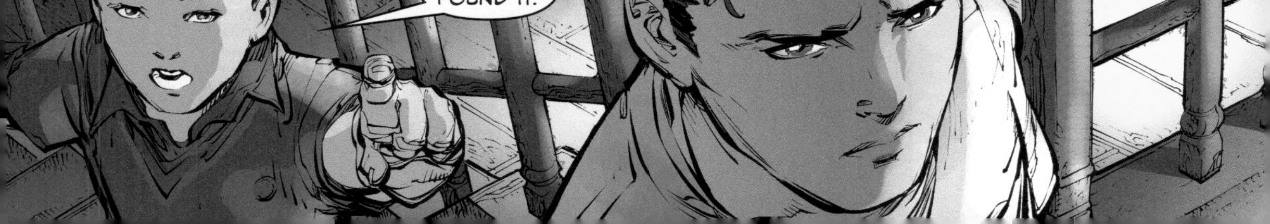
IT'S IN *HERE,* UNCLE HAL--
--HELEN AND JANE FOUND IT.

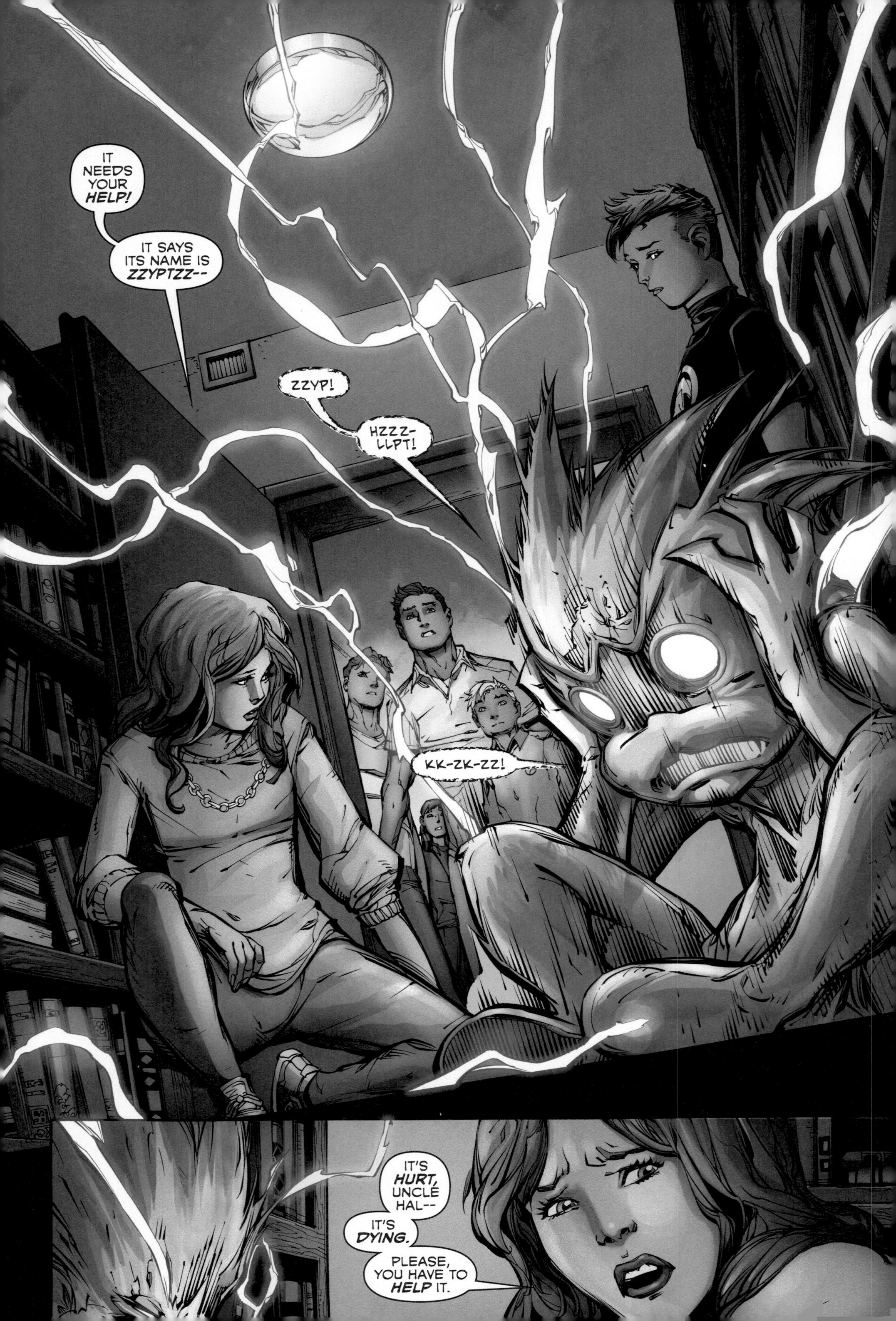
IT NEEDS YOUR HELP!
IT SAYS ITS NAME IS ZZYPTZZ--
ZZYP!
HZZZ-LLPT!
KK-ZK-ZZ!
IT'S HURT, UNCLE HAL--
IT'S DYING.
PLEASE, YOU HAVE TO HELP IT.

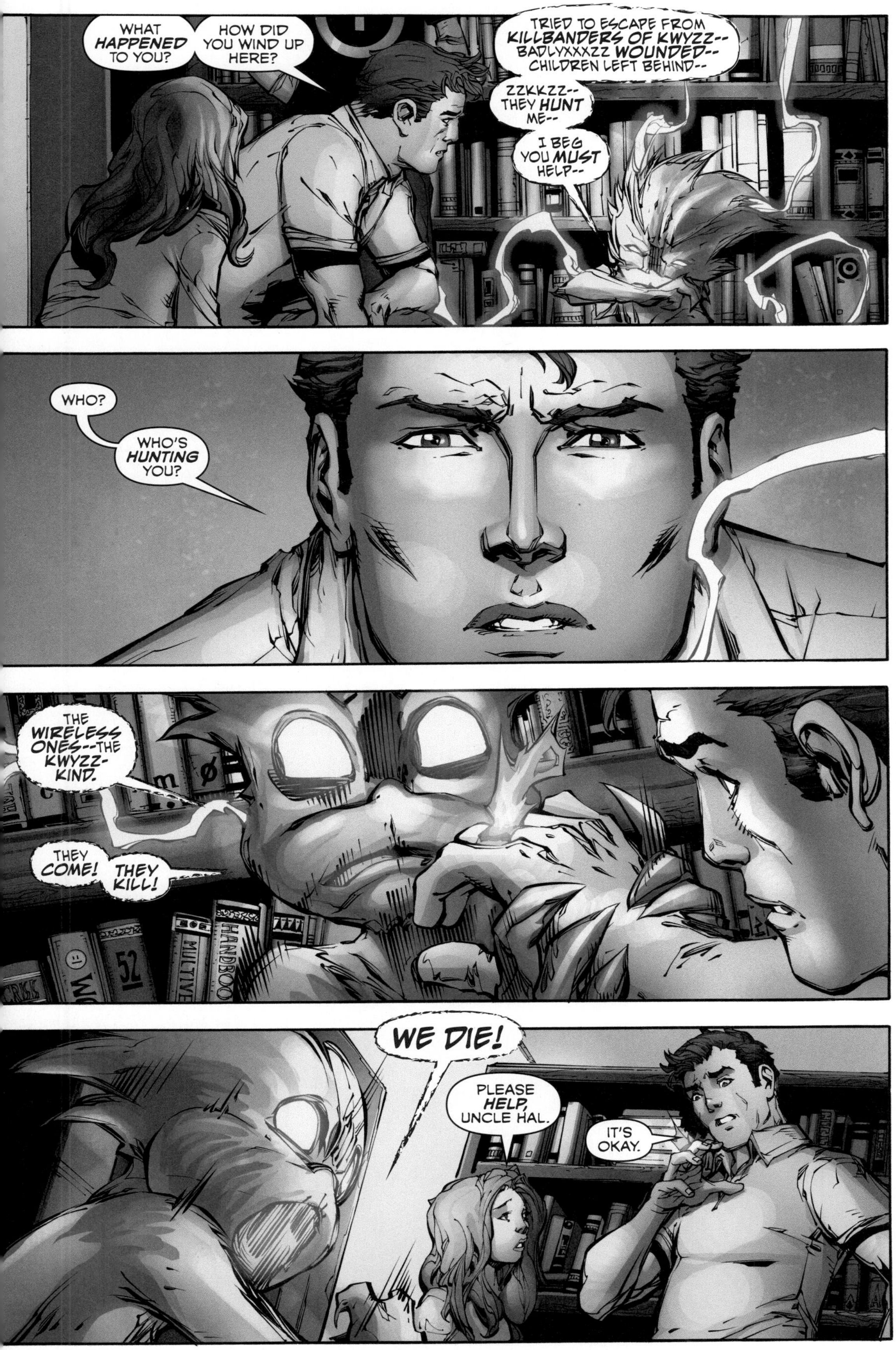
WHAT HAPPENED TO YOU?
HOW DID YOU WIND UP HERE?
TRIED TO ESCAPE FROM KILLBANDERS OF KWYZZ-- BADLYXXXZZ WOUNDED-- CHILDREN LEFT BEHIND--
ZZKKZZ-- THEY HUNT ME--
I BEG YOU MUST HELP--
WHO?
WHO'S HUNTING YOU?
THE WIRELESS ONES--THE KWYZZ-KIND.
THEY COME!
THEY KILL!
WE DIE!
PLEASE HELP, UNCLE HAL.
IT'S OKAY.

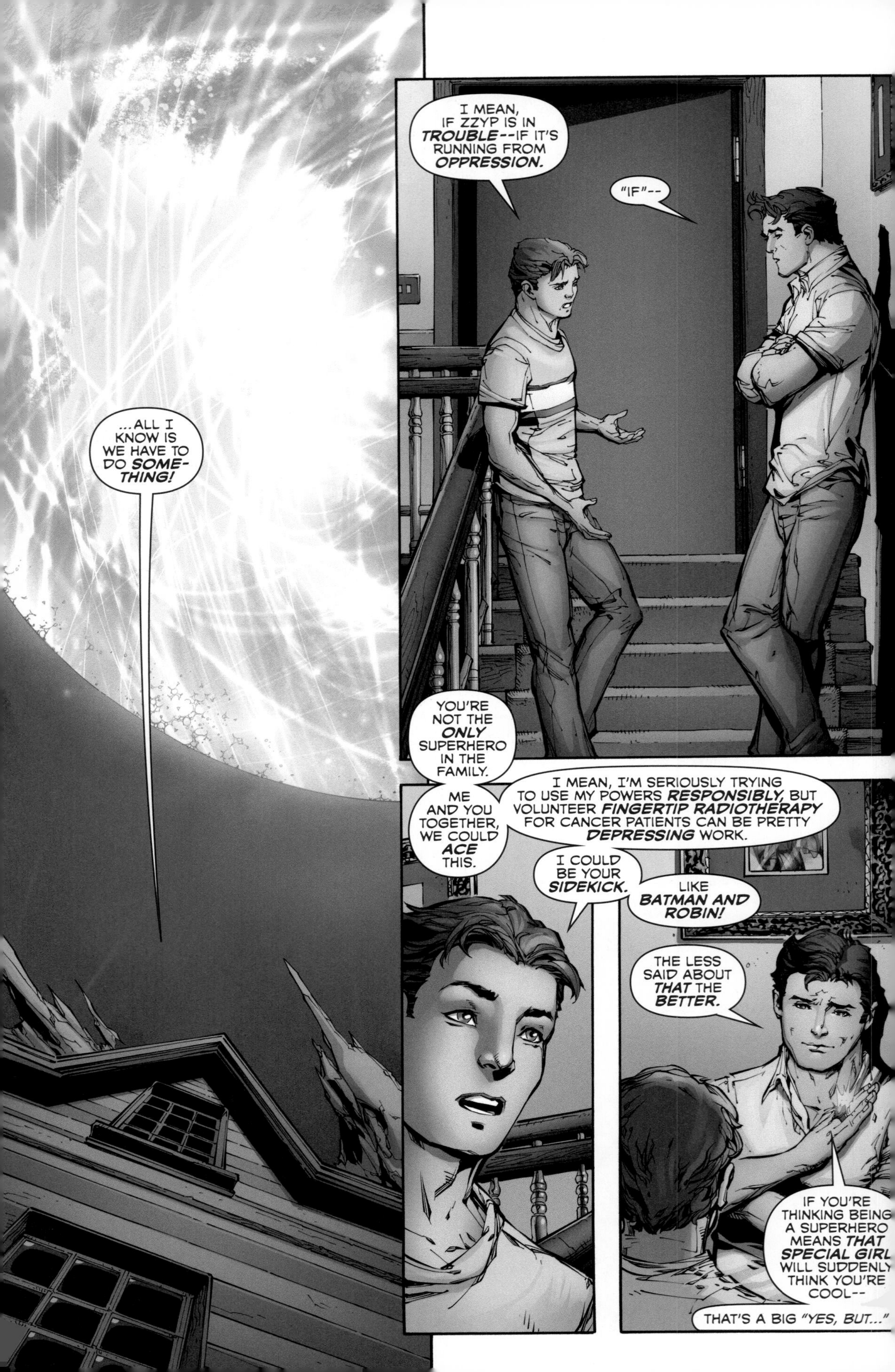
...ALL I KNOW IS WE HAVE TO DO SOME-THING!
I MEAN, IF ZZYP IS IN TROUBLE--IF IT'S RUNNING FROM OPPRESSION.
"IF"--
YOU'RE NOT THE ONLY SUPERHERO IN THE FAMILY.
ME AND YOU TOGETHER, WE COULD ACE THIS.
I MEAN, I'M SERIOUSLY TRYING TO USE MY POWERS RESPONSIBLY, BUT VOLUNTEER FINGERTIP RADIOTHERAPY FOR CANCER PATIENTS CAN BE PRETTY DEPRESSING WORK.
I COULD BE YOUR SIDEKICK.
LIKE BATMAN AND ROBIN!
THE LESS SAID ABOUT THAT THE BETTER.
IF YOU'RE THINKING BEING A SUPERHERO MEANS THAT SPECIAL GIRL WILL SUDDENLY THINK YOU'RE COOL--
THAT'S A BIG "YES, BUT..."

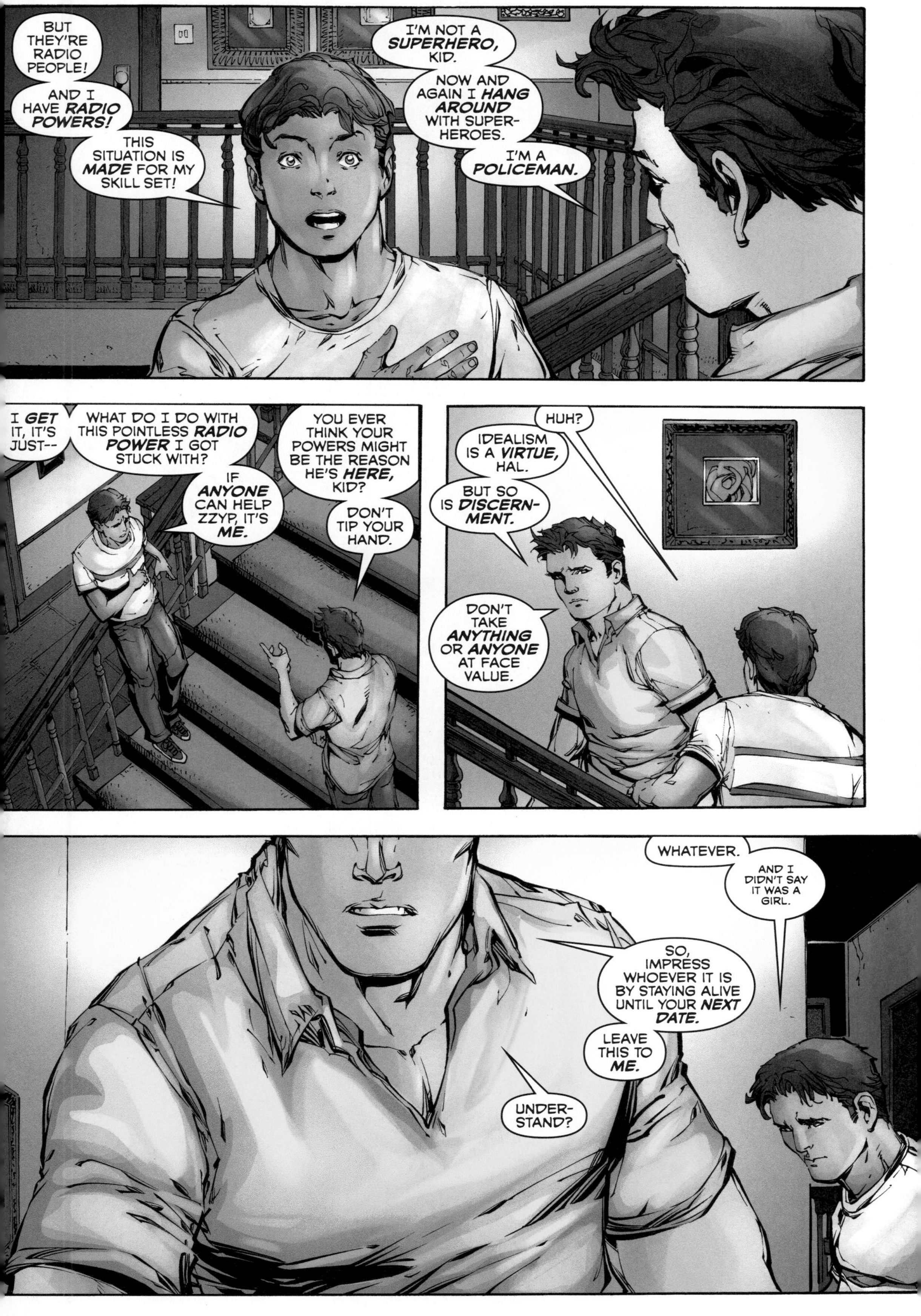

BUT THEY'RE RADIO PEOPLE!
AND I HAVE RADIO POWERS!
THIS SITUATION IS MADE FOR MY SKILL SET!
I'M NOT A SUPERHERO, KID.
NOW AND AGAIN I HANG AROUND WITH SUPER-HEROES.
I'M A POLICEMAN.
I GET IT, IT'S JUST--
WHAT DO I DO WITH THIS POINTLESS RADIO POWER I GOT STUCK WITH?
IF ANYONE CAN HELP ZZYP, IT'S ME.
YOU EVER THINK YOUR POWERS MIGHT BE THE REASON HE'S HERE, KID?
DON'T TIP YOUR HAND.
HUH?
IDEALISM IS A VIRTUE, HAL.
BUT SO IS DISCERN-MENT.
DON'T TAKE ANYTHING OR ANYONE AT FACE VALUE.
WHATEVER.
AND I DIDN'T SAY IT WAS A GIRL.
SO, IMPRESS WHOEVER IT IS BY STAYING ALIVE UNTIL YOUR NEXT DATE.
LEAVE THIS TO ME.
UNDER-STAND?

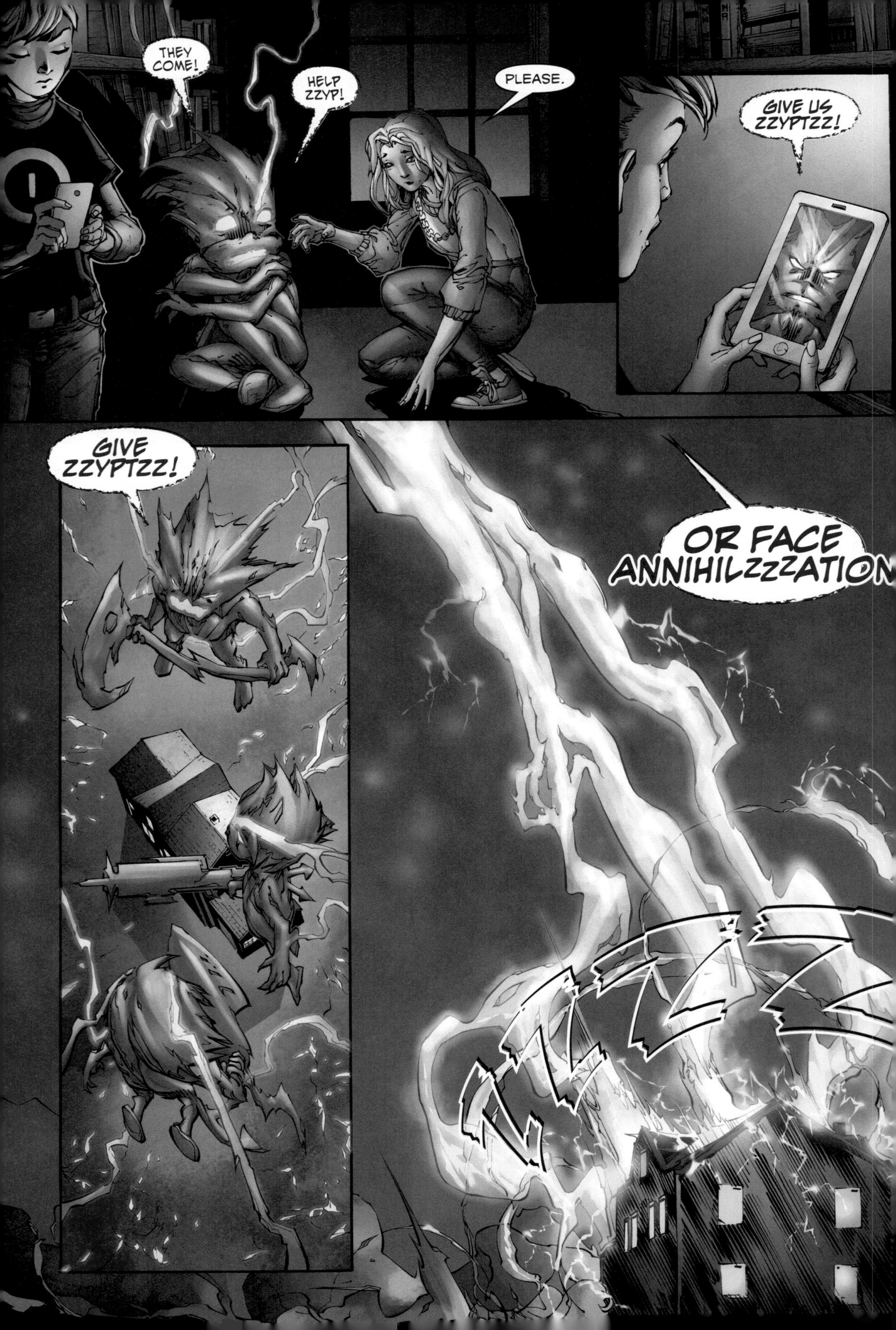
THEY COME!
HELP ZZYP!
PLEASE.
GIVE US ZZYPTZZ!
GIVE ZZYPTZZ!
OR FACE ANNIHILZZZATION
ZZZZ

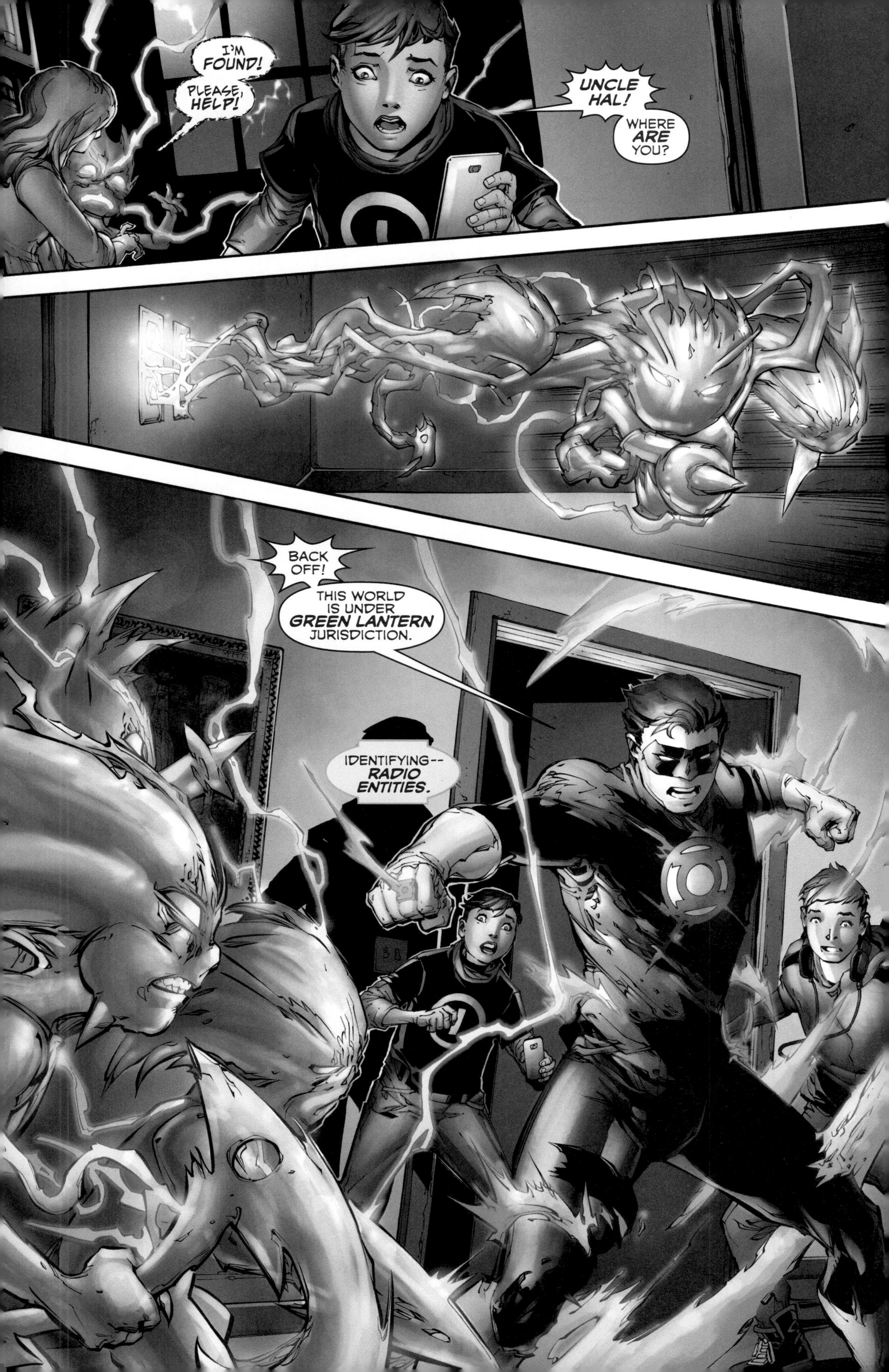
I'M FOUND!
PLEASE, HELP!
UNCLE HAL!
WHERE ARE YOU?
BACK OFF!
THIS WORLD IS UNDER GREEN LANTERN JURISDICTION.
IDENTIFYING-- RADIO ENTITIES.

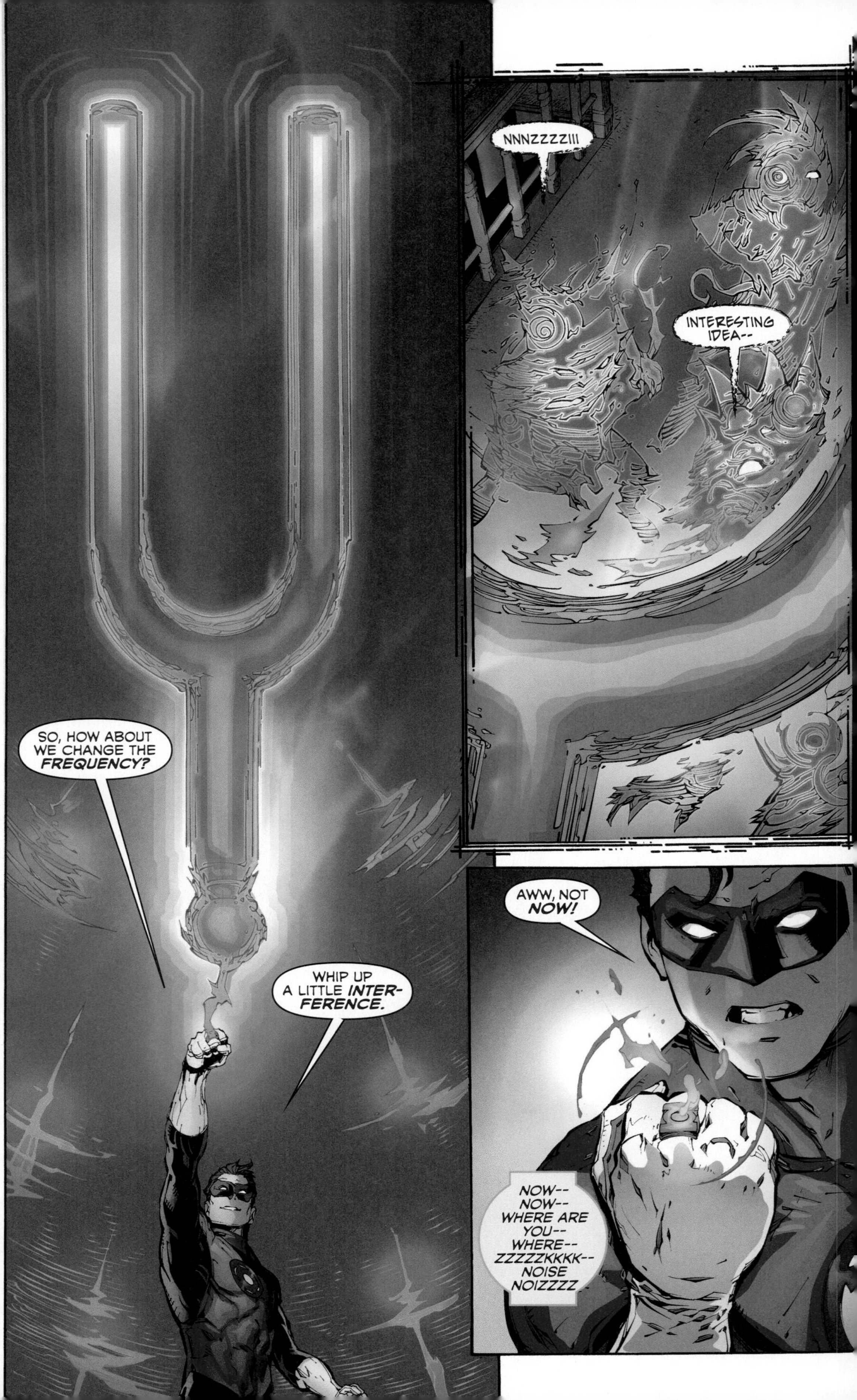
SO, HOW ABOUT WE CHANGE THE FREQUENCY?
WHIP UP A LITTLE INTER-FERENCE.
NNNZZZZIII
INTERESTING IDEA--
AWW, NOT NOW!
NOW-- NOW-- WHERE ARE YOU-- WHERE-- ZZZZZKKKK-- NOISE NOIZZZZ

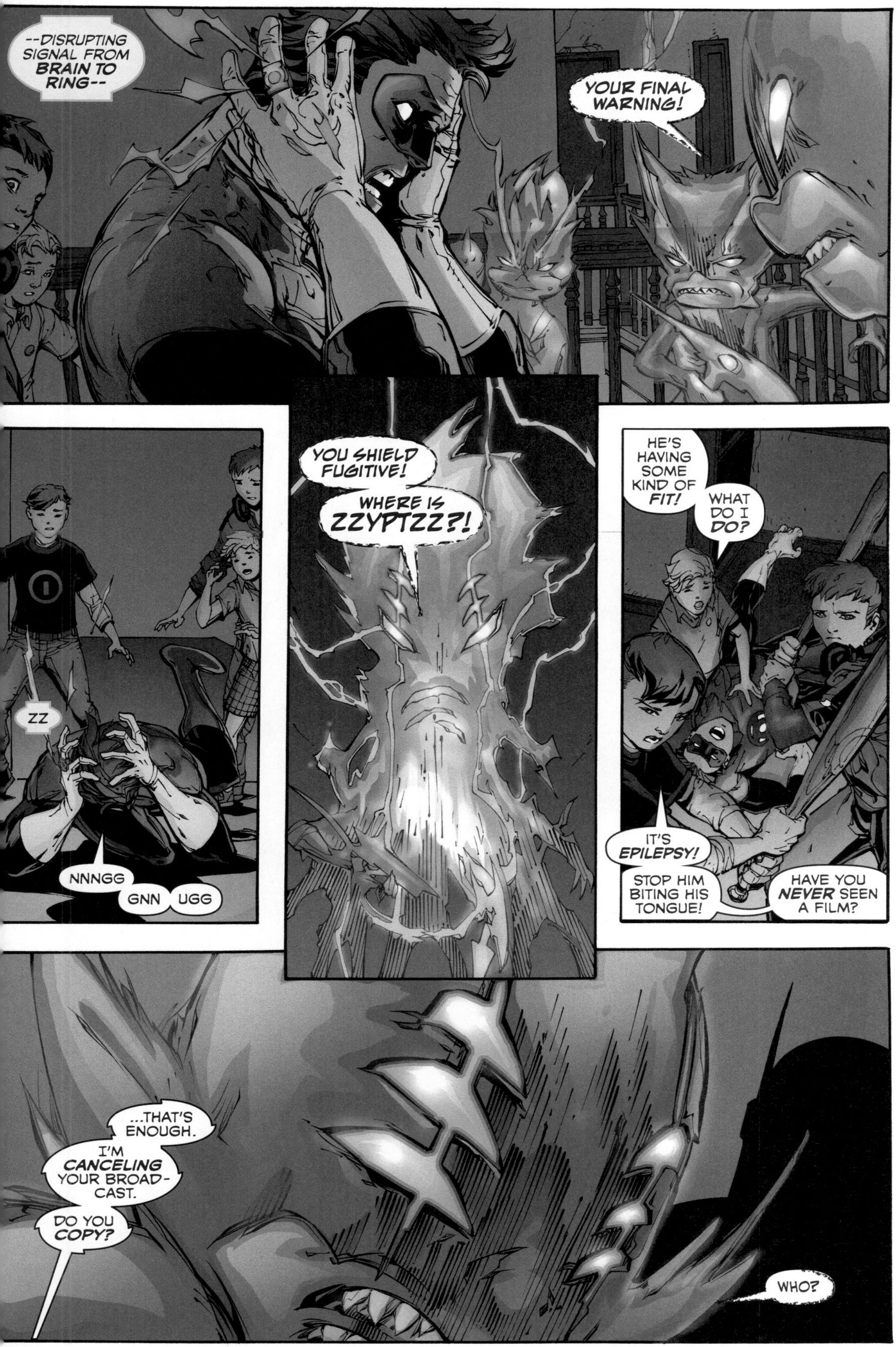
--DISRUPTING SIGNAL FROM BRAIN TO RING--
YOUR FINAL WARNING!
ZZ
NNNGG
GNN
UGG
YOU SHIELD FUGITIVE!
WHERE IS ZZYPTZZ?!
HE'S HAVING SOME KIND OF FIT!
WHAT DO I DO?
IT'S EPILEPSY!
STOP HIM BITING HIS TONGUE!
HAVE YOU NEVER SEEN A FILM?
...THAT'S ENOUGH.
I'M CANCELING YOUR BROAD-CAST.
DO YOU COPY?
WHO?

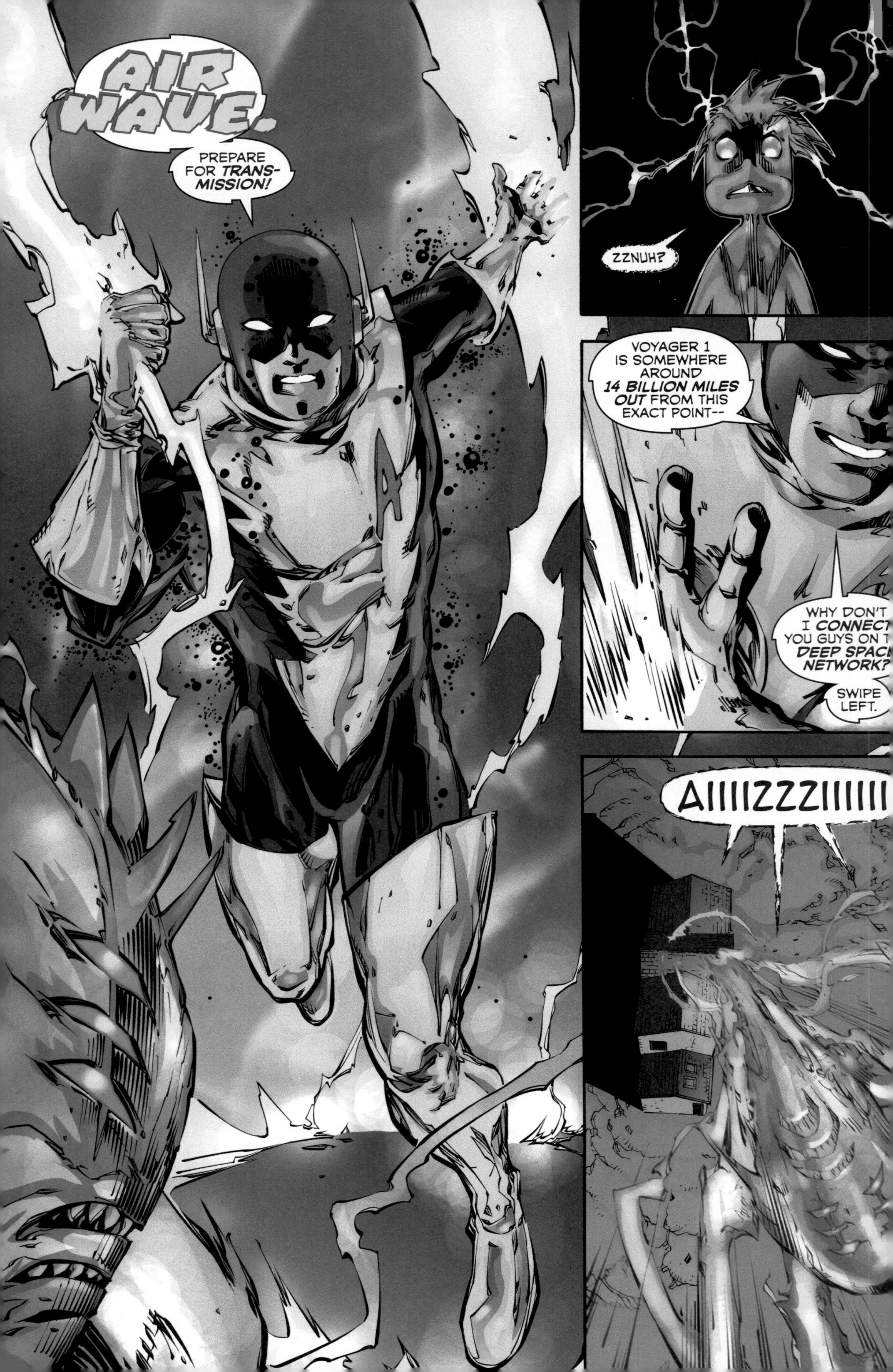
AIR WAVE.
PREPARE FOR TRANS-MISSION!
ZZNUH?
VOYAGER 1 IS SOMEWHERE AROUND 14 BILLION MILES OUT FROM THIS EXACT POINT--
WHY DON'T I CONNECT YOU GUYS ON T DEEP SPAC NETWORK?
SWIPE LEFT.
AIIIIZZZIIIIIII

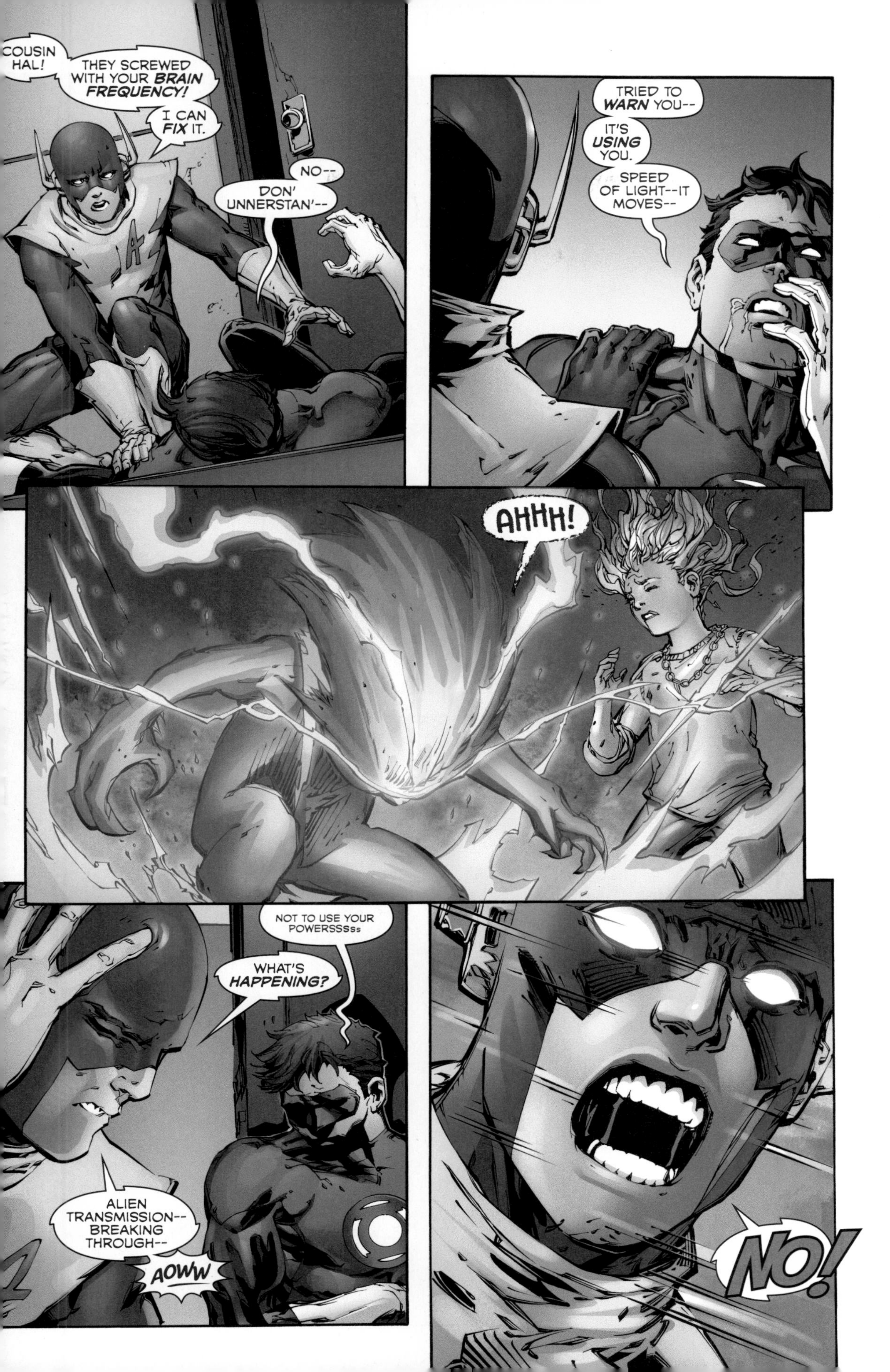
COUSIN HAL!
THEY SCREWED WITH YOUR BRAIN FREQUENCY!
I CAN FIX IT.
NO--
DON' UNNERSTAN'--
TRIED TO WARN YOU--
IT'S USING YOU.
SPEED OF LIGHT--IT MOVES--
AHHH!
NOT TO USE YOUR POWERSSSss
WHAT'S HAPPENING?
ALIEN TRANSMISSION--BREAKING THROUGH--
AOWW
NO!

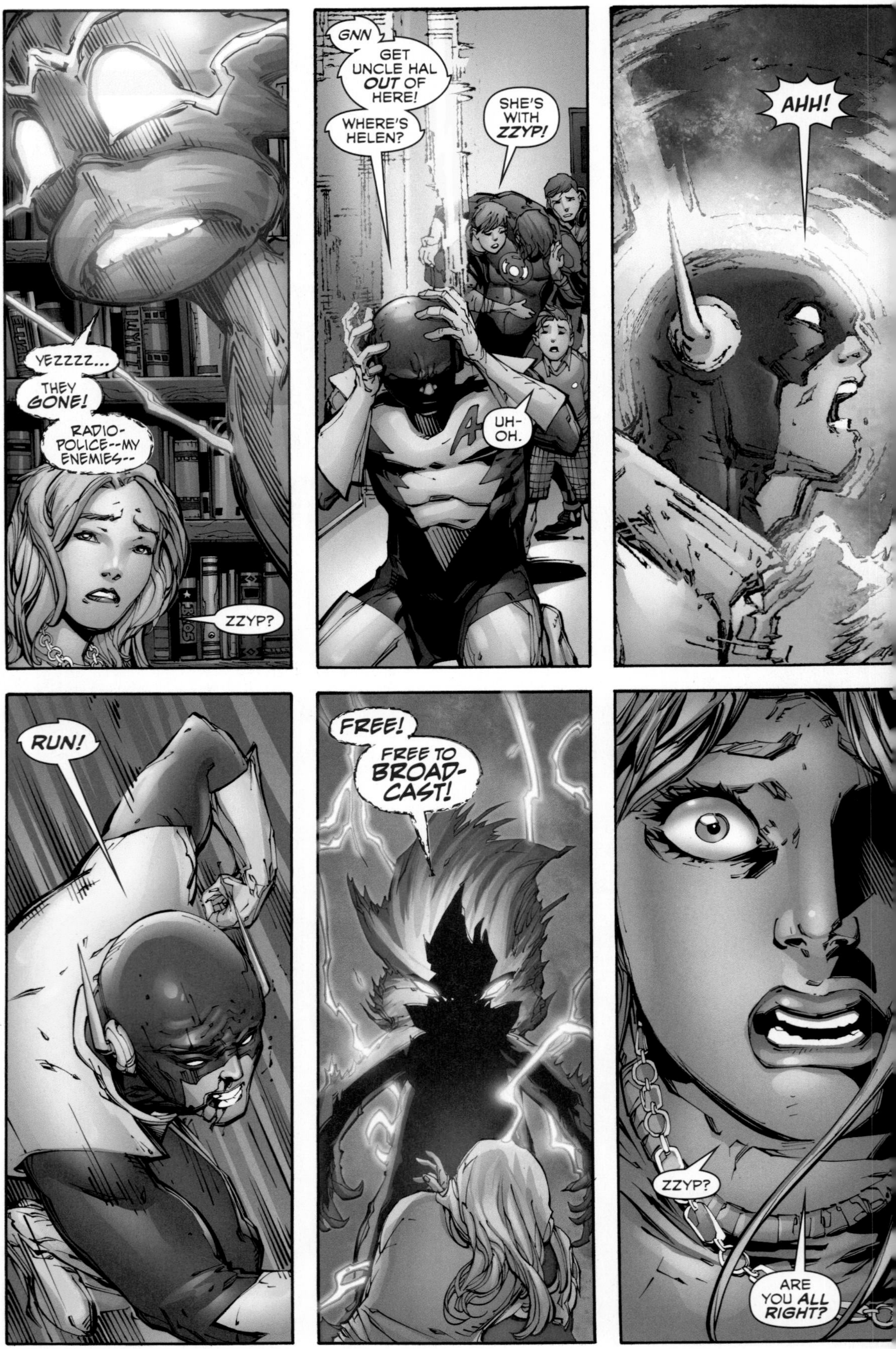
YEZZZZ...
THEY GONE!
RADIO-POLICE--MY ENEMIES--
ZZYP?
GNN
GET UNCLE HAL OUT OF HERE!
WHERE'S HELEN?
SHE'S WITH ZZYP!
UH-OH.
AHH!
RUN!
FREE!
FREE TO BROAD-CAST!
ZZYP?
ARE YOU ALL RIGHT?

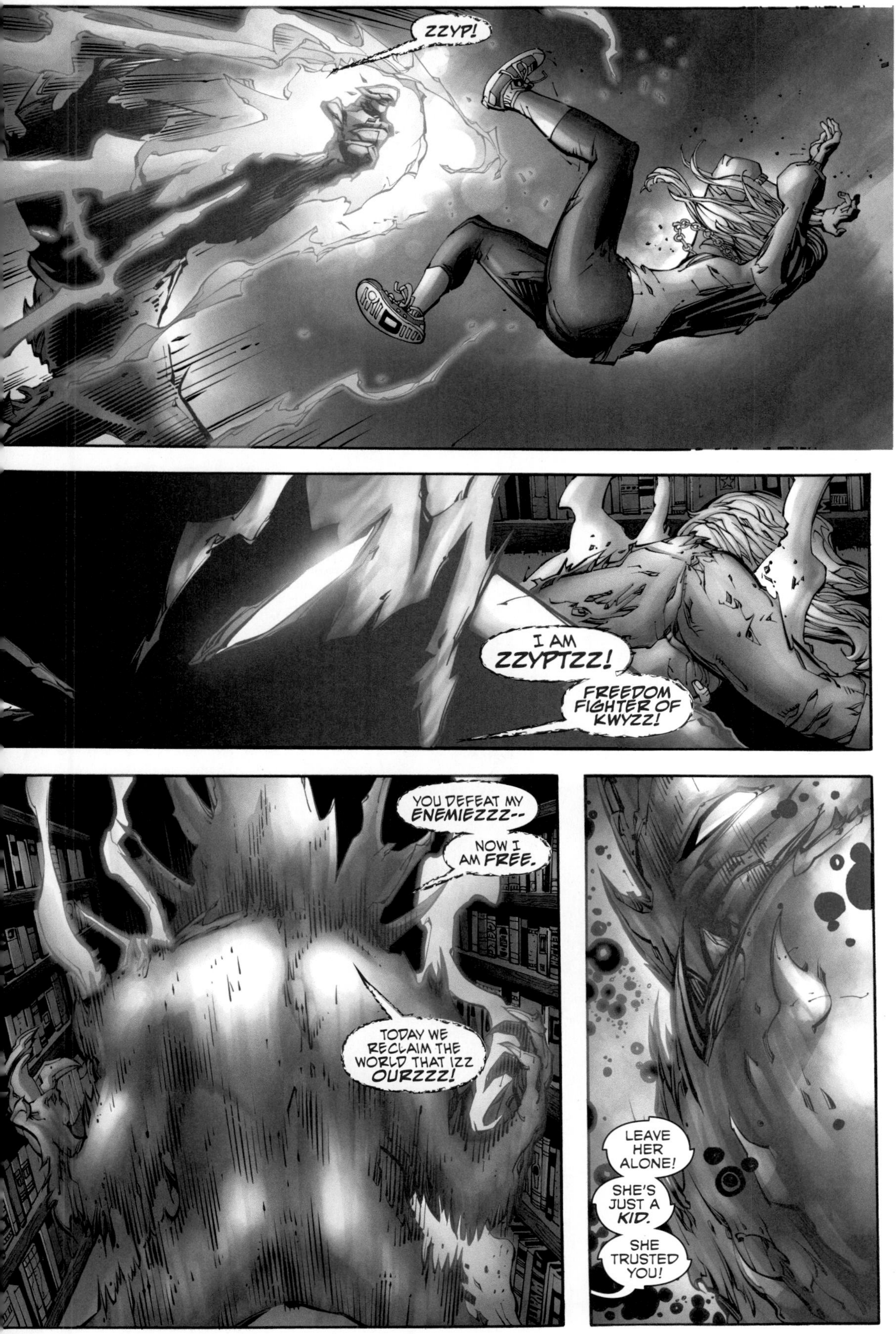
ZZYP!
I AM ZZYPTZZ!
FREEDOM FIGHTER OF KWYZZ!
YOU DEFEAT MY ENEMIEZZZ--
NOW I AM FREE.
TODAY WE RECLAIM THE WORLD THAT IZZ OURZZZ!
LEAVE HER ALONE!
SHE'S JUST A KID.
SHE TRUSTED YOU!

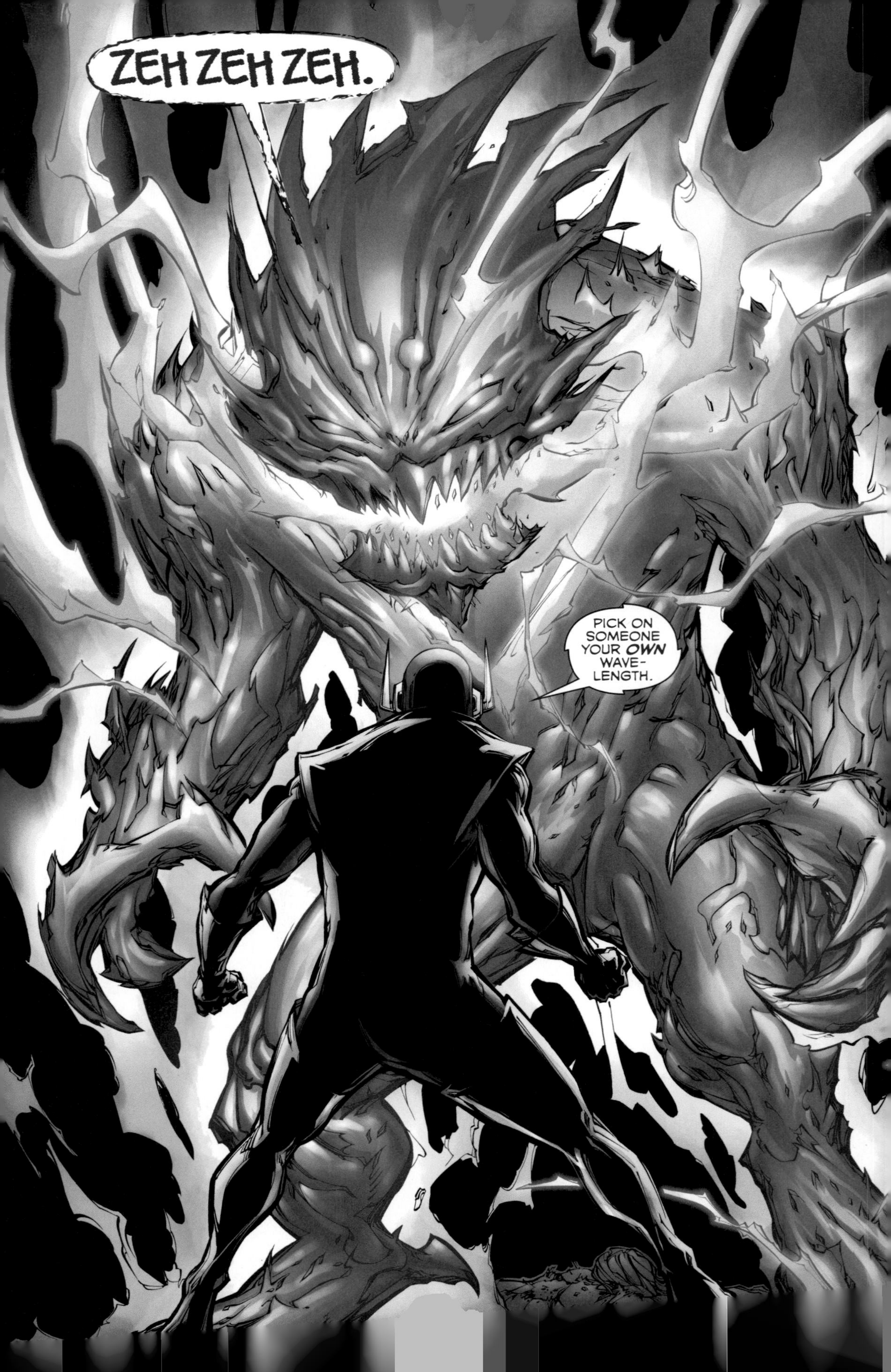
ZEH ZEH ZEH.
PICK ON SOMEONE YOUR OWN WAVE-LENGTH.

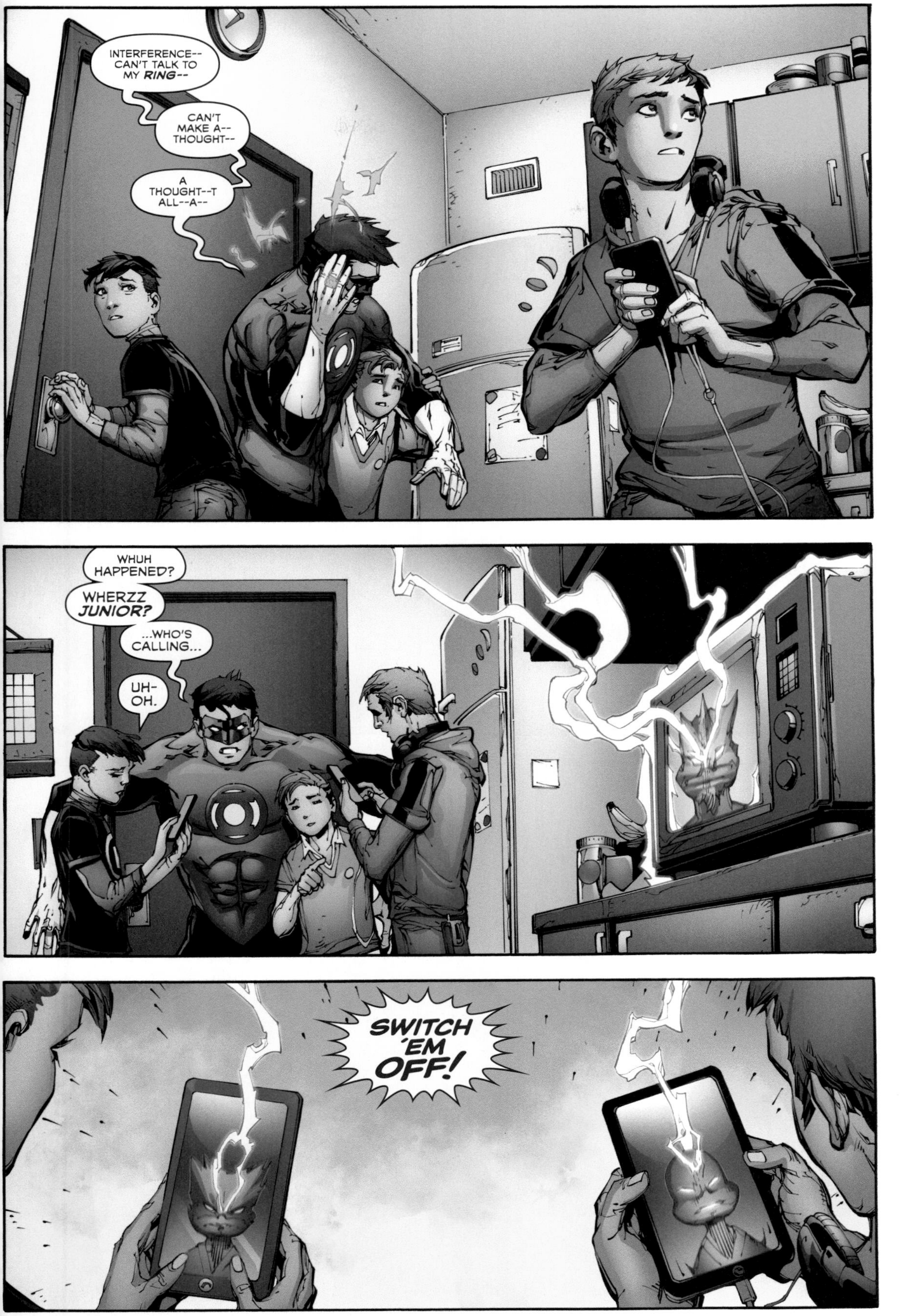
INTERFERENCE-- CAN'T TALK TO MY *RING*--
CAN'T MAKE A-- THOUGHT--
A THOUGHT--T ALL--A--
WHUH HAPPENED?
WHERZZ *JUNIOR?*
...WHO'S CALLING...
UH-OH.
SWITCH 'EM OFF!

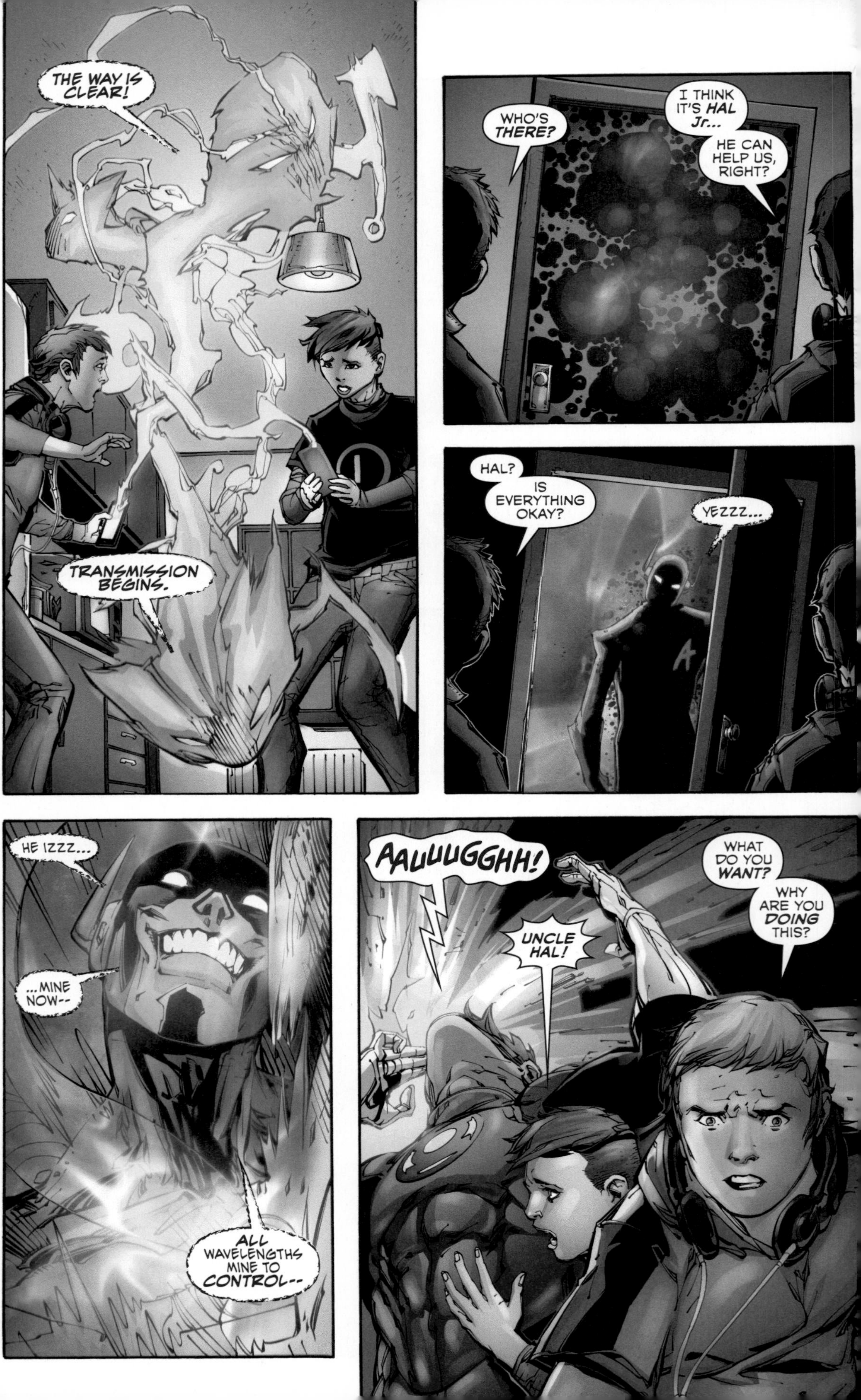
THE WAY IS CLEAR!
TRANSMISSION BEGINS.
WHO'S THERE?
I THINK IT'S HAL Jr...
HE CAN HELP US, RIGHT?
HAL? IS EVERYTHING OKAY?
YEZZZ...
HE IZZZ...
...MINE NOW--
ALL WAVELENGTHS MINE TO CONTROL--
AAUUUGGHH!
UNCLE HAL!
WHAT DO YOU WANT?
WHY ARE YOU DOING THIS?

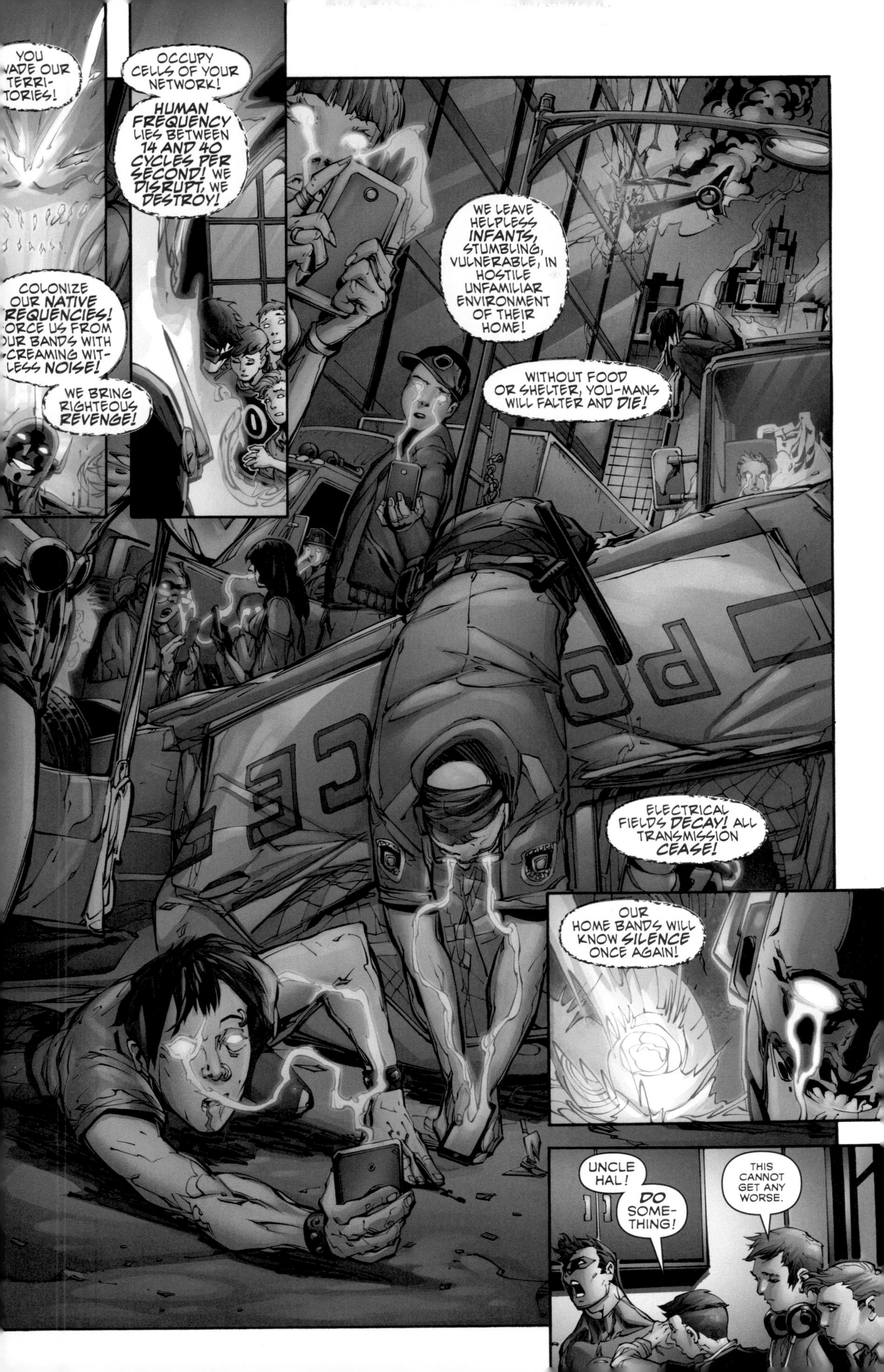
YOU ...VADE OUR TERRI-TORIES!
OCCUPY CELLS OF YOUR NETWORK!
HUMAN FREQUENCY LIES BETWEEN 14 AND 40 CYCLES PER SECOND! WE DISRUPT, WE DESTROY!
COLONIZE OUR NATIVE ...REQUENCIES! ...ORCE US FROM ...UR BANDS WITH ...CREAMING WIT-LESS NOISE!
WE BRING RIGHTEOUS REVENGE!
WE LEAVE HELPLESS INFANTS, STUMBLING, VULNERABLE, IN HOSTILE UNFAMILIAR ENVIRONMENT OF THEIR HOME!
WITHOUT FOOD OR SHELTER, YOU-MANS WILL FALTER AND DIE!
ELECTRICAL FIELDS DECAY! ALL TRANSMISSION CEASE!
OUR HOME BANDS WILL KNOW SILENCE ONCE AGAIN!
UNCLE HAL! DO SOME-THING!
THIS CANNOT GET ANY WORSE.

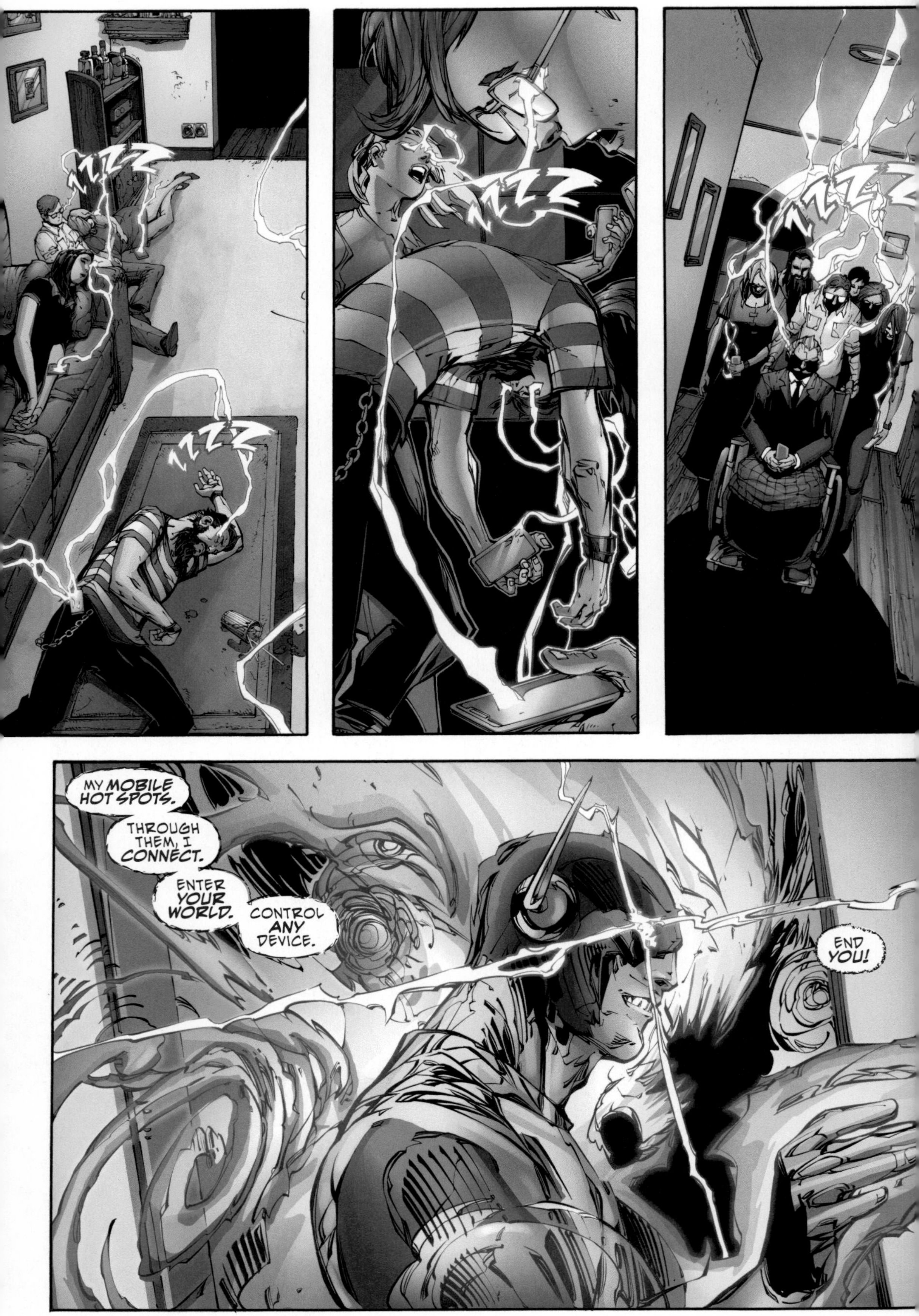
ZZZZ
ZZZZ
ZZZZ
ZZZZ
MY MOBILE HOT SPOTS.
THROUGH THEM, I CONNECT.
ENTER YOUR WORLD.
CONTROL ANY DEVICE.
END YOU!

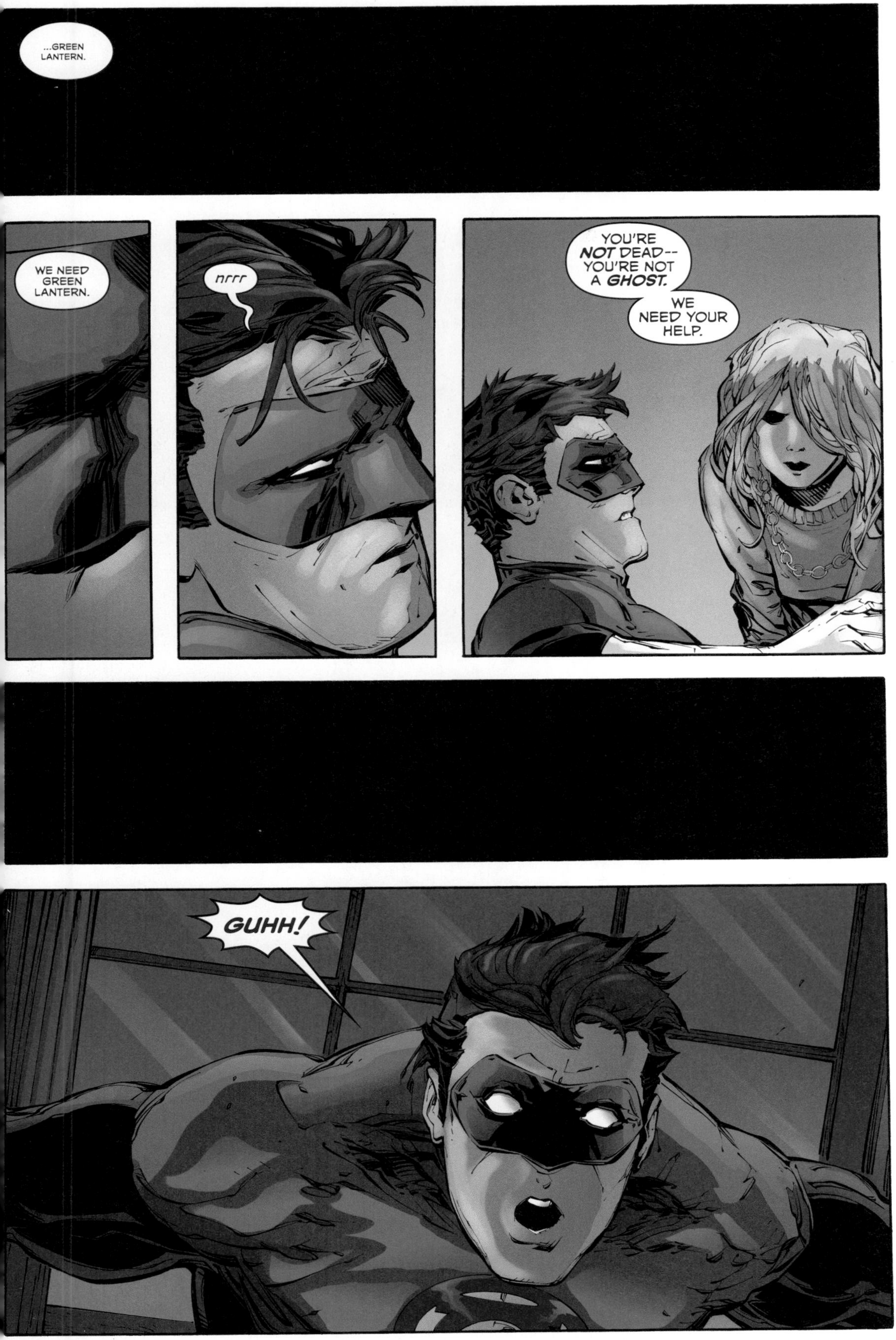

...GREEN LANTERN.
WE NEED GREEN LANTERN.
nrrr
YOU'RE *NOT* DEAD-- YOU'RE NOT A *GHOST.*
WE NEED YOUR HELP.
GUHH!

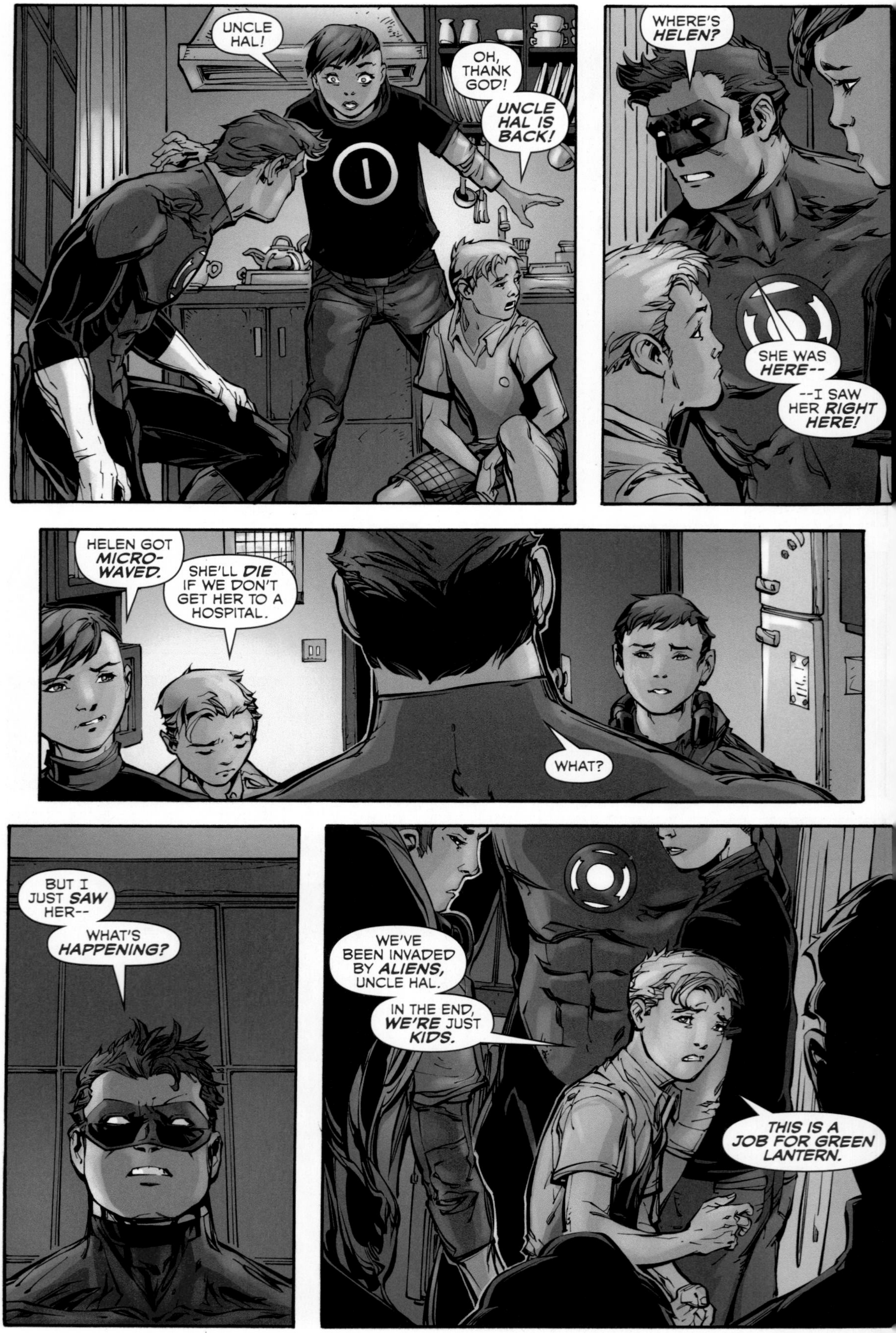
UNCLE HAL!
OH, THANK GOD!
UNCLE HAL IS BACK!
WHERE'S HELEN?
SHE WAS HERE--
--I SAW HER RIGHT HERE!
HELEN GOT MICRO-WAVED.
SHE'LL DIE IF WE DON'T GET HER TO A HOSPITAL.
WHAT?
BUT I JUST SAW HER--
WHAT'S HAPPENING?
WE'VE BEEN INVADED BY ALIENS, UNCLE HAL.
IN THE END, WE'RE JUST KIDS.
THIS IS A JOB FOR GREEN LANTERN.

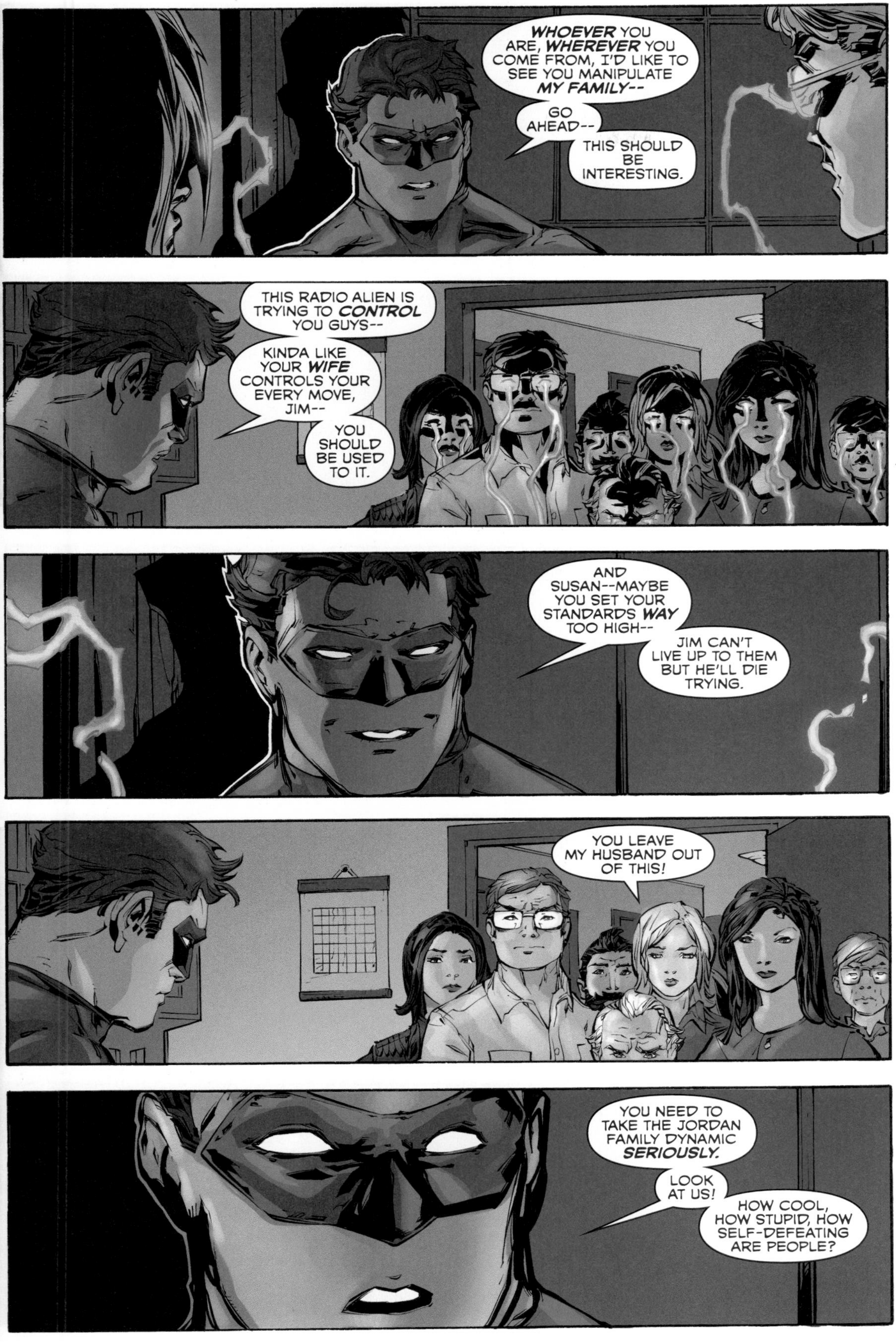
WHOEVER YOU ARE, WHEREVER YOU COME FROM, I'D LIKE TO SEE YOU MANIPULATE MY FAMILY--
GO AHEAD--
THIS SHOULD BE INTERESTING.
THIS RADIO ALIEN IS TRYING TO CONTROL YOU GUYS--
KINDA LIKE YOUR WIFE CONTROLS YOUR EVERY MOVE, JIM--
YOU SHOULD BE USED TO IT.
AND SUSAN--MAYBE YOU SET YOUR STANDARDS WAY TOO HIGH--
JIM CAN'T LIVE UP TO THEM BUT HE'LL DIE TRYING.
YOU LEAVE MY HUSBAND OUT OF THIS!
YOU NEED TO TAKE THE JORDAN FAMILY DYNAMIC SERIOUSLY.
LOOK AT US!
HOW COOL, HOW STUPID, HOW SELF-DEFEATING ARE PEOPLE?

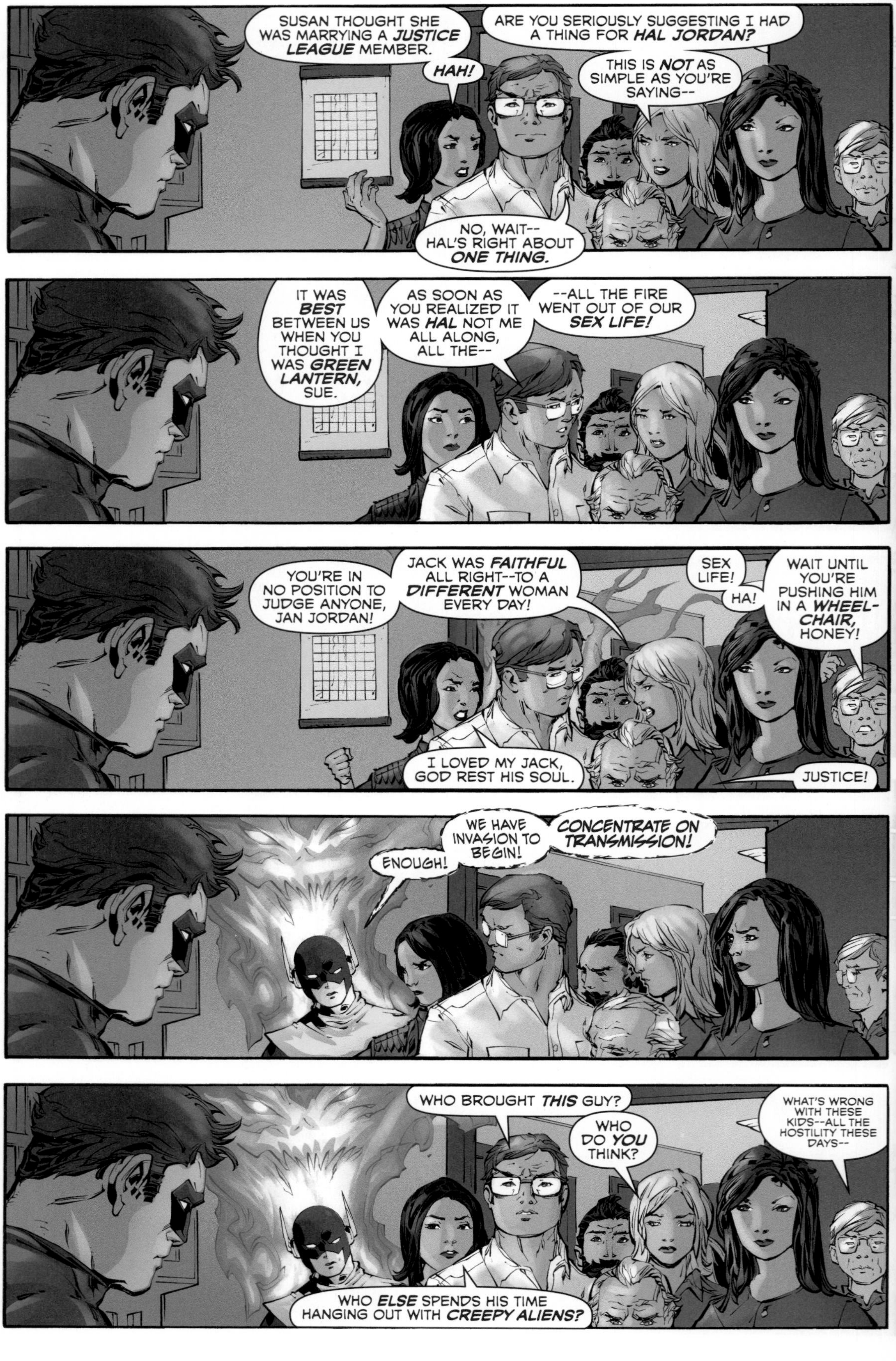
SUSAN THOUGHT SHE WAS MARRYING A JUSTICE LEAGUE MEMBER.
HAH!
ARE YOU SERIOUSLY SUGGESTING I HAD A THING FOR HAL JORDAN?
THIS IS NOT AS SIMPLE AS YOU'RE SAYING--
NO, WAIT-- HAL'S RIGHT ABOUT ONE THING.
IT WAS BEST BETWEEN US WHEN YOU THOUGHT I WAS GREEN LANTERN, SUE.
AS SOON AS YOU REALIZED IT WAS HAL NOT ME ALL ALONG, ALL THE--
--ALL THE FIRE WENT OUT OF OUR SEX LIFE!
YOU'RE IN NO POSITION TO JUDGE ANYONE, JAN JORDAN!
JACK WAS FAITHFUL ALL RIGHT--TO A DIFFERENT WOMAN EVERY DAY!
SEX LIFE!
HA!
WAIT UNTIL YOU'RE PUSHING HIM IN A WHEEL-CHAIR, HONEY!
I LOVED MY JACK, GOD REST HIS SOUL.
JUSTICE!
ENOUGH!
WE HAVE INVASION TO BEGIN!
CONCENTRATE ON TRANSMISSION!
WHO BROUGHT THIS GUY?
WHO DO YOU THINK?
WHAT'S WRONG WITH THESE KIDS--ALL THE HOSTILITY THESE DAYS--
WHO ELSE SPENDS HIS TIME HANGING OUT WITH CREEPY ALIENS?

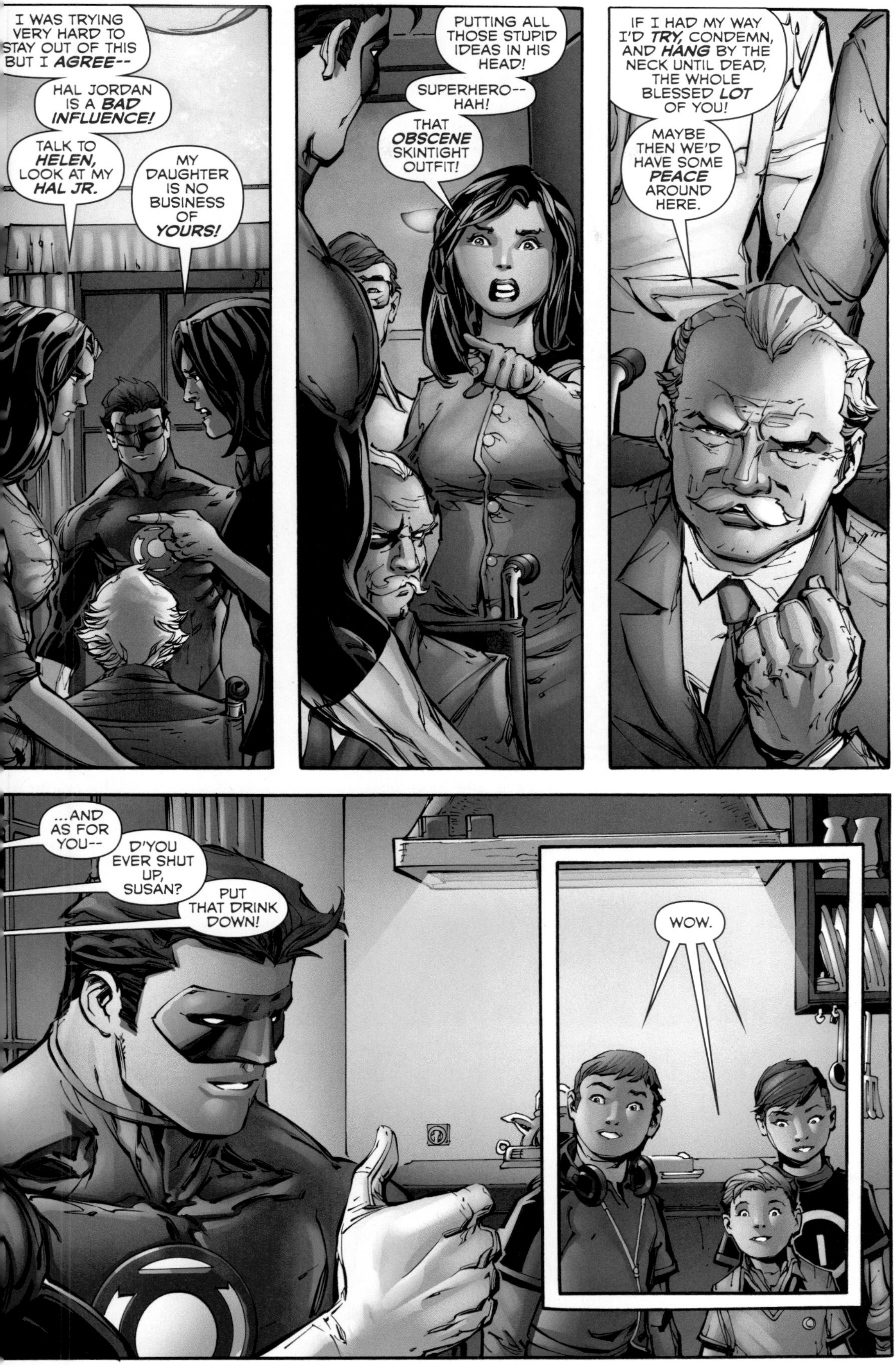

I WAS TRYING VERY HARD TO STAY OUT OF THIS BUT I AGREE--
HAL JORDAN IS A BAD INFLUENCE!
TALK TO HELEN, LOOK AT MY HAL JR.
MY DAUGHTER IS NO BUSINESS OF YOURS!
PUTTING ALL THOSE STUPID IDEAS IN HIS HEAD!
SUPERHERO-- HAH!
THAT OBSCENE SKINTIGHT OUTFIT!
IF I HAD MY WAY I'D TRY, CONDEMN, AND HANG BY THE NECK UNTIL DEAD, THE WHOLE BLESSED LOT OF YOU!
MAYBE THEN WE'D HAVE SOME PEACE AROUND HERE.
...AND AS FOR YOU--
D'YOU EVER SHUT UP, SUSAN?
PUT THAT DRINK DOWN!
WOW.

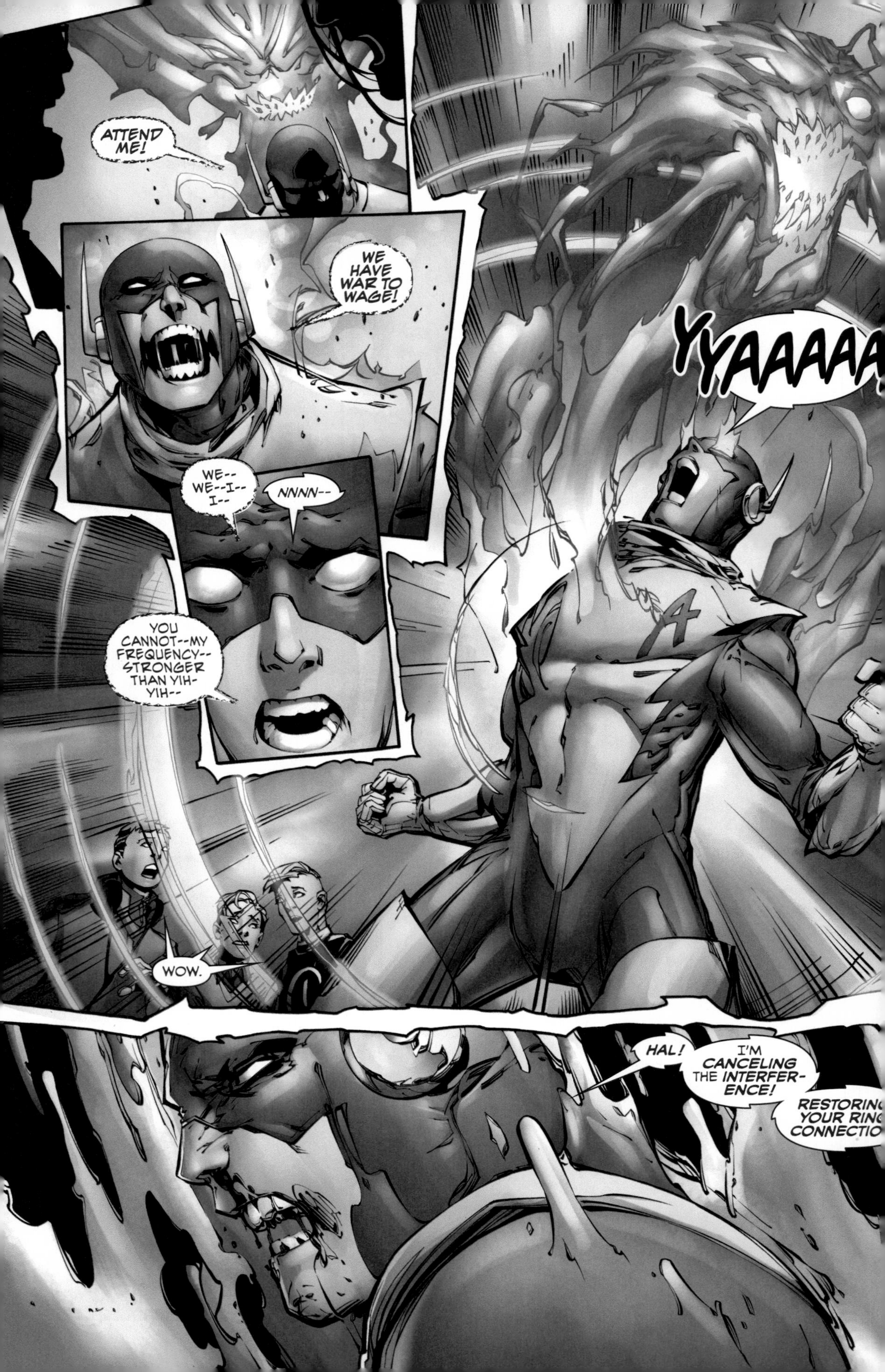
ATTEND ME!
WE HAVE WAR TO WAGE!
YYAAAAA
WE-- WE--I-- I--
NNNN--
YOU CANNOT--MY FREQUENCY-- STRONGER THAN YIH- YIH--
WOW.
HAL!
I'M CANCELING THE INTERFERENCE!
RESTORING YOUR RING CONNECTIO

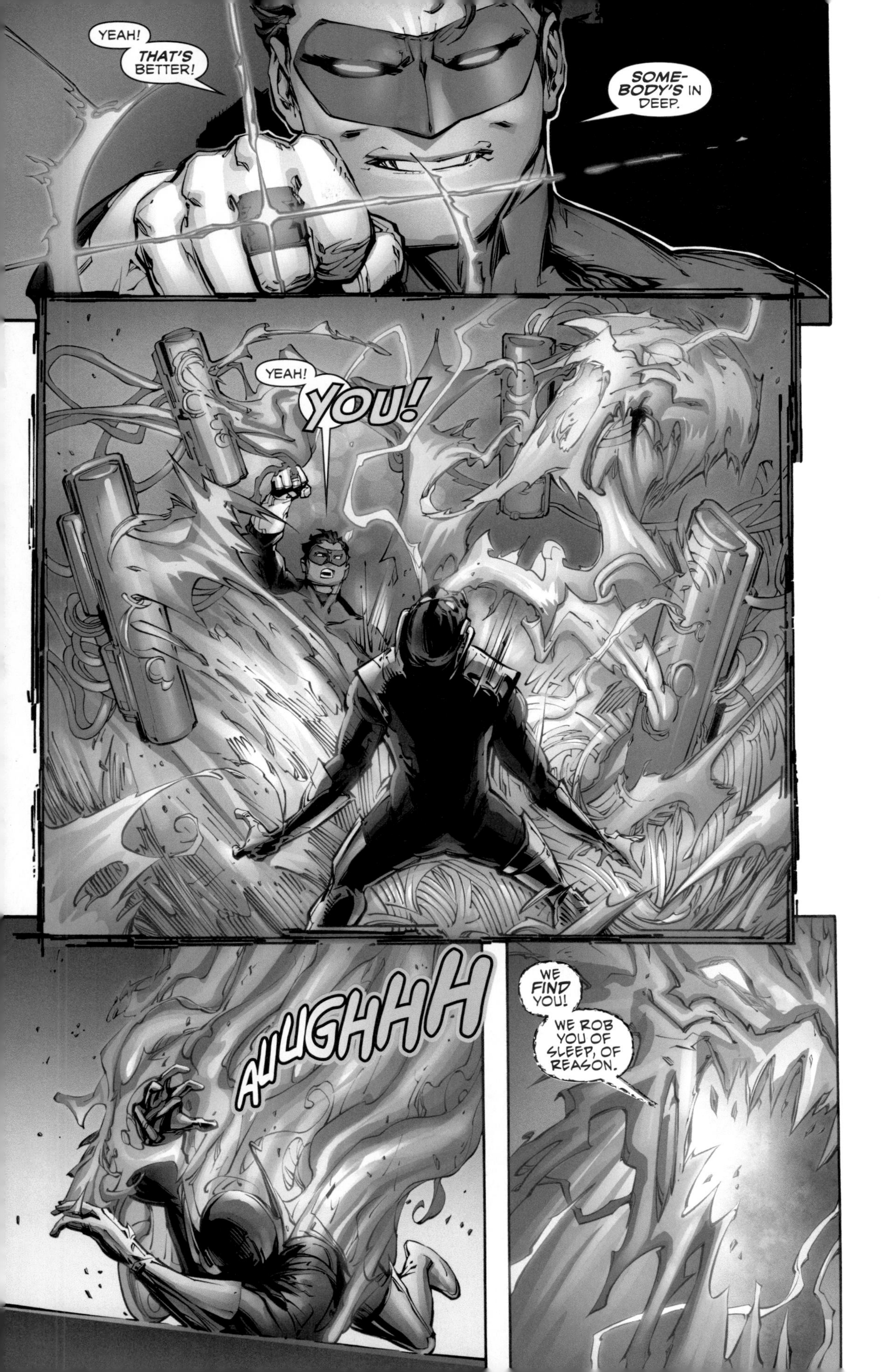

YEAH!
THAT'S BETTER!
SOME-BODY'S IN DEEP.
YEAH!
YOU!
AUUGHHH
WE FIND YOU!
WE ROB YOU OF SLEEP, OF REASON.

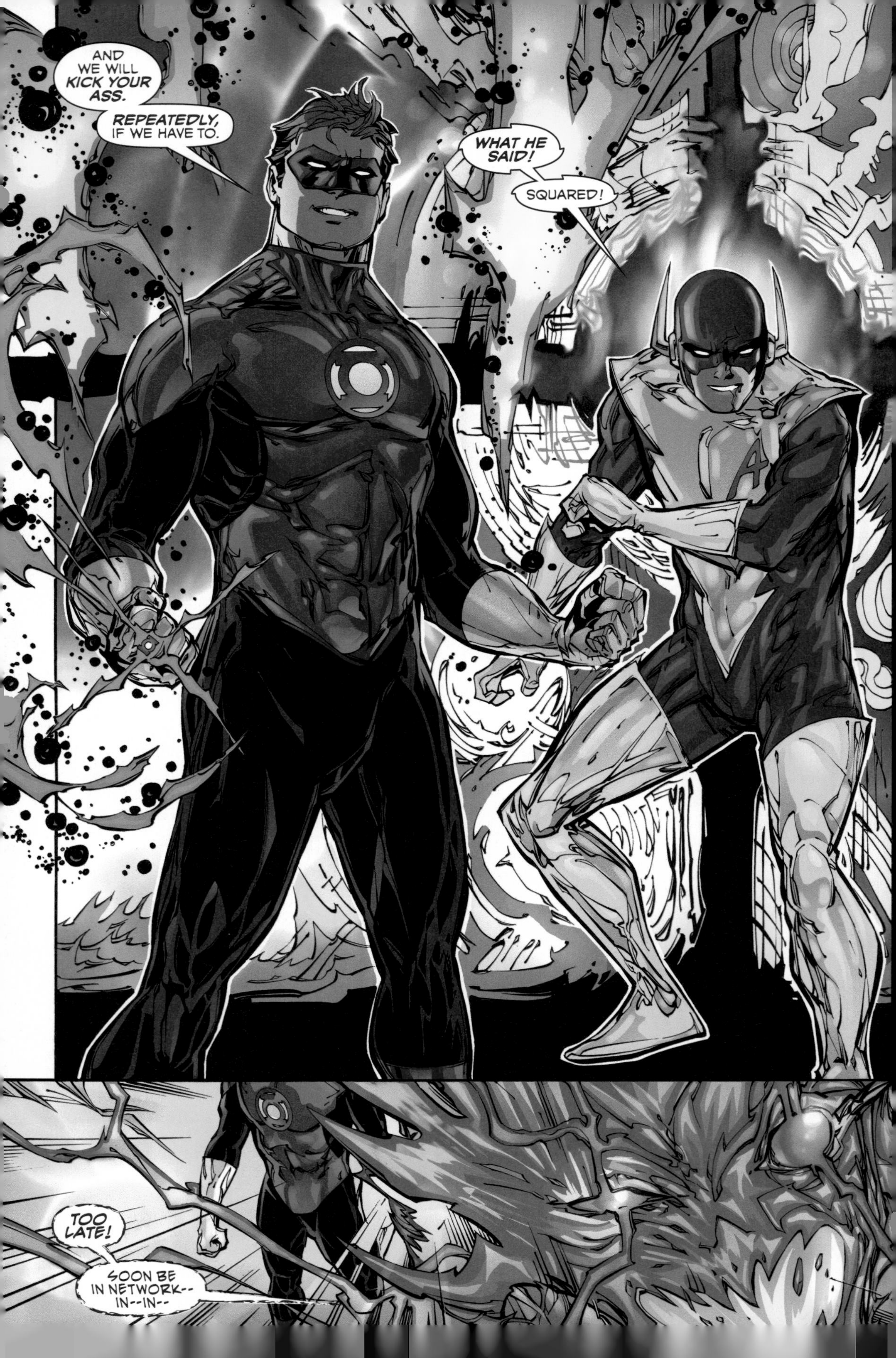
AND WE WILL KICK YOUR ASS.
REPEATEDLY, IF WE HAVE TO.
WHAT HE SAID!
SQUARED!
TOO LATE!
SOON BE IN NETWORK-- IN--IN--

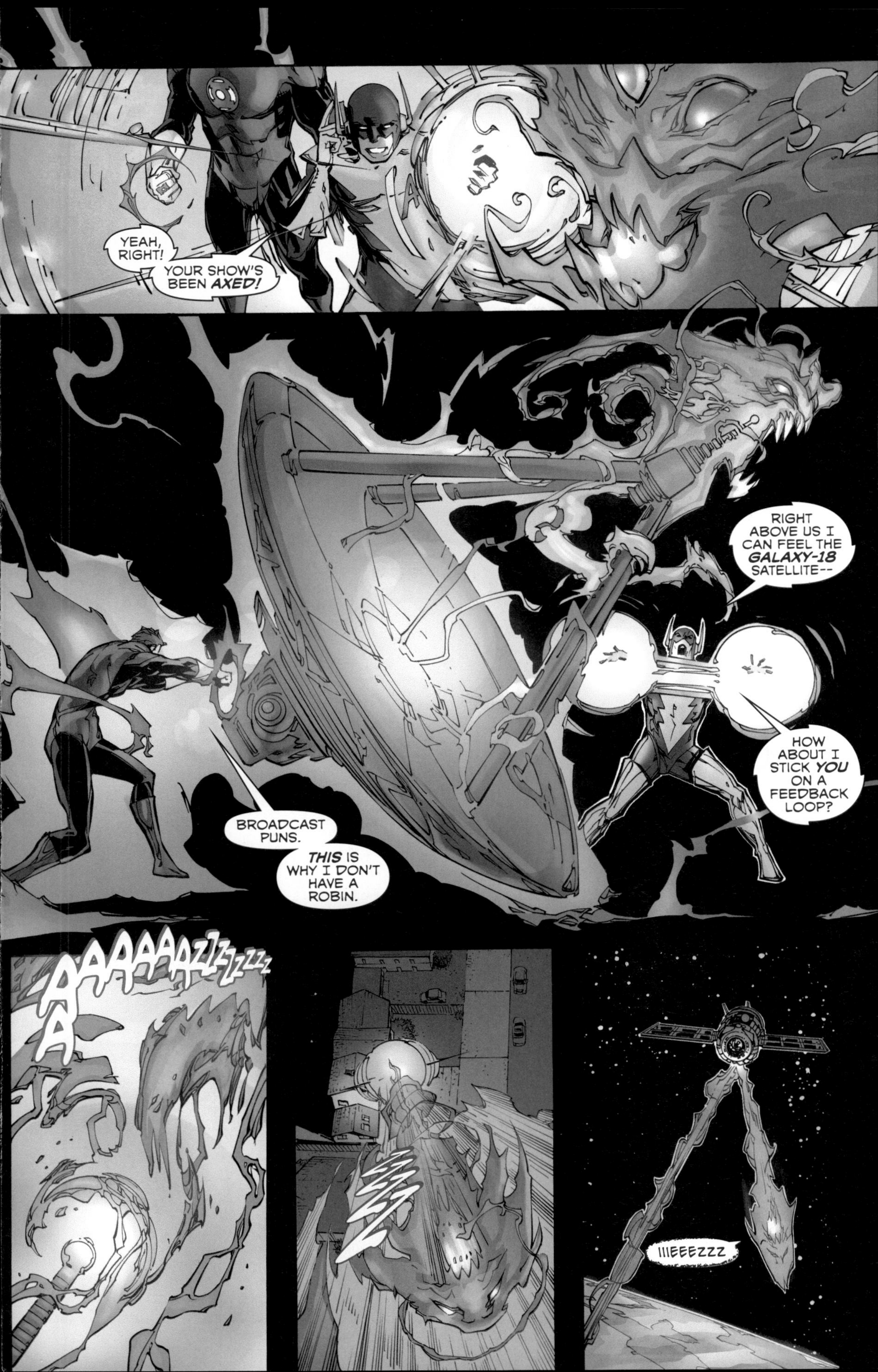
YEAH, RIGHT!
YOUR SHOW'S BEEN AXED!
RIGHT ABOVE US I CAN FEEL THE GALAXY-18 SATELLITE--
HOW ABOUT I STICK YOU ON A FEEDBACK LOOP?
BROADCAST PUNS.
THIS IS WHY I DON'T HAVE A ROBIN.
AAAAAAAZZZZZZZ
IIIEEEZZZ

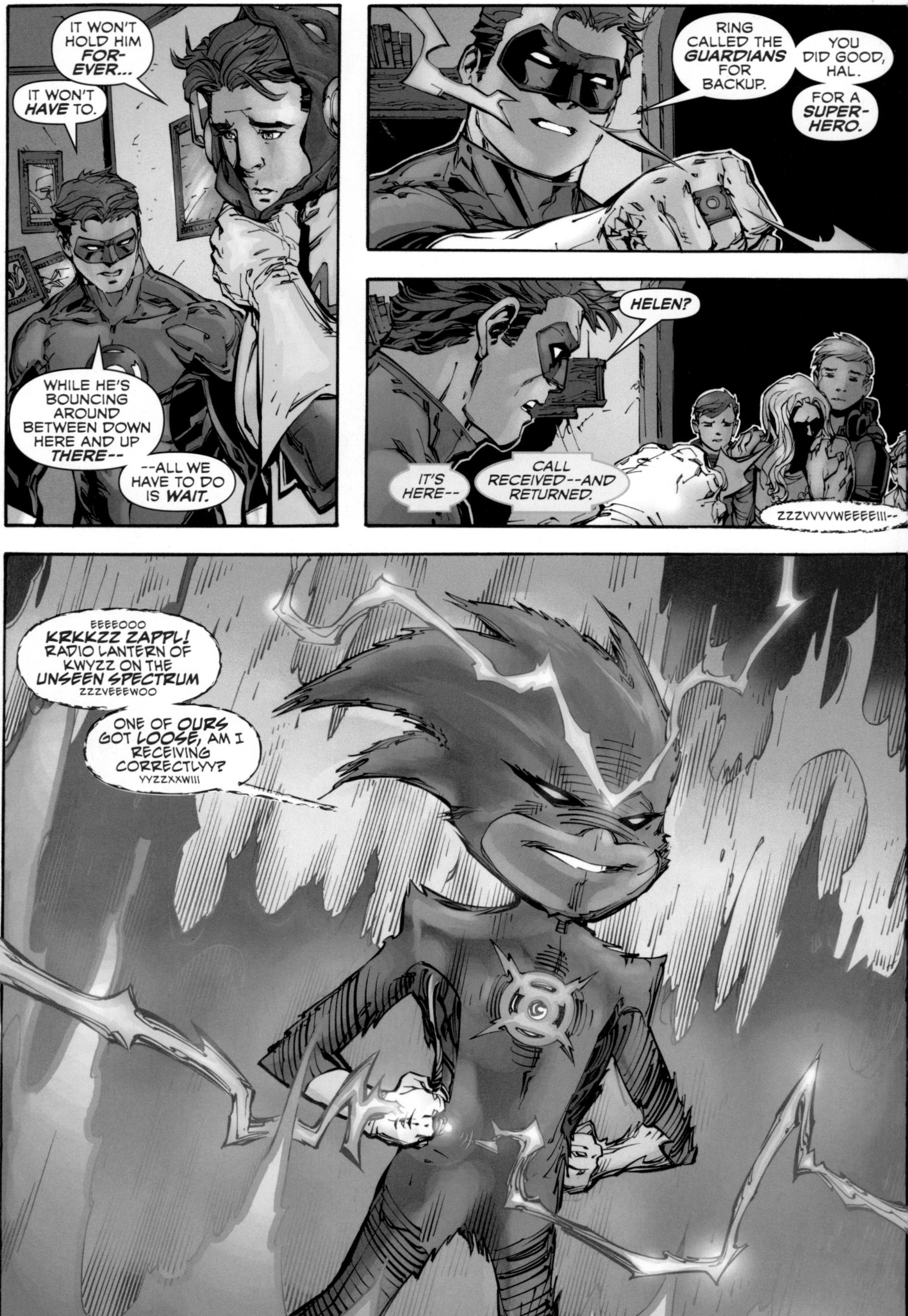
IT WON'T HOLD HIM FOR-EVER...
IT WON'T HAVE TO.
WHILE HE'S BOUNCING AROUND BETWEEN DOWN HERE AND UP THERE--
--ALL WE HAVE TO DO IS WAIT.
RING CALLED THE GUARDIANS FOR BACKUP.
YOU DID GOOD, HAL.
FOR A SUPER-HERO.
HELEN?
IT'S HERE--
CALL RECEIVED--AND RETURNED.
ZZZVVVVWEEEEIII--
EEEEOOO KRKKZZ ZAPPL! RADIO LANTERN OF KWYZZ ON THE UNSEEN SPECTRUM ZZZVEEEWOO
ONE OF OURS GOT LOOSE, AM I RECEIVING CORRECTLYY? YYZZXXWIII

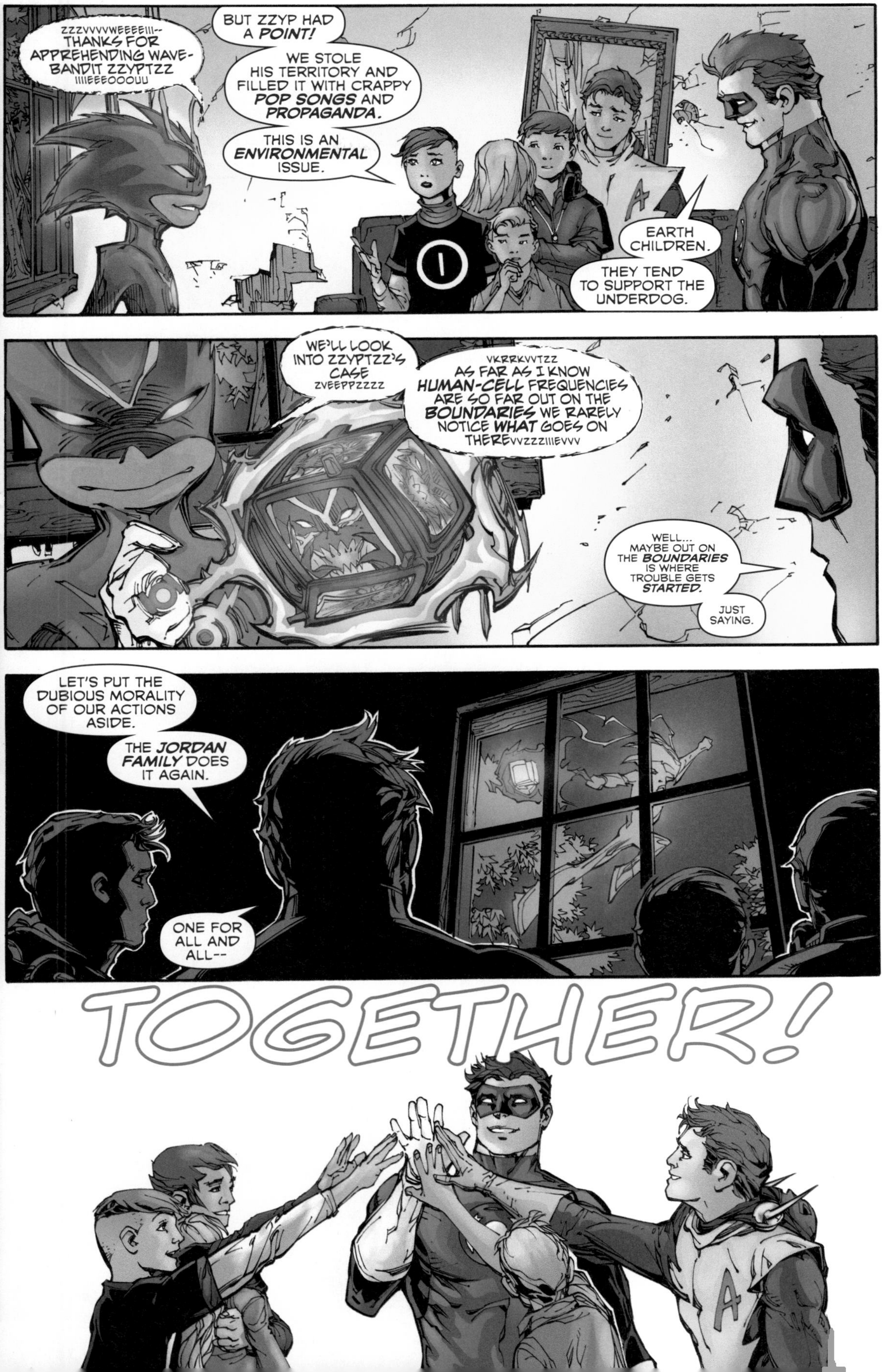
ZZZVVVVWEEEEIII-- THANKS FOR APPREHENDING WAVE-BANDIT ZZYPTZZ IIIIEEEOOOUU
BUT ZZYP HAD A POINT!
WE STOLE HIS TERRITORY AND FILLED IT WITH CRAPPY POP SONGS AND PROPAGANDA.
THIS IS AN ENVIRONMENTAL ISSUE.
EARTH CHILDREN.
THEY TEND TO SUPPORT THE UNDERDOG.
WE'LL LOOK INTO ZZYPTZZ'S CASE ZVEEPPZZZZ
VKRRKVVTZZ AS FAR AS I KNOW HUMAN-CELL FREQUENCIES ARE SO FAR OUT ON THE BOUNDARIES WE RARELY NOTICE WHAT GOES ON THEREVVZZZIIIEVVV
WELL... MAYBE OUT ON THE BOUNDARIES IS WHERE TROUBLE GETS STARTED.
JUST SAYING.
LET'S PUT THE DUBIOUS MORALITY OF OUR ACTIONS ASIDE.
THE JORDAN FAMILY DOES IT AGAIN.
ONE FOR ALL AND ALL--
TOGETHER!

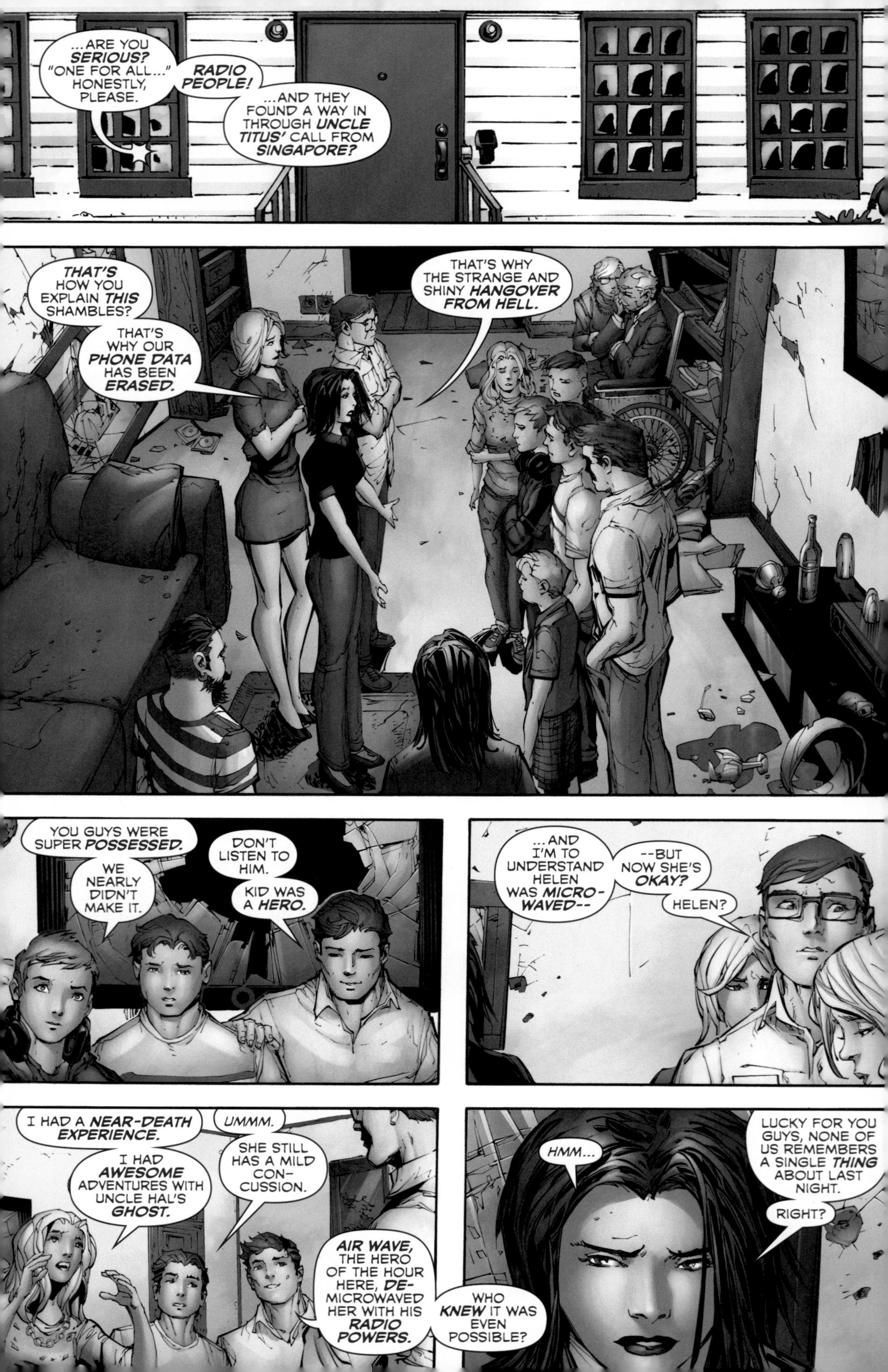
...ARE YOU SERIOUS? "ONE FOR ALL..." HONESTLY, PLEASE.
RADIO PEOPLE!
...AND THEY FOUND A WAY IN THROUGH UNCLE TITUS' CALL FROM SINGAPORE?
THAT'S HOW YOU EXPLAIN THIS SHAMBLES?
THAT'S WHY OUR PHONE DATA HAS BEEN ERASED.
THAT'S WHY THE STRANGE AND SHINY HANGOVER FROM HELL.
YOU GUYS WERE SUPER POSSESSED.
WE NEARLY DIDN'T MAKE IT.
DON'T LISTEN TO HIM.
KID WAS A HERO.
...AND I'M TO UNDERSTAND HELEN WAS MICRO-WAVED--
--BUT NOW SHE'S OKAY?
HELEN?
I HAD A NEAR-DEATH EXPERIENCE.
I HAD AWESOME ADVENTURES WITH UNCLE HAL'S GHOST.
UMMM.
SHE STILL HAS A MILD CON-CUSSION.
AIR WAVE, THE HERO OF THE HOUR HERE, DE-MICROWAVED HER WITH HIS RADIO POWERS.
WHO KNEW IT WAS EVEN POSSIBLE?
HMM...
LUCKY FOR YOU GUYS, NONE OF US REMEMBERS A SINGLE THING ABOUT LAST NIGHT.
RIGHT?

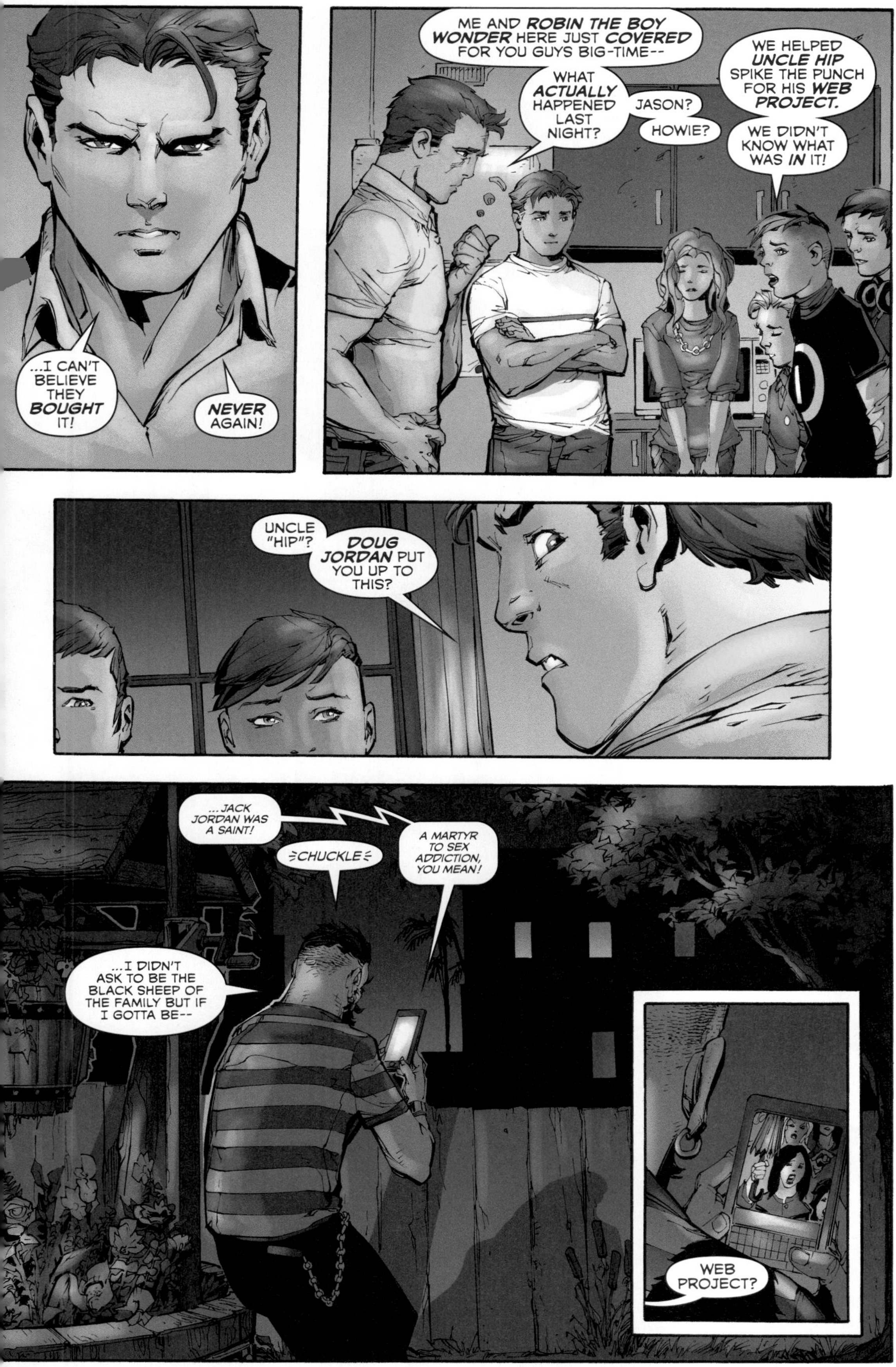
...I CAN'T BELIEVE THEY BOUGHT IT!
NEVER AGAIN!
ME AND ROBIN THE BOY WONDER HERE JUST COVERED FOR YOU GUYS BIG-TIME--
WHAT ACTUALLY HAPPENED LAST NIGHT?
JASON?
HOWIE?
WE HELPED UNCLE HIP SPIKE THE PUNCH FOR HIS WEB PROJECT.
WE DIDN'T KNOW WHAT WAS IN IT!
UNCLE "HIP"?
DOUG JORDAN PUT YOU UP TO THIS?
...JACK JORDAN WAS A SAINT!
CHUCKLE
A MARTYR TO SEX ADDICTION, YOU MEAN!
...I DIDN'T ASK TO BE THE BLACK SHEEP OF THE FAMILY BUT IF I GOTTA BE--
WEB PROJECT?

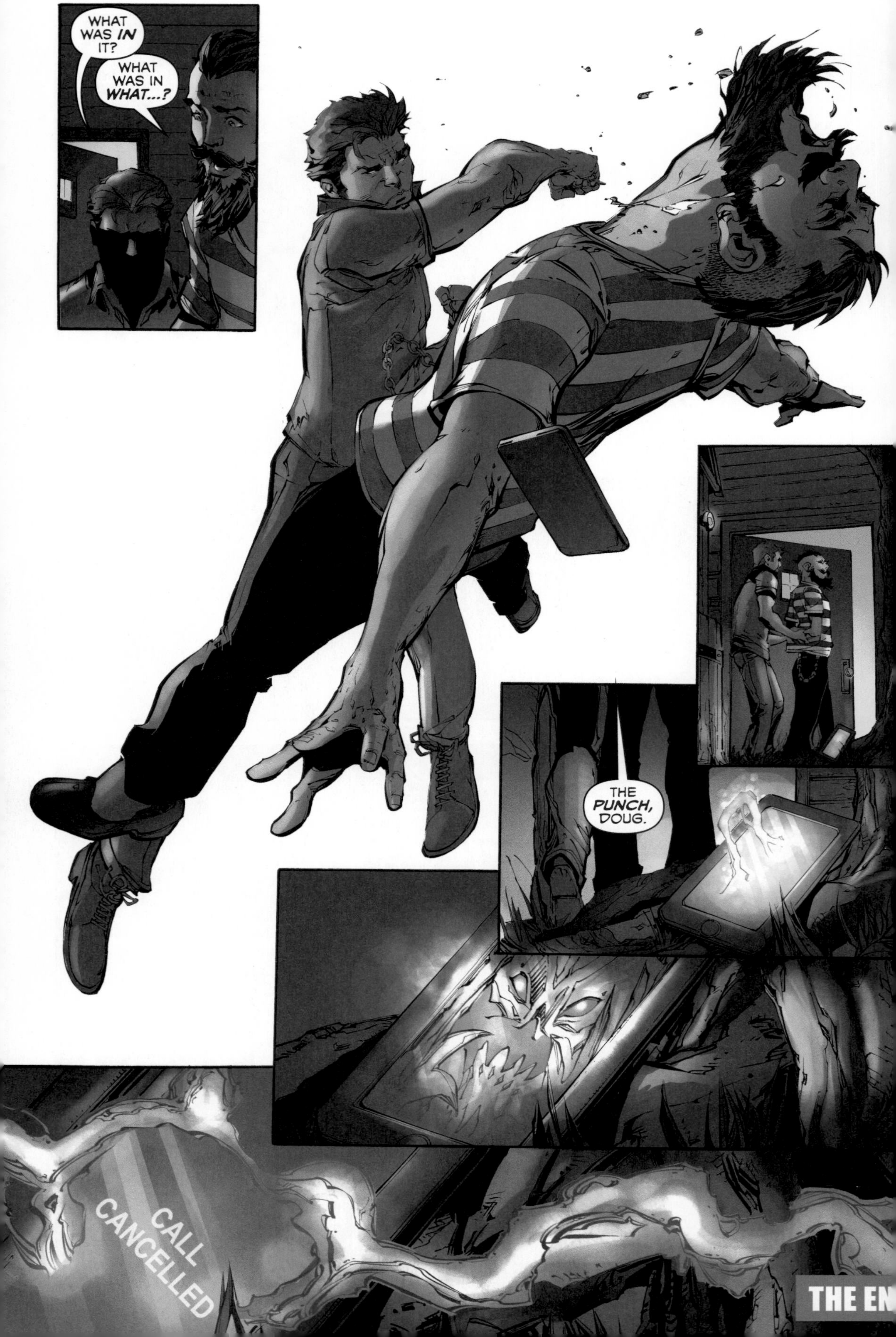
WHAT WAS *IN* IT?
WHAT WAS IN *WHAT...?*
THE *PUNCH,* DOUG.
CALL CANCELLED
THE EN

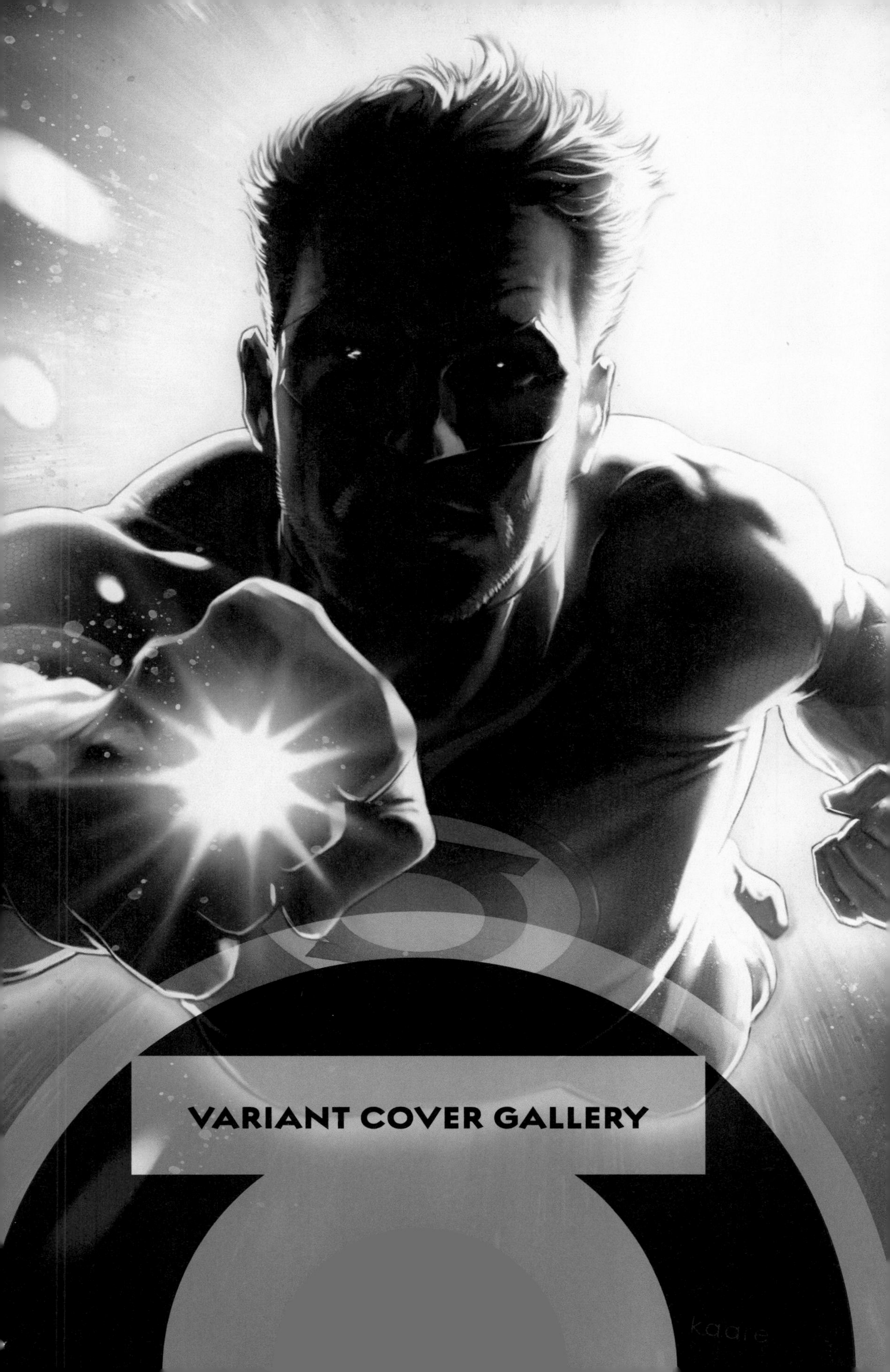
VARIANT COVER GALLERY
kaare

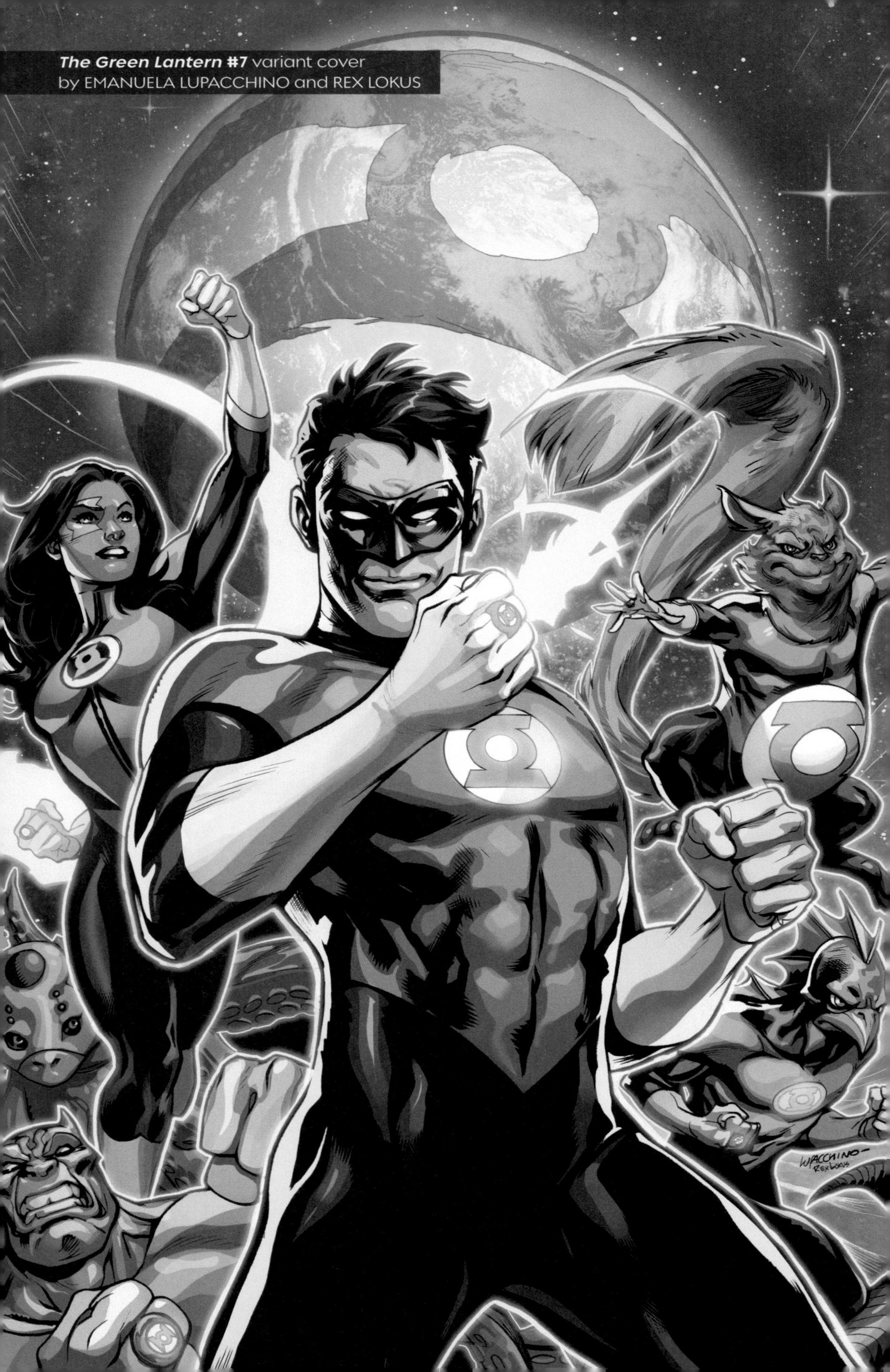

***The Green Lantern* #7** variant cover
by EMANUELA LUPACCHINO and REX LOKUS

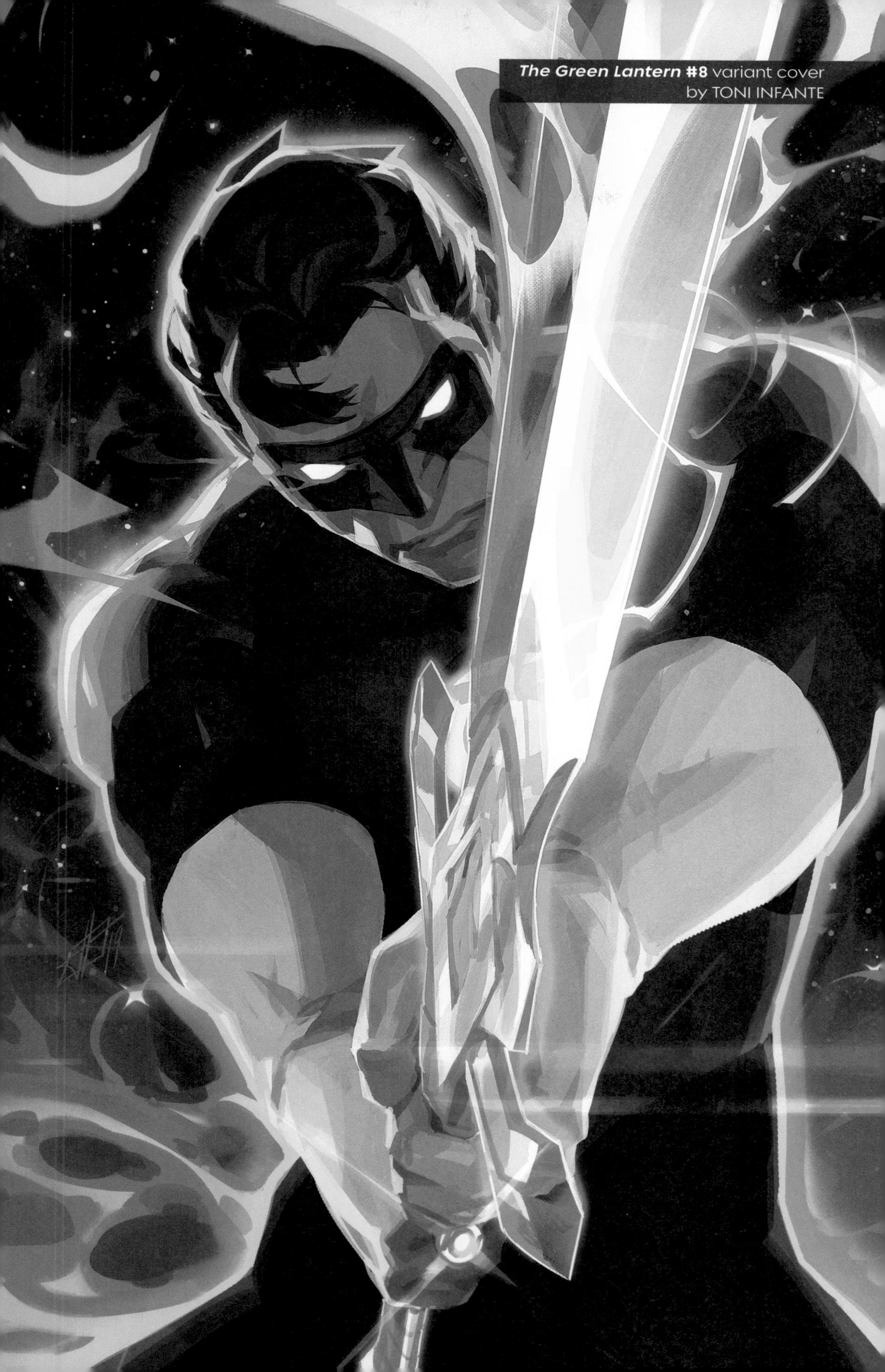

***The Green Lantern* #8** variant cover
by TONI INFANTE

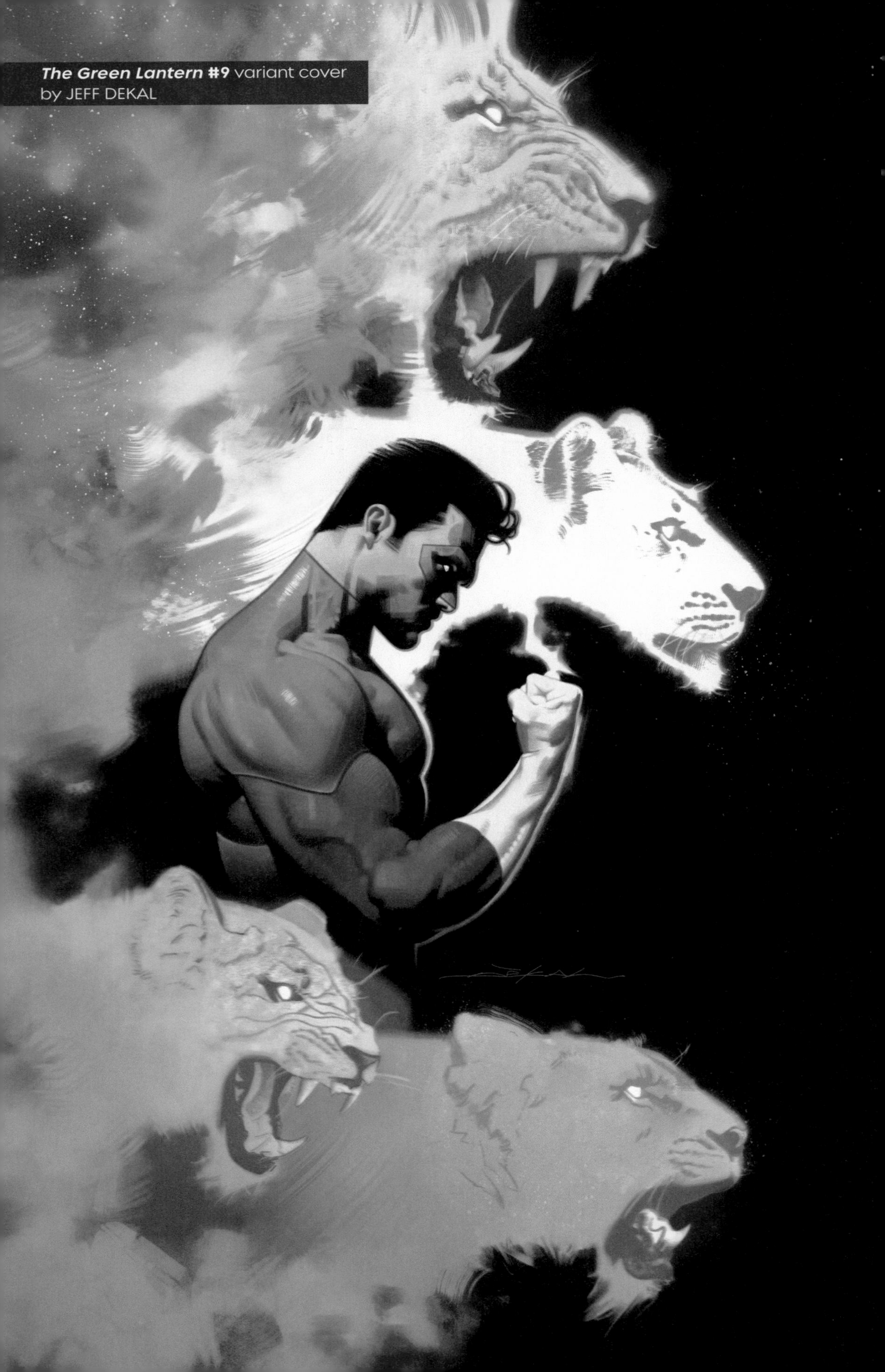

***The Green Lantern* #9** variant cover
by JEFF DEKAL

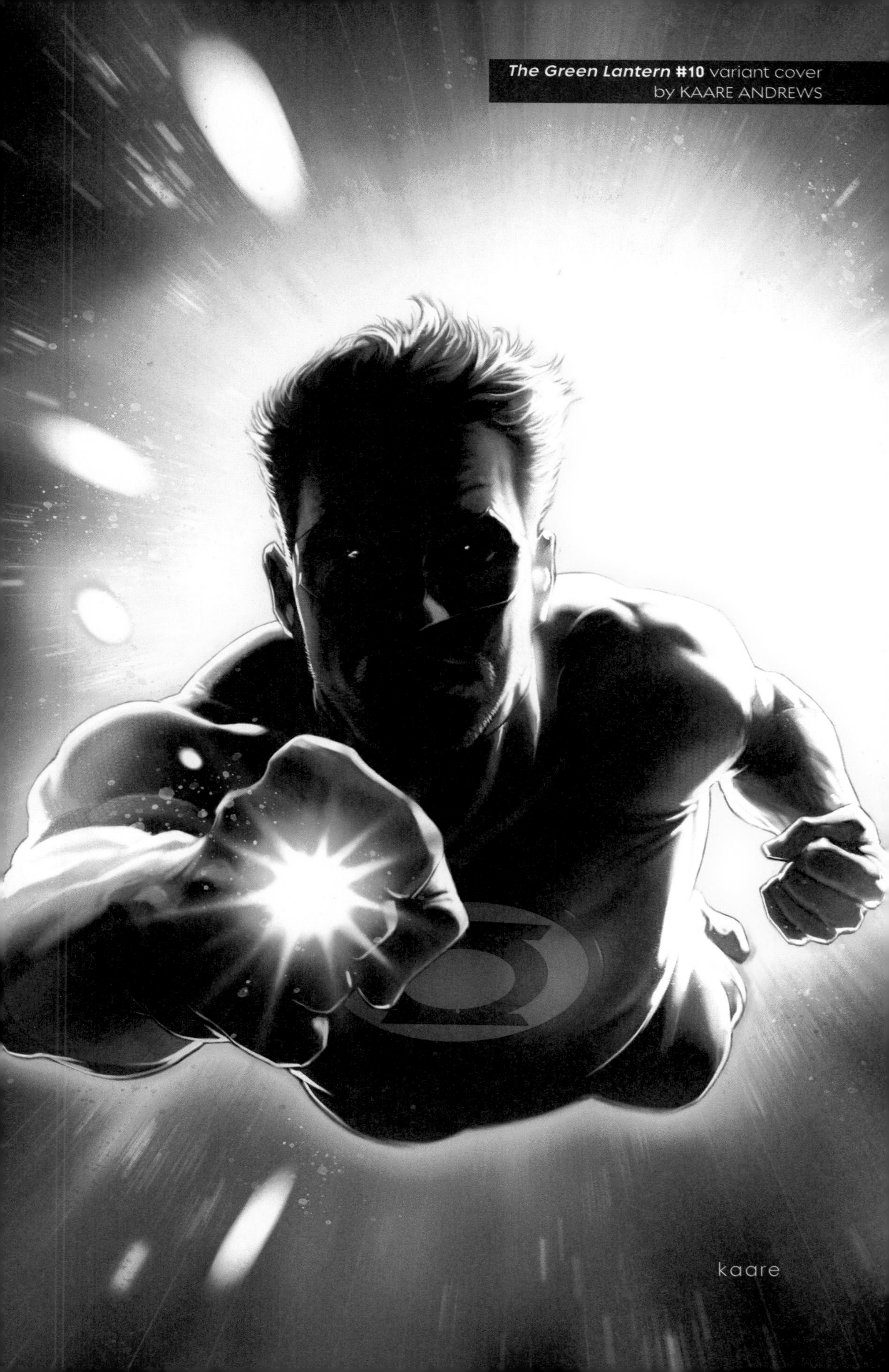
kaare

The Green Lantern **#10** variant cover
by KAARE ANDREWS

The Green Lantern **#11** variant cover
by PAUL POPE with BRUNO SEELIG

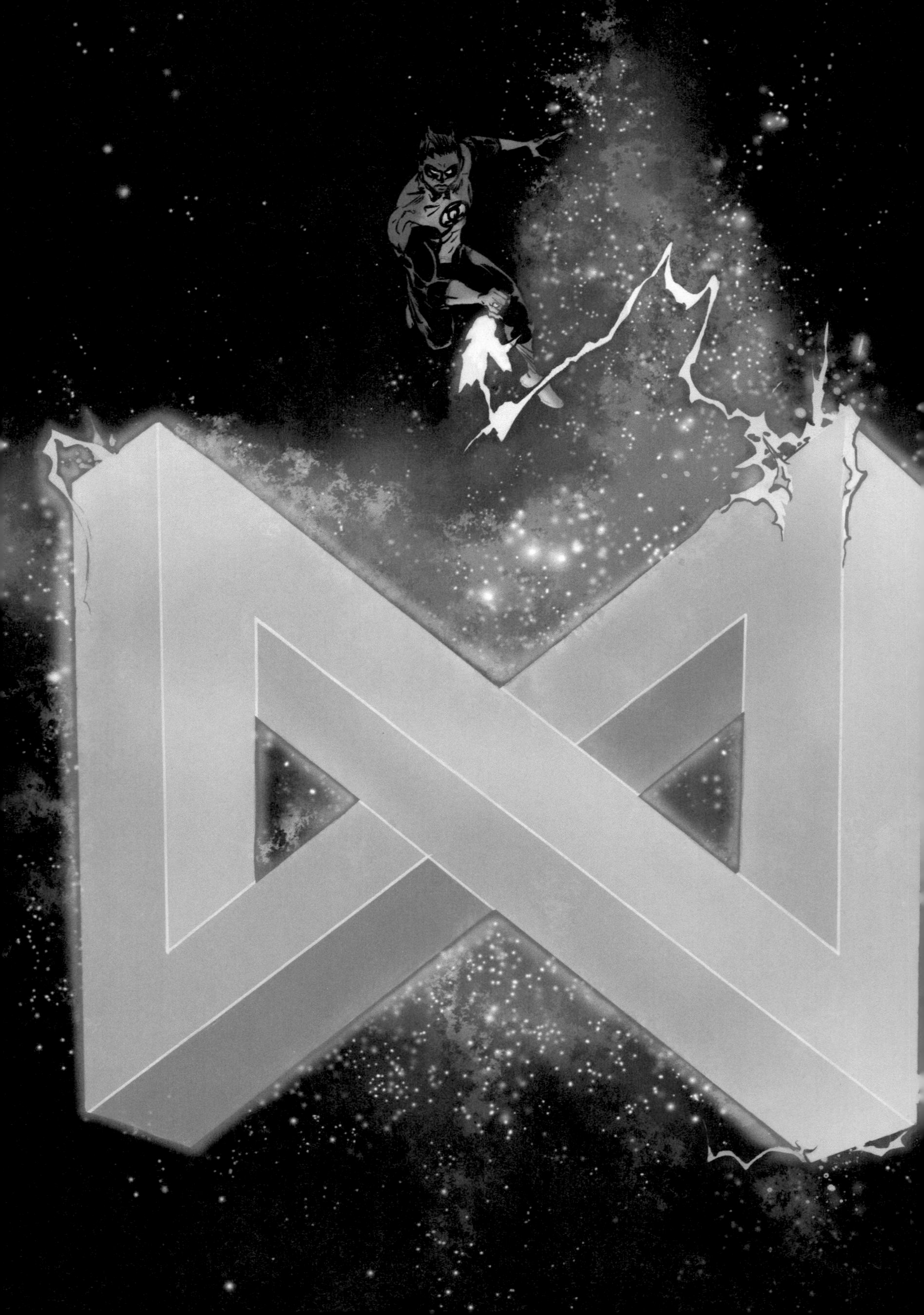

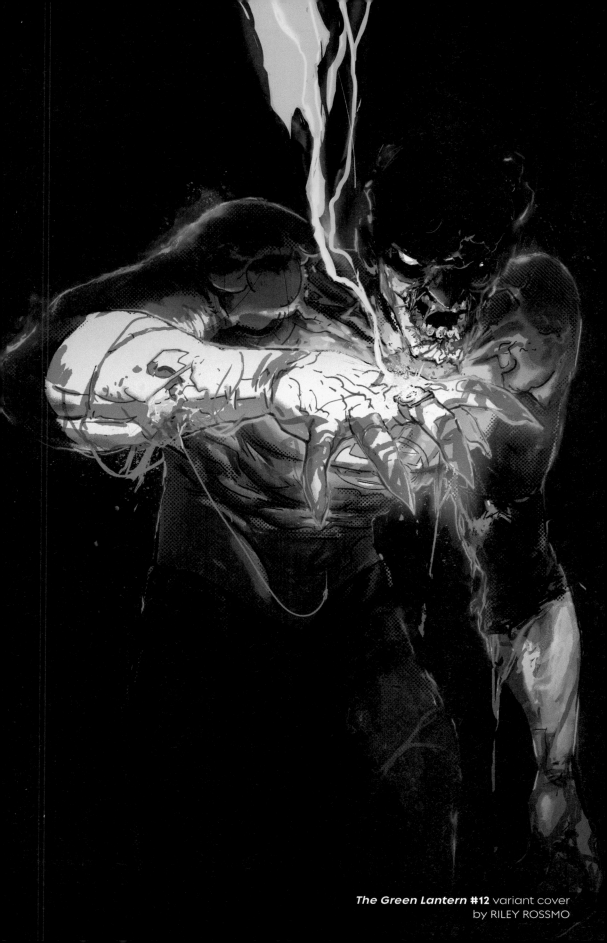

The Green Lantern #12 variant cover
by RILEY ROSSMO

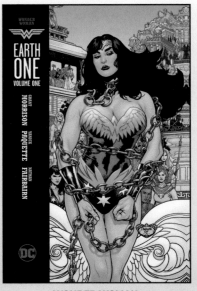
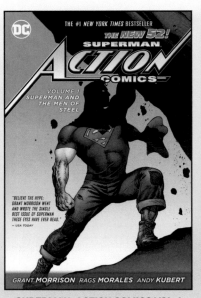
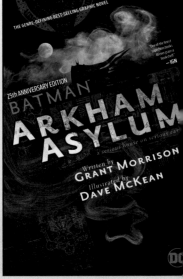

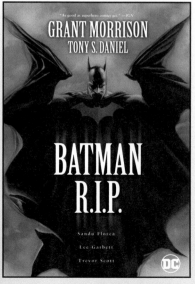

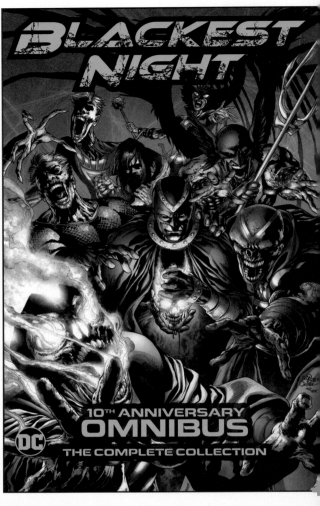